The publisher gratefully acknowledges the gene
Anne G. Lipow Endowment Fund for Socia
of the University of California Press Founda
Stephen M. Silberstein.

Land of the Unconquerable

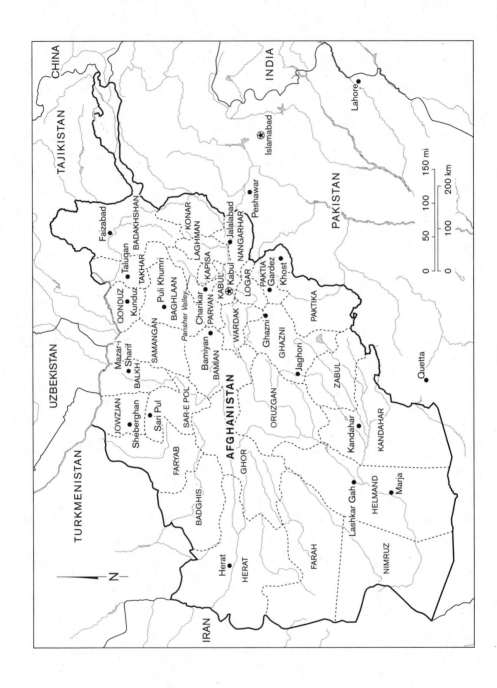

Land of the Unconquerable

The Lives of Contemporary Afghan Women

EDITED BY

Jennifer Heath and Ashraf Zahedi

UNIVERSITY OF CALIFORNIA PRESS

Berkeley · Los Angeles · London

University of California Press, one of the most
distinguished university presses in the United States,
enriches lives around the world by advancing
scholarship in the humanities, social sciences, and
natural sciences. Its activities are supported by the UC
Press Foundation and by philanthropic contributions
from individuals and institutions. For more information, visit www.ucpress.edu.

University of California Press
Berkeley and Los Angeles, California

University of California Press, Ltd.
London, England

© 2011 by The Regents of the University of California

Library of Congress Cataloging-in-Publication Data
    Land of the unconquerable : the lives of contempo-
rary Afghan women / edited by Jennifer Heath and
Ashraf Zahedi.
        p.   cm.
    Includes bibliographical references and index.
    ISBN 978-0-520-26185-3 (cloth : alk. paper)
    ISBN 978-0-520-26186-0 (pbk. : alk. paper)
    1. Women—Afghanistan—Social conditions—21st
century. I. Heath, Jennifer. II. Zahedi, Ashraf, 1947–
    HQ1735.6.L37   2011
    305.48'891593—dc22

                                  2010039318

Manufactured in the United States of America

19 18 17 16 15 14 13 12 11 10
10 9 8 7 6, 5 4 3 2 1

This book is printed on Cascades Enviro 100, a 100%
post consumer waste, recycled, de-inked fiber. FSC
recycled certified and processed chlorine free. It is acid
free, Ecologo certified, and manufactured by BioGas
energy.

Humanity does not gradually progress from combat to combat until it arrives at universal reciprocity, where the rule of law finally replaces warfare; humanity installs each of its violences in a system of rules and thus proceeds from domination to domination.

—Michel Foucault

You cannot solve a problem from the same consciousness that created it. You must learn to see the world anew.

—Albert Einstein

To be hopeful in bad times is not just foolishly romantic. It is based on the fact that human history is a history not only of cruelty, but also of compassion, sacrifice, courage, kindness. What we choose to emphasize in this complex history will determine our lives. . . . The future is an infinite succession of presents, and to live now as we think human beings should live, in defiance of all that is bad around us, is itself a marvelous victory.

—Howard Zinn

Contents

Acknowledgments

There are many to thank, beginning with our contributors—writers and photographers—for their amazing work. Their talents and scholarship are immeasurable, as is our gratitude. All went out of their way, above and beyond the call of duty, to make this book as fulsome, rich, and enlightening as possible.

In addition, we wish to thank, for information, inspiration, help, support, and/or encouragement over the long and short hauls: The American Institute for Afghanistan Studies, Mahnaz Afkhami, Bernard Amadei, Thomas Barfield, David Barsamian, Sarah C. Bell, Michael Carroll, Sam Chen, Christopher Collom, Jack Collom, Sierra Collom, Elizabeth Colton, Nan De Grove, Susan Edwards, Ghada Kanafani Elturk, Nazi Etemadi, Hafizullah Emadi, Asma Eschen, Katrin Fakiri, Ghulam Feda, Wazhma Frogh, Ellen Geiger, Ashok Gupta, Roxanne Gupta, Shahla Haeri, Najia Haneefi, Matthew Heath, Mary Hegland, Nita Hill, Judy Hussie-Taylor, Danish Karokhel, Marda Kirn, Genevieve and Herbert Leggett, Karen Leggett, Marsha MacColl, Shireen Malik, Linda Mansouri, Valentine Moghadam, Idris Mojaddidi, Senzil Nawid, George and Marija Nez, Soraya Omar, Michael Raulli, Denny Robertson, Naomi Schneider, Sheryl B. Shapiro, Mumtaz Soleman, Rickie Solinger, Nadia Tarzi, Beth Wald, Candace Walworth, Barbara Wilder, Andrew Wille, Michael Wolfe, and so many others.

In peace and gratitude,
Jennifer Heath and Ashraf Zahedi

Introduction

JENNIFER HEATH

On October 7, 2001, the United States and its allies launched an assault against Afghanistan in retaliation for the attacks of 9/11 and removed the Taliban from power. The Sunni Islamist and Pashtun nationalist movement calling itself "students" or "seekers" had tyrannized most of the country, especially the women, since 1996.

The 2001 U.S.-led attack began another chapter in the three decades—and counting—of relentless fighting endured by the Afghan people, beginning in 1979 with the Soviet invasion. Across the ten-year Soviet war, more than 1 million Afghans were killed; 1.2 million Mujahedin, government soldiers, and noncombatants were disabled; and 3 million (mostly noncombatants) were maimed or wounded. Five million Afghans, one-third of the prewar population, fled to Pakistan and Iran. Another 2 million Afghans were displaced within the country.[1]

The Mujahedin (who President Ronald Reagan labeled "freedom fighters") had been armed and supported principally by the United States—with ideological and material support provided by Saudi Arabia and Pakistan—in order to fight (and win) a proxy war against the Soviet Union. As is well documented, a call—exploiting a militant, atypical version of Islam—for Muslim men around the world to join a *jihad* (holy war) against "godless communists," led to what the primary author of this scheme, Carter-era national security advisor Zbigniew Brzezinski, labeled "Islamic blowback."[2] Among those who joined the Central Intelligence Agency in its quest to win the Cold War by pitting one ideology against another was, of course, Osama bin Laden. This is an old, elaborate story, much told, but it is essential to repeat briefly here, because the U.S.-led invasion tends to obfuscate the fact that no Afghan was responsible for the tragedy of September 11, 2001, yet all Afghans have been paying for it.

The Soviets left Afghanistan in 1989, although they continued to support the regime of Najibullah in Kabul, while the United States, working through Pakistan with Saudi Arabian aid, continued supporting a coalition of Mujahedin, called the "Afghan Interim Government." It was the first phase of a long civil war. In 1992, declaring an official end to the Cold War, the United States under George H. W. Bush and the USSR under Boris Yeltsin agreed to conclude military and financial aid to Afghanistan, thus introducing the next phase of its civil war, now between Mujahedin factions vying to fill the power vacuum, bringing fresh horrors. Many women report that this four-year period—virtually ignored by the Western media—rivaled, often outdid, the subsequent Taliban era for barbarism and oppression, with rapes, kidnappings, and forced marriages, along with relentless street fighting, looting, and the launching of rockets into quiet neighborhoods, blowing buildings to rubble, and maiming and killing innocent bystanders. The United States, instead of seizing an opportunity to rebuild Afghanistan, had walked away.[3]

The "students," meanwhile, were quietly massing and training in Pakistan. In 1995, they took Herat and in 1996 conquered Kabul, then spread out across most of the rest of the country. Many welcomed them as liberators and bringers of peace. Various Mujahedin fled north, where they formed the United Islamic Front for the Salvation of Afghanistan, or Northern Alliance. It is impossible in this space to give more than a highly abridged version of the twisted geopolitics that have affected Afghanistan across the years. Journalists such as Peter Marsden (*The Taliban, War, Religion and the New Order in Afghanistan*, 1998), Ahmed Rashid (*Taliban: Militant Islam, Oil and Fundamentalism in Central Asia*, 2001), Steve Coll (*Ghost Wars: The Secret History of the CIA, Afghanistan and Bin Laden, From the Soviet Invasion to September 10, 2001*, 2004), and Paul Fitzgerald and Elizabeth Gould (*Invisible History: Afghanistan's Untold Story*, 2009) have written probing, comprehensive histories peeling away the covert layers of U.S. and international collusion in Afghanistan's near destruction.

Between 1994 and 1997, the U.S. government supported the Taliban, again through its allies, Pakistan and Saudi Arabia, its policy motivated by the possibility of an oil pipeline project, as well as its belief that the Taliban would "tighten the noose around Iran. . . . There was not a word of criticism [from the Bill Clinton administration] after the Taliban captured Herat . . . and threw thousands of girls from schools," Pakistani journalist Ahmed Rashid writes. But such incidents did at last begin to enlighten Western consciousness about the misery of Afghan women. Therefore, when it came, Rashid writes, the "U.S. policy turnaround . . . was driven exclusively by the effective campaign of American feminists against the Taliban. . . . [The Clinton administration] could not afford to annoy liberal American women. . . . There was no way the U.S. could be seen as soft on the Taliban." With a prospective U.S.-Taliban oil pipeline deal crumbling (and Pakistan's political situation fast deteriorating), in November 1997, Secretary of State Madeleine Albright publicly condemned the regime's treatment of women during a visit to an Afghan refugee camp in Pakistan.[4]

In 2001, the "liberation" of Afghan women became a justification of the George W. Bush administration for the Afghan invasion. It, too, was a fire fueled by women's rights groups, many of which—good intentions notwithstanding—seemed now to exploit Afghanistan for their own objectives, often painting a distorted portrait of absolutely helpless Afghan women buried alive in their *burqa*s, brutalized by unquenchably savage Afghan men. One sad result of this black-and-white thinking, which overlooks all the nuances and diversity of Afghan life and society, is a severe curtailing of the quality, quantity, and endurance of whatever help Western women try to offer their Afghan sisters.

In shaping foreign policy, Western governments also blunder righteously along, disregarding cultural subtleties. As British academic and Member of Parliament Rory Stewart notes, Western leaders

> rely on a hypnotizing policy language which can—and perhaps will—be applied as easily to Somalia or Yemen as Afghanistan. It misleads us in several respects simultaneously: minimizing differences between cultures, exaggerating our fears, aggrandizing our ambitions, inflating a sense of moral obligations and power, and confusing our goals. *All these attitudes are aspects of a single worldview* and create an almost irresistible illusion.[5]

It was ever thus: from the 1893 British-imposed Durand Line, which split the lands of the Pashtun and Balouch peoples—eventually creating deep territorial disputes between Pakistan and Afghanistan—to the Cold War, when Afghanistan was considered, by Soviets and Americans alike, to be "a perfect listening post," as one former CIA agent put it, and aid sometimes amounted to not much more than popularity contests and bribery for the best positioning, right into the second decade of the twenty-first century, when the country remains, as Fitzgerald and Gould put it, "a victim of the simple-minded Manichean approach to foreign policy forged by America's national security managers."[6]

There are Afghan women who say that the Taliban era was an improvement over the civil war period, for at least there was peace of a sort. Even as women were barred from education and employment, their health care severely restricted, and Draconian laws applied (to everyone), the Taliban era brought comparative quiet and order, a respite from Mujahedin guns and rockets. In 2008, Jason Burke of the *Guardian* interviewed Roshanak Wardak, a gynecologist and member of the Afghan parliament:

> Wardak, whose uncle and grandfather were both MPs in earlier, more peaceful times, has challenging views about life under the last Taliban government. "As a doctor, as a woman, as an Afghan, the last regime was not bad," she says. "They were well-disciplined people. In their time there was security. At midnight, at 2 a.m., I could go to my hospital when I was on call for an urgent operation and come back without any bodyguards. This is a major difference and I will never deny it."
>
> As a woman, however, Wardak says she could never accept the Taliban's restrictions on girls' education. And worse, the new Taliban are very different. "They are criminals. They are thieves and they are not acceptable."[7]

Today, in some quarters—principally in the conservative south and around Kandahar, a Taliban stronghold, but elsewhere as well—women claim they would again prefer the "old" despotism to the current anarchy, mounting deaths, and bloodshed as the United States has escalated its tangled, unfocused war against al Qaeda, the ghostly bin Laden (for whose capture uncounted thousands of innocent Afghans are dying), and the "new" Taliban, now a catchall for drug traffickers, warlords, bandits, ideologues, the impoverished, and the unemployed. Other women fear that withdrawal or a reduction of U.S. and NATO troops from Afghan soil will present an even greater threat to security and women's rights and open the door to another civil war.[8] After a decade of misguided U.S. and international policy, the need for security is undeniable, but there has been widespread agreement that substantial increases in troops continue to radicalize insurgents—as is inevitable in a war of occupation—and generate far more severe problems than ever before. Victories here or there (and it might be wise to question the definition of "victory") by the United States, NATO, and the ill-trained, unenthusiastic Afghan army have been brief and carry no promises for a stable future, the safe return of displaced citizens, a clear understanding of appropriate governance, or negotiations that include women.[9]

In December 2001, with the Taliban defeat, there began a brief period of hope. Yet right from the start, opportunities to salvage Afghanistan were again missed, first with the Bonn Agreement, which set up an Afghan Interim Authority—including the Northern Alliance and other players. The AIA was inaugurated with a six-month mandate to be followed by a two-year Transitional Authority, after which elections were to be held.[10]

Bonn, however, was not a peace agreement, and it did not include the Taliban, who, at that weakened stage, might have been willing to negotiate. Instead, even the more "moderate Taliban"[11] were driven back into the extremist fold and have grown again in strength.[12] Nine years later, a Peace and Reconciliation program to lure away low-level Taliban fighters stalled. A pledge of $250 million from international donors was slow to materialize and Afghan officials could not settle on how to administer the project. The flow of fighters wishing to reintegrate had slowed from 9,000 in 2005 to only 100 by the autumn of 2010.[13]

Nor did the Bonn Agreement address DDR—disarmament (physically removing guns and ammunition from combatants), demobilization (disbanding armed groups), and reintegration (reintroducing combatants into civil society)—which became part of a larger, later plan to address security. The women of Afghanistan, to whom peace and security are critically and obviously important, were not included in the DDR discussions, and they are still left out of negotiations.[14] As Valentine Moghadam writes, because "women are often the special victims of armed conflict, their experiences, perspectives, and aspirations need to be incorporated into negotiation, mediation, and peace-building processes. For the same reason, women experts and leaders must be involved in processes of demilitarization, demobilization, and reintegration of fighters."[15]

For any disarmament process to succeed it must include all warring factions, but Afghan warlords with political clout and tight tribal connections took advantage of a vulnerable situation to disarm competitors and consolidate power. They kept their own weapons and continued to operate with impunity. Some were elected to parliament, have been members of the presidential cabinet, or run whole sectors of government and even entire districts around the country.[16]

The DDR was initiated in 2003 through Afghanistan's New Beginnings Programme, part of the United Nations Development Programme.[17] In order to succeed, it also needed to tie demilitarization to poverty reduction and job creation. Reintegration requires long-term plans and sustained allocation of resources, both of which were lacking. Many ex-combatants have been given opportunities to join the Afghan National Army or the Afghan National Police Force, with limited success. Inadequate efforts have been made to provide former combatants with resources and civilian skills training toward a strong, durable reconstruction, and, with few employment prospects, even men with relatively temperate views increasingly have joined or rejoined mercenary war- and drug-lord armies or the Taliban. The under-funded, under-supported DDR came to an end in June 2006, with little or no real progress toward peace.[18] And, as always, Afghan women have borne the brunt, with few if any improvements in education, health care, and other basic human rights.

When the Taliban fell, governmental and non-governmental organizations flocked to Afghanistan—primarily to Kabul, more or less the country's only safe zone.[19] Hundreds of facilities—schools, clinics, literacy and vocational training programs—were created especially for women. Indeed, funding was more likely when a project was for women, often leaving ordinary men and boys to flounder unaided. Kabul resembled a Wild West gold-rush town—filthy, noisy, and polluted, with rent rivaling Manhattan, traffic jammed with white UN Land Cruisers and yellow taxis, children picking through rubbish and licking plastic bags for remaining crumbs, old folk groveling in the streets, all while the pockets of corrupt government officials, warlords, military contractors, carpetbaggers, and war profiteers were heavily lined. Isolated from the rest of the country, all dolled up, celebrating consumerism for the few while the poor go hungry, and with extortion deeply pervasive, the city is sometimes now called "Little Dubai" and "Fortress Kabul."[20]

In March 2003, the United States invaded Iraq and once again turned its back on Afghanistan. The promised funding for reconstruction dwindled; the profiteers expanded operations into Baghdad. Across the years, particularly in the desperate countryside, many programs and much hope have vanished for lack of money and security. The bloodshed, displacement, starvation, disease, exposure, lack of medical treatment, environmental degradation, and other injustices go on and on. Corruption has expanded, within the government and outside it, a major stumbling block in any peace process.[21]

A young nomad woman grazing her flock of sheep. Courtesy of Afghan Student News and Jennifer Heath, 1966.

In spite of it all, there are institutions doing their best to keep Afghanistan afloat, although most have been driven out of the rural areas as the Taliban have resurged across time and war has intensified. Small humanitarian organizations persist valiantly, many coordinated by returned Afghan expatriates and their non-Afghan supporters—educators, agriculturalists, micro-financiers, physicians, nurses, dentists, social workers, artists.[22]

Sadly, the gratitude that 83 percent of Afghans said they felt for the United States in 2005 had reduced by half and was plunging in 2009, when there were more than 1,000 known civilian casualties in the first six months. And instead of schools or clinics, the United States and NATO have thus far established 700 military bases, of varying sizes, throughout the country.[23] How can a people forced into thirty years of war take more? How, under relentlessly dire circumstances, can they ever begin to shape a stable, just, and humane society?

MAKING THIS BOOK

When Ashraf Zahedi—who has spent years researching, writing, and speaking about gender in Afghanistan—invited me to join her in producing this volume, it seemed an appropriate next step in the relationship I have had with the country since I was an adolescent. But contemporary books about Afghanistan and Afghan women crowd the shelves. Louis Dupree's *Afghanistan* is one of the classics, first printed in 1973, an encyclopedic marvel. The Soviet invasion (addressed in Dupree's 1980 edition) drew hundreds of journalists into the country and inspired distinguished researchers such as Richard S. and Nancy Peabody Newell (*The Struggle for Afghanistan*, 1981). Much was written about the ghastly fate of women during the Taliban years, and in *With All Our Strength: The Revolutionary Association of the Women of Afghanistan* (2003), Anne Brodsky brought to light the "back story," as it were, of their vigor and resiliency.

After 9/11, writers and photographers flooded the country, each apparently with a book contract and a new angle on ways to describe the ever-intriguing, ever-photogenic burqa, or *chadari* as Afghans commonly call it.[24] As Lina Abirafeh, Dinah Zeiger, and other contributors note in this book, the chadari is a dramatic symbol to the West, an obsession that essentializes women, denies their agency, and effectively adds to their oppression. It overpowers urgent issues of poverty, hunger, non-literacy,[25] maternal and infant deaths, acute emotional instability, and war, conditions far more threatening than a piece of cloth.

Among the most thoughtful post-9/11 books is Ann Jones's *Kabul in Winter: Life Without Peace in Afghanistan* (2006). The writings of scholars—including Moghadam, Elaheh Rostami-Povey, Sippi Azarbaijani-Moghaddam, and Deniz Kandiyoti—and activists—Sonali Kolthakar and Sunita Mehta, to name two—have also advanced the causes of Afghan women. Abirafeh, both a scholar and a practitioner, is author of *Gender and International Aid in Afghanistan: The Politics and Effects of Intervention* (2009), based on her experiences establishing and running a non-governmental organization.

Here and there, a few Afghans have managed to get a word in, among them Senzil Nawid and Hafizullah Emadi, whose crucial *Repression, Resistance, and Women in Afghanistan* (2002) is referenced repeatedly here.

The value of day-to-day investigations detailing Afghan life and society conducted on the ground by the independent Afghanistan Research and Evaluation Unit is immeasurable. If Westerners pay close attention to their findings, a solid bridge between worldviews might be built.

It is almost impossible to avoid a topical book about Afghanistan. Events move rapidly. News outlets and the Internet become primary sources. As we gathered contributors we believe best offer reliable representations of Afghan women and their situations, the U.S. elected a new president, Barack Obama, who was determining whether to accelerate the war. While we were assembling the manuscript, Obama—having already sent additional troops—announced a surge of 30,000 soldiers into Afghanistan, escalating U.S. strength in the country to more than 100,000. Hamid Karzai, despite rigged elections in August 2009 and charges of corruption from all sides, was permitted to take back the Afghan presidency, and at a conference in London—where women's voices were silent—he announced negotiations with Taliban leadership, attempts he'd made before, although this time he had the backing of the UN. In June 2010, General Stanley McChrystal was disgraced and replaced by General David Petraeus as top U.S. commander in Afghanistan. In July, 92,000 internal documents describing U.S. military actions in Afghanistan across six years were published by the whistleblower Web site, WikiLeaks. A few days later, the U.S. Congress approved a $59 billion increase in war funding, and the following month, over Petraeus's objections, Obama reaffirmed an earlier promise that U.S. troops would begin leaving Afghanistan in July 2011. Meanwhile, NATO requested 2,000 more troops in an attempt to stave off expanding Taliban forces.[26] And this is merely a very brief outline that neglects other assorted events, including, for example, the daily terrors experienced by Afghan civilians under fire from all sides or U.S.-Pakistan-Taliban convolutions. By the time this book was ready for production, there was little doubt that the war in Afghanistan was an unnavigable quagmire.

Headlines and the mind spin at a dizzying pace. But things also change slowly, so that the collision of Western impatience, the honest urgency to right wrongs, and the need to honor ancient traditions can be—have been—catastrophic.

We have tried to assemble a book that confronts and examines—from pregnancy to poetry, from food security to education, from parliamentarians to prisoners—some of the realities of life for Afghan women: for contemporary women (including women repatriated from countries where they may have had more advantages), glancing toward the West, usually living in cities, where their circumstances are more readily observed, as well as for rural women and those cleaving to custom, from whom we can learn much, yet who are mislabeled as "backward" or deficient. There are and always have been multiple Afghanistans: Kabul, modern, multicultural, and Western-mediated; Herat, Kandahar, Bamiyan, Mazar-i-Sharif, and other cities with quite dissimilar attitudes and populations; and villages and towns isolated in mountains and valleys populated by people—Pashtun, Hazara, Tajik, Uzbek, and others—whose ways of life stretch back long before Islam entered Afghanistan in the seventh century C.E. And there are the displaced, refugees who comprise still another Afghanistan, many of whom may never be able to return to their ancestral homes.[27] The fetishizing and imposition of one-size-fits-all Western-style democracy and Western ideals and ideas are not necessarily appropriate for a tribal, dynastic society and can result—as several of our contributors note—in backlash.

Although this book features some images, we did not want to emphasize the exotic or camera-friendly impoverishment of Afghan women nor sensationalize their plights. We seek a fuller picture: historical background leading to insights, observations, and narratives of women's lives in the present, as close to the ground as we can get, with comprehensive solutions and modest suggestions for social policy toward the future. Reaching for a holistic approach, we called on the expertise of twenty-six accomplished scholars, humanitarian workers, researchers, politicians, and journalists, most with actual, extended experience inside Afghanistan. We could not cover everything and found it impossible and unnecessary to organize the five parts in this book by, say, region, chronology, or studies versus personal accounts. To do so seemed contrived, fusty, unbalanced, and not in accord with the rhizomic and multiple truths of Afghan life. The contributors' distinctive voices, approaches, themes, and backgrounds are meant to be layered, to coincide and converse.

PERCEPTIONS AND REALITIES

We must reevaluate our perceptions if we hope to help Afghanistan come to a new reality—its *own* reality, led by Afghans. This begins with history. Shireen Khan Burki's "Politics of *Zan*" opens the book by guiding us through the frustrating and dangerous maze of Afghanistan's official gender policies starting in 1919, when ideas of equality were introduced, and suggests how future attempts to raise women's status might actually have lasting success.

Afghan societies are primarily rural, agrarian, and inward-looking. As psychologist Willem van de Put notes, "Afghans are born into a set of answers rather than a set of questions. . . . [T]hese 'answers' are rooted in a long history of clan autonomy, codes of honor, and hospitality, gender-related divisions of tasks and roles in society, and religious beliefs."[28] Joan Kayeum—an American educator married to an Afghan, who lived in Afghanistan for more than twenty-five years—insisting that "some generalizations can be made," writes:

A young man sells lilacs outside
the author's Kabul home.
Courtesy of Jennifer Heath, 1965.

It is impossible not to recognize some outstanding characteristics of [the Afghan] people . . . their amazing hospitality, dignity, generosity, good manners, and respect for the elders of their family and community. Theirs is a patriarchal society, yet one is impressed with their love and respect for their mothers, which borders on being a sacred code of behavior. . . . The dedication of Afghans to the honor of their women, their chastity, dominates the cultural scene throughout the land. It is inextricably interwoven with the all-important "good name" that is prized above all else by Afghans.[29]

Afghanistan was once called "Land of the Unconquerable."[30] ("Graveyard of Empires" has lately been a popular if inaccurate moniker.) Afghan men were characterized as (and often considered themselves) eloquent warrior poets—good fathers, good sons, good providers, good patriarchs— and were likely no more vainglorious than men reared in other cultures believing the world revolves entirely around them. Afghan men's ethical codes (based largely on a pre-Islamic system called Pashtunwali), desires, needs, behaviors, and suffering naturally frame the lives of Afghan women, determining their fates and well-being. Dominant in the culture, men are likely to become even more lost than women when the underpinnings of that culture come undone.

Dr. Azam Dadfar, psychiatrist and now minister of higher education, told reporter Elizabeth Rubin that "a new Afghan character type has emerged—a borderline personality characteristic of jihadis. 'Multiple personality disorder is a coping mechanism. . . . A young man who lost his father, his home, he looks to become the cleverest, the most criminal, the lion. In the jungle there are no values but self-preservation. There's no law. And this character learns to lie even to himself.' "[31]

For centuries, Afghans had a successful history of repelling—and absorbing—would-be invaders. But modern warfare has downtrodden the land and its people as never before. Families have been driven permanently from their homes and ways of life annihilated. The solid, secure "we" of Afghan thinking is threatened with extinction. Such desperation easily draws people toward religious zealotry for comfort. And poverty leads to desperate actions, among them the sale of children.

In refugee camps, skills can be lost within one generation: the essential knowledge of farming, for example, disappears. Men are emasculated, shamed, dependent on the kindness of strangers. Boys—once apprenticed to their fathers and other male relatives—must add to the family income or provide for their widowed mothers or orphaned siblings by whatever means necessary. Many have never known peace. Unprotected, they have been conscripted as soldiers and exploited for the sexual gratification of Mujahedin, Taliban commanders, and other men.[32] Veterans suffer from post-traumatic stress syndrome, drug addiction, and alcoholism. Thirty years of war corrupts the soul; violence breeds violence.

"Most people get their information about Afghanistan from *The Kite Runner* and *Charlie Wilson's War*," David Barsamian, producer of the U.S.-based, independent Alternative Radio, said in a 2009 talk. "You can't learn anything from that kind of infotainment." The West, he notes, operates from legends such as "the invasion of Alexander the Great or that Afghans are fierce fighters," by which we characterize and visualize and therefore interact with Afghanistan.[33]

In "Don't Say What, Who, and When, Say How," Wahid Omar suggests that there are ways of understanding the Afghan people other than through a Western filter, to examine how Afghans perceive events or approach a social moment and the decision-making roles of Afghan women within their communities. Learning to know Afghans and Afghan society might improve how development and aid are delivered and boost success.

One way to see beyond what we think we know is through folklore and literature. (It might behoove policy makers and donors to consult the humanities before making decisions, or as Wahid Omar said in a personal conversation, "Let's send ethnographers, not guns.") Among its other accomplishments, Margaret Mills's "Between Covered and Covert" links the female trickster in Afghan oral tradition to women's agency with stories that are "weapons of the weak." Misogyny, she reminds us, is "not inevitable in male speakers, nor is it unheard-of in women's performances."

Neither are women necessarily weak, as Brodsky recalls in "Centuries of Threat, Centuries of Resistance." They have shown their mettle as poets, rulers, educators, politicians, revolutionaries, female Mujahedin, and in daily life.

A WOMAN'S PLACE

... is in parliament ... in the home ... and for too many, an Afghan woman's place is in the streets or prison.

Anna Larson's "Women's Political Presence" contextualizes the process, successes, and failures of affirmative action in the Afghan parliament since the Bonn Agreement established a reserved-seat system to guarantee women's participation. King Amanullah (r. 1919 to 1929) gave women the vote in 1923, but by 1929, they were again disenfranchised, until 1964, when King Muhammad Zahir Shah (r. 1933 to 1973) established a new constitution, even allowing women to enter politics. In 1958, Afghanistan had already sent a woman delegate to the UN, so "no one was startled" Dupree wrote, when four were elected to the *Wolesi Jirga* (Lower House), "two from Kabul, one from Herat, and one from Kandahar."[34] Zahir Shah's prime minister, Nur Ahmad Etemadi, had—as had Karzai during his first term—one female cabinet member, the first minister of women's affairs, Rokya Etemadi. During the civil war and Taliban eras, all bets were off again. Today, as Azarbaijani-Moghaddam says, "The constitution-making process has enjoyed a great deal of attention and pressure from gender equality advocates but it is to be expected that inherent flaws in the mechanisms and processes ... have left loopholes and gaps for the exercise of patriarchy to continue unhampered."[35] In the rural areas, women's participation in political and civil life is hindered by customs and traditions. Rural women, researchers Neamatollah Nojumi, Dyan Mazurana, and Elizabeth Stites note, "face the greatest threats to human security."[36] Seclusion, although anathema to Westerners, can actually mean safety.

Habiba Sarobi is the well-respected governor of Bamiyan Province. During the 2009 presidential elections, when turnout was low throughout the country, but lowest among females, Bamiyan's women voted in droves. Its population is made up primarily of Hazara—Shi'a Muslims—who were known to be more open than other groups to women's public presence. Yet the 2009 Shi'a Family Law, which Larson addresses, sent hundreds of women into the streets protesting this rerun of Taliban-style constraints. In an op-ed for the *New York Times*, Hassina Sherjan wrote, "Even a free and fair election is no substitute for justice."[37]

In "Voices of Parliamentarians," members of parliament, Massouda Jalal, Fawzia Koofi, Azita Rafat, and Malalai Joya (suspended for her outspoken condemnation of corruption), write of their mandates and concerns. Karzai—mistrusted, corrupted, manipulated by fundamentalists, warlords, and family interests—has betrayed women repeatedly, not only endorsing the Shi'a law, but also, for example, pardoning convicted gang rapists.[38]

The Shi'a Family Law formalizes many injustices to which women are persistently subjected and for which, as Lizette Potgieter illustrates in "Nothing Left to Lose," they are imprisoned. There are few female judges and defense attorneys in Kabul, let alone in rural areas, where Nojumi, Mazurana, and Stites found that "the formal, traditional, and customary justice systems . . . purportedly in place to uphold the rights of rural Afghan women often undermine their rights. . . . The lack or complete absence of women in leadership positions within formal and traditional justice systems undermines access to justice."[39]

In "Selling Sex in Afghanistan," Alisa Tang portrays women and girls forced by poverty into sex work, a primary underground source of income for women, as well as for some men and boys, and as Tang notes, even whole families can be involved. There are upwards of 1 million Afghan widows, whose average age is thirty-five. Fifty thousand are in Kabul, often living in abandoned buildings. Many survive by soliciting sex and/or begging in the streets, some with their children.[40] These are Afghanistan's most vulnerable and neglected women. Men are reluctant to marry widows with children, there are few jobs, and, in any case, most are non-literate and unskilled.[41]

There are no concrete figures for the numbers of orphans in Afghanistan, though estimates put them in the thousands.[42] Child labor is a huge concern. Not all poor families send their children to work, but schooling, where it is available, even with minimal fees, can be expensive for a family with little to eat. Nevertheless, some families weigh school costs against future benefits and choose, if they can, to sacrifice for it. And some families see no reason to educate girls, who will one day marry and leave.[43] Researcher Alexandra Reihing writes:

A widow begging in Kabul. Photo by
Sheryl B. Shapiro, 2003.

In Afghanistan, twenty-one percent of child workers are employed in shops;
thirteen percent work as street vendors. Others work in vehicle repair, metal
workshops, tailoring, and farming. In Kabul and other cities there are street
children who shine shoes, beg, and collect and sell scrap metal, paper, and
firewood. The economic pressure to work means that over three million
children are being denied an education.[44]

Deborah J. Smith brings a woman's place—home—into focus with
"Between Choice and Force," based on case studies of marriages, how
they are decided, by whom, and with what results. Not all arranged marriages are unhappy and not all marriages have more elements of force
than choice. In cultures strictly bound by the intricacies of family politics, neither girls *nor* boys have choices, a fact that can impact future
domestic violence. Although girls are certainly married in response to
economic need, we don't want to exaggerate the occasionally sensationalized tales of girls exchanged to pay their family's debts.

TO BE WHOLE IN BODY AND MIND

Without sufficient or nutritious food (tea and naan—flatbread—hardly
make a vitamin-rich meal), education, shelter, work, or decent health
care, there can be no real security. Afghanistan has among the world's

Two small girls sweep sidewalks in Kabul. They are among thousands of Afghan children who must work to help support their families. Photo by Sheryl B. Shapiro, 2003.

worst health indicators—the worst place on Earth for a child to be born—and this, as Sima Samar, currently chair of the Afghanistan Independent Human Rights Commission, writes, constitutes a "hidden war" against women, whose life expectancy is between forty-two and forty-four. One out of four children dies before the age of five.[45] Malaria, cholera, polio, and dysentery account for many deaths. Malnutrition is rampant, particularly as agricultural fields are strafed and sophisticated irrigation systems constructed across millennia have been ruined. Unsafe drinking water, lack of sanitary facilities, and fertilizers from untreated human and animal waste all contribute to Afghanistan's grim statistics.

Increasing combat constrains the ability of professionals to reach rural areas (where 85 percent of the population lives) and has delayed international assistance. Additionally, lack of transportation to the few hospitals or clinics, coupled with restrictions on travel, make it almost impossible for rural women to receive medical attention, particularly prenatal care.

The Taliban are well-known to have severely curtailed women's access to health care,[46] but Nojumi, Mazurana, and Stites remind us that

culture continues to regulate women's access . . . rural women in Kandahar reported that they could *only* see female doctors . . . female informants in

Badghis, Herat, Kabul, and Nangarhar reported that while they could see either a male or female health care provider for basic care, for reproductive care they could *only* go to a woman. Thus, the fact that the majority of rural health clinics have no female care providers means that rural women do not have access to reproductive health care.[47]

Afghanistan's maternal mortality rate is the second highest in the world. In "Challenges to Cripple the Spirit," Pamela Chandler relates her experiences training midwives, showing us the human face behind the statistics.[48]

In 1954, the Shiwaki Project was established as a public health pilot program. Within a year, it had expanded from two to eighty-one villages. Traveling Afghan doctors and nurses provided health services, including sanitation programs.[49] In the 1960s and early 1970s, further strides were made through a multitude of aid organizations, but with the Soviet invasion, those advances halted.[50] Mary MacMakin—a physical therapist who has spent most of her adult life in Afghanistan—was there. In "Women with Disabilities," she shares the breadth and depth of her long experience, describing how women have coped across the decades with physical disabilities, most of which today are the result of war and land mines.

Farm and grazing lands are littered with leftover mines and unexploded ordnance (UXO). It is estimated that there is one mine per Afghan. Thus, hundreds are killed or maimed every year. In Kabul, roughly 85 percent of UXO victims are children. In 2003, 62 percent of Kabulis were living among land mines and UXOs. The process of dismantling them is expensive and painfully slow.[51]

Widespread field studies have been conducted to determine radiation in soil, plants, and human urine from depleted uranium used in precision weapons. In 2002, the Uranium Medical Research Center found Afghans "with acute symptoms of radiation poisoning, along with chronic symptoms of internal uranium contamination, including congenital problems." Some subjects had concentrations of 400–2,000 percent above that for normal populations.[52] In May 2009, there were reports of severe chemical burns possibly attributable to white phosphorus, a flammable material used by combatants to illuminate targets or create smoke.[53]

Afghanistan's environmental damage is incalculable, with observable climate changes such as earthquakes, sandstorms, and unusually harsh winters in the last decade. In 2009, the worst drought in living memory affected all traditional food crops. Afghanistan was rich in

biodiversity—among its many names, it was also called "Land of Lilacs"—
but its fertile lands, its breadbaskets, and its wilderness are now devas-
tated by persistent violence and the weather patterns that follow. Natural resources have been, to say the least, badly mismanaged or simply
not managed at all. In 2002, the United Nations Environmental Programme conducted a basic research project and their findings were
disturbing: "Afghanistan's natural resources—forests, waters, soil, or
wildlife—were clearly in decline or on the brink of irreparable damage,
and the resulting environmental degradation was endangering human
health and compounding poverty."[54]

Afghanistan's mineral wealth, as yet untapped but identified as worth
upwards of $3 trillion, will quite likely only fuel more fighting, corrup-
tion, exploitation, and poverty. And, as in other resource-rich lands,
unearthing the minerals might well unbalance what remains of the
country's ecosystems.[55]

In writings about Afghan women, this tragedy is rarely mentioned
and yet, if environmental degradation is not halted, no other efforts will
ultimately count for much.

In "A Question of Access," Elizabeth Stites—whose co-authored volume
After the Taliban: Life and Security in Rural Afghanistan (2009) is an
invaluable resource—writes here about Afghanistan's history of food
security and how it changed after the fall of the Taliban in 2001.

Only 12 percent of the land is now arable. A great deal of space is
taken up in poppy cultivation, with production spiking after the U.S.
invasion.[56] The multibillion-dollar opium trade has turned Afghanistan
into a full-blown narco state. But attempts at eradicating poppy fields
have been no more successful than the United States's "long war on drugs"
in Latin America. Compensation is not paid to the farmers for opium
crops they are unable to harvest. With every field plowed under or
sprayed, farmers, for whom drug manufacture can be the alternative to
starvation, are left out of work, and more hunger, debt, and economic
tribulations ensue, putting women and girls at further risk.

As Potgieter notes, women are also involved in the drug trade and
some are jailed. Thousands are drug-addicted, a symptom, as psychologist Nahid Aziz writes in "Psychological Impacts of War," of the tragic
degeneration of women's mental health, a consequence of chronic human
rights violations.

A sewing class at the Ministry of Women's Affairs in Kabul. Photo by Sheryl B. Shapiro, 2003.

MAKING THE RUBBLE BLOOM

In "When the Picture Does Not Fit the Frame," Ashraf Zahedi takes a daring step by questioning the merits of "gender mainstreaming" in Afghan development policy. There is no Dari word for "gender." Among people for whom the family means everything, the economic, political, and social lives of men and women cannot be disentangled.

In "Mending Afghanistan Stitch by Stitch," Rachel Lehr recounts the history of Rubia, a grassroots embroidery project she co-founded in 2000. This wonderful, thriving endeavor is not unlike, for instance, the Gee's Bend women's collective in Alabama, which, since the mid-twentieth century, has used quilt making as a strategy for survival and economic development.[57] The respect and care—and shrewdness—with which Rubia works, without predetermination or meddling, account for its success.

There are scores of attempts by non-governmental organizations to help women, particularly in Kabul, create independent enterprises or to export and sell their handicrafts. A few are flourishing. Nevertheless, as Gayle Tzemach Lemmon reported in the *New York Times*:

> Hindered by what development agencies acknowledge has been poor planning, insufficient appreciation of the environment's myriad complexities and

an aid mentality focused on quick cash infusions rather than longer-term investment, many economic programs for women in Afghanistan have struggled to find their footing.

An estimated $16 billion in reconstruction and development funds has entered Afghanistan since 2002, though international donors have yet to distribute billions more in pledged assistance. Exactly how much of this money has gone to empowerment projects for women is hard to know, since two-thirds of the development money has been spent outside the government's budget and much of the aid has never been reported.

Since 2002, the United States, Afghanistan's largest donor, has directed $570 million to programs benefiting Afghan women and girls, with $175 million more likely to be approved for the coming fiscal year [2009–2010]. Women's health programs have received the largest share; $20 million has gone to economic initiatives.[58]

As of 2009, Afghanistan received only about $57 per capita from international aid, as opposed, for example, to Bosnia at $679 and East Timor at $333 per capita. On average, Matt Waldman, former head of policy for Oxfam International in Afghanistan, reported in 2008, donors have spent just "$7 million per day," adding that "since 2001, the United States has appropriated $127 billion for the war in Afghanistan, and the U.S. military is currently spending nearly $100 million a day in the country, some $36 billion a year." In 2010, the Pentagon estimated that the cost of the war in Afghanistan would overtake that of the Iraq war. Forty percent of aid money has funneled back into the donor countries as corporate profits and extremely high consultants' salaries. Although outside expertise is needed on numerous fronts, little money is actually spent on the Afghan workforce, where it can do the most good for the country.[59]

"It is almost impossible to determine where government policies begin and [international financial institutions] end," Bank Information Center consultant Anne Carlin writes, noting how donors can appear to *be* the government. "When significant [United States Agency for International Development] influence is added to the mix, the lines overlap everywhere."[60]

Projects also overlap or compete, despite some attempts by the Afghan government to glean and register the hundreds of NGOs that followed the U.S.-led invasion. There is still almost no oversight and donors continue to bypass the government, which has little enough credibility as it is. For example, in January 2010, the UN reported that Afghans paid $2.5 billion in bribes to public officials during a period of twelve months, across 2009.[61]

Needless to say, the waste is tremendous—so-called "administrative costs" for international organizations alone are breathtaking—and the global financial crisis as well as the cost of war are certain to affect future funding for civilian assistance.[62] Young Afghans told Amina Kator, in interviews conducted for this book's epilogue, that they are fed up with the distorted distribution of aid money, much of which they see as irrelevant or frivolous, with little long-term value.

In "Rural Women's Livelihood," Jo Grace and Adam Pain close the gap with a clear depiction of how women outside urban areas negotiate to benefit themselves and their families and gain power and fulfillment despite inequities. As Wahid Omar suggests, overprescriptive policies and procedures only frustrate potentially constructive projects. Development is hamstrung by many factors, not least a patronizing dedication to saving and empowering women without profound consideration of the steps and stages that might realistically require. Afghan women must not be "othered" nor can they be separated from Afghanistan. (And again: there are various and diverse Afghanistans.)

Building or rebuilding obsolete infrastructures will take billions of dollars and decades to accomplish. In an era when Western countries are aiming for sustainability, aid agencies apply old technology to Afghanistan, where wind and sun are plentiful and indigenous domestic architectural techniques, farming, and irrigation practices could be progressive, "back to the future" models for the rest of the world. Hunter Lovins, president and founder of Natural Capitalism, Inc., writes

> Official proposals for reconstruction make little effort to use state-of-the-art sustainability technologies, despite the fact that they work better and are better suited to poor, widely distributed populations. Instead, most of the reconstruction projects wind up using cast-off equipment and approaches from Pakistan or the West simply because they have a lower up-front cost or vendors are familiar with them. Existing reconstruction efforts approach each problem in isolation, missing opportunities to use whole-systems design to solve multiple problems with the same resources. Using outdated technology and conventional thinking rather than best practice will ensure that Afghanistan remains the sixth poorest country in the world.[63]

There have been small, idealistic, determined, and brave NGOs trying to supply welcome items, such as solar cookers, briquette fuel makers, or ceramic water filters, or exchanging ideas about permaculture, ancient construction materials (e.g., adobe vs. concrete), and traditional agriculture and seed saving.[64] These efforts have been mostly unsupported by

Women and their children in the farming village of Bustan, Afghanistan. Photo by Sheryl B. Shapiro, 2003.

large donor organizations, which are frequently corporate driven, and so far, have not fulfilled their own guidelines to meet environmental sustainability goals. Fulfilling their mandates when there was an opportunity soon after the 2001 invasion might have also begun a process toward stabilizing and improving women's lives.

As is often noted, change is slow for isolated rural Afghans. But what do we mean by change? And why is "slow" unacceptable if it includes "steady" and means that the changes can be sustainable? It is up to Afghans to reconstruct and develop their country based on its cultural and geographic diversity and the desires of each community. What is good for Bamiyan may not be good for Kabul or Nuristan or Jalalabad or Badakhshan or Wardak. Women of all classes must and will be at the forefront of gradual change, although—and it cannot be emphasized enough—without peace, no change can be maintained.

"DON'T ECLIPSE MY HAPPY NEW MOON"

Throughout Afghanistan, where two-thirds of the population over the age of fifteen—and 85 percent of women—are non-literate, people are demanding schools.[65] It is reported that there are approximately twenty-five high schools countrywide in the major cities for girls and boys and about thirty universities in various states of organization, repair, and academic excellence. Untold numbers of children, youth, and adults attend classes in home schools, tents, and cargo containers. After the fall of the Taliban, more than 4 million children returned to school, with girls making up about 35 percent.[66]

Yet, in 2008, 256 schools came under violent attack, up from 236 in 2007. In November 2008, fifteen female students were assaulted in Kandahar. Two were blinded and two injured. In the first six months of 2009, sixteen bomb attacks took place on school premises and by fall, 80 percent of schools in southern Afghanistan were closed.[67]

As Nojumi, Mazurana, and Stites tell us,

Countrywide, percentages of . . . boys and girls attending school are highest in the north and northeast, with the lowest rates in south and south central regions. There are few school-aged rural girls attending school in the south and south central parts of the country; the primary reasons for rural boys and girls not attending school are lack of facilities and distance to facilities . . . ; insecurity is preventing boys and girls from attending schools in rural districts in nine provinces; girls are more likely than boys to be held out of school when areas are affected by physical insecurity.[68]

Traveling distances presents dangers. Coeducation has been frowned upon since Afghan girls first began attending school in the 1920s. Unfortunately, the rush to create girls' schools after the Taliban defeat often neglected boys' educational needs, a mistake considering that a nation of men ignorant of history, literature, mathematics, sciences, languages, arts, political science, and so on, will continue to oppress women, even educated ones, and be unable to participate fully in the creation of a strong and peaceful civil society.

As Sakena Yacoobi illustrates in the opening paragraph of "Empowering Women through Education," even the slightest ability to read can save a life, as well as enrich it. In *Half the Sky: Turning Oppression into Opportunity for Women Worldwide*, co-authors Nicholas Kristoff and Sheryl WuDunn note that

American organizations would have accomplished much more if they had financed and supported Sakena['s Afghan Institute of Learning], rather than dispatching their own representatives to Kabul. . . . The best role for Americans who want to help Muslim women isn't holding the microphone at the front of the rally, but writing the checks and carrying the bags in the back.[69]

Yacoobi, who shares her formulas for achievement, is heroic and is not alone in her valiant efforts. There are many Afghans—and humble non-Afghans usually not associated with massive aid organizations—who are struggling to meet Afghan demands for education.[70]

Enrichment is the basic theme of this book's final part, which takes its title—"Don't Eclipse My Happy New Moon"—from a verse in Zuzanna Olszewska's "A Hidden Discourse," about the strength and comfort poetry has given Afghan women throughout history, whether oral or written, despite the risks of unveiling the truth.

It would be a mistake to assume that the repression of Afghan women's creative expressions is unique. Although Afghans have endured particular and sometimes unspeakable horrors, women poets and artists worldwide, throughout history, and right up to this moment, experience restrictions imposed by their societies. They are undereducated, critically ignored, overwhelmed by marriage and children, or sometimes simply meet the limitations of their creative drives and abilities. If we too adamantly deny Afghan women the commonality of the struggles endured by all artists, we exclude them from the global arts community, isolate them further, and therefore risk undermining their exquisite work.

In wartime, to focus on arts and culture may seem inconsequential (and they are too often considered trivial in any case). Not only do arts and the knowledge of history help shape whole, creative human beings, giving pleasure and beauty and thus enabling peace, not only do they offer lessons from the past and thus innovative visions for the future, but also, as historian Nancy Hatch Dupree emphasizes, it is through culture that national identity is forged and preserved:

> An innate sense of the essence of their culture sustained Afghans through twenty-four years of conflict and displacement. Although they continue to cherish the diversity of regional differences, individuals cling tenaciously to their national identity, upholding traditional values and customs that distinguish them from their neighbors. From the beginning of the twentieth century, attempts to foster unity through nation-building activities in mostly urban areas met with mixed success; the latest attempts to cast Afghans in a puritanical Islamic mould met with disaster. Years of discord stretched taut the fabric of the society and national traits, once honored hallmarks of the culture, were compromised. Yet the fundamentals of the culture remain strong, changed in some ways but readily recognizable as uniquely Afghan. Current expectations aim to engage various cultural elements as bonding vehicles to hasten reconstruction and strengthen peace.[71]

The media also connects people, closing distances and reminding listeners, viewers, and readers of their common concerns. In "From Both Sides of the Mic," Aunohita Mojumdar outlines how media have burgeoned in Afghanistan since 2001, what this means for women, and how women have contributed—sometimes with their lives—to the effort. Of all the forms of media, radio is the most powerful for its reach across the country.

Women announcers and singers first appeared on Radio Afghanistan in 1957, and after only a brief opposition, women were given permanent jobs at the station.[72] Today, however, the challenges and resistance are tremendous and the dangers intense for all journalists. According to Reporters Without Borders—which originally lauded press freedom as "one of the few achievements since the fall of the Taliban, though it remains fragile . . . targeted by religious conservatives"—in 2007, the number of female students in Herat, for example, dropped from 70 percent to 30 percent in journalism.[73]

Nevertheless, despite threats and assassinations, many female reporters and photographers refuse to be intimidated. The work of two young women—Nilab Habibi and Safya Saify—who have found fulfilling vocations as photojournalists in Kabul at Pajhwok Afghan News, graces the title page for part II, "A Woman's Place."

The boom in radio, TV, and print media has helped to keep Afghans informed about everything from politics to pop culture, but there seem to be few national efforts to create distance-education programs in basic literacy and numeracy, the "three R's," for youngsters and adults, particularly isolated girls and women. In remote areas of, for instance, India, Canada, and Australia, people have benefited from radio classrooms.[74] Today, distance learning in the West takes place primarily through the Internet, but this is hardly viable in most of Afghanistan, where there is no electricity. (Radios can be battery-operated and batteries can be purchased almost everywhere.) A government-run effort toward distance learning could carve inroads for formal education to places that cannot now be reached and will not be for years. Of course, much depends, as researcher Sarah Kamal has written, on family politics, that is, the person in the household who controls the radio. But, as "repetition is the soul of education," so is persistence.[75]

A privately owned station such as Radio Sahar (Dawn), which opened in 2003 in Herat—one of a network of independent women's radio stations—is run by a varied community board and offers a wide range of women's programming, primarily on culture, social, and humanitarian issues, with two hours a day of educational programs, but steers clear of politics. Efforts like these, though hazardous, are, as Mojumdar explains, vital to the well-being of women.[76]

Crimes against culture are common in war. Across three decades, Afghanistan has had its share and more, most obviously and deliberately with the Taliban's incineration of films, books, archival volumes and manuscripts, musical instruments, the obliteration of portraits and other figurative images, then, in a grand denouement, the shots heard round the world when the magnificent ancient Buddha statues in Bamiyan were obliterated.[77]

When at last the Taliban retreated from Kabul, musicians, as if offering absolute proof of the human yearning and need for art, returned to Kharabat Street, where for centuries they'd gathered to play. Artisans went back to work relearning and reviving Afghanistan's exquisite ceramics, woodcarving, traditional architecture, calligraphy, or weaving, and theaters sparkled back to life.[78]

In "Painting Their Way into the Public World," Lauryn Oates documents young female artists learning modernist painting, not unheard of in Afghanistan but not expected either, particularly from women. Like poetry, painting has the power to heal and to dissolve rigid certainties, a giant and essential step toward inner and outer peace.

The history of Afghanistan and the lives of Afghan women, their suffering, agency, and empowerment, is complex and too often reduced to one media-convenient dimension. Although each contributor brings open eyes and wider truths to the discussion, this book cannot possibly cover all the nuances, and this introduction can provide only clues to larger contexts in Afghanistan's difficult journey.

We must not abandon Afghanistan, but that is precisely what we do when we attack it with massive firepower, rob it with improperly distributed donor funds, endorse a corrupt, fundamentalist government, and play at treacherous, labyrinthine intrigues.[79] Humanitarian aid is desperately needed and will be for a long time to come. Thirty years of physical, cultural, and psychological damage cannot be repaired overnight. Aid costs less and returns more than fighting, especially if most of the money were to go directly to help the Afghan people rather than into greedy pockets. Conservatives and progressives alike have described the amplified war in Afghanistan as unwinnable, and no one is quite sure of its goals, that is, what would be won if by chance there were a U.S. and NATO "victory."[80]

"Every war," the late historian Howard Zinn reminded us repeatedly, "is a war against children." Rather than a troop surge, what's required are surges of teachers, engineers, medical professionals, environmentalists, organic farmers, social workers, and others—a new and progressive "peace corps"—that can facilitate healing with carefully thought-out programs and support for Afghans to rebuild, led by Afghans themselves, and made to succeed without increased military intervention. But it takes honesty. And patience. And listening. And imagination.[81]

Bombs and guns beget bombs and guns. Myriad ideas have been proposed for how to pull out of the quagmire we have created in Afghanistan and at last accomplish peace.[82] Ultimately, the only sure paths are through dialogue and compromise. Afghan women (and countless men) rightly fear reconciliation with the Taliban. Yet between a corrupt government, powerful warlords, and unyielding conflict, women are still shut out of political decisions, despite constitutional guarantees, and are still desperate for the most fundamental human rights—among them medicine, safe drinking water, sufficient food, warmth, roofs over their heads, safety, sovereignty, and simple dignity.[83]

If anyone understands that war is not the answer, it is Afghan women. Each one is the bravest woman in Afghanistan. Every step—one step at a time—must be taken with consideration for their concerns. Otherwise, there can be no lasting peace, for just as war is fought on the backs of women, peace rests on women's well-being and strength, as well as on justice, good governance, and the rule of law. Any peace agreements, if they are to be durable, must include clear commitments from all sides to respect and protect women's rights.[84] To achieve this, women must sit, fully empowered, in equal numbers, with their brothers at the head of the table.

NOTES

1. Internal fighting had already begun here and there in Afghanistan between the Soviet-backed regimes and anti-communist Afghans shortly before the Soviet invasion. See M. Hassan Kakar, *Afghanistan: The Soviet Invasion and the Afghan Response* (Berkeley: University of California Press, 1995), 32–50. In the 1980s, one out of two refugees worldwide was Afghan. Some 3.7 million Afghan refugees who fled the conflict in the past two decades currently live in neighboring countries: 1.5 million in Iran and 2 million in Pakistan. "The Cost of War in Afghanistan," American Friends Service Committee, http://www.national

priorities.org/auxiliary/costofwar/cost_of_war_afghanistan.pdf. There are no accurate figures for the numbers of civilian casualties in Afghanistan since the United States-led invasion started in 2001, but it is estimated that 2,118 civilians were killed in 2008 alone, compared with 1,523 in 2007, the highest since the Taliban government was defeated in November 2001. Dexter Filkins, "Afghan Civilian Deaths Rose 40 Percent in 2008," *New York Times*, February 18, 2009, http://www.nytimes.com/2009/02/18/world/asia/18afghan.html. At mid-year 2010, the United Nations Assistance Mission in Afghanistan reported that the number of civilians wounded and killed increased by nearly a third in the first six months of the year, as U.S. and NATO coalition forces raised the level of military action. United Nations Assistance Mission, Featured News, "Afghan Civilian Casualties Rise 31 Percent in First Six Months of 2010," August 10, 2010, http://unama.unmissions.org.

2. Zbigniew Brzezinski admitted in an interview in the January 15, 1998, edition of France's *Le Nouvel Observateur* that he and CIA Director William Casey came up with the scheme to provoke the Soviet invasion of Afghanistan by providing covert aid to the Mujahedin via Pakistani Intelligence services. The idea, Brzezinski told the *Observateur*, was to "give the USSR its Vietnam War." The recruitment of Muslim jihadists eventually led to the events of September 11, 2001. See Pankaj Mishra, "The Making of Afghanistan," *The New York Review of Books* 48, no. 18 (November 15, 2001): 3. For further details about the U.S. policy buildup to the Soviet invasion of Afghanistan, see Paul Fitzgerald, Elizabeth Gould, with Sima Wali, *Invisible History: Afghanistan's Untold Story* (San Francisco: City Lights Books, 2009), 85–159; and Juan Cole, "Is Afghanistan Vietnam or Iraq? Arguing with Obama and Rubin," Informed Comment: Thoughts of the Middle East, History, and Religion, September 17, 2009, http://www.juancole.com/2009/09/is-afghanistan-vietnam-or-iraq-arguing.html. Since the fall of the Taliban, many of the old Mujahedin have joined the U.S.-backed Karzai government.

3. The Western media also walked away. With the 1989 Soviet retreat, the Afghan war lost its glamour and U.S. media attention shifted from the warring Mujahedin to focus on Soviet Afghan War veterans, who they likened to American Vietnam veterans. See, for example, Michael Parks, "Counseling in Moscow: U.S., Soviet Vets Share Grief of War," *Los Angeles Times*, October 18, 1988, http://articles.latimes.com/1988-10-18/news/mn-4554_1_vietnam-vets.

4. Ahmed Rashid, *Taliban: Militant Islam, Oil, and Fundamentalism in Central Asia* (New Haven, Conn.: Yale University Press, 2000), 170–182.

5. Rory Stewart, "The Irresistible Illusion," *London Review of Books*, July 9, 2009, http://www.lrb.co.uk/v31/n13/stewo1_.html. (Emphasis mine.)

6. Fitzgerald and Gould, *Invisible History*, 50–52, 104. "A perfect listening post" is from a personal conversation in 1990 with a former CIA agent stationed in Afghanistan during the 1970s, who prefers to remain anonymous. During the Cold War, Soviets and Americans alike courted the Afghan government and Prime Minister Muhammad Daoud Khan often played both ends against the middle. Of interest: Marshall I. Goldman, *Soviet Foreign Aid* (New York: Praeger, 1967) and Nikita Khrushchev, *Khrushchev Remembers* (Bos-

ton: Little Brown, 1970). In 1979, the USSR invaded Afghanistan from the northern border with Tajikistan by tank and truck on the roads it had built, and by plane, landing at the airport the United States had built in Kandahar.

7. Jason Burke. "I Would Never Swap My Country for All the World," *The Guardian*, September 11, 2008, http://www.guardian.co.uk/world/2008/sep11/Afghanistan.gender.

8. Robert Greenwald, "Rethink Afghanistan: Part Five" (Culver City, Calif.: Brave New Foundation, 2009), http://rethinkafghanistan.com/blog/?p=604; Jessica Leeder and Paula Lerner, "Behind the Veil: An Intimate Journey into the Lives of Kandahar's Women" (Toronto: The Globe and Mail, CTVglobemedia Publishing, 2009), http://www.theglobeandmail.com/news/world/behind-the-veil/. See also Gayle Tzemach, "Afghan Women Fear a Retreat to Dark Days," *Christian Science Monitor*, December 18, 2008, http://www.csmonitor.com/2008/1218/p07s03-wogn.html.

9. In late 2009, NATO declared a major victory against the Taliban in the town of Marja in Helmand Province, a brief, "unpredictable" triumph that British Lt. General Nick Parker told the Associated Press had been exaggerated. In future, he said, "the military will be more restrained in forecasting success. . . . The idea was to develop Marja as a model for counterinsurgency techniques in the hope that other communities would turn against the Taliban. Instead, the Taliban have fought back." "General Says Foresight on Marja Was Flawed," Associated Press, September 4, 2010, http://www.nytimes.com/2010/09/05/world/asia/05nato.html.

10. Officially the Agreement on Provisional Arrangements in Afghanistan Pending the Re-Establishment of Permanent Government Institutions, the Bonn Agreement was shaped at a December 2001 meeting in Germany, in order to recreate the State of Afghanistan following the United States-led invasion. Of the twenty-three listed Afghan participants in the United Nations talks, only two were women. Thanks to Ashraf Zahedi for her help researching issues of peace, security, and reconstruction for this introduction.

11. The phrase "moderate Taliban" is not necessarily an oxymoron. The original Taliban leadership is undeniably radical Islamic fundamentalist, trained in the Deobandi and Wahhabi traditions, very unlike the far more tolerant Islam practiced throughout much of Afghanistan before the Soviet invasion. But "moderate Taliban" can refer to those who, out of economic need, have had little choice but to join the fundamentalist ranks, regardless of their own beliefs.

12. An important component of post-conflict accord is the inclusion of transitional justice, a truth-finding process of judicial and non-judicial procedures that seeks to redress the pain and suffering of war victims. It investigates human rights violations and war crimes on all sides. By bringing injustices of the past to the surface, the process of reconciliation and lasting peace is facilitated. The Bonn Agreement does not mention transitional justice but makes general reference to "promoting national reconciliation, lasting peace, stability, and respect for human rights in the country." Instead, the Afghanistan Independent Human Rights Commission was established, which has so far not been empowered to take on transitional justice cases.

13. Rod Nordland, "Lacking Money and Leadership, Push for Taliban Defectors Stalls," *New York Times*, September 6, 2010, http://www.nytimes.com/2010/09/07/world/asia/07taliban.html.

14. Following the April 2002 Geneva Conference on security, different donor nations were assigned to address different aspects of security: the United States, military reform; Germany, police reform; Italy, judicial reform; United Kingdom, counter-narcotics; and Japan, disarmament, demobilization, and reintegration. But the Japanese government did not establish the DDR until February 2003, almost eleven months after the Geneva Conference. Thus a significant block of time was lost, effectively working to the insurgents' advantage and continuing to reflect on Afghan security. Japan—which by 2009 had provided $1.78 billion in vital civilian assistance and in 2010 had pledged another $5 billion—later passed on the responsibility for DDR to the United Nations Assistance Mission in Afghanistan and "Afghanistan's New Beginnings Programme" was established in April 2003. See Mark Sedra, "New Beginning or Return to Arms? The Disarmaments, Demobilization & Reintegration Process in Afghanistan" (paper presented at the ZEF-LSE Workshop on "State Reconstruction and International Engagement in Afghanistan," Bonn, May 30–June 1, 2003), 5, 9. Available at http://www.ag.afghanistan.ed/arg/arp/dera.pdf.

In recognition of the gendered aspects of security and women's roles in the peace process, the United Nations' Security Council Resolution 1325 on Women, Peace, and Security was passed on October 31, 2000. Yet security planning was not drawn upon Resolution 1325 and Afghan women were not invited to participate. Afghanistan's New Beginnings Program aims to demobilize and reintegrate thousands of child combatants in Afghanistan. See "Afghan New Beginnings Programme," *Wikipedia*, http://en.wikipedia.org/wiki/Afghan_New_Beginnings_Programme.

15. Valentine Moghadam. "Peace-Building and Reconstruction with Women: Reflections on Afghanistan, Iraq and Palestine," in *From Patriarchy to Empowerment*, ed. Valentine Moghadam (New York: Syracuse University Press, 2007), 327 [327–350].

16. Following the disputed, fraud-marred reelection of Karzai in August 2009, and with fifteen former cabinet members under investigation for embezzlement, the Afghan parliament refused to confirm seventeen of the president's twenty-four proposed cabinet members, having twice postponed its forty-five-day winter recess in order to review the nominees. They recessed on January 10, 2010, and on January 28, Karzai attended a London conference about Afghanistan without a functioning government. See Hamid Zhalizi, "Karzai Seeks New Cabinet Before London Conference," *NewsDaily*, Reuters, January 10, 2010, http://www.newsdaily.com/stories/sge603oi7-us-afghanistan/.

17. See publications and reports at Afghanistan Peacebuilding, http://www.cmi.no/afghanistan/index.cfm?id=339&Disarmament-Demobilisation-and-Reintegration-(DDR).

18. See "Afghanistan's New Beginnings Programme (NBP)," United Nations Development Programme Afghanistan, http://www.undp.org.af/WhoWeAre/UNDPinAfghanistan/Projects/psl/prj_anbp.htm. See also "US: Taliban Has Grown Fourfold," *Al Jazeera English*, October 9, 2009, http://english.aljazeera

.net/news/americas/2009/10/20091091814483962.html. In 2009 the stated goal of U.S. and allied troops once again was to train Afghan troops at the cost of $7.5 billion a year. It is hoped that a strong, stable Afghan military will provide the U.S. with an exit strategy. Karzai has estimated this will take five to ten years, and indeed recruitment has been a struggle, as has basic training. See Judy Dempsey, "NATO Falls Far Short of Helping Afghans," *New York Times*, February 5, 2010, http://www.nytimes.com/2010/02/05/world/europe/05iht -nato.html; Aamer Madhani, "Afghan Forces' Problems Are a Drag on US Efforts," *USA Today*, November 30, 2009, http://www.usatoday.com/news/ world/2009-09-29-afghan-army_N.htm; Chris Hedges, "Afghanistan Is Worse Off Than Ever, Thanks to the Sham Army We're Propping Up," Truthdig, November 11, 2009, http://www.truthdig.com/report/item/20091109_afghanistans _sham_army/.

19. Security in the provinces has been tenuous from the first and the United States and NATO have never been able to maintain stability much outside the capital city. A common joke among Afghans was that Karzai, handpicked by the United States to lead the country, was merely president of Kabul. This recalls an old Afghan saying that the king controls Kabul, but the tribes control the rest of Afghanistan.

20. In 2003, I traveled back to Afghanistan for the first time since 1977, in the company of photographer Sheryl Shapiro and members of the nonprofit humanitarian groups Afghans4Tomorrow and Engineers without Borders. My impressions were published privately in a report to donors on June 1, 2003. With the exception of a few neighborhoods, the city was in ruins, but Kabul was already overwhelmed with Westerners, so it was not long that all the trappings that please them were provided—shopping malls, restaurants, hotels, ATM machines. Kabul is ranked as one of the most expensive places in the world for expatriates to live (Xpatulator.com, http://www.xpatulator.com/ outside.cfm?lid=1). Administrative costs for organizations such as the UN, World Bank, USAID, Asia Foundation, and others go to pay high rent on houses, some built with laundered drug money. Much of the destruction in Kabul, at least, has been repaired, including historic sites, museums, gardens, schools, and universities, thanks to the efforts of individuals such as Nancy Hatch Dupree (for whom Afghanistan's cultural heritage has been an ongoing concern for nearly fifty years), institutions such as the Aga Khan Trust for Culture and UNESCO, as well as various governments. The poor, however, continue to live in squalid circumstances; the city is overcrowded with people unable to return to their homes throughout the country; and suicide bombers make regular forays into Kabul, killing mostly Afghans rather than expats. See also Mark Dummett, "Hope for Obama Plan in Fortress Kabul," *BBC News*, March 27, 2009, http://news .bbc.co.uk/2/hi/south_asia/7969329.stm.

21. At this writing, there are 70,000 private contractors in Kabul, outnumbering uniformed troops. Many of the groups with interests in Afghanistan are also in Iraq: Halliburton, Bechtel Group, Inc., BearingPoint Group, Inc., Creative Associates International, Inc., Blackwater Security Consulting, LLC, and others. Some are the same companies operating under different names. See The Center for Public Integrity, "Windfalls of War," http://projects.publicintegrity

.org/wow/bio.aspx?act=pro. For more about corruption in Afghanistan, see Stephanie Debere and Michael Sidwell, eds., *Transparency International Global Coalition Against Corruption: Annual Report 2009* (Berlin: Transparency International, 2009), 25, 30, 53. Available at http://www.transparency.org. At the 2001 Bonn Conference to plan Afghanistan's future, many Afghans tried to demand a return to the constitutional monarchy of Muhammad Zahir Shah, who had overseen Afghanistan's most peaceful period. No one listened and Hamid Karzai was appointed to run the country instead. There is still a widespread belief that had the king been reinstated, many problems might have been avoided. See Shireen Burki, "Bold Move to Save Afghanistan: Bring Back a King," *Christian Science Monitor*, June 30, 2010, http://www.csmonitor.com/Commentary/Opinion/2010/0630/Bold-move-to-save-Afghanistan-Bring-back-a-king?, and Michael Hughes, "Corruption Is the Enemy of Afghanistan but Who Is Going to Kill It?" Huffington Post, September 7, 2010, http://www.huffingtonpost.com/michael-hughes/corruption-is-the-enemy.

22. Many Afghan women, such as Rangina Hamidi (http://www.huntalternatives.org/pages/7792_rangina_hamidi.cfm) in Kandahar or Katrin Fakiri (http://www.parwaz.org) in Kabul, have returned to advocate for women. Additionally, myriad Afghan women now "commute" from their homes in exile, collecting and delivering necessities such as blankets, clothing, books, medicines, and more. Some non-Afghan women, such as Kathleen Rafiq (http://www.stasek.com/alittlehelp/programs.shtml) or Sarah Chayes (http://www.sarahchayes.net/), also have settled in Afghanistan to develop humanitarian programs. They follow in the footsteps of American women such as Nancy Hatch Dupree (http://www.dupreefoundation.org/) and Mary MacMakin (http://afzenda.org/about.html), who have worked virtually nonstop in Afghanistan on its behalf since the 1960s. Year after year, with failing security, it has become increasingly dangerous to provide aid. See for example, Rod Nordland, "Security in Afghanistan Is Deteriorating, Aid Groups Say," *New York Times*, September 11, 2010, http://www.nytimes.com/2010/09/12/word/asia/12afghan.html.

23. Gary Langar, "Frustration with War, Problems in Daily Life Send Afghans' Support for U.S. Efforts Tumbling," *ABC News*, February 9, 2009, http://abcnews.go.com/PollingUnit/story?id=6787686&page=1? and "Civilian Casualties in Afghanistan Keep Rising, Finds UN Report," *UN News Centre*, UN News Service, July 31, 2009, http://www.un.org/apps/news/story.asp?NewsID=31636&Cr=afghan&Cr1=civilian. Ruth Rennie, Suhindra Sharma, and Pawan Sen, "Afghanistan in 2009: A Survey of the Afghan People," The Asia Foundation, 2009, http://www.asiafoundation.org/resources/pdfs/Afghanistanin2009.pdf. Nick Turse, "Totally Occupied: 700 Military Bases Spread Across Afghanistan," *Tomdispatch.com*, February 11, 2010, http://www.alternet.org/world/145631/totally_occupied:_700_military_bases_spread_across_afghanistan.

24. For two refreshing points of view regarding the burqa see: Dinah Zeiger, "That (Afghan Girl)! Ideology Unveiled in National Geographic," in *The Veil: Women Writers on Its History, Lore, and Politics*, ed. Jennifer Heath (Berkeley: University of California Press, 2008), 266–280, and Ellen McLarney, "The Burqa in *Vogue*: Fashioning Afghanistan," *Journal of Middle East Women's Studies* 5, no.1 (Winter 2009): 1–23.

25. Throughout this book, I have chosen to use the term non-literate, rather than illiterate, which has pejorative overtones. Although Afghans have a magnificent history of literature, the majority of its population cannot read or write. Nevertheless, there is a vibrant, essential oral tradition.

26. Jerry White, "US, NATO Reach 'Consensus' to Sanction Rigged Election in Afghanistan," *World Socialist Web Site*, September 29, 2009, http://www.wsws.org/articles/2009/sep2009/afgh-s29.shtml; "Barack Obama Orders 30,000 More Troops to Afghanistan," *BBC*, December 2, 2009, http://news.bbc.co.uk/2/hi/8389778.stm; J. Alexander Thier, "Karzai's Taliban Surprise," Foreign Policy and the New America Foundation, January 29, 2010, http://afpak.foreignpolicy.com/posts/2010/01/29/karzais_taliban_surprise; Mark Landler and Alissa J. Rubin, "War Plan for Karzai: Reach Out to Taliban," *New York Times*, January 29, 2010, http://www.nytimes.com/2010/01/29/world/asia/29diplo.html; Dexter Filkins, "U.N. Seeks to Drop Some Taliban from Terror List," *New York Times*, January 25, 2010, http://www.nytimes.com/2010/01/25/world/asia/25taliban.html; Jake Tapper, Martha Raddatz, Huma Khan, and Miguel Marquez, "Gen. David Petraeus Will Replace Embattled Gen. Stanley McChrystal in Afghanistan: Obama: McChrystal's Comments Undermine 'Civilian Control of Military,' 'Erodes Trust,' " *ABC News*, June 23, 2010, http://abcnews.go.com/Politics/gen-david-petraeus-replace-stanley-mcchrystal-afghanistan-obama/story?id=10992188; Nick Davies and David Leigh, "Afghanistan War Logs: Massive Leak of Secret Files Exposes Truth of Occupation," *The Guardian*, July 25, 2010, http://www.guardian.co.uk/world/2010/jul/25/afghanistan-war-logs-military-leaks; "U.S. Congress Approves New Funding for Afghan War," *BBC News*, July 27, 2010, http://www.bbc.co.uk/news/world-us-canada-10784150; Helene Cooper, "White House Reaffirms Afghan Strategy Despite Petraeus Remarks," *New York Times*, August 16, 2010, http://thecaucus.blogs.nytimes.com/2010/08/16/white-house-reaffirms-afghan-strategy-despite-petraeus-remarks/?scp=7&sq=troop%20pullout%20July%202011&st=cse; Christopher Bodeen, "NATO Seeking 2,000 More Troops for Afghanistan Force," *Washington Times*, September 6, 2010, http://www.washingtontimes.com/news/2010/sep/6/nato-seeking-2000-more-troops-afghanistan-force/.

27. About 5 million Afghans have returned since the fall of the Taliban. Some 3 million remain abroad. In 2009, 28,000 Afghan returnees were unable to return to their homes due to insecurity, tribal issues, landlessness, and lack of work opportunities. See UNHCR: The United Nations Refugee Agency, http://www.unhcr.org/cgi-bin/texis/vtx/search?page=&comid=4a5dceab6&&scid=49aea93a61&keywords=statistics.

28. Willem van de Put, "Addressing Mental Health in Afghanistan," *The Lancet* 360 (December 1, 2002): s41–s42.

29. Joan Kayeum, *The Afghan: Hard as a Rock, Tender as a Flower—A Character Sketch Based on Afghan Proverbs* (privately published, March 2007), iii.

30. Afghanistan is located at a crossroads, on the Silk Road, between East and West. Its history of invaders includes Alexander the Great, Darius the Persian, Genghis Khan, and the British, who tried and failed in 1838 and 1878, with the eventual result that parts of the Pashtun homeland were annexed to British India (now Pakistan). Amir Abdur Rahman Khan (1900) called his country—specifically

the tribal belt between British India and Afghanistan—Yaghistan, also "Land of the Unruly," "Land of the Free," "Land of Rebels," "Land of Insolence." See Louis Dupree, *Afghanistan* (Princeton, N.J.: Princeton University Press, 1980), xvii, and for a brief history of European encroachments, 362–410.

31. Elizabeth Rubin, "Karzai in His Labyrinth," *New York Times Magazine*, August 4, 2009, http://www.nytimes.com/2009/08/09/magazine/09Karzai -t.html?scp=1&sq=Karzai%20in%20his%20Labyrinth&st=cse.

32. Unrelated men and women in Afghanistan do not customarily socialize and women are not allowed to dance in public. The custom of *bachabaze* (playing with boys) is an old one that has grown in recent years. These so-called "dancing boys" are often very young, picked off the streets or purchased outright from their parents, offered food, as well as money, and trained to dance for men and provide sexual favors. See Najibullah Quraishi, "Frontline: The Dancing Boys of Afghanistan," *PBS Frontline*, April 2010, http://www.pbs.org/wgbh/pages/ frontline/dancingboys/ and Rustam Qobil, "The Sexually Abused Dancing Boys of Afghanistan," *BBC News*, September 7, 2010, http://www.bbc.co.uk/news/ world-south-asia-11217772.

33. David Barsamian, interview with Brian Drolet, June 2009, Alwan for the Arts, New York, http://www.youtube.com/watch?v=S4UdwsoUV2w. Alexander the Great, aka, Sikander the Greek, invaded Afghanistan in 330 B.C.E. Despite the image of Afghans as fierce fighters then and now, it is important to remember that not all Afghan tribal chiefs and elders are warlords. What's more, all warlords are not alike. For a discussion about levels of warlordism, see Antonio Giustozzi, "Respectable Warlords? The Politics of State-building in Post-Taliban Afghanistan" (Working Paper No. 33, Crisis States Program Development Research Center, London School of Economics, 2003), 2–3.

34. Dupree, *Afghanistan*, 590. When King Zahir Shah fired his cousin Prime Minister Daoud Khan in 1963, he began an era often referred to as the golden age when, as many Afghans like to remember, women—in Kabul—wore miniskirts and those of the elite classes enjoyed relative freedom. Daoud overthrew Zahir in 1973, when the king was visiting Italy. Zahir returned from exile in 2002 with the title "Father of the Nation" and died in 2007. There are still royalists in Afghanistan (see note 21, above).

35. "DG Interview: Sippi Azarbaijani-Moghaddam, Women's Rights in the Afghan Constitution," http://zunia.org/uploads/media/knowledge/sippi.pdf.

36. Neamatollah Nojumi, Dyan Mazurana, and Elizabeth Stites. *After the Taliban: Life and Security in Rural Afghanistan.* (Lanham, Md.: Rowman & Littlefield, 2009), 35–38. For a description of female *shuras* (councils) and participation of rural women in political and civil life, 83–95.

37. Dexter Filkins, "Afghan Women Protest New Law on Home Life," *New York Times*, April 15, 2009, http://www.nytimes.com/2009/04/16/world/asia/ 16afghan.html and Hassina Sherjan, "Apathy Among the Educated," *New York Times*, Opinion, August 17, 2009, http://www.nytimes.com/2009/08/18/opin ion/18sherjan.html?_r=1&scp=1&sq=Apathy+Among+the+Educated&st=nyt.

38. Family ties and hierarchies are vital among Afghans and explain a great deal about Hamid Karzai's entanglements with his brothers, cousins, and vari-

ous kin, whose involvement, not to say interference, contributes to government and other corruption. Clan obligations and tribal loyalties should come as no surprise to anyone with the least knowledge of Afghan society and should have been taken into consideration when Karzai was selected to run the country. Ten years later, in a delayed "ah hah moment," *New York Times* reporter James Risen wrote, "Karzai's Kin Use Ties to Gain Power in Afghanistan," October 6, 2010, describing some of the Karzai government's widespread nepotism, http://www.nytimes.com/2010/10/06/world/asia/06karzai.html?emc=tnt&tntemail1=y. Also see Kate Clark, "Afghan President Pardons Men Convicted of Bayonet Gang Rape," *The Independent*, August 24, 2008, http://www.independent.co.uk/news/world/asia/afghan-president-pardoned-rapists-907663.html.

39. Nojumi, Mazurana, and Stites, *After the Taliban*, 92. In a personal email dated April 9, 2010, Shireen Khan Burki wrote: "In the insurgency areas, i.e., Pashtun majority regions, the traditional jirga system was an effective conflict resolution mechanism that we [U.S. and allied forces] are busy trying to discard to the dustbin of history notwithstanding its historically critical role in maintaining some semblance of the status quo in Hobbesian conditions. Given the destruction wrought on civil society and institutions of 'governance' by the Taliban, building the judicial system is going to be a challenging/time consuming process. One not for the fainthearted nor the fickle. Does Afghanistan need a functioning judicial system? Absolutely. But then it needs a slew of institutions starting with those that can indefinitely protect the population without foreign military hand holding."

40. In 2008, the Afghan government banned begging on streets and called on authorities to send beggars to care homes and orphanages, though this rarely happens, not least because there are few hostels for the needy. See Martin Vennard, "Afghanistan Bans Street Begging," *BBC News*, November 7, 2008, http://news.bbc.co.uk/2/hi/7714735.stm.

41. This is not to undermine the efforts of organizations such as the Business Council for Peace (http://www.bpeace.org/), PARWAZ MicroFinance Institution, PARSA (http://www.afghanistan-parsa.org/), and other earnest NGOs, which help widows, but there are so many, and little if any government support, so the majority are left to their own devices.

42. UNICEF, "Afghanistan," United Nations Children's Fund, http://www.unicef.org/infobycountry/afghanistan_statistics.html. International Orphan Care (http://www.orphanproject.org/about.html), was started in Afghanistan in 1979 with the Soviet invasion and continues today. Notable, too, are Revolutionary Association of the Women of Afghanistan orphanages, started in 1986 (http://www.rawa.org/orphanage.htm), and The Children of War (http://thechildrenofwar.org/web1/component/option.com_frontpage/Itemid,6/).

43. Amanda Sim, "Confronting Child Labour in Afghanistan" (Afghanistan Research and Evaluation Unit, Briefing Paper Series, May 2009), http://www.areu.org.af.

44. Alexandra Reihing, "Child Labor in Afghanistan" (*Policy Innovations*, June 20, 2007), http://www.policyinnovations.org/ideas/briefings/data/afghan_child_labor.

45. For further information, see UNICEF, *State of the World's Children 2009* (New York: United Nations Children's Fund, December 2008). Available at http://www.unicef.org/publications/files/SOWC_2009_Main__Report_ _03112009.pdf.

46. For details see Physicians for Human Rights, *The Taliban's War on Women: A Health and Human Rights Crisis in Afghanistan* (Boston and Washington, D.C.: Physicians for Human Rights, 1998).

47. Nojumi, Mazurana, and Stites, *After the Taliban*, 72. In informal interviews I conducted in 2005 with male nurses at a clinic run by the Italian NGO Emergency, in the Farza District in Kabul Province, I was told that women were not allowed to be seen by men. The nurses expressed a desire for at least an occasional visiting female doctor or nurse. On my second visit, a new supply of medicine had arrived at the clinic (and would be gone before the week was out) and many women stood in line to have their children examined.

48. In 2004, Pashtoon Azfar—the director of Afghanistan's Institute of Health Sciences—founded the Afghan Midwives Association, which was accepted into the International Midwives Confederation in 2006. International Confederation of Midwives, http://www.internationalmidwives.org/AboutICM/MemberAsso ciations/AfghanMidwivesAssociation/tabid/382/Default.aspx.

49. S. Sultan Ahmadi, ed., *Kabul International Exhibition Catalogue* (Kabul: Exhibition Directorate, Ministry of Commerce, 1961). Large development agencies have been reluctant to support or train Traditional Birth Attendants, determining instead that assistance would have to wait indefinitely until hospitals were built in rural areas. Meanwhile, maternal and infant mortality rates have been rising. According to volunteer medical personnel I spoke with in Afghanistan, the simplest of aid—supplies of soap and lessons in soap-making, for example—would reduce illness and deaths.

50. Dupree, *Afghanistan*, 642–643. Of interest, a film by Jill Vickers and Jody Bergedick, *Once in Afghanistan*, recollections of female Peace Corps volunteers who traveled throughout Afghanistan vaccinating against smallpox (Dirt Road Documentaries, 2008), www.dirtroaddocumentaries.com.

51. "Fragile Footsteps: Children and Landmines," Save the Children, undated, http://www.savethechildren.org/publications/reports/landmines.pdf; Nojumi, Mazurana, and Stites, *After the Taliban*, 38–40. Of interest: Oliver Englehart, "The Minefields of Afghanistan," *New York Times*, November 17, 2010, http://video.nytimes.com/video/2009/11/18/opinion/1247465742545/ the-minefields-of-afghanistan.html?emc=eta1.

52. Doug Westerman, "Depleted Uranium—Far Worse than 9/11: Depleted Uranium Dust—Public Health Disaster for the People of Iraq and Afghanistan," Global Research, May 3, 2005, http://www.globalresearch.ca/index.php ?context=va&aid=2374.

53. Jason Straziuso and Rahim Faiez, "Concerns White Phosphorus Used in Afghan Battle," *ABC News*, May 20, 2009, http://abcnews.go.com/Inter national/wireStory?id=7549697.

54. "UNEP in Afghanistan: Laying the Foundations for Sustainable Development," United Nations Environmental Programme, January 2009, http://

www.unep.org/pdf/UNEP_in_Afghanistan.pdf. Unfortunately, not enough has been written about environmental destruction in Afghanistan.

55. A. J. Benham, "Minerals in Afghanistan," Afghanistan Geological Survey, 2006, http://www.bgs.ac.uk/afghanminerals/docs/copper_A4.pdf; United States Geological Survey, "Preliminary Assessment of Non-Fuel Mineral Resources of Afghanistan, 2007," Afghanistan Geological Survey and U.S. Agency for International Development, 2007, http://pubs.usgs.gov/fs/2007/3063/; James Risen, "U.S. Identifies Vast Mineral Wealth in Afghanistan," New York Times, June 13, 2010, http://www.nytimes.com/2010/06/14/world/asia/14minerals.html.

56. Fitzgerald and Gould, Invisible History, 259. With the 2009–2010 military offensive in Marja, Helmand Province, the United States and NATO, under the command of General Stanley McChrystal, would reportedly no longer eradicate poppy fields in the area. Because 60–70 percent of farmers in the area grow poppies, destroying their harvest might naturally alienate them. The decision is controversial among Afghans, and likely temporary. Rod Nordland, "Fearful of Alienating Afghans, U.S. Turns Blind Eye to Opium: Policy Rift Destroying Illegal Poppy Crop," New York Times, March 21, 2010, 1.

57. Collective History of the Quilts of Gee's Bend, http://www.quiltsofgeesbend.com/history/.

58. Gayle Tzemach Lemmon, "Extending the Horizon for Women's Aid Projects in Afghanistan," New York Times, August 15, 2009, http://www.nytimes.com/2009/08/15/business/global/15mall.html?sq=Extending%20the%20Horizon%20for%20Women's%20Aid%20Projects%20in%20Afghanistan&st=cse&adxnnl=1&scp=1&adxnnlx=1256054785-LwF9EWzc8ctA5aNuHeTP8A.

59. Matt Waldman, "Falling Short: Aid Effectiveness in Afghanistan" (Kabul: Agency Coordinating Body for Afghan Relief, March 2008), 1, 3. See also "Afghan War Costs to Overtake Iraq: Pentagon," Defence Talk: Global Defense and Military Portal, May 8, 2009, http://www.defencetalk.com/afghan-war-costs-to-overtake-iraq-in-2010-pentagon-18679/.

60. Anne Carlin, "Rush to Re-engagement in Afghanistan" (Washington, D.C., Bank Information Center, December 2003), 10. Available at http://www.bicusa.org/en/Article.1007.aspx. Also of interest, Susanne Koelbl, "The Aid Swindle," Der Spiegel Online International, April 5, 2005, https://www.spiegel.de/international/spiegel/0,1518,348597,00.html.

61. "Corruption, Not Insecurity, Biggest Concern for Afghans—UN Report," UN News Centre, January 19, 2010, http://www.un.org/apps/news/story.asp?NewsID=33519, and "NGOs Form 'Parallel' Government in Afghanistan: Minister," Afghan News, April 20, 2005, http://www.afghanemb-canada.net/en/news_bulletin/2005/april/20/index.php. Kabul is overrun with NGOs. Some—such as those listed here—are truly effective, albeit among limited numbers, more so than many Afghan government agencies. Others, however, are short-lived or fly-by-night agencies, and still others are covers for proselytizing Christian groups. Recruiting for Christianity seems to be a mission of some in the U.S. military. See, for example, "'Witness for Jesus' in

Afghanistan," *Al Jazeera*, May 4, 2009, http://english.aljazeera.net/news/asia/2009/05/200953201315854832.html.

62. Peter Grier, "Obama's War Plan: How Will He Pay for It?" *Christian Science Monitor*, December 2, 2009, http://www.csmonitor.com/USA/Politics/2009/1202/obamas-afghanistan-war-plan-how-will-he-pay-for-it.

63. Hunter Lovins, "A Vision for a Green Afghanistan: Brief Proposal for a Comprehensive Strategy to Develop a Competitive and Sustainable Afghanistan" (Boulder, Colo.: Natural Capitalism Solutions, 2004). Available at http://www.natcapsolutions.org/publications_files/NCS_VisionGreenAfghanistan_23iiio5.pdf.

64. Of interest: Albert Szabo and Thomas J. Barfield, *Afghanistan: An Atlas of Indigenous Domestic Architecture* (Austin: University of Texas Press, 1991) and Vandana Shiva, *Earth Democracy: Justice, Sustainability and Peace* (Brooklyn, N.Y.: South End Press, 2005).

65. One testament to the desire of Afghans for schools is found in Dexter Filkins, "Stanley McChrystal's Long War," *New York Times Magazine*, October 14, 2009, http://www.nytimes.com/2009/10/18/magazine/18Afghanistan-t.html?ref=magazine. Filkins recorded: " 'What do you need here?' McChrystal asked [in the village of Garmsir in Helmand Province]. A translator turned the general's words into Pashto. 'We need schools!' one Afghan called back. 'Schools!' 'We're working on that,' McChrystal said. 'Those things take time.' " In fact, it should not take time to set up village schools for boys and home schools for girls in areas where there is danger of retaliation. With troops to provide security, these would be the best investments the United States could make.

66. "List of Schools in Afghanistan," *Wikipedia*, http://en.wikipedia.org/wiki/List_of_schools_in_Afghanistan; "List of Universities in Afghanistan," *Wikipedia*, http://en.wikipedia.org/wiki/List_of_universities_in_Afghanistan; and "Education in Afghanistan," *Wikipedia*, http://en.wikipedia.org/wiki/Education_in_Afghanistan.

67. See UNICEF, "UNICEF Condemns Attacks on Schools in Afghanistan," United Nations Children's Fund, November 14, 2008, http://www.unicef.org/emerg/afghanistan_46387.html, and "Lessons in Terror: Attacks on Education in Afghanistan," *Human Rights Watch* 18, no. 6 (C) (July 2006), http://www.hrw.org/reports/2006/afghanistan0706/afghanistan0706web.pdf. Also see Marit Glad, "Knowledge on Fire: Attacks on Education in Afghanistan: Risks and Measures for Successful Mitigation" (study conducted by CARE on behalf of the World Bank and the Ministry of Education, November 2009), http://care.ca/ckfinder/userfiles/files/Knowledge_on_fire-attacks_%20schools.pdf.

68. Nojumi, Mazurana, and Stites, *After the Taliban*, 61.

69. Nicholas Kristoff and Sheryl WuDunn, *Half the Sky: Turning Oppression into Opportunity for Women Worldwide* (New York: Alfred A. Knopf, 2009), 162–165. For further ideas on how to succeed with education in Afghanistan, see Wahid Omar, "From Storytelling to Community Development: Jaghori, Afghanistan," in *Telling Stories to Change the World*, ed. Rickie Solinger, Madeline Fox, and Kayhan Irani (New York: Routledge, 2008).

70. In addition to the Afghan Institute of Learning (http://afghaninstitute oflearning.org/), other long-term and successful NGOs dedicated to education include Afghans4Tomorrow (http://www.Afghans4Tomorrow.org), Afghan Empowerment for a Better Tomorrow (http://www.afghaneducation.org), Women for Afghan Women (http://www.womenforafghanwomen.org), Future Generations (http://www.future.org/international-operations/afghanistan), and Trust in Education (http://www.trustineducation.org/).

71. Nancy Hatch Dupree, "Cultural Heritage & National Identity in Afghanistan," *Third World Quarterly* 23, no. 5 (2002): 977–989, http://www .khyber.org/publications/001–005/culturalheritageafghan.shtml. Dupree has been a leader in cultural preservation for Afghanistan for decades. Her efforts are joined by organizations such as the Turquoise Mountain Foundation (http:// www.turquoisemountain.org), the Aga Khan Foundation (http://www.akdn .org), the Association for the Preservation of Afghan Archaeology (http://www .apaa.info/), and others. In May 2002, the United Nations Education, Scientific, and Cultural Organization and the Afghan Ministry of Information and Culture held an important international seminar on the rehabilitation of Afghanistan's cultural heritage. For "Conclusions and Recommendations," see http:// portal.unesco.org/en/file_download.php/8d14310eab5474b5e28ff25f 57b0a285Recommendations.doc.

72. Dupree, *Afghanistan*, 532.

73. Reporters without Borders/Reporters sans Frontières, "Press Freedom Barometer," December 2005, http://en.rsf.org/. Press freedom has gotten tougher for all Afghan journalists. For example, in 2009, two "fixers," Afghan male journalists traveling with and translating for foreign journalists, were captured and killed, though the foreigners were released. In 2008, a young journalist, Sayed Perwiz Kambakhsh, was sentenced to death and then to twenty years in prison for downloading an article about the rights of women in Islam, then in 2009 secretly pardoned and released. Karzai, citing safety reasons, restricted media coverage on election day 2009. http://www.rsf.org/en-pays50-Afghanistan .html. See also Genevieve Long, "Women on a Mission in Pakistan and Afghanistan," *Quill: Magazine of the Society of Professional Journalists* (May 2009): 14–17. In September 2010, the U.S. military arrested a staff correspondent and a freelance journalist with Al Jazeera, along with a radio reporter, the leader of the Kapisa Province journalists' association. The military would not say what the charges were. The U.S. military frequently arrests journalists in both Afghanistan and Iraq. They were released from custody a few days after being detained. Rod Nordland, "Three Journalists Arrested in Afghanistan," *New York Times*, September 23, 2010, http://www.nytimes.com/2010/09/23/world/asia/23afghan .html, and "Three Afghan Journalists, Two of Whom Were Held By NATO Forces Are Released," *New York Times*, September 24, 2010, http://www .nytimes.com/2010/09/25/world/asia/25kabul.html?scp=8&sq=Rod%20Nord land&st=cse.

74. R.V. Vyas, R.C. Sharma, and Aswini Kumar, "Educational Radio in India," *Turkish Online Journal of Distance Education* 3, no. 3 (July 2002), http://tojde.anadolu.edu.tr/tojde7/articles/educationalradio.htm; Ian Mugridge and David Kaufman, *Distance Education in Canada*, (Kent, England: Croom

Helm, Ltd., 1986), 216. After broadcasting lessons to children in the bush for decades, Radio Australia now offers English as a Second Language. See Radio Australia, http://www.radioaustralia.net.au/learnenglish/. Radio has also been misused to spread the word, for instance, about the importance of chemicals and monoculture in farming and other such marketing.

75. Sarah Kamal, "Disconnected from Discourse: Women's Radio Listening in Rural Samangan, Afghanistan" (Working Paper 27, Massachusetts Institute of Technology, February 2004); "Repetition is the soul of education" is from "Blue Yodel," by Jack Collom (*Blue Yodel, Blue Heron*, Audio CD, Boulder, Colo.: Baksun Books, 2002).

76. "Women's Radio Station is One of the Most Popular in Herat," *Internews Afghanistan*, March 2008, http://www.internews.org/bulletin/afghanistan/Afghan _200803.html.

77. The monumental Buddhas of Bamiyan were carved into the side of a cliff in Afghanistan's Hazarajat region, between the second and fifth centuries C.E., by people of the Kushan Empire. It is a UNESCO World Heritage site. Also of interest, the Association for the Protection of Afghan Archeology, run by archeologist Zemaryalai Tarzi, http://www.apaa.info/. Destruction and looting of the Kabul Museum, established in 1924, took place mostly during the civil war period. In 2003, the Bactrian gold collection was retrieved from a vault in a presidential palace, where it had been hidden for safekeeping since 1988 by museum employees. The museum was rebuilt in 2004.

78. In addition to adult performances and collaborations from experimental theater (Exile Theatre of Afghanistan and New York's Bond Street Theatre, http://www.theatrewithoutborders.com/node/1192) to Shakespeare (Scott Baldauf, "Love's 'Labour' Not a Lost Cause in Kabul," *Christian Science Monitor,* September 1, 2005, http://www.csmonitor.com/2005/0901/p07s01 -wosc.html), U.S. and European children's theater groups, such as Clowns Without Borders (http://www.clownswithoutborders.net/countries/afghanistan/) and No Strings Puppet Theatre (http://www.nostrings.org.uk/), arrived in Afghanistan, bringing laughter and lifesaving advice against land mines, and Theatre of the Oppressed (http://www.theatreoftheoppressed.org/en/index.php ?nodeID=2&country_id=66&continent_id=5, among others.

79. The Cold War years were tangled in intrigue that has endangered the whole world. The CIA has never been able to let go of its spy vs. spy games in Afghanistan, clearly making a bad situation worse. For a contemporary example, see Dexter Filkins, Mark Mazzetti, and James Risen, "Brother of Afghan Leader Is Said to Be on CIA Payroll," *New York Times,* October 27, 2009, http://www.nytimes .com/2009/10/28/world/asia/28intel.html?_r=1&hp. See also CIA historical references in Fitzgerald and Gould, *Invisible History,* 378.

80. Juan Cole, "Top Ten Things That Could Derail Obama's Afghanistan Plan," *Informed Comment,* December 2, 2009, http://www.juancole.com/2009/ 12/top-ten-things-that-could-derail-obamas.html; Graham E. Fuller, "Stretching Out an Ugly Struggle," *New York Times,* December 4, 2009, http://www .nytimes.com/2009/12/04/opinion/04iht-edfuller.html; Mikhail Gorbachev, "Soviet Lessons from Afghanistan," *New York Times,* February 4, 2010, http://www .nytimes.com/2010/02/05/opinion/05iht-edgorbachev.html.

81. It has been suggested that desperately needed security be provided by Muslim soldiers—Turkish, Jordanian, Bangladeshi, Emirati—who the Afghan people are likely to trust and welcome more warmly than European soldiers, particularly in rural areas. "Muslim Troops Help Win Afghan Minds," *BBC News*, March 28, 2008, http://news.bbc.co.uk/2/hi/south_asia/7318731.stm. And as Juan Cole notes in "Top Ten Things That Could Derail Obama's Afghanistan Plan," "The U.S. counter-insurgency plan assumes that Pashtun villagers dislike and fear the Taliban, and just need to be protected from them so as to stop the politics of intimidation. But what if the villagers are cousins of the Taliban and would rather support their clansmen than white Christian foreigners?" This recalls how the first Soviet troops invading Afghanistan by land were Tajiks, who, once over the border, stopped in to visit family members from whom they had been separated. And this point relates again to Hamid Karzai's family fealty and obligations.

82. New World Strategies Coalition, a political and economic think tank founded by Afghans, offers twenty-four non-military solutions to the war in Afghanistan that are well worth taking seriously. See "24 NonMilitary Solutions," New World Strategies Coalition, Inc., http://www.newworldstrate giescoalition.org/24_NonMilitary_Solutions.html.

83. In the run up to the Afghan parliamentary elections on September 18, 2010, Amnesty International reported that many candidates' lives were at risk, particularly women's. They have been bullied, threatened, shot and injured, their campaigners kidnapped, and so on, and they cannot rely on the Afghan police for protection. The Independent Election Commission reported that 938 of the more than 6,000 polling centers would not open due to security concerns. "Afghan Election Candidates in Fear of Attacks," Amnesty International USA press release, September 16, 2010, http://www.amnestyusa.org/document .php?id=ENGPRE201009161867&lang=e&rss=recentnews.

84. At the July 2010 Kabul Conference, hosted by the government of Afghanistan and co-chaired by the UN, and earlier at a Peace Jirga, the Women's 50% Campaign presented statements emphasizing the needs of Afghan women and demanding equal participation in peace negotiations. Those statements can be found at the International Federation for Human Rights Web site at http://www.fidh.org/Recommendations-of-the-Afghanistan-Women-s-50 and http://www.fidh.org/Women-s-50-Campaign-Statement-to-Kabul-Conference. For more about the Kabul Conference—sparsely attended by women—see the United Nations Assistance Mission in Afghanistan Web site at http://unama.unmis sions.org/Default.aspx?tabid=4482. For more about the June 2010 Peace Jirga, see "Afghan Peace Jirga 2010," *Wikipedia*, http://en.wikipedia.org/wiki/Afghan_ Peace_Jirga_2010.

PART I

Perceptions and Realities

Nuristani woman with Kalashnikov, Afghanistan, ca. 1980s. Photographer unknown, courtesy of the Revolutionary Association of Women of Afghanistan and Anne Brodsky.

CHAPTER I

The Politics of *Zan* from Amanullah to Karzai

Lessons for Improving Afghan Women's Status

SHIREEN KHAN BURKI

Women are just like roses: A fresh rose is a happy sight.
—Khushal Khan Khattak, Pashtun warrior poet,
seventeenth-century C.E.

Since independence in 1919, the Afghan state's gender policies have involved a bewildering series of missteps, corrections, and more missteps,[1] resulting in confusion, pain, and suffering for Afghan *zan*.[2] Since the ouster of the Taliban regime, conditions for Afghan women improved under the Karzai government, but if history is any guide, gender policies and approaches are most likely to fail in Afghanistan unless they incorporate into the process the well-entrenched social and cultural norms of a traditional, patriarchal, primarily tribal society. In short, the historical record suggests that a gender template characterized by cautious, incremental efforts at improving female status stands the best chance of improving women's lives in the long term.

A LESSON IN CAUTION—1919 TO 1929

Afghanistan's "modernization" process—including the improvement of women's status—was first set in motion by Amir Amanullah's grandfather, Amir Abdur Rahman (1880–1901) and continued by his father Amir Habibullah (1901–1919), albeit limitedly. During Muhammad Amanullah Khan's reign (1919–1929),[3] ambitious efforts were made to implement drastic social changes to improve women's status. Amanullah's views on women's role in society were not a response to widespread societal demands; rather they were influenced primarily by his in-laws (the highly intellectual Tarzi family) and by unfolding events in the region. Amanullah's gender policies, however, were completely divorced from the social realities of his extremely conservative, primarily tribal, and geographically remote country. Thus, under his father-in-law Prime Minister Mahmud Tarzi's tutelage, he undertook an ambitious and controversial program meant to transform Afghanistan into a modern state in the same mold as Mustafa Kemal Ataturk's Turkey.[4]

Amanullah's government began by emphasizing secular-based (that is, non-madrassa) education and established the first primary school for girls, Masturat School, in 1921 in Kabul, under the patronage of Queen Soraya.[5] From 1920 to 1927, two primary schools and one middle school for girls were established in Kabul, with an estimated 700 students.[6] These numbers, however, suggest that despite strong encouragement by the Amir, most Afghans were reluctant to send their daughters to obtain what was characterized as a secular education. Furthermore, the establishment of girls' schools was limited to urban areas such as Kabul and Herat and thus failed to benefit the provinces.

Although many members of the urban elite welcomed such schools for their daughters, Amanullah's promotion of a coeducational system—with the establishment of the Amaniya School in Kabul (named for the Amir)—was viewed with skepticism and/or disapproval. In 1928, fifteen female graduates of the Masturat Middle School, daughters of prominent Kabulis, were sent to Turkey for higher education.[7] Sending young, unmarried girls out of the country was regarded with alarm in many quarters as yet another sign that the state, in its efforts to Westernize, was willing to push against social and cultural norms.

Queen Soraya, the Amir's only wife,[8] was viewed by most Afghans as a controversial figure. She publicly campaigned for drastic change in women's roles and advocated for women's rights to education, employment, and divorce. Soraya's behavior, however, perplexed most Afghans and frequently was seen as alien and "un-Islamic." In a society where the dominant ethnic group, the Pashtun, adhered to the strictures of Pashtunwali,[9] calls for women's rights made publicly by a woman challenged the embedded religious and cultural beliefs of a tribal society that did not view women as equals but only as property. Furthermore, the queen's advocacy on behalf of women impinged upon Afghan men's carefully nurtured *nang* ("honor" in Pashto), as members of a *khel* (clan) or *qaum* (tribal group). Across time, due to proximity to the dominant Pashtuns, other ethnic groups adopted cultural mores that mirrored the tenets of the ancient tribal codes, valuing family honor and its protection as a true measure of a man's worth and status in society. Pashtunwali stressed the importance of protecting one's *zan* (women), *zar* (gold/wealth), and *zamin* (land), in order to maintain *izzat* (respect). Women were viewed as property whose protection was essential for the preservation of the clan's honor. The notion that women had "rights" was seen as a threat to the status quo and to Pashtunwali itself. Given the very limited support base for gender reforms—primarily concentrated in Kabul among the educated elite—it was indeed a courageous, but overly ambitious, endeavor by the royal entourage to attempt to implement controversial, foreign changes within a short duration.

In yet another controversial move, in August 1924, Amanullah introduced the *Nizamnamah-ye-Arusi* and *Nikah wa Khatnasuri* laws regarding engagements and marriage. Although Amanullah's father had instituted marriage reforms, these were considered far more radical. Whereas the *Nizamnamah* stressed gender equality and established the minimum age for marriage, the *Nikah wa Khatnasuri* specified certain conditions within the marital agreement that were meant to ensure legal protections for brides. The state's encouragement of Afghan women to take legal action if mistreated by their husbands was considered revolutionary and threatening to the cultural status quo.

Both these measures were unpopular, but the provision in the *Nizamnamah* that encouraged girls to choose their own marriage partners without their parents' interference was regarded as pushing the boundaries of modernization at the expense of both tradition and religion. "Love marriages" threatened the alliance mechanism between families or clans, which was the key consideration in strengthening the clan or family's position within the social, tribal structure.

In more traditional provinces, especially the Pashtun belt, which included Kandahar, Nangahar, Khost, Paktia, Paktika, and Ghazni, the new laws fell on deaf ears. They were also viewed with distaste by some of the more secular and better educated urban populace, who were the government's only loyal constituency. Yet the state appeared to be oblivious to the social pulse and continued its ambitious social reforms. These reforms were increasingly seen as the whims and fantasies of elites disconnected from, and oblivious to, mainstream society. In its apparently overzealous stance, the Amanullah-led government sought societal changes that would ultimately fail because they were forced upon the populace without consultation or regard for the tenor of the times. Although the leaders sought to replicate society along the lines of Ataturk's Turkey by advocating for ambitious social change, they did not appreciate the inherent dangers of such precipitous efforts. They did, however, wisely invoke Islam and advocated Islamic due process as delineated by Shari'a courts, which would have jurisdiction over such matters as they sought to transform women's position in society. Thus the *Nizamnameh* stated:

> If the wife of a polygamist man feels that her husband has failed to treat all of his wives fairly and equally, she can file a complaint against her husband in a court of Shari'a, so that the unjust husbands should be punished accordingly. Moreover, punishment will be prescribed for husbands who would prevent their wives from petitioning against them. . . . Article 18 of this document prohibits a forced marriage between adults; it calls the arranger of such a forceful marriage *jabir* (tyrant) and states that the *qazi* (judge) who presides over this contract is to be reprimanded.[10]

Notwithstanding these attempts to rely on Islamic jurisprudence to make the case for female emancipation, the reality in Afghanistan's Pashtun belt was clear: social interaction was first and foremost delineated by the stipulations of Pashtunwali, which took precedence over any Islamic tenets. However, Pashtunwali did not contradict Islamic strictures in matters related to preservation of "modesty," which was, and is, leveraged by Pashtuns in restricting female interaction with the outside world, whether for purposes of attaining education, employment, or marriage. From the perspective of most Afghans, the efforts under Amir Amanullah were considered irresponsible and unnecessary meddling in the internal (social) affairs of an independent people who resented intrusion by the Amir in the best of times. Afghanistan as a "state" still had a very brief history and was essentially a loose confederation under a weak central government that had extremely limited influence in its far-flung, relatively inaccessible provinces. The inability of Amanullah's government to exert control over the periphery all but ensured that efforts to replicate the Turkish social model would fail.

The first wake-up call came in the form of a major rebellion in the province of Khost in March 1924. It was militarily suppressed, but the challenge brought home the threat posed by rapid reform measures that, coupled with the reduction of tribal subsidies, had become untenable. Historically, what little influence any ruler in Kabul was able to exert over the periphery was due to the annual payments dispensed to individual tribes to maintain their allegiances. Amanullah was so caught up in the importance of his social and economic plans, he believed that cutting the subsidies to pay for his programs would be understood, and accepted, by all Afghans.

Widespread, growing discontent in the provinces finally convinced Amanullah of the need to temporarily halt some of his reforms and to modify others. Girls were suddenly directed to receive their educations at home, religious studies were encouraged, and men were once again allowed to have four wives without having to obtain the approval of the original spouse as stipulated in the *Nizamnameh*.[11] This rapid back-pedaling on gender policy by Amanullah's government served only to embolden those who sought to ensure the traditional status quo, while dashing the hopes of many young girls in the urban areas. Nevertheless, although the modernization program never resumed the same pace, the seeds of female empowerment certainly were planted, and credit for this must go to Amir Amanullah and Queen Soraya.

A notorious incident in August 1928 highlighted how detached the royal family had become from the social pulse. Amir Amanullah, presiding over a Loya Jirga, a Grand Assembly of Tribal Elders (who had been forced to wear European clothes provided by the government), brought Queen Soraya to the event along with nearly 100 other women, mostly wives of government employees who supported her. They removed their veils in the presence of the tribal elders, who were shocked, whereas proponents of modernization applauded.[12] This theatrical and provocative act, which had been preceded by unpalatable economic demands, was the last straw. The elders at the Jirga reluctantly endorsed Amanullah's proposals at this public forum but wasted no time mobilizing public opinion against him once they returned home.[13]

The countryside began to take up arms against Amanullah even as elements within the government turned against him. The Amir abruptly shelved his modernization program. Girls who had been sent to Constantinople were recalled and schools for girls in Afghanistan were closed. Women were again prohibited from appearing unveiled in public and from cutting their hair. The center was dissolving. Afghanistan was reverting to its original state as a loose tribal confederation by the time Amanullah was overthrown in March 1929 by a Tajik tribal leader, Habibullah Kalakani, called Bacha-e-Saqqaw ("The Water Carrier's Son").[14] Amanullah's fall from power can be directly attributed to the government's overbearing demands for additional taxes and its reduction of tribal subsidies in order to implement controversial political, social, and economic reforms. These controversial demands in turn led to violence throughout the country, during which Amir Amanullah and the royal family managed to flee into exile.[15]

SLOW AND STEADY PROGRESS—1929 TO 1978

The state's gender policy during the period prior to the communist takeover in 1978 initially reflected a pragmatic, cautious approach to progress for women. Although Muhammad Nadir Shah (1929–1933), who took power from Bacha-e-Saqqaw, was cognizant of the repercussions of inciting the tribal populace and the mullahs, he nevertheless reopened some urban girls' schools, but only after first seeking approval from the tribal and religious leadership. Nadir Shah removed any symbols of Amanullah's era by renaming girls' schools and converting one to a nursing school, all the while justifying his actions as not being contrary to Islamic precepts and with the tacit support of the clerics, mullahs, and tribal leaders. Oversight of school curricula was returned to the clerics in order to ensure that the curricula were in accordance with Islamic teachings. However, members of the royal family and the elite sent many of their children abroad for school. The Sunni Hanifi School of Islamic Jurisprudence (*fiqh*) became the arbiter for civil and criminal laws and repealed Amanullah's ambitious marital and gender relations reforms.

When Muhammad Zahir Shah (1933–1973) assumed the throne after Nadir Shah's assassination in 1933, he continued his father's approach of slow progression on gender and social issues, which would, by and large, remain the blueprint for matters related to female status until 1978. Social, economic, and political conditions for all Afghans improved during the forty-year reign of Zahir Shah. This period was one of development and progress for Afghanistan as a whole, thanks in large part to relative internal tranquility and the absence of foreign aggression. A pragmatist like his father, Zahir Shah began empowering Afghan females by improving access to education through the establishment of elementary schools for girls throughout the country. In 1950, the first women's college was established in Kabul on the premises of Malalai School, formerly called Masturat. In 1957, the first girls' high school was established in Herat.[16] In 1964, women were granted the right to vote and to run for office under the third constitution. In January 1966, Kubra Nurzai became the first female cabinet minister of public health, followed in 1969 by Shafiqah Ziyai. Meanwhile, three women— Dr. Anahita Ratibzad, Ruqiyyah Habib Abu Bakr, and Masumah Ismati

Wardak—became members of parliament, and Humaira Malikyar, Saljuqi Gardizi, and Azizah Gardizi were elected to the Senate.

Employment for women, however, was only encouraged in fields such as education and health care where contact with males could be curtailed. When Zahir Shah's cousin and brother-in-law, Muhammad Daoud Khan, was appointed prime minister in 1953, he accelerated the pace of social reforms. Nevertheless, it was a far cry from Amanullah's precipitous efforts in the 1920s. Thus, in the 1950s began a period of female empowerment that continued until the Soviet-sponsored People's Democratic Party of Afghanistan was forced out of power in 1992. Also, starting in the early 1950s, thanks to large-scale external funding for developmental projects from the United States and the Soviet Union, Afghanistan began to experience unprecedented levels of infrastructure and non-infrastructure development throughout the country. As part of their economic packages to Afghanistan, both superpowers expected "progression" in women's status and funded girls' schools and educational programs that would include females.

Under Prime Minister Daoud Khan (1953–1963), the state again began to encourage women to seek out less traditional opportunities. They were offered positions confined to urban centers as air stewardesses for the national Ariana Airlines, receptionists in government offices, and telephone operators with the national service.[17] With no large-scale public protest, Daoud felt confident the time was right to implement a more ambitious modernization program, á la Amanullah. In what must have seemed like déjà vu, Daoud and the ruling elite, convinced that Afghanistan had reached the point when the social climate was conducive to the abolishment of veiling, began a campaign to end the practice. At the country's independence celebrations on August 24, 1959, wives of military officials and women from the royal household appeared at the review podium of the military parade unveiled. Those military officials who refused to allow their wives to attend unveiled were relieved of their duties and some were even arrested.[18]

Support for Daoud's policies by women of the urban upper and middle classes, coupled with the absence of dissent, led Daoud's government to expand the implementation of "empowerment" initiatives. As in Amanullah's time, Daoud faced stiff opposition when he tried to replicate urban modernization efforts in the rural areas, especially in the eastern and southern Pashtun tribal belt. In places such as Pul-e-Khumri, the capital of the northern province of Baghlan, the predominantly Pashtun population was incensed when the government pressured local taxi and horse-drawn carriage drivers to refuse to transport veiled women. Failure to adhere to this stipulation resulted in fines. Meanwhile, wives of Baghlan factory workers who would not unveil were penalized by being prohibited from shopping at the factory's cooperative society.[19]

Rebellion broke out in December 1959, led by the *maliks*, *khans*, and *mullahs*—tribal and religious leaders—in places such as Kandahar, Jalalabad, Khost, and Wardak. The factors attributed to this outbreak of violence at the local level included the elimination of tribal subsidies and/or taxation and the central government's efforts to impose gender "equality." The level of animosity and the social blowback took the government by surprise. Demonstrations and protests increased, especially in the Pashtun-dominated areas of the east and south. Government buildings were attacked and destroyed and some women who dared to venture out unveiled were killed by mobs. It took lethal methods—the military against its own citizenry—to crush the uprising. Opposition leaders were executed and many others, including prominent clerics, were imprisoned.

Although the state managed to crush any signs of overt rebellion, the experience, so reminiscent of what had transpired under Amanullah, rattled the royal family and the ruling elite.[20] Daoud's stubborn determination to humiliate the clerics and tribal elders in the Pashtun belt only exacerbated the deep schism that had emerged between Kabul and the provinces over modernization schemes involving female empowerment. The state's version of empowerment, modernization, and development had morphed into an ambitious social agenda that included a vision of female rights that challenged the embedded social mores of the majority of the primarily rural populace. Such policy formulations—which reflected an eagerness to get onto the regional Westernizing bandwagon led by Turkey and Iran—once again reflected the whims and ideals of the educated urbanized elite at the expense of those outside of their social strata who struggled to make ends meet.

Daoud's unrelenting stance, in particular his refusal to back down on controversial issues involving *zan*, created ruptures and tension within the royal household and was a primary reason behind his dismissal in 1963 as prime minister by his cousin, Amir Zahir Shah. Daoud's dismissal, however, had to do with more than just controversial, ambitious social policy,[21] so Zahir Shah continued the process of female empowerment, giving women the right to vote and to hold public office. In stark contrast to Daoud's bullying tactics, Zahir Shah's conciliatory and respectful stance toward the tribal *maliks* and *khans* in the Pashtun belt helped mitigate the animosity toward Kabul that had emerged under Daoud's leadership.

When Muhammad Daoud Khan overthrew Zahir Shah in 1973 in a bloodless coup, regime consolidation concerns precluded a more ambitious gender program to end what he saw as extreme inequality. By 1975, a new constitution was enacted that stipulated gender equality.[22] Whereas Afghanistan's first constitution had been ambiguous in its declaration that all *Afghans* were equal before the law, this document went one step further. Article 27 specified that both women and men are equal. Significant legislative changes were enacted again in 1977, in the civil code relating to relations between men and women, including the controversial legal stipulation that women would now be free to choose their spouses regardless of their families' wishes or choices. In reality, however, the enacted laws that specified women's rights were only implemented and/or adhered to among the small elite population of Kabul, Herat, and Mazar-i-Sharif, outside the conservative Pashtun belt. The government had neither the means, nor perhaps the resolve, to implement the new laws, so tribal customs regarding marital and child-rearing issues remained in place.[23]

DISPARATE APPROACHES TO ZAN—1978 TO 2001

During the period of communist rule from 1978 to 1992, under the People's Democratic Party of Afghanistan (PDPA), the state actively sought the support of women in its desperate quest for legitimacy. In its efforts to enact—and implement—what were viewed as un-Islamic social reforms, the state resorted to the use of force to compel females to attend literacy classes in rural communities.[24] Fearing the curriculum intended to convert their daughters to communism and was therefore antithetical to Islam, tribal and rural elements burned schools and other government buildings. Again, the state's use of repressive and autocratic methods only aggravated a volatile situation and led to rebellion in the provinces. Alarmed at the level of hostility, the government backed off and exclusively focused on implementing its version of "female empowerment" policies in the cities of Kabul, Herat, and Mazar-i-Sharif, where the PDPA retained an iron grip. During this period, urban women became essential for the continued functioning of the state. Women comprised more than 70 percent of the teachers, 40 percent of doctors, and 50 percent of university students; they were also prominent in other traditionally male careers, such as law and engineering, because many urban males had either joined the Mujahedin (from the Arabic, *mugahid,* meaning struggler) or had been conscripted into the Afghan National Army.

Meanwhile, the social status quo in rural areas remained firmly in place. The PDPA was unable to mobilize adequate financial and human resources for its social reform agenda. Furthermore, life in the rural areas was characterized by large-scale disruption due to internal displacement and forced immigration, as the Mujahedin-led insurgencies against the PDPA and its Soviet allies. It is estimated that a quarter of Afghanistan's population (around 5 million people) were forced to flee their homes due to Soviet military tactics that made no distinction between combatants and noncombatants.

In 1992, with the overthrow of the PDPA's Muhammad Najibullah, urban women witnessed an overnight reversal of their status. As the country drifted toward failed-state status, the various Mujahedin militias and the warlords (regardless of their ethnic affiliations) battling each other in Kabul, *all* targeted women. In August 1992, Burhanuddin Muhammad Rabbani of the Tajik-led Jamaat-i-Islami party gained control of the Mujahedin-coalition government in Kabul and began instituting a series of measures designed to "Islamize" an already conservative society. In December, when Rabbani's term ended, his Jamaat-i-Islami party refused to turn over the reins, leading to a brutal civil war between ethnic factions that lasted until the Taliban gained control of Kabul in September 1996.

Rabbani's rule was defined by large-scale violence toward women. Rape and killings were commonplace. Furthermore, draconian policies restricted female mobility, dress, and the ability to work outside the home. Urban women's fortunes were dramatically reversed almost overnight. Under the PDPA rule, women had experienced unprecedented freedom that had advocated—at least conceptually—a more egalitarian, and inclusive, role for the Afghan women within their physical sphere of influence. Now, under Rabbani's Mujahedin regime, urban women's gains vanished overnight, causing them and their families considerable economic hardship.

Although not as impacted, women outside the cities also experienced large-scale violence and rape in conditions that reflected the complete breakdown of law and order. In 1996, a relatively unknown group of Islamic madrassa students, calling themselves Taliban (plural of *Talib,* which in Arabic means "student" and implies those who seek Islamic knowledge), took over much of Afghanistan. They drove Rabbani's government from Kabul into the northern Panjsher Valley, where Tajiks, Hazaras, and Uzbeks formed the United Islamic Front for Salvation of Afghanistan, known as the Northern Alliance in the West.

The Taliban, whose leadership is exclusively Pashtun, adhere to an austere version of Sunni Islam, influenced by Salafi-Wahhabi, with origins in Deoband, India. Once in charge, they immediately enacted gender policies that were oppressive even by the standards of Pashtunwali and were based more on the rejectionist ideology of Arab "guests," such as Osama bin Laden.

Under the Taliban, girls' schools were closed; women were prohibited from working and forced into seclusion. Adultery was punished with stoning to death. Widows with no male relatives were unable to venture outside, let alone seek work in order to feed their families. Many resorted to illegal work such as tutoring girls in their homes or prostitution at the risk of execution. The Taliban justified such misogyny—and based their legitimacy—on an argument that they were bound to protect women's sexual honor, which thereby also protected Pashtun male honor, a cornerstone of Pashtun culture. Their denial of any rights specific to women was designed to consolidate power and to control their young and impressionable rank and file, many of whom were orphans raised in Wahhabi-funded madrassas in Pakistan.[25]

Although the Taliban brought a kind of order to a lawless country, their measures (increasingly restrictive with time) were considered oppressive by most segments of society. Many of their cruel, brutal tactics were considered alien to Pashtunwali, which advocated acting to preserve honor. In their zeal to reverse what they saw as corrupting influences of socialists and communists, the Taliban expanded upon Rabbani's already regressive gender policies as they embarked on tactics that were genocidal in nature by targeting those ethnic groups that supported the United Islamic Front.

PROSPECTS FOR EMPOWERMENT UNDER KARZAI AND BEYOND

Afghan women—especially the non-Pashtun—witnessed an overnight improvement in their quality of life following the ouster of the Taliban from power in 2001. Under President Hamid Karzai,[26] the government of the Islamic Republic of Afghanistan took major steps to restore the dignity of its female populace and improve their quality of life with the ratification of a constitution that to an extent mirrors Afghanistan's first constitution of 1964. Article 44 of the new document affirms, "The state shall devise and implement effective programs for balancing and promoting of education for women."[27]

Conditions for Afghan women (especially urban dwellers) have somewhat improved since 2001, but the resurgence of the Taliban has cast serious doubt that this can be sustained.[28] At the provincial level, the situation remains unchanged and/or is deteriorating notwithstanding the influx of billions of dollars of foreign aid to the Afghan government. Lack of security and few "respectable" employment opportunities hinder the pace of progress in gender matters. The failure of an increasingly predatory government to eradicate rampant corruption at all levels, as well as the government's inability or unwillingness to tackle the poppy cultivation industry, which encourages warlordism, criminal mafias, and the insurgency, only emboldens the Taliban and their supporters. These developments are a growing cause for concern among many Afghan women.[29]

A comparative examination of the gender policies of varying Afghan governments since 1919 is a lesson in caution: controversial and/or unpopular social measures have never succeeded unless applied with brute force, as during the Daoud, PDPA, and Taliban eras. In some cases—notably Amir Amanullah and the PDPA—they contributed to the overthrow of the regime. The first lesson for bolstering the position of Afghan women is to no longer construct or attempt to execute social policy as it relates to female empowerment without the agreement of a broad social base. Second, the government must acknowledge cultural, ethnic, urban, and rural dichotomies in gender issues and bridge these gaps by identifying common, unifying goals, such as provision of elementary education and access to health care. Government must be seen as an honest broker in its provision of social services and aid to urban and rural parts of the country. Third, it is essential to understand what the realistic needs of most women are and to address these, rather than mandate incendiary policies such as unveiling, dress codes, coeducation, and other hot-button issues that are destined to fail at the outset and/or may be leveraged for propaganda purposes by those who resist such changes as being un-Islamic. Finally, if efforts toward gender justice are to be sustainable over the long term, they must be primarily homegrown, integrating external assistance only as needed—not the other way around.

The process of abolishing entrenched cultural traditions that limit women's capacity to lead fuller, more productive lives must include much internal, inclusive discussions among Afghans. An empowerment road map for females is needed that incorporates the culture, traditions, and religion of the Afghan people with one important caveat: certain embedded cultural norms that are cruel, inhumane, and widespread, such as domestic violence and child marriage, must be abolished culturally, legislatively, politically, and through effective law enforcement measures, however slowly.

Afghan women are not a monolithic bloc. Since Amanullah, the gender policies of a Westernized elite based in Kabul have been completely disconnected from the issues and concerns of rural women, who have different social/cultural/tribal narratives and limited comprehension of the issues that concern their urban sisters. Furthermore, the empowerment of Afghan women is seen as being a commendable, even essential, endeavor by outside observers in the West, who may never have visited an Afghan village, where there may be no access to, among other things, potable water, schools, or medical care. Destitute women and their menfolk in dire circumstances, more often than not, have different visions of what constitutes "empowerment."

Historically, the gender policies of Kabul have reflected the perceptions, attitudes, and traditions of those in power. Whether the head of the Afghan state has been a Westernized Amir (Amanullah) or a mullah from Uruzgan (Mullah Omar), policies have always reflected the ruler's own social milieu at the expense of the wishes of the larger populace. The notion of compromising on sensitive gender policies has been notably absent amongst these leaders until, and unless, threatening social forces have challenged or confronted the implementation of specific social policies.

Without tangible improvements in both the security and economic realms, Afghan women will continue to be pawns in endless cycles of violence and suffering. As history has repeatedly shown, pragmatic considerations must take precedence over pure self-interest if there is to be a gradual but consistent move toward prosperity and opportunity for all Afghan women.

NOTES

1. Afghanistan is considered to have attained complete autonomy from foreign intrusion officially when it signed the Rawalpindi Treaty, which recognized sole Afghan jurisdiction over its foreign affairs, with Great Britain in 1919.

2. *Zan* is the Farsi, Dari, and Pashto/Pukhto word for "woman." In Pashto/Pukhto it is singular and plural.

3. Muhammad Amanullah Khan (1919–1929) was a Barakzai from the Durrani confederacy.

4. Amir Amanullah and Queen Soraya visited Turkey and were impressed by the determined efforts of Turkey's founding father, Mustafa Kamal, to enact precipitous social reforms that would disallow Muslim customs such as the veil, arranged marriages, and so forth, in order to establish a modern, secular Turkish state.

5. Prior to this period in Afghanistan's history, the only form of education for girls was religious based at local madrassas or at home and focused on learning the Qur'an and Islamic history.

6. Hafizullah Emadi, *Repression, Resistance, and Women in Afghanistan* (Westport, Conn.: Praeger, 2002), 63.

7. Ibid.

8. The fact that Amanullah took only one wife was unprecedented amongst the ruling elite of Afghanistan. His predecessors not only had up to four wives (as allowed according to Islamic precepts) but also had harems full of concubines. If there was one aspect of his life/behavior that bolstered his progressive social tendencies, it was his marital status and his treatment of his wife, Queen Soraya.

9. For more about Pashtunwali (or Pukhtunwali), see Louis Dupree, *Afghanistan* (Princeton, N.J.: Princeton University Press, 1980), 126–127. Pashtuns— variously called Pushtuns, Pakhtuns, Pukhtuns, and Pathans—are historically the dominant ruling ethnic group in Afghanistan, although they do not have a large majority. Afghanistan is a mosaic comprising Tajiks, Hazaras, Uzbeks, Kirghiz, Qazilbash, Balouchis, and the Farsiwan.

10. Helena Malikyar, "Development of Family Law in Afghanistan: The Roles of the Hanafi Madhhab, Customary Practices, and Power Politics," *Central Asian Survey* 16, no. 3 (1997): 393.

11. Emadi, *Repression, Resistance, and Women*, 63.

12. Ibid., 64.

13. Ibid., 65.

14. Habibullah Kalakani, known as Bacha-e-Saqqaw, was a non-literate Tajik who held power for nine months in 1929. Along with Burhanuddin Rabbani (1992–1996), he is the only Tajik to have ruled Afghanistan.

15. Amir Amanullah and Queen Soraya were exiled in Rome, Italy, where he died in 1960 and she died in 1968. They are buried side by side in Jalalabad next to Amanullah's father, Amir Habibullah.

16. Emadi, *Repression, Resistance, and Women*, 69.

17. Fahima Rahimi, *Women in Afghanistan* (Liestal: Stiftung Foundation, Stiftung Bibliotheca Afghanica, 1986), 74.

18. Emadi, *Repression, Resistance, and Women*, 71.

19. Andrew Wilson, "Inside Afghanistan: A Background to Recent Troubles," *Royal Central Asian Journal* 47, nos.3–4 (July–October 1960): 287–288.

20. Hafizullah Emadi, "State, Modernization and Rebellion: US-Soviet Politics of Domination of Afghanistan," *Economic and Political Weekly* 26, no. 4 (January 26, 1991): 176–183, http://www.jstor.org/stable/4397249.

21. Although Prime Minister Daoud's social reform policies were not the litmus test that led to his removal from office in 1963, they did contribute. His

stoking of the "Pukhtunkhwa" (Pashtun State), due to the irredentist connections with Pakistan, were also a factor.

22. For more details on Daoud's rule, see Martin Ewan's "The Return of Daoud and the Saur Revolution," in *Afghanistan: A New History* (New York: Routledge, 2001), 128–137.

23. For more on Daoud's efforts to reduce gender inequality, see Shireen Burki-Liebl, *The Politics of State Intervention: State Policy and the Status of Women in Pakistan (1947–2006) and Afghanistan (1919–2006)* (dissertation, University of Utah, 2007), 177–180.

24. Emadi, *Repression, Resistance, and Women,* 102.

25. Burki-Liebl, *Politics of State Intervention,* 217–218.

26. Hamid Karzai is a member of the Popalzai Durrani Pashtun clan based in Kandahar.

27. "Between Hope and Fear: Intimidation and Attacks against Women in Public Life in Afghanistan" (Human Rights Watch Briefing Paper, October 2004), 10.

28. Jerome Starkey, "Under Taliban Rule: How Insurgents Run Shadow Government in Helmand," *London Times,* October 3, 2010; http://freedomsyndicate.com/fairoooo/timesoo36.html

29. Bula Devi, "Afghanistan: The State of Women's Rights Is Still a Concern," *The Hindu,* September 13, 2010, http://www.thehindu.com/opinion/interview/article627560.ece.

CHAPTER 2

Between Covered and Covert

Traditions, Stereotypes, and Afghan Women's Agency

MARGARET A. MILLS

This discussion considers some longstanding Afghan attitudes about women's nature and capacity for social action, as reflected in proverbs and traditional tales.[1] Contemporary Afghan activist women must confront and work with or around such attitudes in carving out a role for themselves in post-9/11 Afghanistan. To present ways they do so, I examine examples from women's personal experience narratives: interviews with women teachers, an activist's post-9/11 autobiographical narrative, and published quotations of women and girls from topically centered journalists' interviews. Although all three varieties of narrative may predate 9/11 in various forms, as personal memories and as community oral history, such narratives continue to shape the speakers' sense of their place in the world and their options for action.

Why consider folklore in the present Afghan context? While Afghans have experienced vast cultural and physical dislocations in the last thirty years, Afghanistan remains a primarily oral society. Although male literacy may have exceeded 40 percent by 2009, depending on how broadly it is defined, literacy rates and access to education for women and girls still lag far behind those for men and boys, certainly no more than half their rate overall and far less in rural areas, despite the intense interest in schooling manifested in many areas of post-Soviet, and now post-9/11, Afghanistan.[2] In such a predominantly oral society, spoken words matter profoundly in everyday affairs. People's words are their bond; social values are taught orally through folklore and commentary on everyday events; and negative gossip or community criticism has dramatic effects on individual and family decisions about, for example, marriage and career options for young women and men. Yet folklore is not simply a mirror of values. Even the most traditional oral texts provide room for ironic or subversive interpretations.

Afghan traditional speech, like that of many patriarchal societies, includes some very "loud" reservations about women's capacity for moral and social judgment and action.[3] Wherever male dominance is endorsed as natural and the cultural norm, women's spheres of action are circumscribed in particular ways in comparison to men's. Furthermore, whereas women and men may present different assessments of individual women's agency, misogyny is not confined to men. Women also can and do hold negative stereotypes about women.[4] Likewise, not all men's descriptions of women's social behavior (traditional or otherwise) are uniformly negative.[5]

In Afghanistan, a desirable life for a traditional adult woman includes children, health, physical and economic security, reasonable labor demands, and ongoing social bonds and exchanges with her natal and marital extended families, while living within a nuclear or extended-family household. Her social circle is defined as private and domestic, comprising women, children, a husband, and those adult men (fathers, brothers, uncles) who are considered close kin but not potential sexual partners. Women do value the female equivalent of men's extended social networks, seeking to maintain social ties and reciprocal exchanges of gifts and help with a network of women beyond their own households.

The covering a woman wears outside the house (whether a *burqa*—*chadari* in Dari Persian—or other covering) extends the claims she makes to privacy as she moves outside her domestic space, while it also signals her adherence to Islam, in Afghan thought. Being "covered" expresses her observance of *purdah*—an ethic of privacy and sexual exclusivity for the honor of her family. It is also assumed to express the wishes of her *moharram*, the male authority (father, husband, brother) directly in charge of her protection and her social behavior.

The ideal of seclusion, modesty, and "coveredness" (*hijab*) implies that women's social interaction should be out of the view of male non-relatives. Within and alongside this positive understanding of cover, of female privacy and modesty, though, lies the potential for the covert, feeding legends and gossip about women who use institutions of public invisibility to achieve mobility for illicit purposes. The capacity to avoid male gaze or surveillance is thus potentially both pro-social and antisocial, depending on a woman's disposition.

In this connection, probably the "loudest," most widely held negative stereotype about women, not only in Afghanistan but also in Middle Eastern Muslim cultures in general, is the idea that trickery, deviousness, is an essential part of female nature. Using cover for covert purposes is only the most elementary of women's stratagems. The phrase, "women's tricks" (*makr-i zan* in Dari Persian, *kayd un-nisá* in classical Arabic) is proverbial and forms the generic title for a subgenre of folktales and literary anecdotes. In Persian language, when a woman is thought to have done something manipulative or devious, she may be characterized proverbially as a "true daughter of Eve." In Afghanistan, the proverb "Women are seven steps ahead of the devil" supplies a ready gloss for any woman's action that is perceived as antisocial and devious.[6]

In its literary configurations, the idea of women as premier tricksters has its canonical expression in Surah (Chapter) XII, "Yusuf," in the Qur'an, which tells the story of the prophet Joseph in Egypt, including the unsuccessful attempt of his master's wife to seduce him and her subsequent trick, crying rape to cover her own guilt. In this and other literary formations, women are tricksters in pursuit of their own selfish and illicit desires, quintessentially sexual.[7] When Joseph's master confronts his wife's trickery, Surah XII:28 quotes him saying, "Surely, your [feminine plural] guile is great!" Even though the offended husband is the speaker, the traditional interpretation of the verse is that this is also God's evaluation of women in general.

In Dari Persian oral folktales from Afghanistan this author recorded mainly in the prewar 1970s, there are abundant examples of male as well as female trickster figures, both main and supporting characters, good and bad. Tricksterism in males, however, is the special quality of a character type rather than a general personality trait of men. Given the limits imposed on women's agency in patriarchal thought, it is not illogical that women's agency in this fantasy literature prominently involves subterfuge, "weapons of the weak," in James Scott's term.[8] Underdog heroes, male and female, are everywhere in folk narrative. Simply being disempowered, an underdog male or female, and thus forced to resort to tricks or deceptive stories in order to act, is not morally reprehensible; it is rather a generic invitation for Afghan listeners, like folktale audiences elsewhere, to identify with and root for the disempowered, who eventually secure their own rights or retribution for wrongs as a matter of social justice.

What is wrong with women's resort to trickery in the negative stereotype is not trickery as such but (a) their assumption of agency itself in spite of the ideal of patriarchal control, and especially (b) the assumed object of their desires. In the mainly misogynistic written literature on women's tricks, the quintessential woman trickster acts for her own non-procreative sexual gratification, to the destruction of the social order, male authority, and the individual males who come in her way.[9] The word *makarah* ("trickster," feminine noun) is synonymous with "adulterous woman" in everyday speech. Old women tricksters' individualistic, materialistic greed, rather than sexuality, anchors their stereotypical representation as arch-tricksters and meddlers who have no legitimate social wisdom but much experience, and who can thus act as panderers, either to heroes or to villains. Their motives may be either material gain or mere enjoyment of exercising their capacity for mischief. One accomplished male Herati storyteller, Abdul Salam, described such an antisocial, religiously perverted old woman trickster, who is about to enter the plot on the side of the villain, with the following rhyming formulaic phrases: "An old woman, full of schemes, a prime piece, ancient in years, bent-backed, and skinny, who was seven steps ahead of the devil and always cooking sweet rice offerings for the demons."[10]

The emphasis in oral tradition differs somewhat from the dominant misogynist cast of Islamicate literature.[11] Regarding the many female tricksters in tales I heard and recorded from Afghan men and women, misogyny was by no means inevitable or even dominant overall.[12] Both men and women regularly told stories with female main and supporting characters portrayed as pro-social tricksters, women who employ tricks in order to secure justice and repair social order, including patriarchal sexual and family order, normally in the hands of men. Logically, women tricksters act to secure justice and repair social order because the male authority figures who should be doing so have failed, due to corruption, ignorance, incompetence, or sometimes simply their youth. Also, given that women are the preeminent tricksters, an antisocial woman trickster can by logic only be outdone by a more accomplished pro-social woman trickster. In the logic of oral narrative, men never see the trick coming. A folktale told in 1975 by "Madar Zaher," a twenty-nine-year-old married mother of five and accomplished woman storyteller in Herat, illustrates most of these features.

MAKR-I ZANAN, "WOMEN'S TRICKS," TOLD BY SHAHBUBU
GHAFOURY, "MADAR ZAHER"

Three young princes, sons of two different mothers, go hunting. As the youngest leaves with his brothers, his wife asks him to bring her some *makr-i zanan* on his return. As he sets off after their hunt to find this to-them-unknown thing, his brothers warn him against it, but he goes off alone in search of it, keeping his promise to his wife. Arriving at a strange city, he goes from shop to shop asking for it, but no shopkeeper can sell him anything by that name. He is a beautiful young man in princely dress, and his appearance draws attention in the bazaar. Eventually his appearance and strange request draw the attention of a young woman, single head of her own household, who tells him she can help him and invites him home.

After treating him to flawless and totally proper hospitality for three days—when he still asks for help locating some makr-i zanan to take back to his wife as he has promised—she takes him to a bath, shaves him, and dresses him in fine women's clothes, makeup, and jewelry. Covering him with an expensive veil, she then takes him to the royal court and introduces the young man as her brother's wife, asking the king to take "her" into protective custody in his women's quarters until the "husband," her "brother" who is on military service for the king, can return and take custody of "her" again. She has previously told the young man to allow himself to be entertained in female disguise in the women's quarters for a while, then sneak away and come back to her house.

The daughter of the vizier (the prime minister) recognizes on sight that this "lady guest" is actually male though the king's daughters do not. She seduces him, and sends him off to the men's baths, in male dress, after their night of sex. From there, he flees back to the home of his benefactor. His benefactor then takes him, in male dress, back to court where she introduces him as her returned brother and requests the return of the brother's "wife." The "wife" has disappeared and the host princesses infer that "she" has run off with a lover. The vizier's daughter, from whose house the "girl" has disappeared, dresses herself up and presents herself, veiled, as the "girl," but the boy's female benefactor ("sister") insists on looking under her veil to make sure they have not switched some other girl for her "brother's wife." She rejects the vizier's daughter as an inferior substitute for her "brother's" beautiful "wife," at which point the king and vizier beg her and her "brother" to accept the vizier's daughter and one of the princesses as wives in place of the apparent runaway whom they have failed to safeguard.

Thus the boy returns to his female benefactor's house with two royal brides. He still asks her to help him find some makr-i zan he can take home to his first wife, at which point she says, "Don't you understand? All this *was* makr-i zan, and furthermore, your own wife at home is involved in some *makr* (tricks) of her own, sending you off on this quest."

She then packs up her own entire household, the two royal brides and the young prince, and commissions a camel caravan to take them all to his home. On the way, the female storyteller stipulates, the prince's "sister" keeps herself apart from the newlyweds, spending her evenings in prayer.

Arriving outside his father's city gates after curfew, when the gates are locked, they camp outside the city wall, waiting to make a properly ceremonial entrance in the morning. The boy's benefactor "sister" again stays up late to pray and meditate while the prince and his two brides retire to bed. While praying, she notices a female figure climbing over the city wall and heading for the nearby hills. She follows the woman and sees her meet a huge and ugly demon lover, who curses and abuses her verbally. The woman flatters and cossets him and says by way of excuse that she had trouble getting away from the palace. The boy's "sister" waits in ambush for the returning woman, confronts her, and slices off the tip of her nose with a knife, putting the end of her nose in her own pocket. The errant wife flees back to the city with her bleeding nose.

In the morning, in a joyful and courtly reunion with his parents, the young prince tells the story of his adventure acquiring *three* wives (his father receives the sister-benefactor as a daughter-in-law as well, and she accepts this status without comment). The "sister," now wife-to-be, exposes the first wife through the injury to her nose and carefully explains to the prince and to his parents the wife's deception and sexual betrayal of her devoted and attractive husband. The king has the bad wife executed. A gala wedding is held for the prince and his three new brides.[13]

To my query, Madar Zaher replied that she had learned this story when a young, unmarried girl, from an elderly, impoverished woman of good character, who would come to visit them on cold winter evenings:

> ... from one old—she was nearly kin, no—she was like a neighbor, she was very old, and when it was evening and it was winter—and my mother was very good friends with this old woman—she would call her—I really liked tales and I would say, "Grandma, tell a tale," and she'd say, "Forget it, my tongue gets dry," and I'd say, "Nooo—(*high-pitched, fast speech, laughing*)—I *like* them!"—then she'd say, "Fine, I get cold, I'm old, you go make a little tea (*laughs*) and I'll tell a tale." (*Madar Zaher and Mills both laughing*). So my mother had a spinning wheel, and this old woman would tell tales, and I'd quickly make tea, we'd sit and drink, we'd tell tales ... (*with lowered, quiet voice*). She was a very good lady, and a lady of great character ... it's been ten years, about, since she passed away, and we, thank God, are alive, and we tell this tale of hers all the time and that lady doesn't go out of my thoughts or my heart.

In response to my standard field interview question asking where she learned this tale, Madar Zaher offered a thumbnail sketch of the homosocial domestic world of impoverished women in mid-twentieth-century Herat agricultural villages, where a hot cup of tea was valued hospitality, where women spun and wove local cotton, and winter nights were the proper time for such work along with visits and storytelling. Madar Zaher was engaged to her husband from childhood, though. By age twelve, when she remembers learning this tale, she was on the verge of marriage and her fiancé's expectations for her purdah observance were felt. She recalled with regret that her husband-to-be, who was also her cousin, did not like this old woman, a nonrelative, coming around and later forbade her visits. The stereotype of the old woman as an interloper and possible panderer is not far to seek.

Likewise the cutting off of an unfaithful wife's nose, not unusual in folktales but virtually unheard of in real life in the Afghanistan of the 1970s, may seem as fanciful to Western readers as the figure of her demon lover, until confronted with the actual mutilation of a young wife by her jealous husband, publicized on the cover of *Time* magazine in August 2010.[14] For a large majority of Afghans, this degree of retributive violence is a normal part of the folktale fantasy world where witches are burned or other bad actors are chopped in half, and so on (compare many stories from the Brothers Grimm and other European folktales, in our own case), but in the real world, it is horrifically wrong, certainly not supported in any way by the injunctions of the Qur'an on the treatment of women. Madar Zaher pointedly praises her elderly friend's character, though, just as, in telling the story, she defends the character of the pro-social female trickster. Not only does this young, single female head of an affluent household (a fantasy figure in these respects) help the young prince, but also she educates him about women's wiles and appears to have no sexual designs on him (unlike the vizier's clever daughter, herself a trickster, who sees through his disguise). Indeed, during their journey, when the young prince is off to bed with the vizier's daughter and the princess, his two new brides, our heroine spends her nights in *munajat*, prayer and meditation. Only after the boy's father sanctions her status as bride-to-be does she accept it. This pro-social trickster woman both outdoes and exposes the hypersexual, antisocial first wife's trickery, but she leaves the decision on the woman's punishment to the king. The upshot of her intervention is the restoration of patriarchal authority, but it is only by her perspicacity and agency as a pro-social trickster that order is restored and justice served. Potentially subversive messages for traditional women are embedded in this overall conservative plot resolution: the disloyal, hypersexual first wife is destroyed, but the clever vizier's daughter, also aggressively pursuing her own illicit sexual desires, is rewarded with marriage to her desired object by her own clever manipulation of patriarchal responsibilities (the need to compensate for failing to "guard" the "lady visitor"). Likewise, the "sister," the perspicacious trickster, enables herself to marry a young, extremely attractive, innocent, and tractable elite male, whom she has already dominated (adopting and advising him as a friend and "sister"), all this without indulging in any antisocial expression of sexual preferences.

Madar Zaher relishes, and narratively embellishes upon, the idea of a young, affluent, smart, religiously observant, and sexually virtuous single woman head of a household, though no one in her own prior experience fits that description. This pro-social woman trickster is no simple revolutionary, however; her agency is highly conservative in this as in other such stories, directed to upholding patriarchy in the face of men's inability to do so. The young prince may be innocent and therefore ignorant, but responsibility for failure to control an antisocial daughter-in-law then falls on his father, the king, who is both informed and, by inference, chastised by his new daughter-in-law. She seems in position to dominate, by superior intellect and insight, not only her new husband but also her parents-in-law, the proverbial source of authority and object of dread for young wives.

Radical personality, traditional agenda: Where do post-9/11 Afghan women activists come down on such attitudinal matters? Obviously, one size does not fit all; views on cultural feasibility and strategies for social action vary by age, educational and economic status, and rural or urban experience, both of the activists themselves and their clientele. Afghan women activists from different organizations, invited to participate in Afghan Women Leaders Speak, a 2005 conference held at Ohio State University's Mershon Center, were all self-identified Muslims, who nonetheless differed in their own approaches to, for example, modest dress. At the same time, they concurred in a split decision on what they identified as Afghan "traditions": some are good, some bad, in their eyes. They collectively supported the revival and broadcast of Afghan traditional instrumental music, song, and other traditional aesthetic productions and amusements (expressions publicly banned by the Taliban as un-Islamic) and opposed the onslaught of Indian and Western mass-media entertainment, which they called destructive to Afghan culture, identity, and values. At the same time, they strongly criticized traditions of patriarchal authority in the household, such as forced and child marriage, and pointedly, also, the pattern of female-female psychological

and physical abuse, which is all too common, even proverbially expected, from mothers-in-law exercising authority over their coresident
daughters-in-law. The activist women argued the urgent need to educate women in domestic authority to support daughters-in-law in quest
of education, health care, and income generation and to protect them
against domestic abuse.

Even within their critique of traditional women's complicity in abusive patriarchal patterns, these women activists' visions of solidarity
among women for social redevelopment retained a communitarian focus not essentially hostile to the traditional family-based ethos manifested in the folktale above. In the 2005 snapshot of their opinions provided by conference discussions, a major goal of activism was to improve
the family as a support base for the security and vitality of all its members rather than emancipate individuals from the family-centered social
order to pursue autonomous goals. To the extent that Western-style
feminist (or for that matter, democratizing) goals and strategies seem
radically individualist to traditional and some progressive Afghans, male
and female, they may seem "wrong for Afghanistan." In this connection,
the radically selfish and hypersexual individualism of the antisocial
female trickster found in traditional stereotypes, proverbs, and tales,
taints, indeed infects, the image of the Western-style emancipated woman.
To many Afghans, "feminist" implies selfish, antisocial hypersexuality and
its concomitant deviousness. The pro-social individualism of Western-
style feminism seems to some degree an oxymoron and, as such, a
deception.

Insofar as patriarchally inspired forces are incompetent, unjust, or
perceived as un-Islamic, however, those harmed or endangered have not
only the right but also even a duty to intervene. In the absence of authority to intervene, subterfuge is necessary. The Taliban-period clandestine
girls' schools that were ubiquitous and the stuff of legend and staples of
Western media reports in urban Afghanistan are a case in point. Women
who had acted as teachers in such schools—several of whom I met in a
2004 visit—explained their participation in communitarian terms of
need and duty. Some said they taught simply because they needed the
income for their families; others said that teaching was their duty to
their country or to Islam, which mandates education for all believers.

The covert strategies of female teachers were not entirely new in the
Taliban period. In 1994 and 1995, I made two short visits to Herat City
to interview teachers about adult literacy projects and general education reconstruction. I met teachers in girls' schools, trained at the gov-

ernment teachers' college during the Marxist period, who had to engage in subterfuge at times to get to and from their government-run
schools safe from Mujahedin attack. The chadari (burqa), not favored
by the Marxist regime, was useful for this, one strategy being to don a
chadari and leave home in the morning and return in the afternoon
conspicuously carrying a "bath basket," a small plastic mesh carry-all
or string bag with shampoo, soap, pumice stone, comb, scrub mitts, and
other grooming gear required for a protracted session at the public
baths. A full bath, hard to achieve in modest traditional homes without
running water, is not just an aesthetic pleasure, but religiously required
after sex. Traditional "female business" provided a smokescreen for
some urban professional educators.

Stories about clandestine girls' schools became a Western media staple in the latter part of the Taliban period and the months after 9/11.
The Revolutionary Association of the Women of Afghanistan (RAWA),
very active in schooling and other clandestine female-support projects, operated from Pakistan with activists and cells inside Afghanistan
throughout the war years.[15] RAWA remained intentionally clandestine in
both Pakistan and Afghanistan but simultaneously gained wide visibility
in the West through the sponsorship of the Feminist Majority Foundation's Campaign to Help Afghan Women and Girls and its chair, Mavis
Leno. Teachers with or without such organizational support, operating
in their own homes and neighborhoods, knew or assumed they were
under surveillance. Often implied in the accounts of non-RAWA teachers
is a tolerance for the covert, a "mutual unsaid" between activist women
and their neighborhood "minders," that allowed covert schools to function under a fog of mutual uncertainty. In Barry Bearak's *New York
Times* story, "Afghanistan's Girls Fight to Read and Write," Fatima, a
school organizer, tells the reporter, "'It is a sacred task to supply an education to these young girls. . . . This is what is sacred to me, this is my
jihad.'"[16] She is described standing in the alley in front of her house, face
uncovered, to discuss the school she and women friends had opened
three months before: "'The Taliban know,' she said with a slight shrug, a
gesture that meant she herself was unsure what lay ahead. 'We have 250
students. How could they not know? Taliban spies come around, asking
this and that. Some approve, some don't. We'll wait and see.'"

By that time, according to Bearak's information, the United Nations
estimated that 10,000 Afghan girls were attending officially illegal
schools in Kabul alone. Some of Fatima's students, like ten-year-old
Laili, had already engaged in more specifically covert strategies: Until a

month ago, she wore pants and kept her hair closely shorn. "'I pretended to be a boy and studied in the boys' school,' she said triumphantly. 'It was the only way for me.'" Fourteen-year-old Sabira was three years beyond even the school age for girls that was nominally tolerated by Taliban in some places. "'I'm already too tall,' she said. 'But I have a plan. I will wear a burqa and pretend that I am a teacher when I am really still a student.'"[17]

It is noteworthy, Laili and her movie counterpart who assumes the name Osama notwithstanding,[18] that these women and girls used not only transvestite disguise, but also imitations of legitimate female behavior to achieve their necessary deceptions. The distribution of male and female interest in transvestite disguise in traditional folktales[19] similarly suggests that male storytellers, although less imaginative than women about the possibilities for female agency in general, are more narratively engaged by transvestite strategies and much less attuned imaginatively to the ways women may manipulate female identity itself to achieve their purposes.

Another feature of the clandestine-schools phenomenon that connects with other stories of women seeking pro-social agency is the apparent obliviousness of men (such as the young prince in the story above) to women's stratagems and their sometimes seemingly collusive obliviousness, even within families. One woman, deeply engaged in girls' and women's education as a refugee in Pakistan during the Marxist period and continuing the work through the Taliban period and immediately post-9/11 in Afghanistan, told of how she used a physical disability to persuade her reluctant father to let her continue her studies year by year. Her family, she said, was not highly religious but socially conservative; none of the children had much formal education and her older sisters had none. As a disabled youngest child, "I was sitting in a corner all alone and I was playing with books and pens." After fifth grade, "All of the troubles started. According to our culture, I was a grown-up."

Yet as she was too disabled for ordinary household work, each year she cajoled her father into allowing her school attendance for "one more year," up to eighth grade, when they became refugees in Pakistan. Her brothers' wives, whom she supported and with whose childcare she lent a hand, helped conceal her school-going from her critical brothers: "When my brothers would ask, 'Where is [she]?' they would say, 'She's in the toilet. She's in the kitchen. She's sleeping.' So this is the way I completed secondary school." Her brothers were "shocked and amazed."

Soldiers in the street questioned her about where she was going as she went to school. Only her youngest brother supported her higher education plans, and he helped persuade her other brothers that, as a trained teacher, she could make herself useful home-schooling their children and not be an unmarriageable "burden" to the family because of her physical disability.

Anticipating an end to her education if she asked the family for the money needed for fees, covertly, without telling her brothers or father, she contacted a shopkeeper and began making paper flower ornaments for him to sell, earning the money she needed. Her studies of Islam persuaded her to challenge and critique on religious grounds her brothers' view of female education as un-Islamic, as well as their plans to marry off their young daughters involuntarily in childhood. She describes her arts of persuasion:

> I was checking their mood, for when they are happy. Then I was starting from here and there. I was talking about this [and that]. I was making some false stories. I am really sorry for that, but I believe that God will not punish [for that]. Then I was making a story like, "You know one of my friends, she had this sort of problem, she came to me and asked [what Islam says to do] . . ." I told them like this . . . slowly and gradually putting the topic on the table. I was arguing with them. This was the way, through the strength of Islam, that I could achieve.

Eventually, the strategies of discretion, covertness, and tacit "unknowing" came to an end. She was under severe pressure from "my village, my cousins" to accept a marriage offer for her from a wealthy older man with another wife and children, and her father, head of an elite family, felt his and the family's reputation in the community was at stake:

> My father came to me and said, "I know what you feel . . . but this is the pressure from my community, my tribe, that you should accept it for the sake of my respect and honor." And I said, "Okay, Father, for your respect and honor, I am ready to die, no problem. But before I marry that person, I will commit suicide. Because that will be a gradual suicide and it's better [just] to commit suicide."

Suicide has, in recent decades, become an all-too-frequent option for young Afghan women faced with impossible situations, especially disastrous marriages. It is, in that sense, the last form of agency to which a beleaguered woman can resort. This family relented on that marriage plan, but her male relatives still pressured her to stay at home and "take care of the family," offering her a different, more traditionally private kind of agency as a senior woman in an extended household, telling her that her presence had a calming, disciplinary effect on their own (uneducated) wives and children: essentially she was offered the "mother-in-law" position vis-à-vis her sisters-in-law.

Yet she persisted, and with other women friends from college started a modest support project for refugee families in Pakistan. In what she, like the teacher Fatima, describes as "my jihad," she successfully built an education development non-governmental organization that as of 2005 served more than 2,500 women and their families. But when re-interviewed in 2007 about the future she sees for Afghanistan, she replied somberly, "They [the Taliban] will be back, and next time, it will be harder to fool them [to continue women's activism]."[20]

NOTES

1. "Agency," a term used here and widely in women's studies and other disciplines concerned with analyses of social power and empowerment, is here taken to mean perceived or performed capacity for self-initiated action (of various kinds) by a category of persons.

2. The U.S. CIA World Factbook (https://www.cia.gov/library/publications/the-world-factbook) projected overall literacy for those over age fifteen in the year 2000 as 43.1 percent for males, 12.6 percent for females. These numbers should have crept upward somewhat with the reopening of schools.

3. Although not easy to quantify in the absence of systematic research on everyday communications, the "loudness" of a cultural theme might nonetheless be gauged by the number of different communicative forms, genres, or registers in which it is articulated and the relative frequency of its articulation within a form (e.g., in folktales) relative to the frequency of counter-themes in the same genre or medium.

4. Margaret Mills, "Seven Steps Ahead of the Devil: A Misogynist Proverb in Context," in *Telling, Remembering, Interpreting, Guessing: A Festschrift for Prof. Anniki Kaivola-Bregenhøj on Her 60th Birthday*, ed., Pasi Enges (Joensuu: Suomen Kansatietouden Tutkijain Seura, 2000), 449–458.

5. Margaret Mills, "The Gender of the Trick: Female Tricksters and Male Narrators," *Asian Folklore Studies* 9, no. 2 (2001): 237–258.

6. Margaret Mills, "Women's Tricks: Subordination and Subversion in Afghan Folktales," in *Thick Corpus, Organic Variation and Textuality in Oral Tradition*, ed., Lauri Honko (Studia Fennica Folkloristika No. 7, Helsinki: Finnish Literature Society, 2000), 453–488.

7. Fedwa Malti-Douglas, *Woman's Body, Woman's Word* (Princeton, N.J.: Princeton University Press, 1991); Gayanne Merguerian and Afsaneh Najmabadi, "Zulaykha and Yusuf: Whose 'Best Story'?" *International Journal of Middle Eastern Studies* 29:485–508, 1997; Afsaneh Najmabadi, "Reading—

and Enjoying—'Wiles of Women' Stories as a Feminist," *Iranian Studies*, 1999, no. 32: 203–222.

8. James Scott, *Domination and the Arts of Resistance: Hidden Transcripts* (New Haven, Conn.: Yale University Press, 1990).

9. Najmabadi, "Reading—and Enjoying—'Wiles of Women,'" 203–222; Ulrich Marzolph, "As Woman as Can Be: The Gendered Subversiveness of an Arabic Folktale Heroine," *Edebiyât*, 1999, no.10: 199–218.

10. *Yak pir-e zan-e arádeh wo poshti, domb doroshti, dirineh-sál-e kamar hokki, kamar báriki, keh haft qadam az shaytán jelautar miraft, o be shaytun madám shirberenj poxteh mikard*, "Romance of Najmá Shirázi," cassette F37A, March 2, 1976.

11. The term "Islamicate," popularized by the historian Marshall Hodgson, refers to literature, oral tradition, and other cultural properties (e.g., historical memory) that are at home in predominantly Muslim societies but are not necessarily religious in focus.

12. For a discussion of the original 1974–1976 collection of 450 recorded tale performances, 289 by men, 161 by women, see Mills, "Sex Role Reversals, Sex Changes and Transvestite Disguise in the Oral Tradition of a Conservative Muslim Community in Afghanistan," in *Women's Folklore, Women's Culture*, ed. R. Jordan and S. Kalcik (Philadelphia: University of Pennsylvania Press, 1985), 187–213.

13. The story is summarized due to space constraints; a full-length English translation of her performance can be found in Mills, "Women's Tricks," 465–485.

14. Aryn Baker, "Afghan Women and the Return of the Taliban," *Time*, vol. 176, no. 6 (August 9, 2010): 20–28.

15. The Revolutionary Association of the Women of Afghanistan (RAWA), organized at the outset of the Marxist period, opposed both the Marxist and the Mujahedin forms of autocracy, taking as their stated goals equal rights for women and full democratization. See Anne E. Brodsky, *With All Our Strength: The Revolutionary Association of the Women of Afghanistan* (New York: Routledge, 2003).

16. From the Arabic, "to strive," "to exert," "to fight."

17. Barry Bearak, "Afghanistan's Girls Fight to Read and Write," *New York Times*, sec. A1, A6, March 9, 2000.

18. *Osama*, a 2003 film, made in Afghanistan and written and directed by Siddiq Barmak, tells the story of a young girl who disguises herself as a boy in order to survive the Taliban regime.

19. Mills, "Sex Role Reversals, Sex Changes and Transvestite Disguise," 187–213.

20. Anonymous interview, Columbus, Ohio, November 2005. The author reinterviewed this individual in October 2007 in Kabul. Anonymity is provided due to the personal nature of the autobiographical and family information provided; some details have been modified to protect privacy.

CHAPTER 3

Centuries of Threat, Centuries of Resistance

The Lessons of Afghan Women's Resilience

ANNE E. BRODSKY

Throughout the history of Afghanistan, Afghan women have faced seemingly endless threats to their survival. These perils date well before the particularly shocking country-wide oppression of the Taliban that began in 1996 and brought Afghan women to the forefront of international interest. The dangers for Afghan women result from centuries of gender oppression based on conservative interpretations of Islam and Afghan tribal and ethnic customs, particularly Pashtunwali, an unwritten cultural code of conduct that, among other things, assigns women to a life largely isolated from the world outside their homes and essentially under the control of the men in their lives.[1] Under this code, girls and women are simultaneously dismissed as inferior to men, while great effort is paid to their surveillance and control. This is justified and necessitated by the centrality of girls' and women's behavior, reputation, and virtue as a signifier for the honor and stature of the entire family, particularly the men. This customary oppression has been compounded by three decades of war and civil violence, poverty, dislocation of family and community, lack of educational advancement, and political and societal backlash against efforts towards women's liberation. Afghan women's struggle for basic rights continues today in much of the country, despite any claims of post-Taliban liberation.[2]

The strain caused by thirty years of war and unrest, atop a long history of gender oppression, has had a profound impact on Afghan women. By multiple measures of well-being (see Table 1), it is clear that

TABLE I   LACK OF WELL-BEING AMONG AFGHAN WOMEN AND GIRLS

Literacy Rates	15.8 percent for women versus 31 percent for men.
School Attendance	Only 19 percent of schools are designated for girls. One girl attends primary school for every two boys; the ratio is one to four in secondary school.
Economics	38.2 percent of women are in the workforce; generally paid one-third the salary of men. Women's adjusted per capita GDP is one-third that of men; Afghanistan's GDP ranks among the world's lowest.
Security and Government	Women represent 0.6 percent of the National Army and 0.37 percent of the police force, nationally. Women are only 31 percent of the civil service, nationally.
Mental Health	Women report elevated distress and psychological symptoms versus men.
Physical Health Rates	40 percent of basic health facilities have no women staff. Afghanistan has the world's second-highest maternal mortality rate. 64 percent of people with TB are women.
Life Expectancy	Forty-four years for women and men. Women aged fifteen to forty-nine are nearly three times more likely to die than men.
Marriage	57 percent of girls are married before the legal age of sixteen. 70–80 percent cope with forced marriages. One million women are widows.

SOURCE: CIA, *The World Factbook,* "Afghanistan," https://www.cia.gov/library/publications/the-world
-factbook/geos/af.html; Kenneth E. Miller, Patricia Omidian, A. S. Quraishy, N. Quraishy, M. N. Nasiry, S.
Nasiry, N. M. Karyar, A. A. Yaqubi, "The Afghan Symptom Checklist: A Culturally Grounded Approach to
Mental Health Assessment in a Conflict Zone," *American Journal of Orthopsychiatry* 76, no. 4 (2006):
423–433; United Nations Development Fund for Women, Afghanistan—Fact Sheet 2007, "Progress for
Women Is Progress for All," http://afghanistan.unifem.org/docs/pub/07/UNIFEM_factsheet_07.pdf; United
Nations Development Programme, *Afghanistan: National Human Development Report,* 2004, http://www.
undp.org.af/Publications/index.htm; United Nations Development Programme, *Afghanistan Annual Re-
port,* 2006, http://www.undp.org.af/Publications/KeyDocuments/UNDP%20AF%20ANNUAL%20RE
PORT%202006.pdf.

women's and girls' lives have been profoundly negatively impacted by
this context. In 2000, Physicians for Human Rights (PHR) conducted
the most complete physical and mental health survey of Afghan women
during the war years. In interviews with more than 700 Afghan women,
PHR documented extremely high rates of mental health problems
among those living in Taliban-controlled Afghanistan, Northern Alliance (then United Front)–controlled northern Afghanistan and in Pakistani refugee communities. The majority of women in all three settings

reported their mental health to be fair to poor, more than 70 percent of women who were or had been in Taliban-controlled areas met Western criteria for major depression, and 65–77 percent of women from Taliban-controlled areas reported thoughts of suicide. Although there are no known studies of Afghan women's mental health during the Soviet period (1979–1989) or the civil war (1992–1996), undoubtedly the traumas and stresses experienced by Afghan women during these time periods resulted in similar deleterious mental health outcomes. What is most striking and concerning for women in today's "post-Taliban" Afghanistan is the PHR study's finding that even those who had escaped Taliban control reported elevated depression and suicidal ideation, and they saw the Taliban experience as significant to their symptoms. These findings suggest that the nearly continuous history of violence, repression, trauma, and stress experienced by Afghan women over multiple decades may continue to negatively impact their mental health, even if the country moves toward a full recovery.

Two more recent studies of Afghan women's mental health, conducted in Kabul in 2004 and 2005, also show that the 2001 Taliban defeat and promises of liberation, democracy, and peace have not lessened the negative mental health impacts on Afghan women. In one study, psychologist Ken Miller, anthropologist Patricia Omidian, and their colleagues[3] documented indigenous and Western expressions of mental health distress and found women, compared to men, reported higher levels of indigenous distress (e.g., *asabi, jigar khun*—different types of sadness—hitting themselves, quarreling with family and friends); Western-defined symptoms (e.g., depression, anxiety, posttraumatic stress symptoms); and ongoing daily stressors (e.g., roadblocks, air pollution, poverty, unemployment, illness, illiteracy, and lack of adequate housing). Women were also more likely to report that these symptoms impacted their ability to function. Whereas there were no reported differences between men and women on their exposure to past war violence and loss, the high levels of current daily stressors predicted women's levels of depression, anxiety, and current functioning.

Although it is crucial to document and respond appropriately to these negative outcomes for women, these studies only tell one side of the story of Afghan women's responses to past and ongoing violence and oppression. In spite of, and often because of these threats, Afghan women have a long history of spirited resistance and resilience, forging unique, culturally apt solutions to these challenges. These examples of resilience and resistance are often obscured by more numerous representations of Afghan women as silent, nearly invisible (*burqa*-shrouded) victims. Yet this resilience is critically important to document, for it presents a more accurate and complete picture of the indigenous strengths and resources of Afghan women. To understand Afghanistan today and the lives of Afghan women, we need to look not only at the needs and struggles that remain but also at the many examples of strength and resilience offered by Afghan women across the years. These examples are likely to prove more suitable as models for helping other Afghan women than are imported Western "solutions."

The resilience and resistance of Afghan women has a long and celebrated history dating back to at least the tenth century when Rabi'a Balkhi was jailed by her brother, the ruler of Balkh. According to legend, upon discovering her love poems to a Turkish slave, her brother ordered her wrists slashed before she was thrown into a steam bath. Her last act was to use her own blood to write another poem on her prison walls. Her tale and poem have been told and studied for centuries as part of the educated and folk culture of Afghanistan, which has a special regard for poets.[4] Rabi'a Balkhi's name lives on in public institutions dedicated to women's advancement. This includes Rabi'a Balkhi High School, the alma mater of Massouda Jalal, former Women's Affairs minister and the only woman to run against Hamid Karzai for president, and Rabi'a Balkhi Hospital in Kabul, the country's largest women's hospital.

Another historical example is Malalai, renowned for waving her veil as a flag to lead Afghan soldiers to victory in the 1880 battle of Maiwand, during the second Afghan-Anglo war. Fittingly, for a country that reveres poetry, Malalai reportedly further encouraged the fighters by shouting Pashto poetry.[5] Her name lives on in Malalai Lycée, the first high school for girls, founded in 1921 by Amir Amanullah. Malalai Lycée is open again in Kabul, after having been closed to girls under the Taliban, and boasts such graduates as Meena, who in 1977 founded the Revolutionary Association of the Women of Afghanistan—known as RAWA—an Afghan women's political and humanitarian organization.

Poetry is also the language of resistance for the Pashtun women whose landays (two-line, non-rhyming poems with nine and thirteen syllables) on love and war are collected in Sayd Bahodine Majrouh's transcribed and translated collection of this oral tradition. Not only is writing about love a transgressive act,

Put your mouth on mine
But leave my tongue free to speak to you of love[6]

but their fervor for battles exemplifies a more active woman than found in common portrayals of women as silent, depleted victims:

> May you be found cut to pieces by a trenchant sword,
> But may the news of your dishonor never reach my ears![7]

> My sisters, tie your veils around like waistbands,
> Pick up rifles and go off to the battlefield.[8]

Another important woman in promoting Afghan women's advancement is Queen Soraya, who was instrumental in her husband King Amanullah's reform program (1919–1928).[9] Through both their efforts, women gained access to education in Afghanistan and abroad, and a progressive Afghan family code was established, outlawing child and intermarriage and giving women both marriage choice and the right to file legal complaints against unjust treatment by their husbands. The queen presided over numerous related committees, founded the first state-published women's magazine, *Ershad-e Niswan* (Women's Guidance, edited by her mother Asma Rasmiyah Tarzi), and was among the first women to appear officially unveiled in public, as part of Amanullah's campaign to reform *purdah* in Afghanistan.[10] These reforms, however, were short-lived and became part of the backlash against Amanullah that led to his overthrow and exile.[11]

By the 1970s, women in urban centers, such as Kabul, had made considerable progress—42 percent were reported to have formal education and 41 percent were reported to be employed outside the home.[12] This was not however a national trend. A 1975 World Bank survey found only eight percent of Afghan girls enrolled in primary school, two percent in secondary school, and only four percent of women in the labor force, countrywide.[13] Even in 1979, women still lagged educationally, with only 4 percent of women literate versus 30 percent of men.[14]

Despite this uneven progress, Afghan women played a vital, though often forgotten, role in the street protests, civil unrest, and even military activities of the 1970s and 1980s. Women and girls were at the forefront of planning and carrying out numerous student-led pro-democracy protests against then King Zahir Shah in the early and mid-1970s. A striking example is a 1970 Kabul protest of 5,000 girls and women who marched for judicial justice following acid attacks and shootings of young girls and women perpetrated by groups of Islamic fundamentalists who objected to the Western clothing sported by these urban, educated girls and women.[15]

Street protests grew with the takeover of the Afghan Communist Party and the Soviet Union's invasion. Many senior members of RAWA recalled how they learned about and were recruited into RAWA from street demonstrations filled with high school– and university-aged women. One of the creative ways that women distributed anti-Soviet and pro-women's rights leaflets at the time was to take children along as decoys and carry the leaflets hidden in the wrapped bundles normally taken to and from the bathhouses.

Another example of ordinary women's resistance came in January 1980, when thousands of women from all walks of life and educational levels gathered to storm Pul-e-Charkhi prison, after their loved ones were not released, despite President Babrak Karmal's promised political prisoner amnesty. One of the most famous protests of girls and women came later that year, in the spring of 1980, in response to a People's Democratic Party of Afghanistan anniversary celebration of the Saur coup, which brought communist rule to Afghanistan in 1978.[16] Female student protestors in Kabul taunted pro-Soviet Afghan soldiers by throwing their headscarves at them and calling them Soviet slaves and "women." The soldiers responded with gunfire, killing a high-school student named Nahid, who became a martyred heroine for many Soviet resisters, both women and men,[17] and the namesake of many of that generation's children.

During the Cold War–fueled 1980s, stories told in the West of the Afghan freedom fighters were populated by rugged, bearded tribesmen who sparked the imagination of male politicians, war correspondents, and adventure junkies. In my interviews with women refugees in Pakistan at the end of Taliban rule, I heard analogous but less often reported stories of women's roles on the front lines. A woman called Najla in my 2003 book, *With All Our Strength*,[18] spoke of two years on a front line in eastern Afghanistan where she and eight other women were active participants, not only cooking, baking, and doing laundry but also cleaning and loading weapons, sewing face masks to protect against poison gas, providing medical care, teaching literacy classes, and taking part in military operations trainings. Najla's wedding took place on the front during a Soviet aerial assault and she gave birth to her first child a year later under similar conditions.[19] Clearly, this narrative, as well as a photo given to me of an unknown Nuristani woman in traditional garb, her face covered and feet bare, standing on a narrow mountain pass with her Kalashnikov at the ready,[20] demonstrates a continued and bold history of Afghan women's resistance.

Unfortunately, the defeat of the Soviet Union, which brought an end to a bloody ten-year war of resistance and the terrorizing of civilians by an oppressive Soviet police state, did not bring an end to the hardships, particularly for women. Although overshadowed by the officially sanctioned oppression and brutality of the Taliban, between the defeat of the Soviet Union and rise of the Taliban, Afghans suffered a lawless and cruel civil war, with civilians, particularly women, as frequent targets. The regimes that ruled during this vicious civil war had a less-systematic, but equally brutal and repressive effect on women's lives, as warring factions shaped their anti-Soviet tenets and interpretation of Islam into a direct assault on women's rights and lives. In this period, the dangers of assault, kidnapping, rape, and forced marriage were so great, and police or legal protections so lacking, that any attempts at normal daily life for women and girls was done at the risk of harassment, violence, and death. Any strides toward independence that had been made by women and girls up to this point were lost, as many, for their own protection, had to stop attending school and work, went out only when covered (and thus disguised/made invisible) in a burqa, and left the house, if possible, only with a close male relative (*moharram*) for protection.

Afghan women found ways, often at great cost, to resist this repressive period and be active agents on behalf of themselves, their families, and communities. Stories abound from the civil war era of women agreeing to marry men they did not love or even care for, only to save themselves from being forced to marry an even more despicable armed commander. Even harder was the experience, echoed by many other women, of Dashna, whom I interviewed in a Pakistani refugee camp in 2001. To protect her fourteen-year-old daughter from being forced to marry any of the local armed thugs who were eyeing her as she came into sexual maturity, Dashna arranged the marriage of her daughter, against her daughter's will, to a sympathetic cousin.

By the late 1990s, Western feminists and human rights activists had begun to spread word about the work of larger, better organized Afghan women's organizations such as Afghan Women's Network (AWN), Humanitarian Assistance for the Women and Children of Afghanistan (HAWCA), and RAWA.[21] But throughout the entire Taliban era, countless Afghan women actively expressed their resilience and resistance against that oppressive regime. It is important to note that many of these women received aid and support from progressive Afghan men who believed in their cause. Perhaps the most heralded examples of resistance came in the efforts, large and small, to continue the education of girls and women, despite Taliban bans. While some organizations, such as RAWA, were running multiple, underground classes in Afghanistan, and refugee schools in Pakistan, thousands of individual women and small organizations were secretly educating girls in homes, basements, and even in officially closed schools across Afghanistan. Frequently, I have heard stories of women teachers, removed from their jobs by the Taliban, who invited their female students into their homes, where they secretly continued academic lessons, year after year, all the while pretending the girls were learning sewing or studying Qur'an. Other educated women, forced by Taliban to abandon their jobs throughout the workforce, joined other like-minded women to organize and teach neighborhood girls. I was also told of a public girls' school in Parwan Province, which, although under Taliban control and "officially" closed, continued teaching girls, except for those rare weeks when a Taliban official would visit, at which time the school was once again locked shut.

In addition to resisting educational restrictions, Afghan women under the Taliban found ways to earn money through projects done at home, such as sewing, weaving rugs, and even running secret beauty salons. Although underground beauty salons may seem frivolous in a time of great hardship, these endeavors simultaneously earned some money for the beauticians, provided an opportunity for women to gather and enjoy the camaraderie of shared stories, and were a form of resistance in which women attempted to create some sense of normalcy in their lives. All these efforts thus contributed not only to the support of their families at a time of economic ruin but also helped women to keep their spirits aloft in dire circumstances. Women also acted as their families' emotional glue, creating lessons, games, and activities to keep children and other family members entertained in an environment in which countless forms of amusement—movies, TV, music, kite flying, carefree life outside (forbidden for girls, and too dangerous for many boys)—were gone.

Defying Taliban bans on women's work outside the home, many women also continued to work in medical settings, including in major hospitals in Herat and reportedly on and off in Kabul and in small clinics even in the Taliban stronghold of Helmand Province. An obstetrician told me of the jeopardy she faced in reporting the truth to a Taliban official in Helmand about the rape of a nine-year-old girl, committed by one of his men. The official had offered money if she examined the girl and wrote a report saying the child was unharmed. But seeing this young girl's terrible condition she could not do it. So her husband, also a doctor, went on her behalf and told the official not only that she would not write the report but also that the guilty soldier should be punished for his crime. Their actions in standing up for this young girl were heroic but could have had deadly results.[22]

For women involved with RAWA in Afghanistan, resistance activities during the Soviet, civil war, and Taliban eras also involved efforts to impact world opinion and action through their activism, protest, and outreach, such as secretly documenting atrocities. Although the situation was worse in Afghanistan, Afghan women refugees, particularly in refugee camps and impoverished communities of Pakistan and Iran also faced myriad struggles. These included economic hardship, particularly felt by widows and other women who had fled alone with their children; difficulty accessing education for themselves and their family; and violence both inside and outside the family. This violence resulted from a range of factors, including the carry-over of Afghan strife and political animosity into Pakistan.

In Pakistan, especially during the Soviet and civil war periods, thousands of intellectuals were kidnapped and killed in Peshawar, and refugee camps founded and populated by political parties needed fortified walls, lookout towers, and armed guards against rival factions. Family violence, rising above the "normal" level for Afghan family life, resulted from the calcification of tradition that often accompanies loss of homeland; fear of inculcation of foreign values on women and families; and the pressure of refugee life felt by men, who took it out on their families. Although the resulting stress on women showed in their mental distress as measured by PHR,[23] many also responded with the same resilience as their countrywomen in Afghanistan, finding and creating jobs, helping to open Pakistani branches of known Afghan schools (e.g., Zarghona Girls' School), creating and joining Afghan women's organizations such as HAWCA, RAWA, AWN, and Afghan Women's Educational Center,[24] and opening new schools and classes for refugee children and women.

As Lina Abirafeh has noted in her 2005 report "Lessons . . . Learned?" in addition to the increasing danger that women face during times of conflict, there is sometimes a perverse window of opportunity that opens.[25] For some Afghan women, these years of conflict and social disruption provided a chance to show their true capabilities to themselves, their families, their community, their country, and the world. Dire needs called forth Afghan women who filled the void in the social structure, providing hope, assistance, education, and support to others. Whether working as individuals or in an organization, they served as role models and community builders, earning the respect of the children, women, and men who observed their efforts and strength. A male supporter of RAWA explained in January 2002 that for him and other men, observing RAWA members' actions increased their commitment to women's rights and their respect for women's potential:

> What has affected everyone the most in making this commitment is the hard work of RAWA members, especially the understanding that we had and we still have about ordinary women. And we see these women doing activities that we had never seen being done by women, or their opinions or their decisions. All those issues make us support them.[26]

Shazia, a RAWA member, explained how RAWA's activities in Pakistan inspired her to join:

> When I joined the [political] demonstrations I was greatly affected by the bravery. It was the first time I saw that women could do something like this. And after being at a [refugee] camp [where they provided services], I was impressed that they don't care about their own lives, only about other women and children. It was a different world. Six months later, I joined.[27]

In addition to benefiting others, Afghan women's resistance activities benefit the well-being of the women themselves. Humira, a RAWA member who was living in a refugee camp near Peshawar when I spoke with her in June 2002, described this outcome: "When we help others it keeps us busy. It helps us to not think about our tragedies and problems. When you help someone you are satisfied about yourself and life and you become calmer. It impacts my children also. If I am happy they are; if I'm sad they are sad."[28]

Today Afghan women continue to struggle in an Afghanistan where the promises of liberation, peace, rebuilding, and security remain incomplete at best. Although few women mourn the demise of Taliban rule, the new era has produced a hodgepodge of change, simultaneously bringing a smattering of progress overshadowed by disappointment, disillusionment, and a dangerous backlash against women. Although schools have reopened for girls and women, a disproportionate number, particularly outside of the five major, urban provinces, are still not being educated—kept at home by traditional families, security fears, and/or the lack of schools and teachers. While women activists continue trying to change traditional opinions about the worth of girls' education, they are thwarted when parents rightly claim that the security situation makes school unsafe. In June 2007, for example, in a village suburb of the provincial capital of Logar Province, just forty miles south of Kabul, two girls were shot dead and four wounded while leaving Qalai Saida Girls' High School. Three months earlier the school had been firebombed.[29] In November 2008, fifteen girls and teachers on their way to Mirwais Meena School in Kandahar were sprayed with acid in separate coordinated attacks.[30]

Although women from more educated and progressive families, predominately living in urban centers, have returned to work, security fears, the negative talk of neighbors and family, and a lack of jobs that affects both men and women keep many women from economic progress. Women broadcasters, teachers, NGO workers, government workers, and others have been threatened, targeted, and killed. Rather than improving, the threats, restrictions, and violence against women appear to be becoming even more brazen in these supposedly post-Taliban years.[31]

The risk to women is unchecked by the Afghan government and the new Afghan constitution which, while enshrining a number of basic rights for women also places Shari'a law above constitutional law: "No law can be contrary to the sacred principles of Islam."[32] Although Afghan women hold an unprecedented 28 percent of the seats in the lower house of parliament, even if they could vote as a block,[33] they would still be outvoted by the 60 percent of parliamentarians whom Human Rights Watch and the Independent Human Rights Commission of Afghanistan say have ties to fundamentalist warlords.[34] Thus in February 2006, rather than debating pressing issues including security, the economy, or education, the Afghan parliament held a lengthy debate on a law requiring a close male relative to accompany female MPs when their work took them away from home for more than three days.[35] Although the law did not pass, the debate, along with the violence, represents a strong backlash from multiple segments of society, aimed at reversing Afghan women's freedom to participate in society.

Since 2006, President Hamid Karzai's cabinet has included only one woman, lower than the number in his 2004 cabinet. President Karzai explained this shortage, saying the parliamentary elections had shown that "[women's] place was secured," so that representation in the cabinet was no longer necessary.[36] None of this has stopped a number of women MPs from taking outspoken positions on the state of Afghanistan, including Shukria Barakzai, who ran for speaker of the parliament, and Malalai Joya, a representative from Farah Province, who allegedly still faces death threats for speaking forcefully against the participation of warlords in the government.[37] Neither has it stopped countless other Afghan women activists, educators, and social service providers. Women such as Soriya Pakzad of Voice of Women Organization, Jamila Afghani of Noor Education Center, Afifa Azim of Afghan Women's Network, and Orzala Ashraf of HAWCA represent the range of women providing literacy, advocacy, social support, Qur'anic studies, job training, and shelter services to women across many regions of Afghanistan.

Today, Afghan women in and outside Afghanistan continue to express their resilience and resistance while walking a careful line between their demands for progress, respect for tradition, and the threats of backlash.[38] Even now, nine years after the removal of the Taliban from power, some would say that social progress for Afghan girls and women, not to mention the entire population, has been disappointingly slow,[39] whereas others would argue that rebuilding a country and a people after thirty years of war, repression, and trauma takes time. In either case, what is different for Afghanistan now is that any transformations, for better or worse, are taking place with the attention and intervention, also for better or worse, of the world. This outside involvement brings both resources and risks, particularly for Afghan women. Although the struggles and resistance of Afghan women were largely ignored by the West from before the Soviet invasion through much of the Taliban era, the current influx of capacity builders, gender experts, and women's program funders on the one hand bring long-needed resources. On the other hand, these could threaten the resilience of Afghan women, as outside "experts" undervalue and undermine the true experts, Afghan women themselves.

All of the available data points to a complicated picture for Afghan women. Some are surely at risk for succumbing to the negative mental health consequence of past and current threats to their lives and well-being, while others continue to exhibit remarkable strength and resilience despite these dangers. It is these latter women who hold the keys to the promise and progress of the whole of Afghan society, because they, alongside like-minded Afghan men, have always played a crucial role in Afghan life. The results of their actions—providing hope, education, income-generating projects, and a belief in peace, democracy, and women's rights—are visible today at the grass roots, among those girls and women who come out to vote, those who are accepting low-wage jobs to teach or clerk in ministries, the students who pay extra for prep classes and crowd the universities, those who continue to work for the betterment of others despite the threats and risks. Afghan women deserve enormous credit for their strength and the utmost support, from both inside and outside the country, for their continued struggles. But this support must be in service of Afghan women's expertise, not vice versa. Afghan women's resilience has resulted from their ability, under even the most oppressive of conditions, to take some control of their lives, work within their cultural framework and skills, and act as change agents for themselves and others. It is crucial that any outside aid respect Afghan women's expertise and autonomy. Their history of strength and resilience is the best model for how Afghan women, and the country as a whole, can continue to successfully navigate a resilient pathway amongst the progress, disappointment, and backlash in order to ultimately create the Afghanistan of their hopes and dreams.

NOTES

1. Pashtunwali is the tribal code of the Pashtuns, the dominant ethnic group in Afghanistan and the rulers for much of the modern era (e.g., King Amanullah, King Zahir Shah, the Taliban, and President Hamid Karzai). Louis Dupree, *Afghanistan* (Oxford: Oxford University Press, 1997).

2. Unfortunately, neither struggle nor the need to resist set Afghan women apart from countless women across time and place. The Taliban were most unique not for their misogyny, which has been enacted around the globe in numerous appalling forms (e.g., slave-era United States, Saudi Arabia, Iran, Darfur, Bosnia), but for the utter lack of subtlety or facade in their brutal sexist oppression. The national and international reaction to the Taliban also is not an uncommon response where real, along with disingenuous, concern for women's lives is crafted, so that the "women's question" serves a larger political agenda whose aims are not really gender sensitive at all. Afghan women are also not alone in their resilient responses, which contribute not only to their own successes but also to those of their families and communities.

3. Kenneth E. Miller, Patricia Omidian, A. S. Quraishy, N. Quraishy, M. N. Nasiry, S. Nasiry, N. M. Karyar, A. A. Yaqubi, "The Afghan Symptom Checklist: A Culturally Grounded Approach to Mental Health Assessment in a Conflict Zone," *American Journal of Orthopsychiatry* 76, no. 4 (2006): 423–433.

4. Anne E. Brodsky, *With All Our Strength: The Revolutionary Association of the Women of Afghanistan.* (New York: Routledge, 2003); Dupree, *Afghanistan.*

5. Dupree, *Afghanistan.*

6. Sayd Bahodine Majrouh, *Songs of Love and War: Afghan Women's Poetry,* trans. Jarjolijn De Jager (New York: Other Press, 2003), 11.

7. Ibid., 17.

8. Ibid., 44.

9. Queen Soraya, the daughter of Mahmud Tarzi, was a noted intellectual, progressive thinker, and royal advisor to three kings.

10. Hafizullah Emadi, *Repression, Resistance and Women in Afghanistan* (Westport, Conn.: Praeger, 2002); Valentine Moghadam, "Reform, Revolution, and Reaction: The Trajectory of the 'Women Question' in Afghanistan," in *Gender and National Identity: Women and Politics in Muslim Society,* ed. V. M. Moghadam (London: Zed Books, 1994), 81–109.

11. Dupree, *Afghanistan.*

12. Barnett R. Rubin, *The Fragmentation of Afghanistan: State Formation and Collapse in the International System* (New Haven, Conn.: Yale University Press, 1995).

13. Valentine M. Moghadam, *Modernizing Women: Gender and Social Change in the Middle East* (Boulder, Colo.: Lynne Rienner, 1993), 224.

14. Ibid., 225.

15. Nancy Hatch Dupree, "Revolutionary Rhetoric and Afghan Women," in *Revolutions and Rebellions in Afghanistan: Anthropological Perspectives,* ed. M. Nazif Shahrani and R. L. Canfield (Berkeley: University of California, Institute of International Studies, 1984), 306–340; Brodsky, *With All Our Strength.* It cannot be overlooked that this behavior is repeating itself in current "post-Taliban" Afghanistan.

16. The Saur coup, initiated by the Soviet-sponsored People's Democratic Party of Afghanistan, resulted in the violent overthrow and killing of then president Daoud Khan, who five years earlier had peacefully overthrown his cousin, Zahir Shah. The coup brought to power Nur Muhammad Taraki, who initiated Marxist reforms, including those aimed at the emancipation of women, which challenged traditional Afghan values and helped pave the way for the 1979 Soviet invasion (Emadi, *Repression, Resistance, and Women*).

17. Brodsky, *With All Our Strength.*

18. All names are pseudonyms.

19. Brodsky, *With All Our Strength.*

20. Ibid., 59.

21. For more about these organizations, see Afghan Women's Network, http://www.afghanwomensnetwork.org; Humanitarian Assistance for the Women and Children of Afghanistan, http://www.hawca.org; and Revolutionary Association of the Women of Afghanistan, http://www.rawa.org.

22. Brodsky, *With All Our Strength.*

23. Physicians for Human Rights, *Women's Health and Human Rights in Afghanistan: A Population-Based Assessment,* 2001, http://phrusa.org/campaigns/afghanistan/Afghan_report_toc.html.

24. Afghan Women's Educational Center, http://www.awec.info/home.html.

25. Lina Abirafeh, *Lessons from Gender-Focused International Aid in Post-Conflict Afghanistan. . . . Learned?* (Gender in International Cooperation 7, Bonn, Germany: Friedrich-Ebert-Stiftung, 2005).

26. Brodsky, *With All Our Strength,* 200. Quotes in this chapter have been edited for clarity, brevity, and to save space and ease reading. Unless needed to bridge thoughts, ellipses were not added. The important content and meaning of the quotes is unchanged.

27. Ibid., 141.

28. Brodsky, unpublished data.

29. Integrated Regional Information Networks (IRIN), "Afghanistan: Girls Fear to Go to School after Shooting Incident," June 21, 2007, http://www.irinnews.org/Report.aspx?ReportId=72855.

30. Associated Press, "Acid Attack Keeps Afghan Girls Away from School," November 14, 2008, http://www.msnbc.msn.com/id/27713077/.

31. Throughout the lengthy editorial process for this chapter, violence against women has continued and if anything has worsened, as has all violence in Afghanistan. Some examples: Shaima Rezayee, a twenty-four-year-old VJ on a popular pop music TV show, was shot dead in her home in May 2005, following complaints that her work was un-Islamic (*The Times of London* Online, "Female Veejay Who Angered Mullahs Is Shot Dead," May 19, 2005, http://www.timesonline.co.uk/tol/news/world/article524206.ece). In September 2006, Safia Amanjan, the head of Women's Affairs in the Kandahar Provincial Government, was shot and killed by gunmen on motorcycle, as she left her house for work (*BBC News*, "Women Killed in Afghan Bus Attack," June 26, 2004, http://news.bbc.co.uk/2/hi/south_asia/3841845.stm). In June 2007 Zakia Zaki, thirty-five, a head teacher who ran for parliament in 2005 and also directed a U.S.-funded regional radio station called Peace Radio, was killed by seven bullets as she slept in her bed with her eight-month-old son (D. Walsh, "Gunmen Kill Afghan Radio Journalist," *The Guardian*, June 7, 2007, http://www.guardian.co.uk/world/2007/jun/07/afghanistan.declanwalsh). In April 2009 in Kandahar, legislator Sitara Achikzai was shot and killed by motorcycle assailants (*Democracy Now!*, "Prominent Afghan Women's Rights Activist Killed," April 13, 2009, http://www.democracynow.org/2009/4/13/headlines). All had received prior threats related to their work.

32. Afghan Constitution, chap. 1, art. 1; Pamela Constable, "Afghan Constitution Seeks Balance; Draft Document Charts Course," *Washington Post*, September 28, 2003, http://www/w;uml.org/newsfulltxt.shml?cmd[157]=x-157-20350.

33. Many Afghan women parliamentarians unfortunately not only lack the political experience and acumen to come together as a strong voting bloc, but they also have historic personal, constituency, and belief differences that often keep them from creating a strong coalition.

34. David Walsh, "Warlords and Women Take Seats in Afghan Parliament," *The Guardian*, December 19, 2005, http://www.guardian.co.uk/afghanistan/story/o..1670517.oo.html.

35. Scott Baldauf, "Afghan Parliament Debates Chaperones for Women," *Christian Science Monitor*, February 15, 2006, http://www.csmonitor.com/2006/0215/p04s01-wosc.html.

36. Radio Free Europe Radio Liberty, "Afghanistan: Suspended Lawmaker Insists Hers Is Voice of People," May 24, 2007, http://www.rferl.org/content/article/1076690.html.

37. Joya was suspended from the legislature by the assembly in May 2007, after saying that parliamentarians compared unfavorably to barnyard animals. She has not been reinstated (Radio Free Europe Radio Liberty, "Afghanistan").

38. Expatriate Afghan women throughout Europe, Australia, the United States, and Pakistan have been quite active in supporting their sisters in Afghanistan, both before and particularly after the fall of the Taliban in 2001. Many have returned to the country, either permanently or make frequent trips to provide aid and assistance.

39. At the time this chapter was written, the security situation in Afghanistan had deteriorated even more. It is hard to predict what will be the situation when you are reading this. Suffice it to say, however, that military success is only part of the solution, and had social progress in areas of food, shelter, employment, education, legal protection (for men and women), and safety from warlords and drug lords shown more progress in the early post-Taliban years, the Taliban resurgency would not have taken hold in the country as it has as of this writing.

CHAPTER 4

Don't Say What, Who, and When, Say How

Community Development and Women

WAHID OMAR

Non-governmental organizations deal constantly with non-literate populations throughout the world but are not always successful in implementing their projects. Often this is because they fail to recognize the dichotomy between the abstract world and the practical visions of indigenous people.

In Afghanistan, according to a report published by Matt Waldman, far too much aid has been prescriptive and driven by donor priority rather than responsive to evident Afghan needs and preferences.[1] Too many projects are designed to deliver rapid, visible results rather than to achieve sustainable poverty reduction or capacity-building objectives.

In his study of the Soviet psychologist, A. R. Luria—who did extensive fieldwork with non-literate people in remote areas of Uzbekistan and Kirghizstan in 1976—Walter Ong stresses that many cultures that have known writing for centuries have never fully interiorized it.[2] Arabic and Mediterranean Greek, for example, rely heavily on formulaic expressions. Writing differs from speech in that it does not spontaneously rise out of the unconscious. The process of putting spoken words into writing is governed by consciously contrived grammatical rules. Ong tells us that the logic of oral cultures includes: additive rather than subordinate ("and this happened and the next thing happened and . . ."); aggregative rather than analytic; reliance on formulas (Homer: "Son of Laertes and the gods of old, Odysseus, master mariner and soldier"); redundant; conservative (formulas are reshuffled and combined rather than supplanted, so that once forgotten knowledge is gone forever); performative/concrete (no statistics or abstractions); the context is always one of struggle and performance; emotional rather than objectively disinterested; situational vs. abstract.

In Luria's field study in Uzbekistan, the association between abstract object and non-literate subject is exemplified by having non-literate subjects identify geometrical figures by assigning them names of objects. Abstract terms were never used. Instead, a circle was called a plate or moon; squares were called doors. Designs were considered representations of things the Uzbeks knew, concrete objects, and things that seemed practical.

The same is true among Afghans who see the world not in the abstract but in practical and natural terms. In order to further development, it is essential to question how information is processed by the community in question rather than insist on processing it analytically. Quantum physics changed many disciplines and fields by stressing the comprehensiveness of analytical approaches, yet because of its focus on objectivity, it fails to analyze completely the essence of things. The obsession of Western scientific methods with dissecting problems into many parts has detoured and alienated scholars from the objects of their study. In the context of Afghanistan, we must explore and discover how to unfold the intricacies of oral traditions through the lens of Afghan culture, especially among female populations, and understand the difficulties faced by foreigners in delivering assistance due to cultural misunderstandings. Afghanistan is largely an oral culture, so it makes sense to begin with a story I collected in Afghanistan in 2007:

> Maleha, thirty-eight years old, is a female cook working for an expatriate family in the capital city, Kabul. She is honest, hard-working, and gifted with the ability to make anyone smile. She has five children. Her husband is an unskilled worker constantly seeking jobs. The family Maleha works for planted a few pots with seeds from the United States and instructed her to water the flowers from time to time. After a month, some of the seeds germinated, but they were growing slowly, apparently painfully. The soil was not good and other seeds did not sprout at all. Maleha, responding to the frustration and disappointment expressed by the family, decided to plant local wheat seeds in all the pots, all over the house. In a few days, not only were the empty pots lush with green wheat, but so were the pots where mustard, mint, and rosemary were struggling to survive. Maleha happily shared her success with the family, who were left speechless. Why had she decided on her own to bypass the instructions given to her? For them the objective was to grow specific plants for the kitchen, but for Maleha, the important thing was to make everyone happy and brighten the house with greenery. She was

proud of her achievement and said repeatedly how wonderful the pots were now that they were flourishing.

In the household where Maleha worked, everything was arranged for functionality, and the family members expected to find their things where they had left them. Maleha's favorite activity seemed to be to rearrange the décor and surprise everyone with her changes. It was often challenging for the family to find what they needed. Yet no one ever tried to tell Maleha not to shift things around: she was so good-natured and it did not seem worth it to hurt her feelings. She wanted to please, to perform, and that's what counted. Her actions were emotionally oriented rather than objectively disinterested, as might be the actions of a Western worker, to whom work and the workplace are separate from his or her own life.

One day, the local plumber came to fix the bathroom. He needed a receptacle for mixing sand and concrete. Maleha gave him a very expensive and precious glass bowl purchased in Herat. This time, the issue was not emotional, but about solving a problem quickly and practically. To Maleha, the bowl was merely a bowl, available to solve an immediate need. To the family, however, the bowl contained great significance, emotionally, and as a valuable art object.

These stories about Maleha illustrate a larger challenge affecting the differing ways aid workers and local populations in Afghanistan perceive problems, often resulting in negativity despite everyone's good intentions. Most aid workers come from analytical cultures, which value logical reasoning processes. Anything contrary is considered unintelligent and crude. Rather than blaming others for what we see as their ignorance, it is incumbent on us to consider how the way we think might be distancing us from the very people we are trying to help. Afghans have survived wars, diaspora, and desolation. Much of Afghanistan is geographically remote, so that in every era, the ordinary Afghan has had to struggle for subsistence. In general, Afghans see the practicality of things in all aspects of life as the most important and natural approach for development. The notion of practicality is relative to culture and context. In Western society, for example, if a family is poor, it would be seen as "practical" for a mother to go out and work. That may not be true for an Afghan family because a man might be shamed among his people if he could not provide enough for his family. This has nothing to do with not letting women work outside of their homes, which along with the *burqa* and women's subjugation issues have become the favorite topic of people writing about Afghanistan. Any issue must be approached with care and attention to cultural realities. We must avoid generalizations.

In my work as an educator in Afghanistan, I have been privileged to live and work with many people, engaging in countless hours of talking, workshops, and trainings. As an institutional coordinator,[3] I was involved in development planning that featured specific steps through each part of the process, beginning at the area of development, and then moving to objectives, strategies, and finally actions. Very often the training sequence ran off track, because the Afghan counterparts had their own ideas of sequence and would reverse the process without considering whether such change might affect the "logical" flow of events. What if the sequence was not the same, but the end product was? That is, what if the objectives were achieved anyway?

The planning process envisioned by our aid organization to build, for example, a library, began with forming a committee, identifying the development area, setting the objective, establishing strategies, and developing actions such as writing a proposal and submitting it to a donor. Our Afghan counterpart reversed the sequence by starting immediately with proposed action plans, that is, contacting a donor to determine whether funding was available. If it was not available, and there were no resources, then why waste time? This "reversed" planning process is contrary to the principles of most Western development planning, but the goal and the end result were the same: to build a library to increase student knowledge.

It is wrong to assume that tribal societies do not have logical planning processes or are unfamiliar with community development. *Shura* and *jirga*—forms of tribal councils that have been active in Afghanistan for four centuries—are the most common forms of community meetings, where problems are discussed and solved among leaders. The Afghan preference is to build a committee or shura first—a strategy in itself[4]—then discuss the objective, and finally take action. The sequence is very different from the Western development model but the end result is efficient and successful. No formal minutes are taken during shura meetings. Only the power of memory retains all the decisions made by the community.

Westerners tend naively to believe that tribal councils such as shuras and jirgas are the domain of men and that Afghan women do not participate in decision-making processes. Pundits of women's rights have unconsciously contributed to this misrepresentation by focusing fervently, sometimes exclusively, on the persecution of women by Islam and tribal laws. Although there is some truth in their claims, ignoring cultural contexts and social settings limits aid workers' understanding of how people live and behave and therefore reduces our ability to help and empower them. Women's councils in Afghanistan are numerous. Indeed, they surpass the numbers of men's councils, but neglecting to look beyond superficial notions and definitions of what a council is or might be overlooks a vital component of the culture. Women's councils are deeply embedded in Afghan traditions, and they rise organically, so to speak, out of daily life and ancient customs. These must not be ignored for the agency and empowerment they bestow on women within their own grassroots communities—where it counts.

There are two kinds of women's shura in Afghanistan. One is the official council, such as the one that took place in Torkham, Jalalabad, on International Women's Day, March 8, 2008, and was attended by Afghanistan's Minister of Women's Affairs, Banu Ghazanfar.

The second form of shura is not official, but it is more significant in numbers and probably the most effective in solving community problems. This type takes place in informal settings (situational), in oral performance contexts (not concrete), in communication situations (additive), and in cultural contexts involving emotions. Women in Afghanistan are the guardians of oral traditions. The following example describes the traditional way of solving problems, communicating events though community gatherings, and how planning is performed at the level of culture.

In Afghanistan, it is generally believed that *Nazr-e Samanak*, or Festival of *Samanak*, is a religious tradition among women, a pretext for socializing with other people, especially with other women. It centers on relatives and friends working together to prepare a delicacy, samanak, which cooks from night to dawn. It is an opportunity to sing, converse, work, share stories, comfort, and socialize. Some believe it is a ritual that comes down from Zoroastrian ancestors.[5] In this festivity, Muslim and ancient pagan traditions exist in perfect harmony and illustrate how women plan and make decisions together.

The performance of samanak takes place during spring when the last days of winter give way to the first green of spring.[6] This offering is still celebrated throughout Afghanistan, just a few days before *Nawruz* (New Year), among Afghans in cities and rural areas. The performance requires planning, so women divide the tasks a few days ahead of time. A woman especially assigned by the community pours one or two kilos of clean, unground wheat into a large receptacle, places it on a roof under the sun, and covers it with a veil to prevent insects and dirt from entering the bowl and to shelter it from evil eyes. The bowl remains on the roof for a week, absorbing spring rain and sun, which starts the germination process. When the wheat has grown to about four inches, a group of women cut the tender green sprouts. If they fall in pairs, it is considered good luck, but if they fall in odd numbers, it is a bad omen, portending wars, economical difficulties, drought, difficult harvest, many deaths, and other misfortunes. In that case, free bread is distributed to the poor so that the bad omen is counteracted.

The women fix the day of the celebration and everyone prepares their best clothing for the occasion. Someone is assigned to invite relatives, friends, and neighbors. Only close male relatives are invited. Another woman is assigned to calculate the festival costs—for bread, tea, biscuits, and sweets—and to collect the money. A meal is prepared during the day and cooked during the night by the women in the open air of the courtyard. The sprouted wheat is pounded by eight- to twelve-year-old girls. It is then poured into pots, until all the juice is extracted. Older women mix the extract with flour in a huge pot and stir the mixture every five minutes on a wood fire. These tasks are overseen and led by a *kalansal* (female elder), the most experienced person within the group. Young women between fifteen and eighteen years old, dressed in colorful attire, do not work. They sing and garner the attention of future mothers-in-law. Carpets are laid around the fire. Close male relatives and sometimes musicians are invited to join. Meanwhile, the wheat-and-flour mixture has turned brown and become sweet. The samanak cooks until the first signs of sunrise. The woman and the guests are entertained the night long by a special song, whose rhythm is accompanied by the movement of a *chamcha*:[7]

Samanak is boiling and we are dancing
Others are asleep and we are shining

Samanak is a gift of spring
This is the nightly feast of the living

Happiness occurs only once a year
Next year who knows what will happen

Samanak is boiling and we are dancing
Others are asleep and we are shining

The wish for tonight is happiness
Samanak will boil by itself
Happy hearts are wearing a cloak
Next year who knows what will happen

Samanak is boiling and we are dancing
Others are asleep and we are shining

It is sweet without sugar
It is colorful without color

It tastes as good as *firni*[8]
Next year who knows what will happen

Samanak is boiling and we are dancing
Others are asleep and we are shining

Happiness comes from its boiling
It is worth looking at its boiling
Its consistency is like a gum
Next year who knows what will happen

Samanak is boiling and we are dancing
Others are asleep and we are shining[9]

It takes a whole night to perform samanak. Every woman in the household participates in the process: the women sing, talk, perform, and tell stories. They share their problems, discuss issues, and make decisions. I was present at a samanak gathering where women discussed topics ranging from health, children's education, coping with price increases, wedding plans, and attending a funeral. Throughout these discussions, ideas were exchanged that would influence families and how they behave, plan, and make choices in their lives, arrange marriages, preserve tradition, and maintain social cohesiveness.

At dawn, the meal is ready. After the morning prayer, members of the household and their guests are invited to taste the succulent, dessert-like meal. But before it is served, the women lead prayers around the pot, with verses of the Qur'an quietly murmured and wishes made for peace, prosperity, and good health in the new year. The final *ameen* is shouted by the entire group, reaffirming social cohesion. This crucial moment of prayer makes the event sacred and untouchable by conservative Muslim religious standards (despite the samanak's pagan origins) and the whole occasion imparts a unified sense of self and community, the key to evaluating a culture. The ritual culminates after prayers with tasting the long-awaited meal and lavish praise for those who cooked and planned the festival.

Thus, cultural events are planned, budgeted, strategized, and performed in an unofficial council by Afghan women, who use them to discuss issues affecting the whole community. In performing these rituals, women not only are keepers of the religious and cultural events, but also they are real decision makers. Moreover, these events reflect well on how a non-Islamic performance is crafted and blended with Islamic prayers, so that communities are formed, social interactions and bonds are created, and women have an opportunity to change their daily routines. Daniel Taylor, a practitioner of community development, wrote:

> From the daily news to academic scholarship, a growing literature describes and analyzes *what* the problems are, *when* they started, *why* they happened, *who* did what to *whom*, *where* the trends are likely to end—a litany of *w*'s. The *w*'s are helpful, but the list morphs and mounts in a manner that makes it difficult to translate into effective solutions at the community level where action must be shaped.[10]

Clearly, Western aid workers would be more successful if the w's were forgotten and the planning process were instead conducted along cultural lines. The performance of samanak makes clear *how* practicality and simplicity of life are crucial values among Afghans. When the women sing, "Happiness occurs only once a year/next year who knows what will happen," we are reminded of the ephemeral nature of time and the value of life in its present moment. The song recalls the ideals expressed by the eleventh-century Persian poet, Omar Khayyám:

> You are a compound of the elements four,
> The seven planets rule your fevered life.
> Drink wine, for I have said a thousand times
> That you will not return; once gone, you're gone.[11]

Although the plights of Afghan women lead Western discussions about Afghanistan, and aid givers claim gender mainstreaming, community developers regularly ignore the cultural events performed by Afghan women as the base and matrix to bring change into the lives of all Afghans. Westerners judge success by their public influence, whereas for Afghans and others success is measured through the private sphere. Many Afghan women leaders draw their strength and inspiration from their own culture. Confirming this fact, Roshanak Wardak, a renowned gynecologist and member of the Afghan parliament, once said, "On average I help women deliver thirty babies a day besides my parliamentary duties, and my strength comes from believing in my people and my culture."[12]

Identifying the cultural activities and ritual performances among Afghan women is not difficult. But understanding the thinking processes through which Afghan women and men reason and come to conclusions and decisions seems to be problematic for experts in community development.

During field work in 2004, in the district of Jaghori in central Afghanistan, I conducted a needs assessment session with young, novice teachers. I interviewed a student named Zakia,[13] a clever, hazel-eyed fourteen-year-old, wearing colorful, traditional dress. Our dialogue went like this:

-*What kind of trees can you find in the village?*

[*No answer.*]

-*Can you define what a tree is?*

[*No answer.*]

-*Do you have apple trees?*

-*Yes.*

-*Do you have only apple trees?*

-*No, we have apricot, pomegranate, pears, and much more.* (This question was answered by all class members.)

The repeated silences during this conversation puzzled me and re-minded me of another occasion, when I was accompanying a group of American professionals at a girls' school in Kabul.[14] In all six classes, there was complete silence when the question "Why do you study?" was asked. The same thing happened when a group of students were asked in their graduate-study application forms to write essays about why they wanted to be admitted to a master's program. The students wrote about their financial problems, the wars in Afghanistan, disruption of educa-tion, and their professional backgrounds, but the majority did not an-swer the question.

Why define what a tree is, when the Jaghori girls are surrounded by trees? To the girls in the Kabul school, the question of why was merely awkward—and the answer obvious. So are the reasons for being part of a graduate program: everyone knows the financial and personal re-wards of obtaining a master's degree. Abstract categorizations, formally logical reasoning processes, definitions, and articulated self-analysis are a cultural baggage that aid workers bring with them, not realizing that Afghanistan has its own ancient and venerated traditions, and the rules of the game, so to speak, are different.

What matters most to women of Afghanistan is pragmatism. Self-analysis has no place in a culture dominated by community life, humil-ity, and participatory decision processes. The pain experienced by young Afghan women during interview sessions I once attended in Kabul, where they were expected by foreign employers to discuss their quali-ties and "sell themselves," was palpable. Foreign NGOs hire Afghans for jobs such as translators, coordinators, and trainers. They make sure to encourage women when advertising these jobs, but when it is time for interviews, the real challenge starts. Potential employers at the interviews I attended expected the candidates to outline their professional abilities, but instead heard about the difficulties of life in Afghanistan and their desperate need to obtain a job. This is not uncommon. In Afghanistan, sharing problems to describe the real need for work is customary. When one is hungry, feeding the belly comes first and intrinsic motivations come much later. Yet Western employers generally do not hire out of pity. Therefore, many Afghan women are not hired. Instead, young men trained in Pakistan are employed more often because they know, naturally, how to boast about their qualifications. In her study of Pashtun women, Benedicte Grima noted how female storytellers in Afghanistan used emotions in order to garner attention from their audience: "It became clear as I listened and watched the audience that the more personal suffering she could express, aided by tears and outcries and occasional wild verses, the better her tale was esteemed by the small audience of women."[15]

Grima is perhaps one of the rare scholars who by simply observing and participating in Afghan women's lives saw that personal narrative events and live stories are a major active genre among Pashtun women. She understood that live stories are a form of discourse and evidence of how a community of women judges its members and their experiences. Furthermore, she discovered that suffering and its expression (performance) is a sign of respect for Pashtun women.[16] The more a woman suffers in life, the more respect she gains in her community. A woman who does not endure hardship (experience) has no story to tell. A formal interview for an Afghan woman is no different from an informal conversation. Humility and modesty are behaviors expected from respectable women. In the Western interview performance—a ritualized communication between the interviewer and the interviewee (the audience)—the role expected from a woman is to boast and sell herself, but her cultural codes prompt her to choose otherwise. She will perform in accordance with the role assigned by society,[17] that is, to show humility and modesty, and by doing that she will lose the opportunity for a well-paid job.

Many more examples could be cited of situations where instructions are not followed and other solutions proposed, where it is a relentless battle for community developers to implement projects, because the expected outcome is constantly changed thanks to Afghan women and men taking their own initiative to solve problems according to cultural tenets. This is as it should be.

In a country ravaged by decades of war and desolation, in the absence of laws, institutions, and government, and the absence of men who were killed during the fighting, Afghan women have had to make their own decisions and find solutions alone.[18] During the horrifying civil wars and in the midst of explosions, gunfire, and screams, women have had to act quickly to protect their families and abandon their houses and properties. Day after day, they face the harsh realities of losing loved ones. Thousands have walked for miles carrying their children to escape to foreign countries, where they face adversity and uncertainty and have been forced to find ways to feed their families. For the average Afghan woman, struggle has become routine and the result is strength.

It is best to reverse the equation from investigator-informant to informant-investigator in order to understand the many misperceptions and mistakes made by the donor community. We must put aside our analytical, concrete, abstract, and subordinate mode of project delivery and build upon existing aspirations and belief systems. If culture is constituted of knowledge, values, attitudes, hierarchies, and religion (which can all be called knowledge), and it is shared by a relatively large group of people, then it has to affect the way we communicate. It is said that "culture is communication, communication is culture." Like people everywhere, Afghan women and men learn modes of behavior, rules, and customs as they are communicated and passed down through generations. Community development is about communication and the transmission of knowledge and skills. It therefore must take into account cultural practices and accommodate them as much as possible. "The evolution of democracy cannot happen," Mahatma Gandhi said, "if we are not prepared to hear the other side."

NOTES

1. Matt Waldman, "Falling Short," ACBAR Advocacy Series, March 2008, http://www.acbar.org/ACBAR%20Publications/ACBAR%20Aid%20Effec tiveness%20%2825%20Mar%202008%29.pdf.

2. Walter J. Ong, *Orality and Literacy* (New York: Routledge, 1982).

3. From January 2007 to July 2007, I worked throughout Afghanistan with sixteen institutions of higher education belonging to the Ministry of Higher Education.

4. The rule of law refers to all those state and non-state institutions that promote justice and human development through the application of public rules that are fair, applied independently, enforced equally, and consistent with

human rights principles. Shura is a traditional, non-state institution with the authority to settle disputes and enforce justice. Distribution of water, land disputes, breach of contract, criminal cases, and common problems are resolved by its members. The shura is held on a need basis and members are elected democratically.

5. The Zoroastrian priesthood has been the repository of ancient wisdom and many esoteric symbols and actions are a part of Zoroastrian oral training and traditions. Most prayers and accompanying rituals are part of an oral tradition and are recited from memory. Zoroastrianism, the world's oldest revealed religion, was preached in remote antiquity, by the Prophet Zarathushtra, who claimed divine revelation by the one true God, Ahura Mazda, Lord of Light and Wisdom. Zoroastrianism spread throughout Afghanistan before the coming of Islam in 655 CE and is present in every aspect of the Afghan society. Nawruz (Afghan and Iranian New Year), which coincides with the spring equinox on March 21, is just one example of an ancient Zoroastrian tradition celebrated by all Afghans.

6. I deliberately use the term "performance" because the whole event is not about cooking but it is a way to socialize, to share, to learn, to entertain, and to celebrate life. The festivity has songs, performers, and an audience communicating with each other, and as such it should be called "performance."

7. A large wooden spoon, also called *kapcha* (spoken Dari) or *daftcha* (Uzbek).

8. A sweet dish made out of milk, flour, and cardamom.

9. SAMANAK

Samanak dar josh as ma kafcha zanem
Degara dar khwab ma dafcha zanem
Samanak nazre buhar as
Melaye shabe zenda dar as
En khoshi sale yak bar as
Sale digar ya nassib
Samanak dar josh as ma kafcha zanem
Degara dar khwab ma dafcha zanem
Arezo emshab khuroshad
Samanak dar khod bejoshad
Del khoshi jama beposhad
Sale digar ya nassib
Samanak dar josh as ma kafcha zanem
Degara dar khwab ma dafcha zanem
Be shakar shirni darad
Khod ba khod rangi darad
Tam'e khosh tchun firni darad
Sale degar ya nassib
Samanak dar josh as ma kafcha zanem
Degaran dar khwab ma dafcha zanem
Khosh na ayad o ba joshash
Didani bashad khuroshash

Sajeqhaq darad ba doshash
Sale digar ya nassib
Samanak dar josh as ma kafcha zanem
Degaran dar khwab ma dafcha zanem

From a transcript of a tape recorded in June 1976 from Kabul Radio. The source is a story written by Akram Uthman in 1974, "Marjan" (Emerald), and the translation is mine.

10. Daniel Taylor, Carl E. Taylor, and Jesse Oak Taylor, introduction to *Becoming Change* (Oxford: Oxford University Press, forthcoming).

11. Ehsan Yarshater, *Persian Literature* (New York: State University of New York Press, 1988), 154.

12. Personal conversation I had with her in June 2006.

13. I have changed my informant's name to protect her privacy.

14. The school is supported by an Afghan and U.S. non-governmental organization called Afghans4Tomorrow, www.afghans4tomorrow.org.

15. Benedicte Grima, *The Performance of Emotion among Paxtun Women* (New York: Oxford University Press, 1992), 115.

16. Ibid., 126.

17. Rules that are perhaps sometimes assigned by men, but these are not the focus of our discussion.

18. According to a multiple indicator cluster survey conducted by UNICEF in 2003, 3.3 percent of households are headed by women in Afghanistan, indicating that the male member might be dead or displaced.

CHAPTER 5

Afghanistan Blues

Seeing Beyond the Burqa *on YouTube*

DINAH ZEIGER

As the "good war" in Afghanistan began to unravel in 2006 with a re-surgent Taliban, American media again focused attention on Afghan women. Images of women bundled in shapeless *burqa*s reappeared in mainstream media, this time signifying the failed "liberation" promised by the West in its 2001 invasion. One of the most widely viewed was "Lifting the Veil," a television documentary that aired on CNN in September 2007. Produced and reported by Pakistani filmmaker Sharmeen Obaid-Chinoy, the documentary probes the lives, and especially the bodies, of several Afghan women whose condition has not improved in the six years since Western allies drove the Taliban from power. "Lifting the Veil," like many other mainstream media, continues to frame Afghan women as objects of pity and victims of oppression from which Western democracy and capitalism pledged to rescue them.[1]

However, alternative media depictions, especially from Web sites such as YouTube, increasingly challenge this dominant Western interpretation. From the subversive music video "Blue Burka," to nuanced discussions of demands for legal reform and access to education and health care by Afghanistan's current generation of women activists, to entrepreneurial success stories, these new media have provided Afghan women a means of circumventing mainstream mass media to directly address a worldwide audience.[2] The question is whether these alternative outlets are the lever that pries off the lid of tradition or merely a world stage that reinforces a stereotypical Western understanding of the "Orient" as passively locked within ancient custom and religious law.

LOCKED IN A FRAME

The events of 9/11 positioned the war on terrorism as a conflict between good and evil, with Americans as reluctant warriors forced to confront a cruel and treacherous enemy. The problem for journalists was how to represent a war that lacked clearly defined boundaries or front lines. Although most of the perpetrators of 9/11 were Saudis, the Bush administration focused its initial campaign on Afghanistan, where al Qaeda mastermind Osama bin Laden had established terrorist training camps. The attack on al Qaeda justified American bombing raids and allowed Western media to link terrorism with extremism through the radical Islam of the Taliban. Initially supported as part of United States Cold War strategy against the Soviet Union's occupation of Afghanistan (1979–1989), the Taliban gradually began to represent the irrational and oppressive "other" of the East. Certainly the Taliban had left a legacy of brutality and senseless destruction in Afghanistan, but American attitudes had been shaped long before through recurring exoticized, racialized images of the Orient circulated in nineteenth-century popular media, from newspapers to films. These perceptions, according to Edward Said's seminal work on Orientalism, were fundamentally political in nature.[3] The Orient denoted much more than language, geography, and history; rather, it implied a derogatory expression signifying a lesser breed of human being.

The blue burqa—that all-enveloping outer garment worn by many Afghan women—became a symbol of oppression. Many Westerners link the burqa to a host of "uncivilized" cultural practices of Afghanistan's male-dominated Islamic society, in stark contrast to the American ideal of freedom, epitomized by the absence of such covering. Almost every film, photograph, and article produced by American media before and after the 2001 invasion of Afghanistan features an iteration of this perspective. The subtext underlying images of women covered head-to-toe, or begging on the streets, or scarred from a botched attempt at self-immolation is American cultural and moral superiority framed within its ideology of freedom.

Frames help journalists and filmmakers place events within a meaningful context that seems entirely natural in the scheme of things. Images of oppression signaled by the burqa encouraged Western viewers to equate liberty with freeing Afghan (and by extension all Muslim) women from the burdens of their clothing. Frames do more than provide the simple background of a story; rather, they articulate the cultural values and beliefs of their makers. Frames are shaped by events and custom— and also by the interlocking interests and relationships among cultural, political, corporate, and economic elites—which together produce a particular interpretive framework or lens through which to tell stories.[4] Commercially driven mainstream media rely on simplifications and streamlined narratives to clarify complex ideas, often by focusing on an individual. Reducing complicated processes or events to a singular experience allows journalists to fulfill competing constraints of timeliness and professional conventions of storytelling, meaning their stories likely will pass editorial review and make it on the air or into print. Audiences more easily identify with personal experiences—we care about heroes and victims and winners. As Jamison and Campbell point out, "The human connection allows us to imagine ourselves in the situation or create meaning out of the puzzling and complex."[5] In other words, audiences identify and respond in particular ways. However, several problems arise from such decisions: first, this simplified, up-close-and-personal frame distracts from following more substantive questions of context and history; and second, research has shown that the choice of individuals is often driven by their class, gender, race, or ethnicity.

Thus, Western mainstream media filtered Afghan cultural and social conditions through an ahistoric lens of human rights and values already linked to the ideology of liberty. After the United States routed the Taliban in 2001, women were expected to emancipate themselves from the burqa and embrace the new choices available to them. It didn't happen. Most continued to wear their traditional clothing, and, for the most part, their day-to-day conditions changed slowly, if at all. The pace of change attracted scant media attention until the Taliban reemerged; then, the lingering presence of the burqa resurfaced as a symbol of women's inability to attain political and economic equality.

Burqa-clad women pose a problem for Western viewers because of the way photographic images work. We cannot judge the emotional state of or make contact with someone whose face we cannot see, thus we are unable to create a personal relationship with someone covered head to toe. In addition, camera angle and position, whether the subject looks directly at the viewer or avoids engagement, whether it is a close-up or a long shot, all materially affect our ability to "read" images. The position of the camera relative to the subject subtly signals status: a low angle, looking up at a subject, suggests power, whereas a shot from above implies the subject's lesser status. One way Western mass media stabilize perceptions of the oppression of Afghan women is by focusing on individual stories—personal tales of hardship and abuse. Like the mesh face covering of a burqa, this narrows the field of vision to particular circumstances rather than engages whole vistas and ignores complicated inter-relationships. This focus on the individual also implies much neater lines of cleavage than may actually exist and minimizes social, economic, and political complexities.

SPEAKING FOR AFGHAN WOMEN

A study by Shahira Fahmy of Associated Press photographs of Afghan women before and after the U.S. invasion shows that after the fall of the Taliban burqa-clad women were portrayed as more involved, interacting with each other and more socially intimate, often engaged in non-traditional roles, making them more equal to presumed Western viewers.[6] She points out that these latter depictions subtly elevate the women from the realm of the passive and static—the stereotypical Western perception of Islamic culture—to a more dynamic engagement with their environment. "Lifting the Veil," in contrast, eschews subtlety. Self-identified as a "Muslim journalist," Obaid-Chinoy's first documentary, "Dispatches: Beneath the Veil," contributed to the pre-invasion framing of the oppressed Afghan woman. That video aired on CNN in 2001 shortly before the 9/11 attacks and ran repeatedly afterward.[7] It includes the near-iconic image of the execution of a kneeling woman by a man in Taliban dress before a capacity crowd of male onlookers in Kabul's soccer stadium. In "Lifting the Veil," Obaid-Chinoy returns to Afghanistan six years later to find out whether life has changed for women "in this newly democratic state," whether they "have the freedom to live and dress as they please."[8] Of course not: most women still wear burqas; beggar women line the streets; young bartered brides still set themselves on fire to escape the brutality of home life; and education remains elusive for most—for boys as well as girls.

Much of the problem with "Lifting the Veil" lies in the unspoken class difference separating the young filmmaker from her subjects. Her status as filmmaker confers upon her the power to interpret what she sees according to her own knowledge. Born in Pakistan and educated in the United States, Obaid-Chinoy makes films for the United Kingdom's Channel 4 as well as CNN, circumstances that separate her from the lived culture and experience of Afghanistan or Pakistan. What she chooses to focus on, what she edits out or leaves in, how she interprets events or conversations are rooted in her position of privilege and exclusion from events that shaped the lives of her subjects. Obaid-Chinoy appears on camera in each interaction, making direct eye contact with viewers as she interprets the scenes unfolding around her. In many respects, "Lifting the Veil" is about her reactions to conditions and events, some of which she engineers.

Obaid-Chinoy's first stop, an interview with a burqa-clad woman begging on a particularly bleak stretch of muddy rutted road in Kabul, illustrates her approach. With a cameraman in tow, toting her microphone, Obaid-Chinoy advances, talking all the while about her impressions and expectations of the scene. She confronts the woman, who sounds timid behind her coverings; Obaid-Chinoy persists, asking her name (Bibigul) and following her back to her shabby apartment, where she lives with two teenage daughters. Obaid-Chinoy's primary interest seems to be getting a look at Bibigul's face, which the camera exploits in a merciless close-up. Later, Obaid-Chinoy dons a burqa and follows Bibigul back onto the street to discover the harsh realities of begging. Obaid-Chinoy admits she feels "angry and invisible" under the "veil of oppression," which she says attracts the attention of a group of taunting men. The fact is that she is transparent rather than invisible, as she keeps talking into her microphone, followed by a video camera. It's debatable whether the group of men would have gathered absent the camera, and it's difficult to know whether her translation of their comments is accurate, as the film shows one or two giving them money.

Shots of video equipment and other apparatuses of production became a hallmark of television documentary in the 1950s, pioneered by Edward R. Murrow on "See It Now" and quickly adopted by others. Such techniques imply the absence of artifice—viewers can see how, where, and from whom information is gathered. Thus, by extension, the stories must be the real thing. Research shows that television presenters attain authority in viewers' eyes when they actually appear as a person rather than an unseen announcer, fostering a more relaxed and personal relationship with the audience.[9] The presenter becomes the "Prime Knower," the one calling the shots.[10] So, Obaid-Chinoy on camera tells viewers, as she bumps along bad roads to rural villages formerly under Taliban control, that even though some girls have access to education, it is inadequate and overcrowded. In one interview, she asks a group of girls what they think about marriage, in response to which they just

giggle, while Obaid-Chinoy tells us that they dream of becoming teachers. She seems to dismiss the support for women's education of some
village leaders and mullahs but praises the possibility of a bright future
for a school for orphaned girls. The effect of these interpretations and
observations reinforces Western perceptions and desires. They also serve
a disciplinary purpose in setting policy and cultivating popular support
for continued intervention, encouraging the West to stay the course in
the war on terror by linking the battle against oppression to the uphill
struggle of Afghan women to attain liberty and equality.

REFRAMING THE ISSUES

Several films on YouTube challenge this point of view, shifting the focus
from a superficial concept of liberation to propose a more subversive
interpretation of life behind the veil and to the rhetoric of human rights,
justice, and equal access. YouTube constitutes one of the most potent
alternative media outlets worldwide, allowing a wide range of unmedi-
ated voices into a new kind of public sphere, a forum for discussion,
argument, and potential change. It orbits in a new constellation of social networking sites, part of what scholars call Web 2.0, a public video-
sharing Web site where people can watch or share their own videos.[11] It
has evolved from homemade fare into a far more sophisticated platform for alternative voices. Social networks connect people at low cost,
which benefits organizations and businesses as well as individuals. Initially personal forums, they have been appropriated by industry and
government as a way to expand their contact base. These networks help
build customer relationships for companies selling goods and services
as well as offering vehicles for advertising. In addition, they provide a
channel for nonprofits and non-governmental organizations and agencies to connect with a like-minded global community working for social
good. In some ways, YouTube mimics the initial impact of broadcast
television news programs, which offered viewers a novel way of engaging important social and political issues through glimpses of other
people's lives. The difference is that, unlike television's costly and exclusive production and distribution apparatuses, almost anyone with a video
camera or mobile phone can participate on YouTube.

Traditional mass media, television in particular—tangled in a web of
interlocking institutional and political relationships—wield immense
economic and cultural power. They generally support the official version
of events, relying on familiar news narratives and images rather than

independent visual or verbal information.[12] Through selection and exclusion, these media frame both the agenda and interpretation of events, thus structuring how the public understands the issues. However, traditional mass media have less power to control the swarm of alternative media—from Web sites to listservs, blogs, social networking, even e-zines (online magazines)—now available to competing interpretations.[13] These new media offer a space for self-expression, a forum for telling another side of the story, a place to construct alternative identities and build support networks.[14] Researchers attribute their power to the Internet's "many-to-many" form, which allows feedback and generates discussion in a relatively uncensored and unedited forum.[15]

One of YouTube's most salient features is its purported autonomy from state or corporate control. It promotes a raw kind of intellectual critique and debate, encouraging users to comment on the videos posted. Critics point out, however, that it falls short of a traditional public sphere, where political ideas are freely exchanged, because it is increasingly subjected to corporate and government interference and policing by enforcers of intellectual property rights. Moreover, comments generally lack the quality of reflexivity—most are off the cuff and minimally deliberative—and claims and arguments are difficult to verify.[16] In addition, like traditional media, discussions are often dominated by a few individuals, who weigh in on topics and communicate primarily with those who share their interests and values. Research shows their comments offer emotional support, companionship, and advice and reinforce rather than evaluate ideas critically.[17]

Several videos illustrate how YouTube offers different perspectives on the conditions of Afghan women. "Blue Burka," a short video uploaded from fatamorganaclub, at first glance seems to be a subversive commentary on the oppression of the veil. A trio of musicians, covered top to toe in blue burqas, rocks its way through a tune sung in breathless, accented English, translated on screen into German. Whether fatamorganaclub originated the video is unknown, but the gist of the lyrics is that everyone in the family wears a burqa, implying that everyone has something to hide. With the music as background, the video rapidly cuts to a series of shots: the trio dancing on a rooftop framed in a skyline of low houses and minarets characteristic of a Middle Eastern town; shopping in the outdoor market; following burqa-clad women, wearing jeans and high-heels underneath, running errands. One or two scenes are filmed through the mesh face covering, restricting the view of the street.

Irony is the primary mode of address here. Based on the way they move, the members of the Blue Burka band appear to be male rather than female. The lyrics also suggest a gender switch, as does the name of the group that posted the video, fatamorganaclub. Fata Morgana means "mirage," particularly one sometimes seen off the coast of Sicily, so named because it is supposed to be the work of Morgan le Fay, the sorceress half-sister of legendary King Authur. The name Fata Morgana also encompasses European swingers' clubs, as well as fans of the Werner Herzog film and online hive communities. Considered in this light, the verbal and visual cues comment more on Western gender taboos than on oppression. Yet the video's images also suggest the liberating aspects of hiding in plain sight: who knows who is under that covering? It could be one of the guys. And who knows what they are doing under wraps; they may be making a video. That raises another possibility for Western viewers, increasingly confronted with stories about female suicide bombers who hide their deadly cargoes under the cover of a burqa. Who knows what is under that covering? Compounding that problem is the cultural taboo that underlies the burqa in the first place—to shield from others' eyes the bodies of women—which forestalls a too-close inspection. So, this silly but subversive little video presents a layer cake of counterarguments: 1) even clad in a burqa, it is still possible to play in a rock band; 2) a burqa may be as liberating to some as it is oppressive to others; 3) can you really know who is under that thing? and 4) can you tell exactly what someone is doing under there?

THE INSIDE STORY

A short video titled "Afghanistan: Women Entrepreneurs," from ILOTV, the United Nations–sponsored International Labour Organization, suggests an even more subversive idea: Afghan women succeeding in business. Burqas are simply not the issue. Instead, the video focuses on the activities of women who have turned traditional women's work into economically viable businesses, some even with global ambitions.[18] Some of the businesses are handicraft-based, requiring the needlework skills of an army of women laborers. One segment in an earlier version features the reemergence of local bread bakeries, traditionally an occupation reserved for widows, which was banned under the Taliban. An unseen narrator explains how, against the odds, women are finding their place in the rebuilding of Afghanistan. And several women talk, through an interpreter, about how they are achieving independence through ILO assistance and contacts.

The video narrative reflects the values and structure of the ILO, which was created at the end of the First World War and inherited by the UN at the conclusion of the Second World War. The ILO grew out of the European and U.S. union movements and emphasizes "decent and productive work in conditions of freedom, equity, security, and human dignity."[19] Its tripartite structure—representing governments, employers, and workers—ensures that it addresses the particular conditions of each country. The video's images of Afghan women at work or seated around a boardroom table discussing a financial plan subvert the Western mainstream media narrative of hopelessness and oppression. The camera shows the possibility of progress toward economic independence, not the unrelieved oppression that undoubtedly exists. It suggests an alternative narrative, not on a sweeping scale but on a human one, a slow progress.

"Fear Behind the Veil," a film by independent filmmaker Zarghona Rassa, presents a slightly different picture of progress, recycling the time-tested rhetoric of the Western women's rights movement of the nineteenth and twentieth centuries.[20] The push for women's rights in Afghanistan did not begin with the American incursion; women's rights have been at the center of nationalist conflicts since the early twentieth century. Afghanistan remains a country fragmented by warring tribal factions fighting over land and water and sometimes women and "honor." Geography constrains development and partly dictates the country's tribal-feudal economy based on land ownership and kinship ties. Islam is one of the few things that unite Afghans, and its laws, blended with tribal customs, structure its system of justice. Women function as chattel within this social structure, representing a family's honor, whose labor is bought and sold through marriage. Economist Hafizullah Emadi points out that in Afghanistan women are regarded as resources, reproducers of labor, part of the property of the male-dominated household. In common with most patriarchal societies, female education and literacy rates are low, and fertility is high.[21] To protect a family's honor, the virtuous woman behaves appropriately by covering her head and body. These restrictive codes conflict with Western capitalism and modernization and precipitated women's emancipation movements in Afghanistan in the 1920s, the 1950s, and the 1980s. Each time, reform efforts collapsed when confronted by deeply entrenched traditions and tribal loyalties that forcibly blocked attempts to universalize education and change marriage practices.

Rassa's film, distributed by U.K.-based Journeyman Pictures, allows a range of Afghan women to speak for themselves. Rassa—a middle-aged Afghan woman who fled to Britain following the murders of two brothers by the Taliban—never appears on camera, nor does she verbally interpret anything said or shown. It is unknown whether she is the unseen narrator who sets the opening scene and bridges the narrative between interviews. The difference between "Lifting the Veil" and "Fear Behind the Veil" is who is telling what story. The latter focuses on Afghan women explaining the conditions of their lives and arguing for rights. They are not primarily the oppressed, brutalized women of many mainstream media accounts, although a few do tell such stories. Rather, the majority of women on camera are social activists, lawmakers, and teachers, as well as wives, widows, and mothers. Some sit behind desks surrounded by computers and other symbols of Western organization, some stand in front of blackboards in classrooms, and others run clinics and shelters. Several speak to the camera in English; for others, subtitles translate their comments. Most of the women cover their hair: one wears a filmy *dupatta* draped over only her hair, another a nurse's cap, and others the traditional close-fitting black or white cowl that covers the head and shoulders. In general, the camera is positioned at eye level, creating a point of contact with viewers, as if sitting face to face in conversation.

These women talk about the slow pace of change. They acknowledge their growing access to education, health care, and jobs outside the home but observe that it is still dangerous for women to travel between home and work. Najia Haneefi, director of the Afghan Women's Education Centre, points out in the film that in such a fundamentalist society, "change needs a long time." Afghanistan's newly minted constitution reserves 68 of its 248 parliamentary seats for women, but few have run, and those who do so find themselves marginalized, constrained by traditional values and practices. As the women's rights activist Nooria Haqnagar observes, the Afghan constitution is one of the best for women's rights, *if* it were implemented. The problem, she says, is that many men accuse women activists of importing modern Western values.

Violence remains the single most critical issue, exacerbated by a legal system that regards women as second-class citizens. As Haneefi points out, the system doesn't consider women "human." Afghanistan's laws and legal system exist for men, many of whom reject the term "violence against women" and insist that if a woman is doing something wrong she should be beaten in order to maintain family stability. "They are not considering justice in families," Haneefi says. "They are pro-stability. It [violence] is not considered injustice."

Haqnagar, looking directly into the camera from her position behind a desk, says that Afghanistan's courts, judges, and tribunal do not believe in gender equality. Increasingly, however, women's shelters provide access to legal aid as well as skills training and education and a safe haven for widows and wives harassed and threatened at home. Several of these women tell their stories on camera. One weeps uncontrollably, only her eyes visible behind the scarf she pulls across her face. She says she has brought fuel with her that day to set fire to herself outside the shelter to draw attention to her abusive husband. Another has been abandoned by her family because a mullah said she brought bad luck, threatening two lucrative marriage contracts. One widow, however, stood up for herself, telling a brother-in-law wielding a knife that he could not force her into marriage.

The priorities for these Afghan women's rights activists are security and access to economic self-sufficiency. Sima Samar, director of the Afghan Independent Human Rights Commission, sums it up: Respect for human rights must be at the center of any policy seeking peace and security. This parallels arguments made in the nineteenth century by the nascent women's rights movement in the United States, which claimed that no country could call itself a democracy if half its citizens were disenfranchised. They, too, advocated for a woman's right to equal access to education and employment; equality within marriage, the family, and religion; and a married woman's right to property, wages, control over her own body, and custody of her children. The fight for voting equality in the United States took seventy-two years, from the Seneca Falls meeting in 1848 to passage of the Nineteenth Amendment in 1920. And another fifty years elapsed before women won equal rights in the workplace. Rights activists had to marshal alliances and arguments to counter deeply held beliefs, by women as well as men.

All media—mainstream or populist—have the potential for good or ill. Social networks are replete with examples of vicious, morally repugnant claims and counter-claims. In fact, they may be more awash in such ideas than mainstream media, which package their news products in familiar narratives, often reliant upon key insiders, to appeal to the broadest possible audience. The larger the audience, the greater their access to financial resources and the more closely woven they become in the political power structure. The mainstream media's rush to push Afghan women out of their traditional roles, their lamentation over the slow pace of change, may alert audiences to certain conditions, but it ignores Americans' own history and overlooks the vast cultural and structural differences between these two societies. Constant repetition of images of burqa-clad women also deflects attention from the larger issues confronting most Afghan women—access to health care, education, and jobs. Furthermore, such images quell any potential linkage to those same issues at home, where access to education, health care, and jobs is blocked for many American women. The recurring trope also dismisses the changes that have occurred and the ways that Afghan activists have mobilized on behalf of women's rights there. Afghan women confront a deeply entrenched traditional patriarchal structure underpinned by religious law and tribal culture. Its social norms are not comparable to Western ideals. Yet, after the U.S. invasion in 2001 and the initial rout of the Taliban, enormous cultural and structural changes occurred, driven largely by Western desires.

Alternative media offer Afghan women a venue from which to communicate their issues and interpretations sans the filter of mainstream media, which use female oppression as a tool to sustain Western interest and maintain the flow of funds toward a military solution. Although marginal in relation to traditional structures of power, new media increasingly attract the attention and have begun to reshape the agendas of mainstream media. They constitute a vital source of new ideas, although, as one study pointed out, there is no guarantee that new media report the truth and mainstream media do not.[22] One shortcoming of social networking sites such as YouTube is that they often are preaching to the choir; viewers probably already share the point of view being expressed. The difference for women is who is speaking. The relatively inexpensive costs of a video camera and an Internet connection allow the voices of Afghan women to be heard. Through this platform they can present the conditions of their lives without the filter of Western expectations, addressing the dangers and difficulties as well as the small steps toward progress in their lives. It is sometimes difficult for Westerners to see beyond the burqa—not behind or beneath it, but past it. It becomes the filter through which the West measures progress, but it is a meaningless yardstick for Afghan women.

NOTES

1. Sharmeen Obaid Films Web site, http://sharmeenobaidfilms.com/ar chives/88.

2. Fatamorganaclub, "Blue Burka," http://www.youtube.com/watch?v=bpH83 Vi7b9E.

3. Edward Said, *Orientalism* (New York: Random House, 1979), 204.

4. Todd Gitlin, "News as Ideology and Contested Area: Toward a Theory of Hegemony, Crisis, and Opposition," *Socialist Review* 48 (1979): 12.

5. Kathleen Hall Jamieson and Karlyn Kohrs Campbell, *The Interplay of Influence: News, Advertising, Politics, and the Mass Media* (Belmont, Calif.: Wadsworth/Thomson Learning. 2006), 44.

6. Shahira Fahmy, "Picturing Afghan Women: A Content Analysis of AP Wire Photographs during the Taliban Regime and After the Fall of the Taliban Regime," *Gazette: The International Journal for Communication Studies* 66, no. 2 (2004): 107.

7. Sharmeen Obaid, "Dispatches: Beneath the Veil," Google video. http://video.google.com/videoplay?docid=-4201322772364661561#.

8. Sharmeen Obaid, "Afghanistan: Lifting the Veil," CNN: Special Investigations Unit Transcript.

9. Peter Dahlgren, "TV News as a Social Relation," *Media, Culture and Society* 3 (1991): 293.

10. Ibid.

11. "Web 2.0," Wikipedia.

12. Yeslam al-Saggaf, "The Online Public Sphere in the Arab World: The War in Iraq on the Al Arabiya Website," *Journal of Computer-Mediated Communication* 12 (2006): 312.

13. Ahlam Muhtaseb and Lawrence R. Frey, "Arab Americans' Motives for Using the Internet as a Functional Media Alternative and Their Perceptions of U.S. Public Opinion," *Journal of Computer-Mediated Communication* 13 (2008): 622.

14. Patricia G. Lange, "Publicly Private and Privately Public: Social Networking on YouTube," *Journal of Computer-Mediated Communication* 13 (2008): 362.

15. Muhtaseb and Frey, "Arab Americans' Motives," 636.

16. L. Dahlberg, "Computer-Mediated Communication and the Public Sphere: A Critical Analysis," *Journal of Computer-Mediated Communication* 7 (2001), quoted in al-Saggaf, "The Online Public Sphere in the Arab World," 314.

17. Ibid.

18. ILOTV, "Afghanistan: Women Entrepreneurs," International Labour Organization. A two-minute clip.is available at http://www.youtube.com/user/ILOTV#p/search/o/frfyJXrP3-E.

19. International Labour Organization Web site, http://www.ilo.org/global/About_the_ILO/lang—en/index.htm.

20. Zarghona Rassa, "Fear Behind the Veil," Journeyman Pictures Web site, http://www.journeyman.tv/57790/short-films/fear-behind-the-veil.html.

21. Hafizullah Emadi, "State, Modernization and the Women's Movement in Afghanistan," *Review of Radical Political Economics* 23 (1991): 231.

22. Muhtaseb and Frey, "Arab Americans' Motives," 625–626.

PART II

A Woman's Place

ABOVE: A gathering at the Ministry of Women's Affairs in Kabul. Photo by Nilab Habibi for Pajhwok Photo Service, Pajhwok News Agency, 2009.

LEFT: A woman in Kabul casts her vote in the August elections. Photo by Safya Saify for Pajhwok Photo Service, Pajhwok News Agency, 2009.

CHAPTER 6

Women's Political Presence

A Path to Promoting Gender Interests?

ANNA LARSON

Afghanistan ranks in the world's top twenty countries for numbers of women in parliament.[1] In the *Wolesi Jirga* (Lower House) alone, women hold sixty-eight seats, comprising 27 percent of the plenary—partly due to a reserved seat system established during the Bonn Process.[2] This is a considerable milestone in the struggle for equal opportunities in Afghanistan. Nevertheless, although political space has been created for women in parliament, the question remains as to how this space is being used.

The benefits and shortcomings of reserving seats for women in legislative bodies are continually debated. The positive effects of this kind of affirmative action include marking the first step toward achieving some form of equity. Preferential treatment for certain social groups can compensate for their past exclusion, contributing to a process of righting historical injustices.[3] Affirmative action can also be used to overcome barriers that would otherwise prevent women or other marginalized groups from participating in political institutions,[4] and in fast-tracking their political presence, it can quickly redress quantitative social imbalances within these institutions. Further supporting this stance is the assertion that a critical mass of 30 percent of women in parliament is needed in order for women's political influence to be effective.[5] However, although this idea implies that influence can be quantitatively determined, it does not allow for factors that obscure the link between women's access to politics and their capacity to influence decision making, let alone the link between women's presence and their ability or willingness to promote their gender interests.

Central to the debate on affirmative action is the recent shift, in terms of political representation in general, from a "politics of ideas" to a "politics of presence."[6] Demands for women's (and other minority groups') greater political participation have replaced the concept of a representation through ideas, political platforms, and corresponding policy.[7] Indeed, this appears to be the case in Afghanistan's Wolesi Jirga, in which considerable emphasis has been placed on the question of which social groups are represented and where very few platform-based alliances exist that cut across social groups. A further problem with the "politics of presence" discourse is the frequent assumption that all members of a minority group share identical interests.[8] This assumption proves inaccurate when considering the women of the Wolesi Jirga, who, contrary to the often romanticized portrayals in Western media of the solidarity of a persecuted group,[9] are far from united as a homogenous bloc but are instead divided across ethnic, class, linguistic, political, and regional lines.[10]

In 2007, the Afghanistan Research and Evaluation Unit (AREU) conducted a study of the ways in which women's gender interests were being represented in the Wolesi Jirga.[11] Through interviews with male and female members of parliament, AREU found that affirmative action to fast-track women into the legislature had affected their perceived legitimacy in office. AREU also found that women's gender interests have not been substantively represented in parliament since its first term began in 2005. This short summary of updated findings of the 2007 study details key challenges concerning women's presence in the Afghan parliament, the representation of "women in general," and the nature of women's collective agency and influence during its first term (2005–2010).

WOMEN IN AFGHAN POLITICS

Women's political participation is not a new phenomenon in Afghanistan. The third Afghan constitution, drafted under King Zahir Shah in 1964, gave women the right to vote and to enter parliament as elected candidates for the first time. Although women's subsequent relationship with political participation has been turbulent, to say the least, their potential contribution to national-level politics has been recognized at different points over the last forty-five years.[12] However, the effects of the exclusion of women from political space during the Mujahedin and

Taliban eras are still apparent—primarily in terms of prevailing conservative perceptions that would limit women's role in the public sphere.

Nevertheless, the government of Afghanistan has taken steps to redress the inequalities imposed on women during previous regimes. Indeed, following the Bonn Agreement (December 2001), and subsequent global conferences such as Beijing +10,[13] the government made a series of commitments to Afghan women including the establishment in 2002 of the Ministry of Women's Affairs, the signing of the Convention for the Elimination of All Forms of Discrimination against Women in 2003, and the constitutional introduction in January 2004 of sixty-eight reserved seats for female candidates in legislative elections.[14] In May 2008, President Hamid Karzai ratified the National Action Plan for the Women of Afghanistan. Gender equity is also a key cross-cutting theme in Afghanistan's National Development Strategy, finalized in 2008, with gender mainstreaming identified as the preferred mechanism to achieve this goal.[15]

The international community has played a key role in encouraging these steps,[16] to the extent that the national ownership of and political will to promote the gender equity agenda in Afghanistan can be called into question in some cases. With a policy framework that promotes women's gender interests at least on paper, key constitutional and other legal milestones can be seen as the foundations for the promotion of women's gender interests. However, considerably more needs to be done in order to ensure that these provisions are internalized, implemented, and mainstreamed throughout legislative processes.[17]

The Politics of Women's Presence in Parliament

Women's presence in parliament is perceived in a number of ways by MPs themselves. On the one hand, the majority of male and female parliamentarians interviewed between 2007 and 2009 considered women's presence to be a positive step forward for the Afghan legislature.[18] On the other hand, their sizeable presence is often equated, by men and women parliamentarians alike, with the achievement of "women's rights." As one male MP stated, "There are twenty-eight percent of seats for women in the Wolesi Jirga, and this assures us that they have their rights."[19] This approach could lead to the conclusion that, if women's rights have already been "accomplished," there is no need to further promote women's gender interests in parliament.

Another issue concerns the attitudes of some (primarily male) MPs toward women's political presence and the way in which they acquired parliamentary seats. Indeed, the reserved seats system appears to have generated a degree of resentment from male MPs, who, even in 2007 (eighteen months after the elections) were still vocal about the disparity between male and female candidates' final vote counts. Other male MPs voiced the need to "take things slowly" with women's rights and their presence and influence in parliament, so as not to incite conservative reactions. This is perhaps understandable given Afghanistan's history, in which a series of these reactions to relatively liberal policies can be identified.[20]

Finally, and significantly, the reserved seats system was largely misinterpreted in the 2005 parliamentary elections. While the constitution clearly states that at least two seats on average must be reserved for women,[21] the minimum of sixty-eight reserved seats became a glass ceiling above and beyond which successful female candidates were not allocated parliamentary space. Almost 30 percent of women won their seats in their own right and not as a result of the reserved seats system,[22] and yet these seats were included in the sixty-eight finally given to women after the elections. Moreover, in parliamentary discourse, the notion of "women's seats" and "men's seats" is commonly referred to, as if there were seats reserved for men also. In this way, general seats—in theory open for any candidate to contest—have become men's seats in public perceptions. This is emphasized by the way in which many MPs (male and female) who were interviewed talked about sixty-eight seats being "not enough" for women. This common perception could significantly hinder women's chances of winning more seats in future elections.

Representing "Women in General"

Having discussed challenges concerning women's presence in parliament, it is pertinent to look briefly at who they represent therein. Officially, MPs are elected by provincial constituency, and thus in theory they represent their province. However, through interviews with MPs it became clear that many had mobilized village- or district-level voter support networks, and that these more localized areas were instead considered the focus of MPs' representational responsibilities. Some female MPs in interviews expressed the desire to support women of a particular ethnicity from their own district, for example.[23] This is not unsurprising, of course, but it is particularly significant when compared with the notion of representing "women in general"—a task often expected of women in legislative bodies. Furthermore, MPs for the most part represent the elite strata of society and have limited connections with "ordinary" women and men. This is true in many legislative bodies worldwide, but in Afghanistan it is emphasized by the fact that many parliamentarians have returned recently from overseas and have not experienced the direct effects of conflict. Female MPs often claim to be assisting ordinary women in responding to their practical needs, providing blankets or establishing clinics, for example. In describing these activities, however, they often present themselves as benevolent benefactors undertaking charitable tasks, which emphasizes the class divide and calls into question MPs' ability to understand, let alone represent, ordinary women's interests.

WOMEN'S COLLECTIVE AGENCY AND INFLUENCE

In spite of the nuances within and between different women's gender interests, these interests are nonetheless collective at a basic level, and as such they are most successfully represented by issues-based blocs as opposed to individuals. However, neither solid issues-based blocs nor collective political platforms have been strongly consolidated in parliament to date. Parties exist, and some exert considerable influence in parliament, but they are far from "institutionalized" in the conventional sense; they are not formally recognized as plenary blocs and their membership remains fluid and informal.[24] Moreover, for the most part they do not hold solid, issues-based platforms that would categorize voting patterns in parliament; these are instead largely determined by factors such as ethnicity and personality. A "parliamentary groups" system has been instigated in parliament to compensate for this lack of formal parties, but the formation of these groups has been highly problematic. Unfortunately, a situation in which more than 240 voices contend for audition in plenary sessions is still in place. As such, potential spaces for the substantive representation of women's gender interests have not emerged.

One recent example of the lack of an issues-based bloc promoting these interests is that of the parliamentary reaction to the conservative and highly controversial Shi'a Family Law, which prompted international outcry in April 2009 due to its apparent denial of women's conjugal rights, among other issues. This law had been discussed in plenary sessions on a number of occasions throughout 2008–2009, but, according to one female MP, not in its entirety: details concerning sexual relations, for example, had been "missed out" of the debate.[25] Various changes have been made to the law since its initial appearance in parliament, and by mid-2010 a new but still controversial version had been published by the Ministry of Justice. During the legislative process, a number of women MPs, who are not usually noted for their conservative leanings, took a public stance in favor of the law.[26]

Women's gender interests are clearly brought into question in this law, and thus it is necessary to explore why female parliamentarians did not emerge as a unified bloc to protect them. Specific factors include the tensions that exist between individual women, and especially between those who have significant connections to international agencies and donors (usually due to proficiency in English) and those who do not. These rifts have constituted significant barriers to the consolidation of collective gender interests over the last five years. It is not suggested here that women MPs should necessarily form a close-knit group by virtue of their gender, however, the power struggles between some individuals nevertheless impede productive cooperation when interests do coincide.

Another factor is women's allegiance to diverse parties or influential individuals, which can be prioritized over and above any commitment to promoting women's gender interests. In some cases, women were put forward by parties during the 2005 elections as a means to gain "easy" seats, and their decision making has been subsequently under the direct control of these parties; but in other cases, women MPs have used their party connections to their strategic advantage. Examples of this include women having accepted funding from parties for their electoral campaigns but once in office refusing to align with these parties' interests and simultaneously refusing to pay back the funds they initially received.[27] Moreover, while a number of parties have women's wings, they lack the institutionalization, the formal connections to the legislature, and essentially the political will to provide platforms for the effective promotion of women's gender interests. Ethnicity also plays a significant role in determining male and female MPs' allegiances. With women parliamentarians, it is often the case that ethnic and *qaum*-based identities are prioritized over and above gender identities,[28] undercutting any sense of unity between women over issues that otherwise might invoke solidarity.

Lastly, echoing the concerns of some of their male colleagues, during interviews a number of female MPs voiced a concern to keep the peace and a disinclination to disrupt any sense of "national unity," however superficial, attained in parliament. This was particularly the case regarding controversial issues, about which one female MP described the need to "speak gently": "We should use the mechanism of speaking gently and not against the men, so that they don't get angry with us; this will help to change their minds slowly."

Although this kind of caution is evidently strategic, and perhaps wise, one can nonetheless wonder when and over what issues female MPs will feel comfortable standing openly and speaking *un*gently to promote their gender interests. Furthermore, it is necessary to ask why, and why now, women and men are so concerned not to upset conservative sensibilities in parliament.

In responding to these questions, it is evident that security is an essential, underlying consideration affecting all aspects of the functioning of Afghanistan's legislative processes. In a climate of decreasing security levels in which MPs are targets of both anti-state activists and those who would oppose their views inside parliament, it is not surprising that there is a considerable reluctance to promote women's gender interests when association with these interests can prove quite frankly dangerous. Moreover, because sentiments against international intervention in Afghanistan appear to be increasing, particularly as a result of apparently accumulating civilian casualties attributed to international military forces, any sign of support for "Western values" and what is perceived as "foreign interference with Islamic principles" is highly political and can involve considerable risk.[29]

In sum, it is clear that women's presence in Afghanistan's legislature has not led to the collective representation of women in general or the promotion of women's gender interests to date. A number of factors pose key challenges: attitudes toward the legitimacy of their very presence in parliament, assumptions concerning who they represent therein, and the existence of cross-cutting identities and allegiances that fragment efforts to mobilize as a collective bloc. Underpinning these factors is the essential consideration of decreasing security, which is rendering the concept of free speech essentially meaningless in 2010. Technical measures to improve the functioning of parliament are necessary and may provide the mechanisms needed to encourage bloc formation and the representation of collective interests. However, until MPs feel secure enough to broach and vote on controversial subjects such as women's gender interests—with the confidence that their opinions will not generate violent opposition—the chance of these interests being promoted substantively will remain elusive.

NOTES

1. Andrew Reynolds, Lucy Jones, and Andrew Wilder, *A Guide to Parliamentary Elections in Afghanistan* (Kabul: AREU, 2005), 10. http://www.areu.org.af.

2. Officially, the system used in Afghanistan is a reserved seats system. This differs from statutory quotas in that it marks a constitutional provision to allocate a certain number of seats to women legislators, rather than regulating the specific proportion of male and female candidates by all parties seeking parliamentary representation. Pippa Norris, *Opening the Door: Women Leaders and Constitution Building in Iraq and Afghanistan* (Cambridge, Mass.: Harvard University, John F. Kennedy School of Government, 2006).

3. Deborah Smith, *Finding Power: Gender and Women's Political Participation in Rural Rajasthan, India* (PhD thesis, London School of Economics and Political Science, 2005), 39.

4. Drude Dahlerup, "Using Quotas to Increase Women's Political Representation: New Trends in Gender Quotas," in *Women in Parliament,* ed. Julie Ballington and Azza Karam (Stockholm: International IDEA, 2005).

5. Thirty percent was put forward as the critical mass target for women in decision-making posts as prescribed in the United Nations-facilitated Beijing Platform for Action, 1995. IPU, *Women in Parliament in 2006: The Year in Perspective* (Geneva: IPU, 2007), http://www.ipu.org. However, approaches toward the critical-mass idea have shifted in the last decade, with the UN now emphasizing that it will take more than increased numbers of women in parliament to overcome barriers to gender equity (UNRISD "Women in Public Office: A Rising Tide," in *Gender Equality: Striving for Justice in an Unequal World* (Geneva: UNRISD, 2005), http://www.unrisd.org/80256B3C005BCCF9/httpNetITFramePDF?ReadForm&parentunid=12F166540C09D163C1256FB1004C0156&parentdoctype=documentauxiliarypage&netitpath=80256B3C005BCCF9/(httpAuxPages)/12F166540C09D163C1256FB1004C0156/$file/GE_11Chap9.pdf.

6. Anne Phillips, *The Politics of Presence: The Political Representation of Gender, Ethnicity and Race* (Oxford: Clarendon Press, 1995).

7. Ibid.

8. Phillips critiques this assumption in ibid., 24.

9. Such is the perspective given in Natasha Walter, "We Are Just Watching Things Get Worse," *The Guardian,* November 28, 2006, http://www.guardian.co.uk/afghanistan/story/0,,1958707,00.html.

10. The concept of multiple identities is important here, as people's interests are often determined by the particular aspects of the identities they choose to prioritize at a given time.

11. Anna Wordsworth, "A Matter of Interests: Gender and the Politics of Presence in Afghanistan's *Wolesi Jirga*" (Kabul: AREU, 2007). Available at http://www.areu.org.af. Updated findings focus on the Wolesi Jirga's first term (2005–2010) and do not cover the beginning of parliament's second term (2010–2015), which had not begun at the time of writing.

12. For detailed background information, see Deniz Kandiyoti, *The Politics of Gender and Reconstruction in Afghanistan* (UNRISD Special Events Paper 4, UNRISD, Geneva, 2005), 31. Available at http://www.unrisd.org.

13. This 2005 conference was attended by an official delegation from Afghanistan, led by then minister of Women's Affairs Massouda Jalal, and preempted the drafting of the National Action Plan for the Women of Afghanistan. UNAMA, *Gender Issues*, Issue 1, March 2005, http://www.iiav.nl/ezines/email/GenderIssues/2005/No1.pdf.

14. Constitution of Afghanistan, Chapter 5, Article 83, printed in The *A to Z Guide to Afghanistan Assistance 2009* (Kabul: AREU, 2009), 84–113. Available at http://www.areu.org.af . The constitution states that an average of two seats for each of the thirty-four provinces be reserved for women. The actual number of seats per province depends of the population of that province—for example, in Balkh, of the eleven WJ seats available, three are reserved for women; in Kabul, of the thirty-three WJ seats available, nine are reserved for women; and in Uruzgan, of the three WJ seats available, one is reserved for women. In total across thirty-four provinces, sixty-eight seats are reserved. Reynolds, Jones, and Wilder, *A Guide to Parliamentary Elections*, 11.

15. For further information on gender mainstreaming, NAPWA, and the ANDS, see Anna Larson, *A Mandate to Mainstream: Promoting Gender Equality in Afghanistan* (Kabul: AREU, 2008). Available at www.areu.org.af.

16. Ibid., 9–19 and 45–47.

17. The president's initial ratification of the contentious Shi'a Family Law in March 2009 is a case in point here, given that it clearly contradicts previously ratified provisions for women, such as the NAPWA or CEDAW.

18. Interviews, male and female MPs, December 2006–February 2007.

19. Interview, male MP, January 2007.

20. Kandiyoti, *The Politics of Gender*, 3.

21. Constitution of Afghanistan, Chapter 5, Article 83.

22. Andrew Wilder, *A House Divided? Analyzing the 2005 Afghan Elections* (Kabul: AREU, 2005), 1. Available at http://www.areu.org.af.

23. Interviews, female MPs, December 2006–February 2007.

24. For more on political parties and their role in parliament, see Anna Larson, *Afghanistan's New Democratic Parties: A Means to Organize Democratization?* (Kabul: AREU, 2009). Available at http://www.areu.org.af.

25. Interview, female MP, April 2009.

26. Interview, female MP, April 2009. For more information on the process through which the Sh'ia law was passed, see Lauren Oates, *A Closer Look: The Policy and Lawmaking Process Behind the Shia Personal Status Law* (Kabul: AREU, 2009), available at http://www.areu.org.af.

27. Interviews, female MP, June 2006 and January 2007.

28. *Qaum* in Dari refers to a kinship group, often used to denote a wider family group or subtribe.

29. Interviews, female MPs, April 2009.

CHAPTER 7

Voices of Parliamentarians

Four Women MPs Share Their Thoughts

MASSOUDA JALAL, MALALAI JOYA, FAWZIA KOOFI,
AND AZITA RAFAT

Four female members of the Afghan parliament from across the country were invited to write about their experiences in government and/or to address the possibilities and impediments for women in political office.

In 2004, Massouda Jalal campaigned for the presidency, the first female candidate in Afghanistan's history, in the first elections since before the 1979 Soviet invasion.[1] Parliamentarians Fawzia Koofi and Azita Rafat have labored on various fronts by advancing laws and policies—as guaranteed in the constitution—to improve the status of Afghan women and Afghan society. In 2007, Malalai Joya was suspended from parliament on the grounds that she had insulted fellow representatives in a television interview. She nevertheless continues her struggles to protect women against injustice.[2]

CHALLENGES AND OPPORTUNITIES
Massouda Jalal

By studying the history of Afghanistan, we realize that men's and women's existence is intertwined and like the two wings of a bird, they complement each other. History and experience have shown us that reconstruction, progress, and development of Afghan society depends on cooperation between men and women.

Widespread marginalization of Afghan women in education, health, the economy, the legal system, leadership, management, and social planning are serious problems, causing serious concern. But the marginalization of women in politics is the most difficult and important of all.

Afghanistan is trapped in the early stages of development and over the centuries has regarded its female citizens, unjustly, as second class. Men adhering to patriarchal views and in positions of power have deliberately pushed women to the edges of society and often refused to assist them even in small measures.

In light of the unpleasant experiences of the past, it can be said with certainty that as long as women do not hold political offices or leadership positions and have no role in high-level decision making, their problems will never be resolved. The only way women can influence politics, succeed in society, and gain access to leadership is through democratic processes. We must be involved and actively participate in presidential, parliamentary, and municipal elections—to fulfill our roles as citizens.

Politically active Afghan women are well aware of the challenges and obstacles. The first are patriarchal customs and practices that have been in place for centuries. It is believed that women must be obedient and not work outside the home, let alone run for political office. In Afghanistan, political organizations and parties are run by influential men with large resources, who seek to monopolize power. Women, however, lack even a political party of their own.

Money is another challenge. Women have had no role in corruption and backroom dealings. Candidacy requires a great deal of money, and most women do not have access to sources of financial support. Few can build alliances. Those who have achieved political office have served with devotion, dignity, and honesty.

Security is a great hindrance, preventing women from campaigning in safety and freedom. Women also lack access to the media and thus cannot disseminate their publicity and communicate their campaign messages.

Perhaps most painful of all is the lack of cooperation between female politicians. Because the political environment is so unfavorable and divisive, they have difficulty choosing a candidate among themselves, lending support to the most qualified, and then campaigning. For a variety of unfortunate personal reasons, some women will even undermine female politicians.

Although the second presidential election since the 2001 fall of the Taliban has taken place, women have not yet been able to overcome these challenges. But it is high time that Afghan women, led by female politicians and policy makers and supported by the international community, play an active role and advance the cause of women to end their marginalization. The country's problems can never be solved without women's involvement. Today, more than ever before, women all over the world are deeply concerned about the status of Afghan women, which can only improve with our active participation in the socioeconomic, political, and cultural spheres.

The Bonn Agreement in December 2001 set the foundation for governing the country after two and half decades of war.[3] The tasks and duties of public office were determined and a timetable for creating a new constitution and holding parliamentary and presidential elections was identified. Because most victims of the wars are women and children, the Bonn Agreement placed special importance on their status. Equal rights, affirmative action, and preparation for women's participation in the social, political, economic, and cultural lives of Afghans were some of the objectives.

Following the Bonn Agreement, more than 176 women participated for the first time in provisional government, and for the first time in history, a woman sought the presidency. In the 2004 elections, 600 women, from various states and regions, sought election to parliament and 90 were elected.

In many ways, conditions for women have improved and they are beginning to compete with men for government jobs. In a short period of time, the ground has been prepared for women's participation in social institutions. Yet with all this progress, fundamental problems remain: powerful, violent forces continue to attack the Afghan women's movement and isolate high-profile politicians.

A WOMEN'S RIGHTS CATASTROPHE
Malalai Joya

Society is like a bird whose one wing is men and the other is women. The sick Afghan bird has not been able to fly because its "female wing" is severely injured and her wounds constantly salted.

In the 1960s and 1970s, doors were opened for women's progress and freedom, but in the past three decades of war and fundamentalist domination, any achievements were smashed. From the Russian stooges in the 1980s, to the fundamentalists fighting a civil war from 1992 to 1996, to the Taliban from 1996 to 2001, Afghanistan has become a living carcass, brutalized and torn down by killings, rapes, lootings, kidnappings, and other horrendous crimes. And women were the most vulnerable victims of this social, political, and cultural blackout.

In 2001, the United States and its allies invaded under the banners of "democracy," "women's rights," and "peace," but these were just fake slogans, serving as a façade for the geopolitical strategies of the White House. The Taliban were replaced by the criminal warlords of the Northern Alliance. Under Hamid Karzai's puppet government and the heavy military presence of more than forty countries, led by the United States, Afghanistan remains stuck in the dark ages. Although the United States and its allies used the awful plight of Afghan women as an excuse to occupy Afghanistan, women's conditions have not improved but instead grow worse hourly.

Women and children are the first victims of U.S./NATO bombardments. Thousands of Afghan civilians have lost their lives since they began on October 7, 2001. Villages, schools, and weddings are hit and the innocent murdered. With each new surge of U.S. troops in Afghanistan, more such deadly attacks are inevitable.

Afghan women have been betrayed. They are still deprived of their basic rights and needs, oppressed by men who exploit religion and deep-rooted superstitions. Millions of dollars flooded into the country for girls' education, but as of 2008, more than 650 schools have been torched in the Taliban-dominated areas, so that girls are completely deprived of their educations. According to the Afghan Independent Human Rights Commission, only 5 percent of girls enrolled in school are allowed to pursue their educations through the twelfth grade.[4] They are threatened, kidnapped, poisoned, raped, and even killed on their way to school. An incident in Kandahar, when acid was thrown on schoolgirls, became headline news, but it was not an isolated event; it happens persistently.[5] Only education and, at a higher level, political awareness, can enlighten and emancipate women. I believe this can only happen if all reactionaries and fundamentalists are completely wiped out and uprooted as military and political forces and a democratic and secular government installed, whereby religion remains a strictly personal matter and people are free to choose their beliefs.

Afghan women are exposed to extreme domestic violence. Beatings, insults, and torture by husbands and families are the horrific norm. Thousands of such cases happen in Afghanistan daily, but the rotten judicial system does not punish those who commit such crimes against women. Many rape victims come to me for help. The Afghan government's indifference to them is shocking. According to the United Nations, about 31 percent of Afghan women suffer physical violence, 30 percent suffer psychological violence, and 25 percent are subjected to sexual violence.[6]

Rape is common, though "rape with impunity" might better describe the phenomenon in Afghanistan, where women and children as young as three years old have been violated by fundamentalist warlords. Equally, if not more disturbing, in August 2008, President Karzai pardoned three convicted rapists.[7]

Fifty-seven percent of Afghan girls are married before the legal age of sixteen. Between 70 percent and 80 percent must endure forced marriages, often to an older man who has another wife and children.[8] Afghanistan provides 93 percent of the world's opium.[9] Armed warlords with private armies engage in looting, killing, and other crimes associated with drug-trafficking and girls as young as nine are sold as "opium brides," given by their impoverished fathers to pay off debts.

Around 20 million people out of Afghanistan's estimated 26 million live below the poverty level.[10] Extreme poverty pushes women into prostitution, and their cultural and political weaknesses make them easy targets for sex trafficking. Most prostitutes are widows with children, who often feel suicide is their only alternative. According to the United Nations Development Fund for Women, in Kabul alone an estimated "50,000 Afghan women are widows and heads of household. Sixty-five percent of women surveyed by the Physicians for Human Rights reported suicidal tendencies and a staggering sixteen percent actually attempted suicide."[11]

Suicide rates are exploding among Afghan women as terrifying hardships continue to mount. The most common method is self-immolation: sixteen cases in 2008 have been reported in Badghis Province, and in Herat, forty-seven cases were reported.[12] The numbers are actually higher and on the rise drastically everywhere. It is the result of rampant corruption and mafia-like regional governments, judiciaries that ignore all justice for women. The slightest demand for justice brings disgrace to families and threats to the women themselves. Self-immolation occurs because there is no law and no support for women; rape occurs because there is widespread impunity and rapists are backed by paramount rulers; domestic violence occurs because fundamentalism and ignorance are meshed with the ruling elite; and on and on.

The constitution grants equal rights to men and women, but this is merely a piece of paper to be shaped according to the whims of the powerful. The government blossoms with slogans of "women's rights" and "equality," but it is in fact extremely anti-woman. Of the sixty-eight women in parliament, most are pro-warlord and U.S.-backed. Their presence is a true mockery of democracy. Many are engaged with fundamentalist parties and try to portray the situation of Afghan women as less tragic than it really is. They are themselves part of the problem. The Ministry of Women under the Karzai regime is merely a showcase and fails to take action against the oppression of women.

Politics is dangerous for Afghan women. I was suspended from parliament for unmasking the true nature of the criminals and their manipulation of parliament for their own gain. I was threatened in the *Loya Jirga* (grand assembly) and have since undergone countless efforts to silence me, including four assassination attempts and hundreds of death threats. There are only a handful of serious groups and non-governmental organizations working for women's rights. The oldest and most important is the Revolutionary Association of the Women of Afghanistan, which has been struggling on behalf of women's emancipation since 1977.[13]

I strongly believe that the only way to end the suffering of Afghan women is to completely uproot every brand of fundamentalism and ignorance, ending the rule of warlords and Taliban (which deeply plagues Afghanistan with lawlessness and corruption) and ending the U.S. occupation (which threatens to intensify and which supports the criminals).

Democratic, secular, freedom-loving, and women's-rights movements must be supported morally and practically. I believe firmly that freedom of women (and men) is something that cannot be donated or imposed by bomb or at gunpoint. No matter how many countries surge Afghanistan with their troops, there will be no freedom until the people themselves rise up and demand it.

WORKING TOGETHER: ARTICULATING A COMMON VISION

Fawzia Koofi

Throughout the twentieth century, the debate about women's rights and women's role in Afghan society has been closely linked with the national destiny. Gender has been one of the most politicized issues in Afghanistan over the past 100 years, and attempts at reforms have been denounced by opponents as un-Islamic and a challenge to the sanctity of faith and family.

During nearly thirty years of conflict, armed factions turned traditional norms of honor and shame into weapons of war, engaging in rape and sexual assault against women of opposing groups as the ultimate means for disgracing entire communities and reducing people's capacities to resist military advance.

Women suffered serious human rights violations during the conflict. While it justified itself on the basis of protecting women, the Taliban regime's retrogressive views about gender resulted in the opposite. Women were not allowed to work or receive even basic education, and restrictions on their mobility obstructed their access to medical care, education facilities, and any human rights and dignities. With the overthrow of the Taliban in 2001, Afghanistan embarked on a new beginning, recognizing the contributions of the female half of society.

But despite constitutionally mandated gender equality, Afghan women's lives are still influenced more by the notion of complementarities between male and female roles than by equality. Differences of ethnicity, region, socioeconomic status, education, and residence—urban or rural—are significant. Overall, women's lives center on family and household, which are seen as their main areas of activity.

The 2001 Bonn Agreement called for specific attention to the role of women and established a dedicated government structure for this purpose. Core strategy for women's advancement is defined as "gender mainstreaming" in the national and development framework.[14] The Constitution of Afghanistan, passed by the constitutional Loya Jirga in 2003, proclaims that any kind of discrimination or privilege is prohibited (article 22), and that Afghan citizens have equal rights and duties before the law (article 23). The Constitution calls for sixty women to serve in the lower house and twenty-one women in the upper house. All this highlights the need to recognize women's role in society and politics.[15]

I believe that leadership potential exists within every individual and can be developed and harnessed. Academic achievement certainly plays an important role in individual growth, particularly if it is used jointly with courage, decisiveness, and commitment. Most women parliamentarians are role models. They enter the public sphere in order to contribute to social change.

Some women MPs' main focus has been human rights, especially for women and children. Some key women's initiatives that have been championed include working with the Ministry of Interior to increase the number of policewomen. On the one hand, this will help build trust for the rule of law, and on the other hand, it will help reduce violence, especially domestic violence against women, as women victims are sometimes afraid to call for help from male police or demand justice in the courts. They may, instead, kill themselves, often by self-immolation. There were 129 documented cases of self-immolation in Herat Province alone in 2008.[16] The number of women in the police force varies from region to region, due to traditional security barriers. As I wrote this in 2009, Badakshan Province in the northeast was relatively calm. Since 2007, thirty women have been trained in police work. In Kandahar, an insecure province located in the south, the lives of female police officers are at risk. Women become targets as they grow stronger and more outspoken. In 2008, renowned Kandahari policewoman, Malalai Kakar was shot to death by the Taliban.[17] Despite horrific challenges, women's involvement in police work increases day by day, a great achievement not only for the policewomen themselves, but also for the female MPs who support this process.

There has been some improvement of women's living conditions in Afghan prisons through resolutions introduced and approved by women MPs. I established a commission to work on the issue of violence against children, notably sexual abuse, which has increased in recent years. There is a culture of impunity toward the perpetrators, due to political favors and powerful criminals who interfere with the judiciary process. We are advocating the amendment of laws that are too lenient in the punishment of perpetrators.

In addition, we have promoted education for women and girls, by advocating access to good schools, as well as creating opportunities for informal education for out-of-school children in Afghanistan.

To come this far in this heavily traditional country, we have battled male domination, imposition of men's selective religious interpretation on the rights of women, and issues of political power between men and women and between old and new generations. Young people are seen as a threat by traditional power holders, who do not want them to organize and oppose their authority. Young people face other challenges, which come from the lack of resources and constraints imposed in a post-conflict situation. In the face of these challenges, women are networking, organizing, and working together on advocacy and communication, and they are articulating a common vision for the future of Afghanistan.

HOPE: LOST AND FOUND
Azita Rafat

Corruption, rising extremism, sexism, confinement within the four walls of the house, and deprivation from all that is approved by Islam—such as education and knowledge—have, like sharp blades, left their deep marks on Afghan women's bodies across the past three decades, even during the rule of the Taliban, who claim to be the true followers of Prophet Muhammad. Yet there are brave women not only who have been undeterred by these obstacles but also who have sacrificed their lives in the cause of freedom, equality, and women's rights.

The new Afghan political process embellished with fairness and democracy—witnessed and approved in 2001 by the most powerful countries in the world—opened a window of hope for many Afghans, especially our daughters, sisters, wives, and mothers who have been burdened by deprivation and injustice. Re-establishment of the parliament after thirty years of war, approval of the new constitution, formation of a ministry charged with designing appropriate and practical policies, and most important, the presence of women in the parliament were all impressive achievements and for awhile seemed like soothing medicine to ease the mental pain of the Afghan people.

But as so often has happened in Afghanistan's history, this much-praised and highly promoted process soon lost its momentum and failed to deliver. Once again, Afghans are faced with insecurity, poverty, and all manner of violence against women, including continuing political violence against female MPs, faced with rigid beliefs strengthened by all the years of war: intolerance of opposing views, male superiority, and the privileging of men in the laws. It is important to note that the majority of members of parliament are male and approval of the law is based on the majority vote. Male MPs accuse female members of not being committed to Islamic issues and thus do not cooperate with them. What is more, government interference in legislative matters and preference for male members as political investment, in turn, weakens female MPs. Meanwhile, ironically, the government emphasizes justice and equality for all.

Yet this is not to say that these obstacles, which lead to disappointment, have prevented us from reaching for our legitimate goals. With each day our beliefs and determination grow stronger and our efforts for unity and cooperation intensify. The formation of women's committees in parliament and our cooperation and active participation demonstrate our achievement.

Afghan women's struggles are part of the woman's movement worldwide. Cooperation of the international community, particularly political women, will strengthen us. No country can be successful without the complete presence of women.

NOTES

1. Of the many presidential candidates in the 2009 election, only two women were officially on the ballot: Frozan Fana, a forty-year-old surgeon, and Shahla Atta, a member of parliament, who ran on a Socialist platform. Reports about voter turnout in the 2009 presidential election varied from 10 percent to 17 percent. In the south, in Taliban-dominated areas such as Kandahar, the turnout among women was next to none. But in the Hazara stronghold of Bamiyan, where Habiba Sorabi is Afghanistan's only female governor, the turnout among women was strong. See Stephanie Hegarty, "Low Voter Turnout Reported in Afghanistan" (*New Statesman*, August 27, 2009, http://www .newstatesman.com/2009/08/afghanistan-security and Nasrat Shoib, "Women Voter Turnout Sinks in Afghanistan," Associated Press, August 23, 2009), http:// www.google.com/hostednews/afp/article/ALeqM5humB26GvOkzPulyhaZo_ nk8mNKcw. Of further interest about Afghan elections generally, see *Afghanistan's Presidential Election: Power to the People, or the Powerful?* (London: International Council on Security and Development, April 2009), http://www .icosgroup.net/documents/power_to_the_people.pdf. Due to the proximity of Afghan elections in August 2009, women's rights activists and civil society actors launched the Five Million Afghan Women Campaign to support women's political participation. See "Afghanistan: Women's Participation in the Election Process & in Political Leadership," Women Living Under Muslim Laws: News and Views, http://www.wluml.org/english/newsfulltxt.shtml?cmd%5B157 %5D=x-157-565131; also see Women's UN Report Network, http://www .wunrn.com/.

2. "Challenges and Opportunities" by Massouda Jalal and "Hope: Lost and Found" by Azita Rafat were translated from the Dari by Ashraf Zahedi.

3. Officially the Agreement on Provisional Arrangements in Afghanistan Pending the Re-Establishment of Permanent Government Institutions, the initial series of agreements intended to re-create the State of Afghanistan following the U.S. invasion of Afghanistan in response to the September 11, 2001, terrorist attacks, an invasion that ended the twenty-plus-year-long Afghan civil war. A number of prominent Afghans met under United Nations auspices in Bonn, Germany, to decide on a plan for governing the country; as a result, the Afghan Interim Authority (AIA)—made up of thirty members, headed by a chairman—was inaugurated on December 22, 2001, with a six-month mandate to be followed by a two-year Transitional Authority (TA), after which elections

are to be held. Under the Bonn Agreement the Afghan Constitution Commission was established to draft a new constitution in consultation with the public.

4. Afghanistan Independent Human Rights Commission, Research and Policy Unit, "The Right to Education," in *The General Situation of Children in Afghanistan* (Kabul: AIHRC, 2007), 14–16, http://www.aihrc.org.af/2008/April/Rep_eng_Chi_Nov_2007_U_Apr_2008.pdf.

5. On November 12, 2008, men on motorbikes in Kandahar, Afghanistan, sprayed acid on a group of girls and their teacher walking to school. Ten men were arrested for the crime.

6. United Nations Statistics Division, April 1, 2010, http://data.un.org/Search.aspx?q=afghanistan+women.

7. For further details, see among others, Kate Clark, "Afghan President Pardons Men Convicted of Bayonet Gang rape," *The Independent*, August 24, 2008, http://www.independent.co.uk/news/world/asia/afghan-president-pardons-men-convicted-of-bayonet-gang-rape-907663.html.

8. UNIFEM Afghanistan, Factsheet 2007, http://www.unifem.org/afghanistan/docs/pubs/08/UNIFEM_factsheet_08_EN.pdf.

9. United Nations Office on Drugs and Crime and Government of Afghanistan Counter Narcotics Directorate, "Afghanistan Opium Survey 2004," November 2004, http://www.unodc.org/pdf/afg/afghanistan_opium_survey_2004.pdf.

10. According to the Human Development Index, Afghanistan ranks 181 out of 182 countries. See RAWA News, "Factsheet of Human Development Report 2009," http://www.rawa.org/temp/runews/2009/10/05/human-development-report-2009-factsheet-afghanistan-ranked-181-out-of-182-countries.html.

11. Noeleen Heyzer, "Reconstruction Assistance to Afghanistan," United Nations Development Fund for Women, January 21, 2002, http://www.unifem.org/news_events/story_detail.php?StoryID=147.

12. medica mondiale, "Dying to be Heard: Self-Immolation of Women in Afghanistan Research Report," 2007, http://www.medicamondiale.org/fileadmin/content/07_Infothek/Afghanistan/Afghanistan_Dyingtobeheard_self_immolation_medica_mondiale_2007.pdf.

13. RAWA, founded in 1977, is the oldest political/social organization of Afghan women. See http://www.rawa.org/index.php.

14. Gender mainstreaming is the public policy concept of assessing the different implications for women and men of any planned policy action, including legislation and programs, in all areas and levels.

15. For a full text in English of the Constitution of the Islamic Republic of Afghanistan see "The Constitution of the Islamic Republic of Afghanistan," France Diplomatie, http://www.diplomatie.gouv.fr/en/IMG/pdf/The_Constitution_of_the_Islamic_Republic_of_Afghanistan.pdf.

16. medica monidale, "Dying to be Heard."

17. For further details, see, among others, Tom Coghlan, "Leading Policewoman Malalai Kakar Shot Dead in Afghanistan," *Times Online*, September 29, 2008, http://www.timesonline.co.uk/tol/news/world/asia/article4842498.ece. For a brief profile of Kakar, see Dina Temple-Raston, "Kandahar's Top

Cop Is A Woman: The Taliban Leave Death Threats on Her Door at Night, but for Malalai Kakar, Kandahar's Top Cop, Fear Is Not an Option," *Marie-Claire*, n.d., http://www.marieclaire.com/world-reports/news/international/kandahar-cop, and for a ten-minute video remembrance of her, see "Lt-Col Malalai Kakar—Remembering Kandahar's Policewoman," posted by Fahard2000, VideoSift, http://www.videosift.com/video/Lt-Col-Malalai-Kakar-Remembering-Kandahars-Policewoman.

CHAPTER 8

Nothing Left to Lose

Women in Prison

LIZETTE POTGIETER

The taxi driver attempts to drop my Afghan interpreter and me off at Badam Bagh Central Prison for Women Offenders, but the prison guards wave us off repeatedly, shouting that we are not allowed to stop at the entrance. Guards and police are on the front lines of suicide bombings, which are increasing in Kabul, so they are naturally terrified of explosions and view every passerby with suspicion. It is March 2009.[1]

When we are at last allowed to get out at the gate, the guard squints at my prison admission letter. "You look OK," he says, and gives us directions to the Badam Bagh commander.

"You chose the right day to interview the women," the commander says.[2] "An NGO has organized Women's Day celebrations for them. They will all be happy."[3]

THE PRISON

In May 2008, all women prisoners were moved from the notorious Pul-e-Charkhi prison to Badam Bagh, whose construction was undertaken by the United Nations Office on Drugs and Crime (UNODC) and United Nations Office of Project Services.[4] Ninety-three women prisoners and their seventy-two children are under the commander's supervision. External security is provided by males, and the ten staff members inside the prison are female.

At Pul-e-Charkhi, "the rooms were overcrowded and conditions were very bad," the commander says. "The situation is better here. We don't want to call it a jail. We want to create a home for the women."

Badam Bagh, a big, rectangular, three-story building, with six rooms on each floor, is hardly homey. Women and children move around freely during the day.[5] Each cell has three or four bunk beds. There are shelves against the walls where the women store kettles, irons, and other paraphernalia. Prison food is inadequate—rice three times a day with a few lentils and an occasional piece of fatty meat. The cells have gas stoves, pots, and oil, enabling the women to cook on a small scale. Those who have money can buy items such as bread, biscuits, and tea, which the guards acquire for them. Visiting families also bring food, shared with fellow inmates. Foreign prisoners are separated from Afghans, with the Chinese women—sex workers arrested during raids on bars that front for brothels—all in one cell and African and Pakistani drug dealers in other cells.

A small TV blares loudly in each room. Children share the space, sleeping on the carpeted floors or in their mothers' beds. Mothers have created hammocks with sheets strung from bedposts for their infants.[6] Each cell has a small bathroom with a squat toilet and a basin. Badam Bagh looks and smells clean. There is a large laundry room, with huge basins and two washing machines. Washing is hung in a small yard outside the prison entrance or from cell balconies. On the top floor, a cell serves as a classroom for children five years and older, mostly boys. It is compulsory for the mothers to send their children to classes, though some seem to attend sporadically. A female teacher—aided by a girl of about eleven, who also teaches the younger children—offers basic reading, writing, and arithmetic. Next door is a nursery for children between two and four years old, overseen by a middle-aged warden.

Presently, all activities are organized by non-governmental organizations, funded by international donors, with some supported by the United Nations Office on Drugs and Crime. Education and vocational training is provided by Afghan Women's Education Center, which also organizes family visits and monitors prisoners' children placed in orphanages or with relatives. The Italian NGO, Emergency, provides medical care to female prisoners in Badam Bagh and supplements the diets of those who are pregnant or breast-feeding. The UNODC currently monitors treatment of the prisoners. Conditions are slowly improving in Kabul prisons, as well as those in other cities, such as Herat, Jalalabad, and Mazar-i-Sharif. There is little reform in the provinces, particularly in the war-torn south.

Literacy classes for the prisoners are held upstairs and there are six computers for teaching computer skills. The women can learn crafts and some have completed courses in vocational education, English, and tailoring. "Sixty-three certificates were issued last week," the commander says proudly.[7]

But some women tell me they're not interested in improving their educations, because when they are released there will be no opportunities, thanks to lack of employment and social stigma. And there are women here who lie on their beds all day, depressed and lonely.

There is no exercise program, but the prisoners are permitted to sit outside during the day on a patch of grass next to the entrance surrounded by the wall. *Badam Bagh* means "Almond Orchard" in Dari, yet there is not an almond tree in sight.

CRIMES AND PUNISHMENTS

The commander keeps a list of the approximately ninety inmates under a plate of glass on his desk. Twenty-six have been convicted for murder, five for kidnapping and killing children. The women I interview tell me these are false accusations by male members of their families.[8] Eight women reported that they themselves had been kidnapped, four said they were kidnapped and raped, twenty-six had run away from home and been raped, fourteen admitted they are drug traffickers, and one Pakistani prisoner had planned a suicide bombing. Afghanistan currently has a death penalty for men only. Women convicted for murder are in general sentenced to eighteen years of imprisonment.

There are many reasons Afghan women are in prison. Their situation and the challenges they face on release cannot be fully understood without reference to their social and economic status and the provisions of legislation and practices that lead to their imprisonment. Most women and girls are non-literate and face poverty, limited access to health care, and continued and widespread violence. Under the Penal Code of 1976, which is still in force, women can be punished for offenses defined as "moral crimes." Moral crimes are mainly adultery and running away from home. The majority of female prisoners at Badam Bagh are being held for violating social, behavioral, and religious norms.[9]

Many international and Afghan NGOs strive to defend Afghan women's rights, but they have little power and no legal staff. Medica mondiale Afghanistan provides lawyers in order to ensure the women get fair trials.[10] There are few female defense lawyers in Afghanistan and no public defense pool of lawyers as in the United States.[11] At Badam Bagh—where free legal aid is provided by medica mondiale Afghanistan and the Afghan NGO Da Qanoun Goshtunky—prisoners complained that female defense lawyers have little clout in court. Husbands are said to bribe judges to put or retain their women in prison.[12]

Neither Afghan women nor men have access to lawyers at the police station during their first interrogation and may wait in detention for months before arraignment. Some never get a hearing. Time limits for detentions are rarely applied.[13] The Supreme Court in Kabul, which covers the whole country, is responsible for thousands of cases referred from the secondary courts of Afghanistan's thirty-four provinces, many of which offer no access to legal counsel whatsoever.[14] When time limits expire, detainees are not released, as provided by legislation.

The Family Court in Kabul is the only one in Afghanistan with a small number of female judges. Rahima Razai is the head judge of the Family Court. She is assisted by two senior female judges and one male judge. It was extremely difficult for me to set up an appointment with Judge Razai, who fears for her life and therefore did not want to reveal personal information. Judges have been killed outside their homes by suicide bombers or fundamentalists or family members angered by convictions.

"My job is very difficult," she says. "I have to deal with complex family problems, corruption, and traditional culture." Judge Razai is not so much concerned with discrimination against Afghan women working in the current judicial system as she is worried about those who are imprisoned for so-called "immoral acts" and those who remain in prison while others who can afford to bribe criminal justice agencies are released. "Many women who have been raped are beaten, rejected, and put in jail," Razai says. "Those who pay the bribes are released. Illiterate women with no power, connections, or independent means suffer particularly. A national policy to stop moral crime victims from going to jail and to improve the civil laws has not yet been implemented. Various ministries are working on this and it should be complete in six months. The Supreme Court, the Afghan Human Rights Commission, and Parliament will then test it on society. Depending on its success rate, the new laws will be implemented."

Nabila Naibkhail, a medica mondiale defense lawyer, who, since 2002, has worked as a prosecutor in Kabul, agrees that there has been some improvement in divorce laws, but she complains that "in general most Afghan women have lots of legal problems. For example, when a husband goes abroad to earn money, his family will sometimes treat her badly. In some cases wives are even killed. There is lots of violence toward women. This leads them to become violent. Men aggravate these women to commit crimes.

"The marriage laws also need to be amended," Naibkhail says. "A man has the right to marry more than one wife. It is difficult for women to accept the new wives and this causes a lot of friction. Democracy doesn't really exist in Afghanistan. There have been some improvements in Kabul, but in the provinces a woman would not dare utter the word democracy."

The central government has minimal authority in many parts of the country. "Just try to imagine what is happening out there," Razai says. "Customary laws rule."

In all regions of Afghanistan disputes and crimes are tried and resolved by councils of elders composed exclusively of men. Afghans regard *jirga* (tribal council) decisions as the law and condemn those who refuse to accept these decisions.[15]

Najiba, head of the Kandahar Central Jail for Women, confirmed that 80 percent of cases are solved by jirgas or *shuras* (tribal councils) in the provinces, although the AIHRC visits prisons once a month to inspect cases and to inform women and men of their basic human rights.[16]

"It is the women who suffer the most when crimes and disputes are settled by the shuras," she says. "Especially in the practice of retribution (*qissas*) and blood money (*diyat*).[17] Forced marriages occur for the settlements of feuds (*badal*), restitution for a crime, by giving a young girl to the victim's family (*baad*), and forcing widows to remarry someone from her deceased husband's family. Rape may be treated as adultery and punished according to the Shari'a (Islamic law), if a settlement cannot be reached between the two families concerned.

"Honor crimes are still happening in the provinces," Najiba says. "These are committed by male members to cleanse the honor of the family. It is very difficult to determine how many women are being affected by this. Women simply disappear."

There are ten women in Kandahar prison. Some have been there for two years without legal representation and their cases are pending.[18]

Officially, criminal procedure is governed by the Interim Criminal Procedure Code of 2004.[19] According to this code, a person can spend a maximum of ten months in detention, from the moment of arrest to the end of the period in prison, before a final sentence is passed.

"But this law is not followed in Afghanistan," says Najiba.

THE PRISONERS

Women mill around, some dressed up for Women's Day, while the children run back and forth. The noise quiets down as the celebrations commence. The UNODC has organized the event, including speeches about women's rights, but the prisoners look a little bored. In lieu of flag waving or cake, I am becoming the main attraction. Word has spread quickly that I'm here to record the women's stories and a queue forms outside the wardens' observation room, where I'll conduct my interviews. Within an hour the room is crowded with upwards of twenty-five women, talking, weeping, laughing. They range from late teens to late fifties, some heavily made up in tight-fitting tops and pants, others in traditional Afghan dress, with white or black lace-bordered pantaloons peeping from under long, full skirts. The young girls are unveiled; the older women, especially those from tribal areas, bear dark blue tattoos on their faces and deep orange henna on their fingernails, toes, and feet.

Zarmina, a petite twenty-six-year-old, is nervous and shy. She stares at her tattooed hands and twists her ring. The tattoos are the names of her six children, living with her mother-in-law in Ghazni, in Central Afghanistan.

> I was very small when my mother died. When I was thirteen, my father sold me to a forty-five-year-old man. I was exchanged for his daughter, who was married to my brother. My husband was an opium addict. I told my father I wanted a divorce, but he didn't care about me. My husband brought another woman into the house and had sex with her. He told me I should do the same. "Find a man and have sex with him," he said. I was with my husband for twelve years. He beat me and often attacked me with a knife. Look at my scars.

Toward the end of their marriage, the couple moved to Iran, where Zarmina's husband contracted HIV/AIDS. When they returned to Afghanistan, he at last agreed to a divorce.

> I thought my life would change, but it got worse. I went to live with my brother in Kabul, but he beat me all the time because I was divorced. I then left for Mazar-i-Sharif to be trained as a police officer.[20] I wanted a job. My sister followed me to Mazar and tried to convince me to return to my brother's house. She said, "If you refuse, I will report you to the police and tell them that you tried to kidnap me."

Nevertheless, Zarmina refused to return to Kabul. Her brother had her arrested on charges of kidnapping. She was imprisoned in

Mazar-i-Sharif, where she spent a few weeks, before attending a court hearing in Kabul, where a male judge chose to believe her brother and sent her to Badam Bagh.

> I've tried to commit suicide three times: once when I was a child and twice while I was married. Every day I pray to Allah to let me die. A few days ago, I pushed a burning cigarette into my upper lip to kill the pain I feel in my heart. No one has come to visit me here. My brother threatens to kill me when I'm released. I don't have a future.

In prison, Zarmina is safe from her brother, and there are a few women's shelters where she can be taken in secret to stay a few months while attempts are made to reconcile her with her family and/or find her a job.[21] She makes full use of the prison literacy classes. She has met only once with a defense lawyer during her ten-week stay. She says the lawyer has no information on her, "doesn't care and isn't helping me."

Shahpari, a thirty-year-old tribal woman from northern Afghanistan, is soft spoken with thick black kohl lining the lids of her light green eyes. She clutches her seventh child, a month-old baby born in her cell.

> I was twelve when I was married to a forty-year-old man. Six months ago I was kidnapped by two of my male relatives during the night at gunpoint. I was pregnant. They brought me to Kabul, where I was raped repeatedly for four to six days. The men told me they were going to sell me. I managed to escape and immediately reported them to the police in Kabul.

Shahpari was sent to prison, she says, because "the rapists said bad things about me to the police." She originally received a sentence of one-and-a-half years, but for reasons she does not know, the term was increased another six months. A Supreme Court judge disregarded her plea for release. "My husband has told me that when I'm free I can come back home, but he will not accept me as his wife, because I've been raped. 'I will keep you to take care of my children,' he said." The prisoners listening to Shahpari's story all shake their heads in sympathy. "We are being kept here for no reason at all," one says.

The door swings open and a feisty redhead bursts in.

"God bless you!" Soraya says in English. "I'm a Christian, you know." She pauses to wink at the other women before she adds: "Don't believe all the stories you're told." And promising to bring us tea, she dashes off.

"She's a drug trafficker, from Pakistan," the prisoners inform me.[22]

While we wait, nineteen-year-old Mariam tells us that she ran away from her thirty-year-old rug-maker husband to live with her young boyfriend, who owns a cosmetics shop. The couple's liaison didn't last long. A night watchman reported them to the police. Mariam was sentenced to two years and six months. Her boyfriend is serving two years in Pul-e-Charkhi.

"My boyfriend's family has accepted me and they visit me here," Mariam says. "We are hoping to get married when we're free." Both Mariam's parents are dead. Although it may prove impossible, Mariam believes fervently that she will get the divorce she seeks.

Soraya returns with tea. "I'm guilty," she says. "I got involved with the wrong people and took the risk to smuggle heroin across the border." She was sentenced to seven years, most of the time already served in Pul-e-Charkhi.

"There is a lot of bribery in the judicial system," she says. "A woman who murdered her husband was with me in Pul-e-Charkhi for only eight months. The family paid a bribe of 1,000,000 Afghanis (US $20,000) and she was released."[23]

Soraya leans forward confidentially: "Women are paying other women for sex," she whispers. "And I know of a few others who are close with one of the female wardens, who arranged to have sex with the male wardens. They pay them money. Some of the prisoners try to build up cash to bribe their way out of jail. The male wardens also bring in hashish and opium for the women, to support their drug habits. Some really need it and can't go without it."[24]

The women ask me to take their pictures to send to their families, and Farida drags me into her cell. While she changes into traditional Afghan dress for a photo, she tells me that she set her sister alight when she caught her having sex with her husband.

Farida is twenty-seven. "I want to keep these photographs so that when I'm released, I can look back at how young I looked today," she says.

She changes clothes again, for another shot, this time wearing her prayer shawl. She sits on the ground holding a small, leather-bound Qur'an. "This photograph is for my husband. I'm going to send it to him."

The following day, a fight breaks out. Women scream on the first floor as the battle moves downstairs. The two prisoners pull hair and bite, then one removes her sandal and hits the other on the head. "You are a criminal," she shouts.

"We're both criminals, you fool," the other yells. The wardens pull them apart and send them to their rooms.

Most of the female wardens here have worked in prisons for an average of twenty-five years. Pashtoon earns 3,250 Afghanis (US $65) a month and receives no benefits. "I don't like my job," she says, "but I don't have a choice. I have to work." She recently completed a two-month course on how to treat prisoners, with the promise that she will get a salary increase.[25]

Salia was recently among a group of Afghan lawyers and judges, sponsored by the United States Corrections Sector Support Program, to observe prisons in the United States. "The jails in Afghanistan are better than the ones in the States, which are too strict," Salia says. "But law enforcement is better there." She was impressed that American wardens are able to watch the prisoners on monitor screens. "We also need such a system. We don't know what is happening inside the women's rooms and cannot observe the use of drugs and other violations."

Psychologist Zarghona Ahmed Zia, who is trained in trauma, sexual violence, and rape, provides individual and group counseling to women and girls in prisons and rehabilitation centers.

"We create a safe space," Zia says. "They have been stigmatized by their families and society and feel helpless and lonely. The women are guided to identify their problems and needs. We encourage them and give them the power and ability to move on in life."

The bigger issues involve coping with why they are in prison. "When the women arrive, they have many problems," Zia says. "Step by step we first sort out the small problems and then deal with bigger issues. The women have conflicts with each other. We teach them how to resolve the conflicts.

"If a prisoner's children are with the family, we try to find a way for her to meet with them. Recently we made an arrangement so that an imprisoned mother could send her veil to her children," Zia says. "Now they have something tangible to remind them of their mother."

"My children are illiterate and picking up bad habits here in jail," says Shirin Gul. "But what can I do? My husband was hanged during Ramazan last year."[26] Three of her six children—including a baby born in prison—share her room, and the other three are on the street, begging.

A notorious murderer, Shirin Gul is thirty-five, originally from Jalalabad, an eastern provincial capital of Afghanistan. She was convicted for killing twenty-eight men in collaboration with her husband and his in-laws. She has served five and a half years of her twenty-year sentence and claims she is innocent. The story broadcast on Afghan national television goes that Shirin Gul lured taxi drivers to her house for sex, then she, her husband, and in-laws robbed and killed them. Shirin Gul's husband was accused of being part of a gang that kills for money, moving from province to province. Shirin Gul said she was living in Peshawar, Pakistan, unaware of her husband's activities. But it is rumored in the prison that Shirin still runs a mafia-style operation from her cell.

REFORM

Extensive work is ongoing to implement legislation to reform existing laws in line with the constitution, Afghanistan's international human rights obligations, and Islamic law.[27] Meanwhile, equal rights for women—especially those in prison or accused of crimes—are not yet reflected.

The failure of the judiciary, police, and the wider society to treat forced marriage as a criminal offense appears to stem from the deep-seated acceptance of customary over statutory law,[28] ensuring consistent failure by the state to initiate criminal proceedings against perpetrators. Their interpretation varies according to different judges, prosecutors, and legal experts.

The UNODC recommends that prison-based activities and post-release support activities be regarded as part of a comprehensive package of measures to address the issue of social integration in holistic and sustainable ways. It therefore covers many areas that may affect the success of social reintegration measures directly and indirectly from the moment women come in contact with the criminal justice system.

With the support of the United Nations, other international agencies, and donor nations, penal legislation is being reviewed and revised, judges and prosecutors are receiving training, access to legal counsel is improving, courthouses and prisons are being constructed, and the capacity of justice institutions is being developed. Varying degrees of progress have been made in all these areas, though much remains to be done.

"Only two basic points will solve the current situation in Afghanistan where women to a great extent are still regarded as 'commodities,'" says Judge Razai. "Teach the men about human and women's rights at the mosques; and teach boys and girls at school that they are equal."

NOTES

1. I live in Kabul, Afghanistan, where there are no libraries for research. Thus, my primary sources included staff members of medica mondiale Afghanistan, the Badam Bagh prison commander, female prison wardens, prisoners, and the head judge of the Kabul Family Court. I also conducted telephone interviews with members of the Afghanistan Independent Human Rights Commission, who regularly visit women's prisons throughout the country.

In 2009, I visited Badam Bagh for two days to interview the prisoners for this chapter. A few months later, I visited for a photo assignment for medica mondiale Germany. I interviewed many women, but space limitations prevent my using them all. It is difficult to gain access to Afghan prisons and involves numerous visits to the Ministry of Justice to obtain letters of permission, after which the guards outside the prison must be convinced to let you in, followed by an informal interrogation from the commander. Once in, the trust of the female wardens must be gained. Each prison official seems to have a separate set of rules, making it hard to move around the prison.

Dr. Husn Banu Ghazanfar, Minister of Women's Affairs in Kabul, was not available for comment though I tried to contact her numerous times. MoWA is notorious among journalists for refusing interviews.

2. Most of my sources asked to be anonymous, so I changed their names. However, some women welcomed their real names in print, a small act of defiance. Many Afghans use only one name.

3. During my first prison visit, all seemed relatively well. But on my next visit, I found quite a few prisoners lying listlessly with blankets covering their heads, complaining of illness. "Feeling sick" is a phrase commonly used by Afghan women to disguise feelings of despair and depression.

4. Pul-e-Charkhi was begun in the 1970s by order of then president Mohammed Daoud Khan. Construction was completed during the Soviet invasion of Afghanistan in 1979–1989. The prison was notorious for torture and other abuses. Living conditions were brutal. Afghan communists executed 27,000 political prisoners there. A mass grave was discovered in 2006 and is believed to hold some 2,000 bodies.

The UNODC, with financial support from the Italian government, undertook the rehabilitation of a number prison facilities, including parts of Pul-e-Charkhi prison.

5. This casual situation poses potential problems. There is little control inside the prison and the wardens might easily be overpowered by the prisoners. Serious criminals live in the same cells as innocent women and children. There are many fights over seemingly petty issues. One woman tried to commit suicide by cutting the arteries on her right leg, leading me to wonder why she was allowed to have a knife in her cell.

6. Many women are pregnant when they are convicted. If there is not enough time to get laboring women to hospital, they give birth in their cells. Hospitals and doctors sometimes refuse to attend prisoners because of the social stigma.

The law allows women to keep their children in prison up to the age of three, but there are children at Badam Bagh who are older. Not all women have their children with them in prison. Some families are broken and scattered. Some children are on the street with no one to care for them. In some cases, fathers want the children to be in jail with their mothers and in other cases they will take the children back, without their mothers.

7. Dressmaking is a skill that provides women with real prospects for income and is work that can be conducted at home.

8. According to the head judge of the Kabul Family Court, medica mondiale Afghanistan, and AIHRC, many women have been imprisoned because they have had no legal assistance, have been used or framed by male relatives, were forced to confess, or blamed because they happened to be with their husbands or fiancés when the crime was committed. Very occasionally a desperately impoverished woman will kidnap a child, usually to sell for money.

9. Other chapters in this volume address the constitution; discrimination in the areas of marriage, divorce, and inheritance; equal rights; and customary law versus statutory law, which often lead to women's imprisonment. See also "Adultery, Pederasty and Violation of Honor," *Penal Code*, Official Publication of the Government of Afghanistan, Issue 13, Serial no. 347, October 7, 1976, Section iii, chapter 8, 127. Available at http://aceproject.org/ero-en/regions/asia/AF/Penal%20Code%20Eng.pdf/view.

Rape as a crime is not clearly defined within the Penal Code but is covered under adultery, as is prostitution.

The German NGO, Frauen die Helfen, is among the groups working toward human rights for women traumatized in post-conflict situations In her book, *Kabul in Winter: Life Without Peace in Afghanistan* (New York: Metropolitan Books, 2006), Ann Jones describes her work in Afghan women's prisons in conjunction with Frauen die Helfen.

10. In numerous cases—through interventions with legal authorities and judges and conversations with the families—medica mondiale staff members have been able to obtain releases or substantially lesser sentences than those demanded by the state prosecutor. Since May 2007, medica mondiale has had its own counseling center in Badam Bagh, where families and imprisoned women can work with counselors to find ways to manage conflicts. Medica modiale's psychosocial project supports women affected and traumatized by violence in war and conflict zones and assists women with mental health problems and illnesses in prisons and rehabilitation centers throughout Afghanistan. This NGO, founded in Germany by Dr. Monika Hauser in 1995, provides specialized training for defense lawyers, psychologists, midwives, social workers, and medical staff in Gardez, Jalalabad, Kabul, and Herat. "Medica mondiale Afghanistan: Project Information," medica mondiale, http://www.medicamondiale.org/fileadmin/content/07_Infothek/Projektinformation/Projektinformation_Afghanistan_-_englisch_-_09-2008.pdf.

11. The constitution and the Interim Criminal Procedure Code provide for legal assistance to indigent defendants. In practice, detainees in most parts of the country rarely have access to legal representation. Constitution of the Islamic Republic of Afghanistan, Chapter Two: Fundamental Rights and Duties

of Citizens, Article 31 http://www.diplomatie.gouv.fr/fr/IMG/pdf/The_Consti-
tution_of_the_Islamic_Republic_of_Afghanistan.pdf .

12. As is well documented, bribery is rampant in Afghanistan. See, among
many others, Dexter Filkins, "Bribes Corrode Afghans' Trust in Government,"
New York Times, January 1, 2009, http://www.nytimes.com/2009/01/02/world/
asia/02kabul.html?hp. The issue is also addressed in the 1976 *Penal Code*, "Bribery," section ii, chapter 3, 75. Adding to the corruption are judges unqualified
for their jobs, appointed through powerful family connections, a common practice in the Afghan government, where entire departments might be run by one
family alone.

13. Tomris Atabay, *Afghanistan: Female Prisoners and Their Social Reintegration* (Vienna: United Nations Office on Drugs and Crime, March 2007), 23.
Available at http://www.unodc.org/pdf/criminal_justice/Afghan_women_prison_
web.pdf.

14. In the absence of lawyers, there nevertheless are police and prosecutors
in all provinces, thus arrests and investigations can continue.

15. Ancient tribal codes, such as Pastunwali and Islamic law, or Shari'a, are
discussed at length in other chapters in this volume.

16. In a telephone interview, March 2009.

17. *Qissas* is based on Islamic jurisprudence and refers to retribution, ap-
plicable to physical injury, manslaughter, and murder. *Diyat* refers to compensation. The laws of qissas and diyat provide that the punishment must be com-
mensurate with the offense committed.

18. Atabay, *Afghanistan*, 27.

19. As of this writing, the 2004 Criminal Procedure Code is being redrafted.
"Interim Criminal Procedure Code for Courts 2004," International Committee
of the Red Cross, http://www.icrc.org/ihl-nat.nsf/6fa4d35e5e3025394125673e0
0508143/2ee7715e48bfca37c1257114003633af/$FILE/Criminal%20Proce
dure%20Code%20-%20Afghanistan%20-%20EN.pdf .

20. The total Afghan police force is about 80,000, with no more than a few
hundred women. "As Afghan women seek a balance between new opportunities and tradition, the Kabul Police Academy is a unique proving ground. In a
profession dominated by men, it offers both the first glimpses of independence
and a frustrating lack of opportunity." Mark Sappenfield, "Female Cops Test
Traditional Gender Roles in Afghanistan," *Christian Science Monitor*, January
7, 2009, http://www.csmonitor.com/2009/0107/p01s03-wosc.html.

21. If their families refuse to take them back or if they are in danger of being
killed, released prisoners are referred to shelters. Safehouses are few and far between, and women can stay in them only until they get married, reunite with their
families, or in the unlikely event they find jobs. When they leave, they drop off the
radar. Officially, post-release support for women prisoners in need of shelter is
the responsibility of the women's ministry, assisted by various NGOs, including
the Afghan Women's Education Center, Humanitarian Assistance for Women
and Children in Afghanistan, and medica mondiale. Atabay, *Afghanistan*, 36.

22. As a non-Afghan, Soraya was shunned as a foreigner in the prison. She
was reared by missionaries in India, married a Pakistani man when she was fifteen, divorced him, and, since her release from prison, is back in Pakistan.

23. As of this writing, fifty Afghanis equals one U.S. dollar.

24. The UNODC estimates that 509,000 Afghan households—or 14 percent of the total population—are involved in opium cultivation. Of the 920,000 drug users living in Afghanistan in 2005, 120,000 were women. "Afghanistan Opium Survey," (United Nations Office on Drugs and Crime, November 2005), http://www.unodc.org/pdf/afg/afg_survey_2005.pdf, 85.

25. All the female wardens I spoke to were unhappy with their small salaries, no extra benefits, and long work hours. The United States Corrections Sector Support Program conducts training on the treatment of women prisoners. Female wardens indicate that they need training in basic and mental health issues.

26. Ramadan—an Islamic religious observance of fasting that takes place during the ninth month of the Islamic calendar, the month in which the Qur'an, according to tradition, was revealed to the Prophet Muhammad—is called Ramazan in Dari, Farsi, and Turkish.

27. United Nations Assistance Mission in Afghanistan (Afghanistan's Justice Sector Overview, November 2006), 1.

28. Abject poverty, armed conflict, and draught are cited as reasons for the increasing practice of marrying girls at pre-puberty level; it serves to reduce the number of dependents within a household and to raise cash through the receipt of a bride price. M.A. Drumbl, "Rights, Culture, and Crime: The Role of Rule of Law for the Women in Afghanistan," (*Columbia Journal of Transnational Law* 42, no.2 (2004). http://papers.ssrn.com/sol3/papers.cfm?abstract_id=452440, 359.

CHAPTER 9

Selling Sex in Afghanistan

Portraits of Sex Workers in Kabul

ALISA TANG

Aisha was eleven when she was molested by a man with no legs. He paid her five dollars. She was forced into sex work in one of the world's poorest and most conservative countries, where the penalty can be death.[1]

A dangerously taboo subject in Afghanistan, sex work is strictly forbidden, and many Afghans claim it is only an imported foreign vice, practiced by women brought into the country to serve Western men. Punished as adultery in the Afghan Penal Code,[2] sex workers can face five to fifteen years in prison. Convicted adulterers have been subjected to lashing or stoned to death, though these punishments have been rarely applied since the fall of the Taliban in 2001. Afghanistan has been under intense scrutiny and wary about upsetting the international community and donors.[3]

The Afghan sex trade appears to be thriving, with girls like Aisha operating underground in a country where jobs are scarce to nonexistent, particularly for women. They ply their trade in various Kabul neighborhoods and in an area known as Shoor Bazaar in the old city, which was the red-light district through the late 1970s, before the 1979 Soviet invasion. There are also a number of cinemas that attract young boys used for homosexual prostitution, musicians, and male dancers also known to provide sexual services, as well as hotels where truck drivers and other travelers stay.[4]

According to reports, only a minute fraction of women know about condoms or sexually transmitted diseases.[5] Reliable statistics about sex workers or any other population group are hard to come by in this unstable, violence-plagued country, yet indicators point to the likelihood of an increase in sexually transmitted diseases, including HIV.[6]

Many sex workers have borne their client's children. Abortion has been permitted in Afghanistan since 2002, if there is a medical risk, but research is lacking about the numbers of women who have sought the procedure.[7]

General Ali Shah Paktiawal, Kabul's chief police investigator, said there were only twenty-six Afghan sex workers arrested in 2007, but the head of the sexual crimes department, Zia ul-Haq, said he has come across at least two per week.[8] They include married and single women, runaways, and boys and girls sold by their families. Some men, he said, hire their wives and daughters out for sex.

"Prostitution exists in every country that has poverty," said women's rights activist Orzala Ashraf, founder of the Kabul-based aid organization Humanitarian Assistance for the Women and Children of Afghanistan. "But Afghan society has black glasses and ignores these problems. Tradition is honor, and if we talk about these taboos, then we break tradition."[9]

STREET CHILD

At thirteen, Aisha speaks four languages—the Afghan languages of Pashtu and Dari; Urdu, which she picked up as a refugee in Pakistan; and English, which she is learning from a $2.40-a-month course she pays for herself. She knows that being multilingual will eventually help her find work and she is frequently the only breadwinner in her family of ten. She does not know what a condom is, and she has not heard of HIV/AIDS.

I met Aisha through a policeman working on juvenile cases, and I gradually sketched out her story in a dozen meetings across four months. During the first several interviews, she insisted she was a "good girl"— and cited a doctor's check-up confirming she was still a virgin. Nevertheless, she was able to describe in detail the lives of others involved in the sex trade and knew how children were forced into the sex industry, where they waited for customers, who they were, and how they conducted their business or were pimped out. Trafficking of women and boys for sexual and other exploitations (such as drug and gun running), particularly across the Afghanistan-Pakistan borders, was rampant during the years of war and the Taliban regime (1996–2001) and continues unabated.[10]

Trysts are often arranged by mobile phone, which Afghan police and aid workers say has become the key link between sex workers and clients. "Don't think bad things of me because I have this phone," Aisha said. "My dad gave it to me so he could keep in touch with me, but sometimes my friends use it to keep in touch with their clients."

Aisha grew up in Pakistan, where her family fled during Afghanistan's bloody civil war (1992–1996). She cleaned cars to bring her family money and was regularly attending school, which ran only a few hours a day. After the United States–led invasion toppled the Taliban regime, her family joined the flood of refugees returning home. But her father earned only about forty dollars a month doing odd jobs, so, like hundreds of other children were forced to do, Aisha sold chewing gum and newspapers and cleaned car windows in the muddy, pothole-riddled streets of Kabul. She made about three dollars a day.

That was where she met Uncle Lang—a nickname that means Uncle Legless. He was a landmine victim, and Aisha and one of her friends helped him by bringing tea and food. Police say he forced himself on them. "I didn't know anything about sex, but it happened" Aisha said, looking down as she spoke. She tucked her hair repeatedly under her headscarf and nervously fiddled with her *shalwar kameez*, a matching outfit of baggy trousers and loose-fitting tunic, worn by most Afghans. "I used to be a very good girl, but now I have very bad friends." One of them, she said, recently invited her to the home of a shopkeeper. He pays two dollars, and likes to be with more than one girl at a time.

Uncle Lang was careful not to damage the girls. "They were doing it from the back because he didn't want them to lose their virginity," said Ghulam Siddique, the Interior Ministry's chief police investigator for child protection.[11]

In November, Uncle Lang took Aisha and other girls to the northern city of Mazar-i-Sharif to beg and sell sex. "They stay in one place for two to three months. Then when the neighbors learn of their business, they move, sometimes after five or six days," said Esmatullah Nekzad, a policeman formerly with the department of moral crimes.[12]

Within days of the group's arrival in Mazar-i-Sharif, neighbors became suspicious. The police raided the place, arrested the girls, but Uncle Lang fled. Aisha agreed to become an informant. She told police about boys and girls who were part of a child prostitution ring.

An Afghan social worker—whose organization shelters battered women and sex workers and teaches them skills so they can seek legitimate jobs—offered to help Aisha.[13] For a few weeks, she visited daily, arriving in the morning, working in the kitchen, and receiving an hour of counseling before leaving at 4 p.m. Her spirit became noticeably lighter.

Her parents had been encouraging her to work with Uncle Lang, she said. Now that she'd stopped seeing him, her ten-year-old brother was sent to him. One day, staff from the aid organization spotted Aisha with Uncle Lang on a popular street lined with kebab and ice-cream shops. When the social worker confronted her, she said she was only trying to stop her brother. The next day, Aisha stopped going to the organization and has not been seen or heard from since.

FAMILY-BASED SEX INDUSTRY

Families encouraging sex work is not uncommon, according to the study by Ora International, which reports that 39 percent of the sex workers interviewed found their clients through their relatives—including 17 percent through their mothers. This is linked to vast problems of child labor in Afghanistan, where, according to recent estimates, one in four Afghan children aged seven to fourteen is engaged in some form of work, including sex work.[14]

The Ora International report also found that nearly four out of five of the girls and women surveyed were married. Fifteen percent of sex workers found clients through their husbands and the average number of clients per week was seventeen, with the maximum being forty-nine and the minimum one client per week.[15]

During my visit to the brothel in the old city, I met and briefly interviewed about a dozen sex workers, most married with several children. They said they had only one or two regular clients who paid around fifty dollars—almost the equivalent of a teacher's or policeman's monthly salary of seventy dollars—or they might get a bag of grains, beans, or a piece of meat to feed their families. Some said their husbands did not know they were doing sex work, and that a few of their clients were actually relatives. One woman said that she often was not paid at all.

The aid worker told me she knew of a client who visited a family-run brothel but who had refused sex with an orphaned girl after seeing how young she was. He paid and left. The girl escaped her kidnappers and alerted the Afghanistan Independent Human Rights Commission.[16] Police raided the house where she'd been held and discovered a fourteen-year-old whose parents were involved in the sex trade and another eleven-year-old orphan, who had been sold several times.

THE RUNAWAY

Samira ran away from home when she was fifteen and has been homeless since. I met her through a Kabul-based women's aid agency, which provided her a place to stay at their underground shelter.

Born in Iran, Samira moved to Herat with her family after the fall of the Taliban. In her new life as a young Afghan woman, she was forbidden from going to school, whereas across the border in more affluent Iran, she had been allowed to pursue her education. Now her family insisted she dress conservatively in shalwar kameez, though she preferred fitted blue jeans and tight knit sweaters.

After running away, she spent two years homeless in Herat and three years in Kabul. She has had no contact with her family. She told me she had forty-five clients. She was reluctant to share her story.

"They think that if they tell us the truth, we will return them to their families, and their families will kill them, or that we will send them to an institution and they will be put in prison," said Jamila Ghairat of the aid organization Women for Afghan Women. "The girls are afraid of their families, the government, and everyone."[17]

A woman organized Samira's first client, a young man about eighteen years old, with whom she spent an hour at his home. She earned anywhere from ten dollars for half an hour to one hundred and fifty dollars for the night. She spent nine months with a married man whose wife beat her. She lived in a house rented especially for her and a Thai woman by an American man who came and went. A few years ago, she was imprisoned for four months for adultery because police caught her in a car with a man to whom she was not related. "I don't want to continue. I'm looking for someone to spend the rest of my life with," she told me. "When I find him, I will stay with him. I don't want to go outside anymore."

Samira left the shelter in early 2008. The aid group does not know her whereabouts.

IMPORTED

Thousands of Westerners, many on fat salaries, poured into Afghanistan after the fall of the Taliban in December 2001, and brothels sprang up to serve them. While most of Afghanistan's secretive flesh trade involves Afghans serving Afghans, this money-spinning, underground sale of sex and smuggled alcohol to foreigners has a much higher profile. A government crackdown reduced the early numbers of foreign brothels, and authorities periodically raid the bars that continue to front them. In 2008, 154 foreign sex workers—most of them Chinese—were arrested in Kabul.

The International Organization for Migration assisted ninety-six Chinese women who were deported in 2006—all of whom claimed to have been deceived by a travel agency in China. They told IOM they were promised employment in a restaurant for three hundred dollars a month, but when they arrived, the Chinese restaurant owner denied them salary and forced them to provide sexual services by night. An IOM staffer said one Chinese woman thought she was going to work in Dubai and had no idea that she had instead landed in Kabul.[18]

BURGEONING CYCLES

Three decades of war and conflict have left about 1 million widows to support broken families in a deeply impoverished and divided country,[19] where it is still frowned upon for women to leave home or take jobs, so that sex work too frequently becomes the only possible source of income. Afghanistan has reeled into ever increasing violence as the insurgency has flared in recent years, so the number of widows continues to rise.

Furthermore, since the fall of the Taliban, neighboring countries have closed refugee camps and forcibly repatriated Afghan migrants. Four million returnees live in Afghanistan today,[20] and there are somewhere around 500,000 internally displaced persons. According to the Afghan Ministry for Counter Narcotics, a large number of addicts are returning refugees from Iran and Pakistan.[21] Afghanistan is the world's largest producer of opium, which is used to make heroin. A 2008 World Bank summary on HIV and AIDS in Afghanistan noted there are an estimated 1 million drug users, including 19,000 intravenous drug users, and that "Afghanistan's emerging epidemic likely hinges on a combination of injecting drug use and unsafe paid sex." Three percent of intravenous drug users were found to be HIV positive, and nearly one-third used unclean needles. Sixty-nine percent paid for sex.[22]

The World Bank summary indicates 478 HIV cases have been reported in Afghanistan, although the United Nations World Health Organization estimates there could be between 1,000 and 2,000 people living with HIV.[23] Reliable data are sparse.

A handful of aid agencies are trying to help Afghan sex workers move on to safer professions. Because a large portion of the population is uneducated, joint non-governmental organization and Afghan government public information campaigns include posters, speeches, and marches for awareness that have been covered by the local media. So far—although condoms and clean needles are also distributed—these appear to be most effective in teaching that HIV can be spread by intravenous drug use and unsafe sex.

Profound sorrow and guilt seem to plague many of the sex workers I interviewed in Kabul. The trajectories of their lives are inextricably linked to the decades of violence, diaspora, and severe poverty. Like sex workers everywhere, they are too frequently perceived by their society to be sex addicts, condemned as morally corrupt women beyond salvation.

NOTES

1. The names of the sex workers have been changed to protect their identities. The terms "sex work" and "sex workers" are employed here instead of "prostitute" and "prostitution" in order to define commercial sex and de-eroticize the work, while claiming for women the dignity of the job.

2. See "Adultery, Pederasty and Violation of Honor," *Penal Code* (Official Publication of the Government of Afghanistan, Issue 13, 15 Mizan 1355 [October 7, 1976], Serial no. 347, Section iii, chapter 8), 127. Available at http://acepro ject.org/ero-en/regions/asia/AF/Penal%20Code%20Eng.pdf/view.

3. In April 2005, a twenty-nine-year-old woman was publicly killed in what Amnesty International reported was alleged to be the first execution of a woman for committing adultery since the fall of the Taliban. "Afghanistan: Stoning to Death—Human Rights Scandal" (Amnesty International Press Release, April 26, 2005, http://www.amnesty.org/en/library/asset/ASA11/005/ 2005/en/doe6f33a-d4f7-11dd-8a23-d58a49c0d652/asa110052005en.pdf; IRIN, "Afghanistan: Woman Executed for Adultery," May 3, 2005, http://www .irinnews.org/Report.aspx?ReportId=28576. On the night of July 12, 2008, the Taliban in central Ghazni Province shot to death two women accused of "taking pure and innocent Muslim women of this province to the Americans and other foreigners (a United States military base in Ghazni city), as well as to local Afghans, to earn money through prostitution," a Taliban commander told the Associated Press Television News. Associated Press Television News, http://www .aptnvideo.net/Browse/SearchResults_Player.do;jsessionid=12ED2FB 4090E86E798205DF4D7B50AA0?itemID=97390&siteSystemRole=APTN& searchString=ghazni&pageNum=1&sortDirection=desc&sortKey=score& pageSize=20&action=Script.

4. Ora International, "Survey of Groups at High Risk of Contracting Sexually Transmitted Infections and HIV/AIDS in Kabul," April 2005, http://www .ora-international.org/.

5. Ibid.

6. Ibid.

7. Agence France Presse, "Abortion Legal in Afghanistan in Early Pregnancy," January 16, 2002.

8. In interviews in 2007 and 2008.

9. In an interview in 2008. For further information see Humanitarian Assistance for the Women and Children of Afghanistan, http://www.hawca.org/main/index.php.

10. International Organization for Migration, "Trafficking in Persons in Afghanistan: Field Survey Report," *RAWA News*, September 13, 2008, http://www.rawa.org/temp/runews/2008/09/13/trafficking-in-persons-in-afghanistan-field-survey-report.html. In 2007, I interviewed Rukhma in a women's prison in eastern Nangarhar Province. She told me she had been trafficked with her three-year-old son from her home in Pakistan's tribal areas across the border into Afghanistan, where she was sold to an Afghan man who claimed her as his wife and raped her for three months. She was about to be sold to another man who did not want her son, so she tried to run away. She said she was viciously beaten and her son battered to death. The man was imprisoned for murder, and Rukhma was serving a five- to seven-year sentence for running away, a crime found under "Adultery, Pederasty and Violation of Honor" in the Penal Code.

11. In an interview in 2008.

12. In an interview in 2008.

13. Some women's aid organizations prefer not to be identified for fear they will be accused of harboring and facilitating sex workers, as has happened.

14. Amanda Sim, "Confronting Child Labour in Afghanistan" (briefing paper, Afghanistan Research and Evaluation Unit, Kabul, May 2009).

15. Ora International, "Survey of Groups at High Risk."

16. Since its establishment in 2002, the Afghanistan Independent Human Rights Commission has become known through media, public service announcements, and word of mouth as a trustworthy venue for women to seek help.

17. In an interview in 2008.

18. In an interview in 2006.

19. "HIV/AIDS in Afghanistan" (The World Bank, August 2008), http://siteresources.worldbank.org/SOUTHASIAEXT/Resources/223546-1192413140459/4281804-1231540815570/5730961-1235157256443/HIVAIDSbriefAF.pdf.

20. Ibid.

21. Rafiq Maqbool, "All But Forgotten: Kabul's Drug Addicts Live Amid Detritus of War" (Associated Press, December 27, 2007), http://www.aegis.com/news/ap/2007/AP071251.html.

22. World Bank, "HIV/AIDS in Afghanistan."

23. Ibid. Also see "Afghanistan," United Nations World Health Organization, http://www.who.int/countries/afg/en/.

CHAPTER 10

Between Choice and Force

Marriage Practices in Afghanistan

DEBORAH J. SMITH

This chapter presents findings from a research project conducted by the Afghanistan Research and Evaluation Unit on Family Dynamics and Family Violence in Afghanistan.[1] Data for this study, which are purely qualitative in nature, were collected in both rural and urban areas of four provinces of Afghanistan: Bamiyan, Herat, Kabul, and Nangarhar in 2006 and 2007. The findings presented here relate to one aspect of this study: how decisions are made about marriages and how marriage is practiced. The research has been concerned with both actual events and respondents' opinions on how marriage should be and is practiced in their communities.[2]

The chapter focuses on five themes that emerged from the data: first, the manner in which individual's opinions and desires frequently run counter to the demands of cultural norms; second, diversity in how marriages are decided; third, the notions of force and choice in relation to marriage decisions; fourth, aspects of marriage practices that can act as precursors to violence in the marriage; and fifth, the amount of awareness found across the communities as to the negative consequences of particular marriage practices.

INDIVIDUAL OPINIONS—CULTURAL NORMS AND A READINESS FOR CHANGE

I understand your question and now I am going to make it all clear for you. In the past people didn't ask their children, but in the future

I will ask my children about their lives. As I said before it is not our custom to ask them, but we hope it will change in the future. We now let our sons and daughters go to school to become intelligent and through this knowledge our children will make their own decisions in the future. You know I am very hopeful that our people will change their ideas. I wish that my children seek education; after that we will let them plan their own futures, we will guide them but this is my wish. I am not sure that we can adopt it, because right now in our society it is not our custom. I am not literate, but I know if our people seek education, I am sure, their minds will change. Look, my husband is educated, just he is under the pressure of his culture—so let's see what happens—but we are very hopeful for the future and I hope my children have successful lives.

The divergence between perceived cultural norms and individual desires is clearly explained by this woman in her early thirties, who lives in Jalalabad, Nangarhar, when speaking about the role children should play in decisions regarding their marriages. She struggles to negotiate between her understandings of the demands of cultural norms and her own desires for her children's futures. Indeed, many respondents, both male and female, and from different socioeconomic groups, explained how their own opinions differed from what they saw as the cultural norms of their communities.

This discrepancy between personal opinions and cultural norms can be seen both as an indicator that cultural norms are in flux and as a particularly important space for change. It is evident that there is desire and readiness for change in the communities where the research was conducted. Actual change is also in process and is evidenced, for example, by those families aiming to involve their younger children, more than they did their older children, in decisions about their marriages.

As with many aspects of social change, it is difficult to identify exactly what has brought about this discrepancy. It is likely that a combination of inter-linked factors came together at particular points in time. War, and more specifically migration, was identified by respondents as an impetus for change in opinions and practice. External migration exposed people to new ways of being and new ideas, which have been brought back to Afghanistan as people have returned.[3] It is possible to surmise that the past few years—at least in the areas where the data was collected—have been the first time in a generation that people have felt relatively settled and in a position to think about a future for themselves and their families.[4] These two factors then combine exposure to different ways of being and relative stability, to create an opportunity for change.[5]

MAKING DECISIONS ABOUT CHILDREN'S MARRIAGES

The importance of looking in detail at the decision-making processes leading up to a marriage was highlighted by the examples respondents gave of how "mistakes" led to conflict, including physical violence between a couple. Marriage decisions are influenced by a multiplicity of factors both internal to the family and originating externally. Factors internal to the family include the structure of and the gender and generational dynamics of individual households and families, as well as the individual characteristics and life histories of family members. External factors include gender and generational dynamics in a given community; the current political, economic, and social situation; as well as more specific things, such as when a proposal comes.[6]

A vast array of family dynamics and household structures were found across the research sites. Correspondingly, a substantial variance in the levels and forms of different family members' participation in and influence on decision making about marriages was found. It is, therefore, argued that although social rules apply and provide an overall context in which families operate, the way in which they function is complex and adaptable to different circumstances.

The role and influence of women in family decision-making processes tend to be more complicated and variable than men's. Men often have more overt roles, whereas women must use more covert methods to influence decisions. Despite this, men and women of different ages expressed the belief that women in the family should play a role in decision-making processes about their children's marriages. However, this does not mean that all women are in a position to substantially influence marriage decisions. Instead, particular women in particular families play a role, whereas others are excluded.

The amount of influence a woman has changes throughout the course of her own and the wider family's life. A woman who at an earlier stage in her life may have found it difficult to influence decisions usually gains more authority as she becomes older. This is particularly the case if she is an elderly widow and is then perhaps the eldest person in the household.

Women's influence in decision making can also increase over the course of a family's life cycle as the men in the family come to realize they need the advice of their wives. Several examples were found in which men made decisions about their daughters' marriages that they later regretted. In response to this, they had either handed the entire responsibility of decision making about marriage to their wives or had become more inclusive in how they made such decisions. In some cases, women themselves demanded a greater role in response to their husbands' regrettable decisions.

Under other family circumstances and household structures, women who are younger can be influential. For instance, Bas Bibi,[7] from the capital city Kabul, was at the time of her marriage the only married woman in her in-law's household. As such—although she reported her father-in-law taking the ultimate responsibility for who his children would marry—her father-in-law relied on Bas Bibi to visit the families of potential spouses and discuss the possibility of engagement with the women in these families. This process inevitably gave her considerable ability to shape the outcome. This is typical of the way in which women influence decisions in families where the male head of household is perceived to be the ultimate decision maker, the person *who* makes the decision. *How* the decision is made, the process undertaken to make a decision about a marriage, provides women with substantial opportunity to influence the final outcome.

It was found that women who have particularly domineering and/or violent husbands can be excluded from this role in the decision-making processes. For example, Zeba, who lives in a relatively wealthy family in Bamiyan City, was prevented by her husband from socializing in the community. Her adult son explained how this led her to be excluded from playing a role in selecting potential spouses for her children.

In the same way that individual family circumstances and a woman's position in the family can increase her level of input into marriage decisions, so too can it limit it. The role for older women in the decision-making processes can be at the expense of younger women and particularly the mothers of the children whose marriages are being decided on; a mother-in-law's counsel may be taken instead of a mother's.

The amount of influence men have in decision-making processes about children's marriages also varies from family to family. The overall greater degree of power and influence men have in Afghan society usually places them in a less-constrained position in the family than women. Despite this, not all men, any more than all women, have equal levels of influence within families. While fathers, grandfathers, uncles, and brothers may all have substantial influence, the different levels of influence they have are determined by individual relationships between family members and family structure at the time a marriage is being decided on.

On occasion, fathers, like mothers, may be excluded from or have less influence than other older men in the family over decisions about their children's marriages. For instance, Saghar, who lives in urban Kabul, reported that her father- and mother-in-law decided on her eldest daughter's marriage, excluding both her and her husband from making the decision. In other families, it is clear how uncles, most usually older uncles, can have considerable influence over decisions about their nieces' and nephews' marriages. This is particularly the case where grandparents are elderly or have died and left neither a woman nor a man of an older generation in the household. This was found to be true even when brothers had separated their households from one another.

Male siblings can also have substantial influence regarding their brothers' and sisters' marriages. This is particularly the case where fathers have died and elder brothers move to playing a key decision-making role in the family, often alongside their widowed mothers. For some this may mean that brothers make decisions against their sisters' wishes. In other cases, brothers can be advocates for their sisters' well-being. Examples were found of brothers attempting to prevent the marriages of their sisters to men either they were not happy with or their sisters were not happy with.

FROM CHOICE TO FORCE AND CHILDREN'S ROLES IN DECISIONS ABOUT THEIR OWN MARRIAGES

A lot of attention is given to the notion of forced marriage in Afghanistan. However, less attention is given to understanding what constitutes a forced marriage and what causes forced marriage.

The archetypal presentation of a forced marriage and the image the expression "forced marriage" conjures in many imaginations is of a young girl being married against her will, usually to a much older man. It is usually used to refer to marriages seen as abusive and/or illegal.[8] If a girl had no say in her marriage, did not want to get married, or was married to a particular man but in the end the marriage is relatively nonviolent—described as happy by the couple who also may be close in age—it is rare that this is highlighted in the literature as a forced marriage. (Indeed a number of respondents describe their marriages as forced but added that they are now happy.) Is forced marriage only seen as a problem if the marriage is violent, the wife is abused, or the man considerably older than the woman? Likewise, is it only girls who are forced into marriages against their will? Further, whole families may be forced to marry a child against their wishes. It can also be argued that cultural norms force individuals to marry their children in a manner that is contrary to their personal desires. These different forms of forced marriage were recognized and expressed by respondents, both male and female, from the different provinces.

A standard definition for forced marriage is marriage in which "one or both of the partners do not give free or valid consent to the marriage"[9] or "a family [determines] who a daughter should marry without her consent."[10] However, it is important to recognize that a person can be unwilling to marry but still give consent for a variety of reasons. In a social order where obedience to elders and particularly parents is deeply entrenched, it is very difficult for a child, male or female, to object to such a decision. Consent may only be sought from a girl or boy once their respective families have already agreed to the engagement, leaving them no real option but to agree. Likewise, although children in the family may consent to a marriage, they may not have enough knowledge about what marriage means, their future spouse or in-laws, or the arrangements for the marriage in order for this to be considered *informed* consent. However, young people do express the desire for their parents to make the decision and so, even though their consent may be tokenistic and ill-informed, they may still be willing to be married.

Individuals may feel emotional or social pressure to marry at a time that or to a person who is not in accord with their own desires or wishes. For instance, little pressure may be exerted by parents or other family members but children may still not want to upset them by refusing a proposal that their parents deem to be good.

A major factor impeding children's ability to give informed consent is that many are far too young when their marriages are decided for them to have a meaningful role in the decision-making process. Although not impossible, as a number of cases from the research demonstrate, it is extremely difficult to break an engagement. Although many parents said their children should consent to their marriages, their behavior did not conform to this. Examples were found of parents who gave this opinion but had decided on their children's marriages when they were still babies. As such, it is not the age at which children are married that necessarily bears the most influence on their ability to be part of the decision-making process, but the age at which their marriages are decided on.

Older children may influence decisions about their own marriages in ways other than verbal consent or overt participation. Indeed, watching how a child reacts to suggestions of marriage partners or that a marriage will happen is potentially more influential than the often superficial verbal consent. Mothers and fathers both reported to the research team that they examined the faces of their children, girls and boys, to see if they were happy at the suggestion of a marriage partner. Likewise, some fathers, knowing that their daughters would feel compelled to agree to any suggestion they made of an engagement, would ask another woman in the family to see if the girl were really happy with it.

The way in which women are sent to ask girls in the family about who they would like to marry, or the manner in which mothers may simply watch for their daughters' unspoken reactions to proposals, allows people, when they so desire, to take their daughters' opinions into consideration without crossing perceived cultural norms not to consult with daughters about their marriages. While boys may have more room to protest a suggested marriage, tactics of looking for unspoken reactions are also used by some families, particularly when they think their sons or brothers might be too shy to voice their preferences.

FORCING BOYS INTO MARRIAGES AND ITS IMPACT ON FUTURE VIOLENCE IN THE FAMILY

Much has been written about the effects of forcing girls into marriages against their wills, but there is little information about the effects of boys being forced into marriages. Throughout the research it was common for men to describe their marriages as forced. Examples were found of men who felt they had been forced into their marriages taking out their anger and frustration on their wives. A link has been identified between men's violence against their wives and their feelings that they were forced into the marriage to begin with. Similarly, being forced into a first marriage leads some men to want to take a second wife. Many don't necessarily object to the woman who was selected for them but are averse to the timing of the marriage. Several younger men explained that they had wanted to continue their educations or apprenticeships but their families had insisted they get married. Cases were also found in which a family's fears that their sons would engage in sexually or romantically deviant behavior led them to marry their sons to girls the boys did not want or at a time when the sons did not want to get married. In two families studied, marriages were arranged for sons who were having a relationship with a girl the family felt was not suitable and so it was arranged for the boy to marry someone else. In both these cases the men became abusive and neglectful of their wives. Further, these boys' family members identified the way in which they were married as the cause of the current levels of violence in the marriage.

It is important to note that the levels of influence family members have over marriage decisions were found to be determined primarily by household structure and individual's personal histories and characteristics rather than by gross demographic factors such as education levels; economic position; place of residence, whether urban or rural; and ethnicity.

FAMILIES FEELING FORCED TO MARRY THEIR CHILDREN AGAINST THEIR WISHES

Not only are children pressured to agree to marriages by their immediate family members, but also examples were found where families as a whole were pressured to marry their children at times and in manners that were against their better judgement.

Gender and generational dynamics play a strong role in determining who in a family can impose a proposal on another member of the family. With first-cousin marriages being prevalent, parents may feel it is rude or disrespectful to refuse a proposal coming from members of their own families. Older brothers in particular can put pressure on younger sisters to marry their children to their children's cousins.

Times of war and insecurity were also identified as creating situations wherein parents felt pressure to marry their children quickly and in ways that did not correspond to their ideals. A man from rural Bamiyan explained how he had to marry his daughters in haste to "protect their honor":

> We were migrating; we were going to Yakowlang [in northwestern Bamiyan Province], when we received a message from Ahmad's sister to give the girls in marriage; the girls were old enough and something might have happened to them. . . . We exchanged them in Yakowlang and did the *nekah* [acceptance agreement]. We did their wedding party in their old and dirty clothes while migrating.

In rural Herat, a father explained how, when his family members were internally displaced, the commander of the area where they stayed decided who the girls in the village would marry and when. To avoid the com-mander deciding for his daughter, he hurriedly married her to her cousin.

It was not only the marriages of daughters that were organized due to the exigencies of war and displacement. In Bamiyan Province, a number of families reported that they had married their sons in an effort to stop them from going to fight. It is not being argued here that married men did not fight during the different wars in Afghanistan; instead, marrying sons was reported to the research team as a strategy families used in attempts to stop their sons from going to fight.

With so many different factors influencing the levels of choice and force both families and those being married have in decisions about their marriages, it is argued that marriages in the Afghan context are better understood as operating along a range from force to choice. Some marriages may have larger elements of choice than force, and some may have more elements of force. Some marriages fall at one extreme of this range with both spouses either choosing each other and the timing of their marriage or being in full support of the partner and timing chosen by their parents or other family members. Some marriages fall at the other end of the range and correspond to the stereotypical presentation of a forced marriage, as described above. However, many marriages fall at different places along the range and comprise elements of both force and choice.

MARRIAGE PRACTICES: *BADAL* OR EXCHANGE MARRIAGE, BRIDE PRICE, AND POLYGAMY

Badal, the practice of exchanging women between families in marriage, is recognized by all the different groups researched as a practice that perpetuates a cycle of violence and abuse toward the women who have been exchanged in marriage.[11] Some also recognized it as un-Islamic.

Case studies of exchange marriages revealed that many are, indeed, a precursor to abuse and violence, with violence toward or mistreatment of one woman married through an exchange marriage being met by violence or mistreatment of the woman she was exchanged for. Some men explained that their powerlessness to help a sister being abused by their own wife's brother—the husband of the sister—led them to be violent to their own wives. It was apparent that men's violence toward their wives can simply be an act of revenge on their wives' natal family for mistreatment of their sisters. Families may also hold a newly married wife as ransom for better treatment for the woman from their own family, for instance, not allowing a new wife to visit her family until their sister/daughter is allowed to visit them. Violence toward a daughter-in-law because her husband's sister is being abused by her own in-laws is so normal that women themselves may use this as a threat in an attempt to protect themselves, as did this young woman in rural Nangarhar: "You know at that time I cried a lot because my whole body was in pain. I said to my mother-in-law, 'Do you feel good now! Look, he beat me, and I will tell my mother to beat your daughter because your son beat me.'" Despite people's awareness of the detrimental consequences of exchange marriage, it continues to be one of the most common practices used by the communities researched. This contradiction in opinion and behavior can be explained by a combination of factors. First, people perceive themselves as lacking options: paying a bride price or conducting an exchange marriage is seen as the only means through which to conduct marriages. Indeed the most frequent reason given for marrying sons by exchanging daughters is to avoid paying a bride price. It should be noted however, that not only the poorest families use exchange marriages. Second, although parents recognize that their daughters might suffer very badly if they are married through an exchange, ensuring sons are married can take priority over concern for daughters.

People are also generally aware of the negative impacts of the practice of bride price, despite its widespread use. Respondents to the research pointed to the detrimental consequences of bride price, including how it may motivate families to make decisions about their daughters' marriages, with economic concerns of the whole family overriding the well-being of their daughter; the economic consequence for the bridegroom and his family; and the treatment of a woman by her in-laws when she is first married due to their feelings about the amount they had to pay for her.

For some, taking a bride price is acceptable if it is a small amount and is primarily used to buy things for the girl getting married to take with her to her in-laws' home. However, in reality, it is far more common to hear that families use the bride price to meet basic needs or for wealthier families to invest in assets. It is clear that collecting a bride price is a key livelihood survival strategy for some. Some families reported seeking a bride price to cushion economic shocks to the family. One young girl was reportedly married to a much older man in order to pay for her father's medical treatment. Although her family members were reluctant to do this, they saw no alternative. Another girl was married in order to pay for the treatment of her brother's drug problem.

Likewise, the livelihoods of boys' families are equally affected by having to raise a bride price. Examples were found of families' productive assets being sold to marry a son or brother. Many men travel abroad to Pakistan or Iran to work for a number of years to raise their own bride price.

Paying a bride price, particularly when demands are relatively high, or when it increases over the period of the engagement, can make the boy's family feel bitter and angry toward the girl. Jamila, who was married to pay for the treatment of her brother's drug problem, explained how her husband directed his anger toward her as a response to her father having demanded a high bride price. A group of older men during a focus group explained how a girl is intricately linked to the bride price that her family demands for her by telling of a woman whose in-laws called her "Afs 60,000," the amount of her bride price. The bride price also contributes to in-laws believing that they own the woman and have ultimate rights over her.

With the negative impacts of bride price widely recognized, it is important to ask why the practice continues. One reason is that there is an expectation that, regardless, a newly married girl will face problems and be abused and constantly pressured. Despite the fact that the bride price may be recognized as a contributing factor to the ill treatment of daughters-in-law and that for boys' families it can present a huge economic burden, taking a stand against it is difficult for individual families to do and still be able to marry their sons without wider community agreement.

As with exchange marriage and bride price, polygamy is also recognized by respondents to the research as a common and highly problematic practice. At the least it is seen as a difficult family dynamic to manage, usually associated with destructive family relationships and violence. A woman in Jalalabad also referred to it as un-Islamic:

> I do not agree with having a second wife, because their husbands can't give them their rights. . . . Of course they will make arguments at home, so it is better to have only one wife. You know, Allah said that you have a right to marry again if you can make a balance between them [your wives]; otherwise it is better to have only one. Of course, it is really difficult to make a balance between them, so Islam also prefers one wife.

However, most people disapprove of the practice because of its potential to create conflict in the family, particularly between different co-wives. It should be noted that although most of the case study data confirmed this, there are exceptions whereby co-wives provide a source of support to one another, particularly by resisting a husband's violence.

Despite the general view that polygamous marriages can be fraught with difficulties, they are extremely common. Three reasons were identified as to why a man would take a second, third, or fourth wife. First, if a man and his current wife or wives have no children or only daughters, it was said that he should marry again. For many people, a woman not having sons is seen as a suitable reason for a man to marry again, but a number of female respondents said that the sex of a child was of Allah's making and therefore it was not wholly acceptable to marry again if a woman had no sons. There was also some—though limited—recognition voiced by women that infertility might be caused by the man in the relationship, although this was not usually discussed or recognized by men. There was one exception where a concerned man investigated his own fertility status before marrying a second time. He and his first wife were reluctant for him to marry again but saw it as an unavoidable necessity. Indeed, his first wife took the primary role in choosing the second wife. Other examples were found of first wives insisting their husbands marry again because they had no children. The need to have children is so essential that a woman is prepared to share her husband.

Second, a man might be obliged to marry the widow of a male family member. In virtually all examples of this, the women had become widows as a result of war. In common with marrying another wife for reasons of infertility, marrying a widowed woman in the family is seen as an unavoidable necessity for both the men and women involved. It was reported to be shameful for a widow to marry outside her husband's family. For many widows there is little choice, as they are likely to lose custody of their children to their in-law's family if they do not marry again within their in-laws' family. Men also felt they had little choice but to marry a dead brother's widow. Not all widows who marry their brothers-in-law are marrying a man who already has a wife. Neither do all these men take another wife after marrying their sisters-in-law.

Finally, a small number of cases were found where a man took a second wife or wanted to take a second wife because he or his family were dissatisfied with the first. Examples of this were found when men felt they had been forced into their first marriage.

Contrary to common perceptions, respondents did not cite a man's wealth as a reason for polygamy. Instead, wealth was reported by only a few men and women as potentially enabling a man to treat his wives more equally and reduce conflict, as he would be able to provide separate living spaces for them. However, others noted that wealth does not necessarily guarantee equality in the treatment of wives and therefore cannot be used to justify polygamous marriages.

Gender, generation, status, and household structure all affect how much influence individuals within the family have over marriage decisions. There is a great deal of diversity and complexity in the ways individuals agree to marriage and in their motivations for accepting a particular suggestion of marriage. Most attempts to describe marriages in Afghanistan as forced tend toward oversimplification. Marriages are better conceptualized as operating along a range from force to choice. At one end is a stereotypical presentation of forced marriage and at the other end are marriages in which both spouses choose each other or are happy and willing to give sufficiently informed consent. Not only do women suffer from prevailing gender norms but so too do men. Although the terrible suffering of women who are the victims of their husbands' violence is not to be forgotten, it is important to recognize that men too are compelled to marry against their wishes, ending up in bad marriages, depressed, and frustrated.

The majority of people in the communities where this research was conducted are aware of the negative consequences of not including children in decisions about their marriages, as well as the problems wrought by the practice of exchange marriage, giving and taking a bride price, and polygamy. Similarly, individual's opinions and desires were often found to be in conflict with cultural norms and practices. Individuals present their personal opinions as more constructive and progressive than the culture norms and practices they often feel compelled to comply with.

These findings all point to important spaces for positive change in the way that marriages are practiced in Afghanistan. The diversity and complexity found in decision- making processes show that cultural norms are not fixed but open to change. The awareness communities have about the negative consequences of certain marriage practices and the stark differences between many individual's opinions and cultural norms also point to a desire for change.

NOTES

1. The author wishes to acknowledge the research teams in the different provinces: in Bamiyan—Ali Hassan Fahimi, Sakina Sakhi, Mohammad Hassan Wafaey, and Zara Nezami; in Herat—Asila Sharif Sadiqi, Homa Salehyar,

Faqrullah Niksad, and Azizullah Royesh; in Kabul—Sakhi Frozish, Leena Waheedi, Yama Qasimyar,and Saghar Wafa; and in Nangarhar—Hanifa Gulmiran, Abdul Jalil Nooristani, Abdul Manon Sadiqi, and Parwana Wafa for their dedication, attention to detail, and resilience, under what were often difficult conditions and when researching such a sensitive subject area.

AREU publications from this study are D.J. Smith, *Love, Fear and Discipline: Everyday Violence toward Children in Afghan Families* (Kabul: Afghanistan Research and Evaluation Unit, 2008); D. J. Smith, *Decisions, Desires and Diversity: Marriage Practices in Afghanistan* (Kabul: Afghanistan Research and Evaluation Unit, 2009); D. J. Smith, *Challenging Myths and Finding Spaces for Change: Family Dynamics and Family Violence in Afghanistan* (Afghanistan Research and Evaluation Unit, 2009).

2. For further details of the methodology used for this research see Smith, *Decisions, Desires and Diversity.*

3. AREU's research on second-generation Afghans in neighboring countries and their experiences of return explores further the differences between life in Pakistan and Iran and life in Afghanistan; see Mamiko Saito, "Searching for my Homeland: Dilemmas Between Borders—Experiences of Young Afghans Returning "Home" from Pakistan and Iran" (AREU, July 2009), http://www.areu .org.af/index.php?option=com_search&Itemid=112&searchword= Mamiko+Saito&searchdata=author&submit=Search&searchphrase=all&or dering=relevence.

4. It is recognized that in some of the research sites, since the data was collected in 2006–2007, security has rapidly declined, particularly in Nangarhar Province.

5. See Smith, *Love, Fear and Discipline,* for a fuller discussion on changing attitudes, specifically in relation to violence toward children in the family.

6. The term "children" is used here to describe their position in the family and does not imply that those being written about are necessarily under the age of eighteen.

7. All names have been changed.

8. For examples, see the stories provided after a brief discussion on forced and child marriages in Amnesty International. In these examples there are either extreme age differences between the couples, thirty-six years in one case, or the husbands are described as becoming particularly violent. "Afghanistan: Women Still Under Attack—A Systematic Failure to Protect" (Stop Violence Against Women, Amnesty International, 29 May 2005), http://www.amnesty.org/ en/library/asset/ASA11/007/2005/en/21078ed1-d4e7-11dd-8a23-d58a49c0d652/ asa110072005en.pdf.

9. "Forced and Child Marriage," Stop Violence Against Women, http://www .stopvaw.org/forced_and_child_marriage.html. Similarly the UN "Convention on Consent to Marriage, Minimum Age for Marriage and Registration of Marriages" states that "no marriage shall be legally entered into without the full and free consent of both parties" (http://www2.ohchr.org/english/law/convention.htm).

10. "Women's Rights Unit," Afghanistan Independent Human Rights Commission, http://www.aihrc.org.af/womenrights.htm. Note in this definition, it is only a daughter who is referred to.

11. In the vast majority of cases, it is two daughters of roughly the same age who are exchanged with each other as wives for their brothers. However, examples were also found of fathers exchanging their own daughters in order to get new wives for themselves and of girls being exchanged who are of considerably different ages.

PART III

To Be Whole in Body and Mind

A woman in Kunduz Province bathes her child in water from a stream. Photo by Sheryl B. Shapiro, 2003.

CHAPTER 11

The Hidden War against Women

Health Care in Afghanistan

SIMA SAMAR

Afghanistan has the second-highest maternal mortality rate in the world, with 165 women dying for every 1,000 live births. One woman dies every twenty-nine minutes in child birth. Access to reproductive health care is minimal. One in five children dies before the age of five.[1]

Health care—along with sufficient good food and a healthy environment—should be a social service to which every human being is entitled. Not having an active war in a country is not the only measure of security. Without proper health care, especially for women, human security and peace are unattainable. Among sickly populations, every kind of crime is possible. Wherever maternal and child mortality and morbidity are high, there is a hidden war taking place against the lives of half of the population.[2] Women are the primary victims when health-care facilities are not adequate. When the mother is not healthy, the child will not be born healthy. Where women are not healthy, the family is not healthy. Where the family is not healthy, the nation is not healthy. Where the nation is not healthy, the world is not healthy.

The hidden war against women is waged worldwide,[3] but its effects are nowhere more apparent than in Afghanistan, where women's health is closely linked to peace, sickness, and war, and where adequate health care, basic social services, social justice, and education are missing. Poverty, too, plays a large role in the violent conflict that has continued in Afghanistan across three decades.

The Soviet invasion in 1979 began a nine-year period of destruction while the Cold War was fought on Afghan territory. All sides trampled the rights of Afghan women, each in its own way. Islamic fundamental-ism was supported by outside forces as a strategy against the commu-nists, and it had horrible implications for women, who were forced to take responsibility for upholding Afghan culture and so-called Islamic values. In the civil war that followed the Soviet Union's withdrawal in 1989 from Afghanistan, violence against women increased to an unpre-cedented level.[4] What few health-care facilities existed were destroyed and hospitals looted. Kabul University's medical school was decimated and "the violence left thousands of unqualified, uncertified, under-paid health workers, a dearth of clean reliable health-care facilities, adulter-ated drugs sold from unlicensed pharmacies, and some of the worst health indicators in the world."[5]

The Taliban took over the city of Kandahar in 1994, then Herat, and finally Kabul in 1996. In September 1997, their Ministry of Public Health banned female personnel, including physicians, nurses, pharma-cists, and technicians from working in Kabul's twenty-two hospitals and suspended medical services to the city's half million women, with the exception of the poorly equipped Rabi'a Balkhi facility, which had thirty-five beds and no clean water, electricity, surgical equipment, X-ray machines, suction, or oxygen. After months of negotiation with the International Committee of the Red Cross, the Taliban reversed the edict and agreed to readmit women into most hospitals and permit female hospital staff to work. But by June 1998, they had reissued the order forbidding physicians to treat women not accompanied by a male relative. They also shut down the public baths for women, abol-ishing an important, traditional means by which women maintain hy-giene and health.[6]

There had not been many health-care facilities in Afghanistan before the Soviet invasion, but in the 1960s and 1970s, a system of rural health care and assistance had been developed by CARE-MEDICO, the Medical Assistance Program (which sponsored a mobile health unit), the United Kingdom's National Organization of Ophthalmic Rehabili-tation, and others.[7] Nevertheless, some remote areas of the country never received health-care centers at all. And what little development was taking place in rural regions came to a complete halt because of the fighting. Medical professionals, along with others in the educated classes, fled the country, leaving women who, to this day, have never seen a doctor in their entire lives.[8] Family planning was not on any government's agenda and indeed, even women who escaped into neighboring countries were denied access, to a large extent because fundamentalists, who opposed all women's rights including health care, were influential in running the refugee camps.

The years passed with little help for women from the international community. Historically, there has been a lack of donor interest in funding for refugee women's reproductive health care. Clinics in the camps in Pakistan were inadequate, lacking female staff with virtually no reproductive health care or contraception available. Some camps were as many as six hours away from the cities and many women died on their way to hospital. This is still the case today inside Afghanistan. The few hospitals that have been restored are mostly in Kabul and other cities, far from the rural areas.[9] Clinics run by non-governmental organizations find it difficult to get and stock medicines and health-care workers are mostly men. Even today, a small percentage of births in Afghanistan have skilled attendants present, and only a relatively few women receive professional prenatal care.[10]

In the 1980s, when I began my work as a physician in the refugee areas of Pakistan, there were virtually no maternity or other hospitals for Afghan women. The only health care available was for male members of political parties. There was little education at all among refugee women, especially about health care. Aid agencies provided no family planning information or contraceptives.

Even with the establishment of some hospitals for women, such as the ones I opened in 1989 in Quetta, Pakistan, reproductive health care for women was restricted by lack of resources and political opposition. Requests by our newly formed Shuhada Organization, even for minimal help from international donors, were largely ignored. For example, one of the United Nations agencies refused to print our literacy course books, because we included information on family planning.[11]

Afghan women's health has suffered greatly across three decades and has a long way to go to overcome these conditions. The average women's life expectancy in Afghanistan is only forty-four.[12] According to Article 52 (chapter 2) of Afghanistan's 2003 constitution,[13] women can now seek medical care without official restrictions, but most have little to gain from this new freedom. Afghanistan is and has always been a patriarchal and conservative society. The social subordination of girls and women results in discrimination and control of every aspect of their lives. For example, if a male member of the family needs medical care, the family will take him to the hospital in another city. But this may not be the case for girls. Girls are counted as not belonging to the family because when they marry—57 percent under the legal age of sixteen[14]—they become the property of another family.[15] Sexuality and reproductive issues are social taboos and not discussed. This puts a girl in a difficult situation. She cannot ask questions or discuss her concerns, particularly around the men in the family, lest she be labeled a bad girl.

Nutrition is a problem as well. The best food—and nutritious food is often difficult to obtain for anyone—goes first to the male members of the family, including the boy children. In some conservative areas of Afghanistan, girls are not counted as children with the privileges of childhood. Women and girls eat after the men and receive the leftovers. They are often forced to survive on tea and naan (unleavened bread) or scraps. As a result, 48 percent of women are iron deficient, resulting in anemia and putting menstruating, pregnant, and lactating women at high risk.[16]

Malnutrition, which predisposes women to infection, may also be a factor in the high death rate from tuberculosis. Out of the 25,000 Afghans who die from TB each year, 16,000 are women. Tuberculosis in Afghanistan affects an estimated 325 new cases per 100,000 people a year. Inadequate access to health care and shortage of female health workers also affects the numbers.[17]

In addition, Afghanistan is confronted by high incidences of water and sanitation-related diseases—cholera, dysentery, scabies, trachoma, for example. Half of the deaths of all children under five are related to diarrheal disease caused by inadequate sanitation, lack of clean drinking water, and poor hygiene practices.

The production of opium poppies creates further health problems. According to a United Nations Office on Drugs and Crime survey, of 920,000 reported drug abusers in Afghanistan, an estimated 120,000 are women and that figure is rising.[18] Baad—or the exchange of girls or women in marriage to pay a debt or settle a dispute—is frequently practiced among men unable to meet their obligations in the drug trade.[19] The security and health consequences of child and forced marriages can be drastic. Women are underfed, overworked, and depressed, and they give birth too young.

In 2006, Afghanistan's Ministry of Women's Affairs registered 2,133 cases of sexual and gender-based violence, including 1,011 cases of beatings.[20] These numbers account only for the reported cases. The majority of women in Afghanistan believe that they must be beaten by their husbands, that it is part of their daily lives and marital obligation. They may not complain or seek medical care after the beatings. Poverty, lack of job opportunities for men, and post-traumatic stress syndrome among veterans and war victims certainly exacerbate the violence by Afghan men against women, as it does elsewhere in the world.

Women's issues are political issues. Eighty-five percent of Afghan women are uneducated and uninformed about their own bodies, reproductive health, and options.[21] They are unaware of sexually transmitted diseases and thus vulnerable to them. Although in 2006 there were only forty-nine reported cases in Afghanistan, foreign soldiers and workers, including prostitutes, along with drug use and lack of information have heightened the risks of HIV and indeed all STDs.[22] Most Afghan women are taught, and believe, that they have to serve men and to produce children. Among those lucky enough to be informed about contraception, the majority must have the permission of their husbands and sometimes their mothers-in-law to use it.

On average, women bear seven to ten children, though some of those children, as we have seen, die at birth or before the age of five.[23] Because women perform unpaid labor in the home, they earn no cash, have no money of their own, and are entirely dependent on male members of the family, who are sometimes unwilling to pay the cost of their medical treatment.

After the fall of the Taliban in 2001, programs to repair and build hospitals and clinics began. As of 2006, emergency obstetric care services were supported in twenty districts; the Society of Obstetricians and Gynecologists was founded; Malalai Hospital—the largest maternity hospital in Kabul—was refurbished and renovated; many agencies have been training female health-care workers and facilitating the return of female doctors from exile.[24] In 2003, the new Department of Women and Reproductive Health was established within the Ministry of Health. By 2007, the number of health-care workers increased to 15,001, 49 percent of them women.[25] Nevertheless, the numbers of educated medical staff are very low, contributing to a lack of trust. Equipment and resources everywhere continue to be at a premium, particularly outside urban centers and in ongoing conflict areas.

Although there has been some improvement since 2002, it is barely sufficient and is largely centered in urban areas.[26] In rural Afghanistan, the majority of women still cannot access health care.[27] Most parts of the country still have no health facilities whatsoever. The people are not near hospitals or clinics and have no adequate means of transportation, nor are the roads accessible to motored vehicles. Security is dwindling, even in the capital city of Kabul, where most of the aid activity takes place. Many aid workers have evacuated the rural areas where Taliban and other fundamentalist factions are once again taking precedence.

Lack of security and political will, continuing war, and the financial aid that was promised, but has barely materialized, contributes to the ongoing problems. In spring 2004, five employees—three foreigners and two Afghan staff—of Medecins Sans Frontieres were killed in their car, while on the way to their base from a rural clinic in north Afghanistan. After twenty-five years of work in Afghanistan, through the Soviet occupation, the civil war, and the Taliban, MSF finally pulled out of the country.

Officials talk a lot about gender mainstreaming and equality, but little has been done. There have been few women in leadership positions in the government. If women are not part of the decision-making process, then women's problems will not likely be addressed. Ultimately, this begins with education. Education is the key to women's empowerment, so that they can understand and, wherever necessary, change their choices and make decisions accordingly.

As long as we do not count women as human beings and women's rights as human rights, and as long as women are casualties of the hidden war, we will not solve the world's distresses and diseases, and we will have no chance for world peace. The crisis of the women of Afghanistan is a crisis for the entire world.

NOTES

1. The United Nations Development Fund for Women reports that one woman dies every twenty-nine minutes in childbirth (1,600 to 1,900 deaths per 100,000 live births) and has the second-highest maternal mortality rate in the world). "UNIFEM Afghanistan Fact Sheet 2008," *United Nations Development Fund for Women Afghanistan*, http://afghanistan.unifem.org/media/pubs/08/factsheet.html.

The World Food Programme reports that the province of Badakhshan has the highest maternal mortality rate ever recorded—6,500 per 100,000. "Highest Maternity Mortality in the World in Northeastern Afghanistan (World Food Programme, 27 June 2005) http://www.wfp.org/stories/highest-maternal-mortality-world-northeastern-afghanistan. According to the World Health Organization, the mortality rate in 2004 of children under five years old was 275 per 1,000 live births: 258 male, 256 female. One in four children who succumb before the age of five dies from a preventable disease, the highest infant mortality rate in the world. "Infant and Under Five Mortality in Afghanistan: Current Estimates and Limitations" (Bulletin of the World Health Organization, April 7, 2010), http://www.who.int/bulletin/volumes/88/8/09-068957/en/index.html.

2. "Of the estimated total of 536,000 maternal deaths worldwide, developing countries accounted for 99% (533,000) of the deaths," "World Poverty Day 2007: Investing in Women—Solving the Poverty Puzzle" (United Nations Development Fund for Women, 2007) , http://www.womenfightpoverty.org/docs/WorldPovertyDay2007_FactsAndFigures.pdf.

3. Women compose 70 percent of those living in poverty worldwide and 75 percent of non-literate adults. Two-thirds of the children who do not receive an education are girls, and 80 percent of refugees are women and children. "World Poverty Day 2007."

4. Lauryn Oates, "Taking Stock Update: Afghan Women and Girls Five Years On" (Report of WOMANKIND Worldwide, October 2006), 11–16.

5. Nellie Bristol, "Reconstructing Afghanistan's Health System," *The Lancet* 366 (December 17, 24, and 31, 2005): 2075–2076. Bristol interviewed an Afghan-American physician, Homaira Behsudi, who returned to Kabul University, where she had earned her medical degree. "There was no equipment, no training materials, and few books. The chairs and ceilings were gone. Even the electrical wiring had been pulled out of the walls. 'The shocking thing was the anatomy lab,' she says . . . 'the models, the human models didn't have any heads.' . . . Taliban law banned human figures that could be construed as idols. 'How would you train a medical student without knowledge of brain and head and neck?' "

6. Physicians for Human Rights, *The Taliban's War on Women: A Health and Human Rights Crisis in Afghanistan* (Boston: Physicians for Human Rights, 1998), 65.

7. Louis Dupree, *Afghanistan* (Princeton, N.J.: Princeton University Press, 1980), 642–643.

8. According to UNIFEM, depending on the location, today between 30 percent and 90 percent of Afghan women in rural areas cannot access health care. "The Situation of Women in Afghanistan" (United Nations Development Fund for Women, Afghanistan Fact Sheet, 2008), http://afghanistan.unifem.org/media/pubs/08/factsheet.html.

9. The Italian NGO Emergency is an exception. In 2003, a Maternity Centre was established inside the Emergency hospital compound in the Panjshir Valley. In September 2004, Emergency opened a hospital in Lashkar-gah, the capital of the Helmand province. All hospitals are connected to First Aid Posts and Primary Health Centres located in heavily mined areas or in remote villages where there is no other medical facility. Emergency Activity Report, 1994–2007, EMERGENCY, 4, http://www.emergency.it/img/report/lasten.pdf.

10. "UNIFEM Afghanistan Fact Sheet 2008: HEALTH," *United Nations Development Fund for Women Afghanistan*, http://afghanistan.unifem.org/media/pubs/08/factsheet.html#health.

11. Today, with the support of the Norwegian government and Novib (Oxfam Netherlands), the Shuhada Organization's twenty physicians and 1,000 other staff run four hospitals, twelve clinics, and sixty schools in Afghanistan.

12. Statistics on life expectancy vary. The United Nations Development Fund for Women reports forty-four years of age, "Fact Sheet on the Situation of Women and Girls in Afghanistan" (November 30, 2009), http://afghanistan.unifem.org/media/news/detail.php?storyID=830. The World Health Organization reports forty-two years of age, "Gender Health and Ageing" (World Health Organization, November 2003) http://whqlibdoc.who.int/gender/2003/a85586.pdf.

13. Article 52 (chapter 2), "Health Care, Hospitals, Physical Education, Sports," of the 2003 constitution of the Islamic State of Afghanistan states:

1. The state is obliged to provide free means of preventive health care and medical treatment, and proper health facilities to all citizens of Afghanistan in accordance with the law.

2. The state encourages and protects the establishment and expansion of private medical services and health centers in accordance with law.

3. The state in order to promote physical education and improve national and local sports adopts necessary measures.

14. Some children are married as young as six years old. Many girls, if not married, are betrothed without their consent and sometimes without their knowledge during childhood. Statistics from Afghan Women's Ministry of Affairs, as cited in Oates, "Taking Stock," 13.

15. Article 54 (Chapter 2) of the 2003 Constitution of the Islamic Republic of Afghanistan makes the legal marriage age of girls sixteen and of boys eighteen.

16. Median requirements of absorbed iron are estimated to be 1.36 and 1.73 mg per day among adult and teenage menstruating females. However, 15 percent of adult menstruating women require more than 2.0 mg per day, and 5 percent require as much as 2.84 mg per day. The superimposition of menstrual losses and growth in menstruating teenage girls increases the demands for absorbed iron; 30 percent need to absorb more than 2.0 mg of iron per day; 10 percent as much as 2.65 mg, and 5 percent 3.21 mg. These requirements are very difficult, if not impossible, to satisfy even with good quality, iron-fortified diets. Vitamin deficiencies lead to scurvy, and iodine deficiencies cause goiters in mothers and a thyroid condition called cretinism in their babies.

17. "The Situation of Women in Afghanistan" and Department of Gender and Women's Health, Family and Community Health Cluster, "Women's Health in Afghanistan," World Health Organization, March 2002, 3, http://www.who.int/mip2002/index.pl%3Fid=2094&isa=Item&field_name=item_attachment_file&op=download_file.

18. Afghanistan Independent Human Rights Commission Research and Planning Section, "Effective Factors Associated with Drug Addiction and the Consequences of Addiction among Afghan Women" (February 2008), 3.

19. Of interest: Sami Yousafzai, "The Opium Brides of Afghanistan" (Newsweek, March 29, 2008), http://www.newsweek.com/id/129577?from=rss.

20. "The Situation of Women in Afghanistan."

21. Oates, "Taking Stock," 21.

22. According to the World Bank: "Reliable data on HIV prevalence in Afghanistan is sparse. To date, 478 HIV cases have been reported, however,

UNAIDS and WHO estimate that there could be between 1,000 and 2,000 Afghans living with HIV. The HIV epidemic is at an early stage in Afghanistan, and is concentrated among high risk groups, mainly injecting drug users (IDUs) and their partners. Afghanistan's emerging epidemic likely hinges on a combination of injecting drug use and unsafe paid sex. According to a 2006 study, 3 percent of IDUs in Kabul were HIV positive. Almost one-third of the IDUs participating in the study said they used contaminated injecting equipment. In addition, large proportions of these (male) drug users also engaged in other high-risk behavior. For example, 32 percent had sex with men or boys, and 69 percent bought sex. Only about half of the IDUs knew that using unclean syringes carries a high risk of HIV transmission or that condoms can prevent infection." "HIV/AIDS in Afghanistan" (The World Bank, August 2008), http://siteresources.worldbank.org/SOUTHASIAEXT/Resources/223546-1192413140459/4281804-1231540815570/5730961-1235157256443/HIVAIDSbriefAF.pdf.

23. The overwhelming responsibility involved in rearing this many children is another reason women are prevented from taking part in social activities or politics where they might increasingly have a voice in their own lives.

24. Oates, "Taking Stock," 27–28.

25. "The Situation of Women in Afghanistan."

26. In June 2008, the Japanese government awarded the Afghan Ministry of Public Health $4.33 million. Under the agreement, approximately 7.5 million children will receive vaccines to prevent and control infectious diseases and to further accelerate ongoing polio eradication efforts.

27. "The Situation of Women in Afghanistan."

CHAPTER 12

Challenges to Cripple the Spirit

A Midwife's Experiences

PAMELA CHANDLER

In the spring of 2005, three and a half years after the fall of the Taliban, I had an opportunity to travel to Afghanistan as a midwife working with a human rights organization.[1] The country was experiencing its first break in violence after decades of war, and although there was a very cautious optimism in the air, the challenges involved in rebuilding on every level were abundantly clear. I had been drawn there to try to aid in some way with the enormous obstacles facing child-bearing women— obstacles that contribute to some of the highest levels of maternal mortality that have ever been documented. The exodus of medical professionals as the fighting dragged on, the lack of any education for women during the Taliban regime (and even before), the traditional importance that women be attended by women during childbirth when there was a total paucity of skilled individuals to do so, the remoteness of so many villages in a country of forbidding landscapes—all of this I knew something about before I arrived, and I hoped somehow that I could help.

What I did not know was how profoundly my own life would be touched by the amazing women I met while I was there. I have been haunted ever since by my memories of their courage, perseverance, and grace in the face of challenges that would cripple the spirits of most of us. My experiences put a human face on the grim statistics that represented life for child-bearing women in Afghanistan—a situation that can only have become much worse since the resurgence of the Taliban and the increase in violence.

The numbers alone are startling. What does it mean to have the highest maternal mortality rate in the world? It is estimated that 1,800 women die of complications related to childbirth for every 100,000 live births (or one maternal death for every fifty-five births), and that one in eight women will die from complications related to childbirth.[2] In Afghanistan overall, a woman dies of pregnancy-related causes every twenty-nine minutes, and in some parts of the country more than 6,000 women lose their lives for every 100,000 babies born. That is 600 times the risk of dying from childbirth in North America.[3] Infant mortality (death before the age of one) is estimated to be an astounding 165 deaths per 1,000 live births compared with numbers in the single digits where women have access to adequate care. One in five children will die before his or her fifth birthday.[4]

Almost all Afghan women give birth at home, but by some estimates only 8 percent get help from a trained birth attendant. When something goes wrong, getting help can be arduous and even treacherous, as some of these stories show. In the United States and Europe, people take safe childbirth for granted, but every pregnancy represents a significant risk to the women of Afghanistan.

I spent a few days in Kabul—a city of incredible traffic, congestion, frenetic reconstruction, and rubble—before I left for the countryside where I would be working. One night, I was seen observing a wedding party at a nearby house in the neighborhood, and I was spontaneously invited to join the festivities and to partake of the feast. As the food was served, I realized that only the young couple, their parents, and I were seated in chairs, whereas everyone else gathered on the floor to eat. Why should I, who had essentially crashed the party, be treated with such honor? I was a guest in the country, and that is the Afghan way, insisted the father of the bride. That startling hospitality was the essence of my experience throughout Afghanistan.

My work outside Kabul involved providing technical support to a regional midwifery training program in a remote part of the country. After the United States invasion in 2001 and the defeat of the Taliban, the new government recognized the urgent need for more female care providers skilled in obstetrics and had started hospital and community-based programs around the country. I was to be a liaison between the program in the community where I was assigned and the local hospital. The hospital itself was still a work in progress, with ongoing construction to replace older, damaged buildings, and many functions still taking place in tents. The village, a regional center, had a bustling bazaar but still lacked electricity, a sanitation system, and clean water. Many buildings had been burned by the Taliban and were now abandoned, but there were generators and even a few satellite dishes on the roofs of the compounds where the aid workers were housed. Ditches carried water along either side of the main dirt street, and the donkeys tied at the upper end did not keep people from washing dishes or even brushing their teeth in the water as it passed their stalls. Fortunately, a large river also provided for the water needs of most of the town.

The midwifery program was located in a building in the bazaar. The young women had been recruited from the surrounding communities and, as they were to be there for many weeks, several had brought their families. Everyone lived together on the ground floor and the classes were held upstairs. I was very impressed by the depth and breadth of the material that was taught, and the use of sophisticated teaching aids, including some procedures beyond the scope of midwives in the United States, such as vacuum suction to manage an incomplete miscarriage. These women had to be prepared to handle all kinds of obstetric emergencies by themselves when they returned to their villages.

One could only wonder if they would have the supplies they would need to deal with the inevitable crises they would have to manage. It seemed unlikely that the tools they had access to in the classroom would be readily available in those villages. My colleagues and I had brought to Afghanistan several duffel bags filled with basic medications and medical supplies that were dearly needed by the hospital. How much more in need must the outlying and often very remote villages be? I would eventually have a chance to find out.

Although I was only in the country for a number of weeks, it seemed like every day brought a new and at times unimaginable disaster for the women I was seeing. There was one patient, right after I arrived, whose near-term fetus saved her life when she inadvertently threw unexploded ordinance into the cook stove with the wood she had gathered. There was the mother of an unmarried pregnant fifteen-year-old, who forced her way into our clinic and refused to leave until we heard her pleas on behalf of her daughter, and whose ingenuity eventually saved her daughter from being killed to preserve the family honor. There was the woman who arrived severely infected and near death after lying at home in a remote village for twenty days with a retained placenta. There was Lila, who nearly died trying to give birth to the baby so desperately wanted by her elderly husband and his other two infertile wives. Her story and those of the other women who came to our hospital are the focal point of this chapter, which speaks as well to an enormously committed group of local physicians and foreign-aid workers.

Lila was about seventeen and an outpatient at the hospital when I first arrived, having already been sent from her remote village several times to be monitored for elevated blood pressure, a potentially serious problem in pregnancy. As an outpatient, she had a bed with a mattress covered in plastic on a small ward with other pregnant or laboring patients. The families of these women supplied them with their only bedding and brought in meals from the bazaar or from home if they were lucky enough to live nearby. Many patients walked or rode donkeys for hours to get to the hospital, and if they were admitted as inpatients for any length of time, family members often had to return to their homes and other responsibilities. Furthermore, visiting hours were highly restricted, especially for the men; and when the families had left, the women, all non-literate, had only one another's company for entertainment.

Saddiqa, one of Lila's roommates who had been there for weeks already, was being managed for preterm labor, buying precious time for her unborn infant. Shy at first, she clearly longed for companionship and quickly bonded to our interpreter, a young Afghan American. When Saddiqa was alone on the ward, the interpreter made it a point to spend time with her, and Saddiqa loved hearing stories of life in the West. All the patients were deeply impressed that someone who had made it to the United States would want to return to help their country.

A few days after I arrived, late one evening, Lila went into labor, and as it happened, I was on duty with another American midwife. She progressed rapidly, her blood pressure remained fairly stable, and we soon moved her to a rudimentary delivery room where she gave birth to a healthy male child. Unfortunately, she was also bleeding profusely. Without access to medications that are common in developed countries— such as Cytotek, a single pill that, when placed in the rectum, quickly controls bleeding—our initial efforts to stop the bleeding were unsuccessful, and she rapidly progressed into shock. Even with the help of an obstetrician from Tajikistan, who was resting nearby, we were unable to start intravenous fluids as her veins had collapsed from the blood loss. Thankfully, there happened to be an anesthesiologist in another part of the hospital, and he was able to get there in time to open a vein and insert the line of life-saving fluids.

Although we were able to control the initial acute hemorrhage, Lila continued to bleed throughout the night, despite all our efforts. The cause of the bleeding was never fully determined, but as she was already severely weakened and in a guarded condition, it was ultimately decided to take her to the operating room and remove her uterus. The fact that this family had finally been blessed with a viable baby boy made the decision easier, and with her uterus gone, Lila's bleeding stopped. Now began the effort to find the blood she would need to recover from the surgery and survive to parent her child. This would become a theme during my stay. Although the hospital had the capacity to do blood typing, the blood itself was woefully scarce, and family members were often reluctant to donate, apparently due to beliefs around giving one's blood to another. I never fully understood this: in some cases a family member would gladly donate blood, whereas in most cases they would simply refuse to do so. Fortunately for Lila, her husband, although quite elderly, was more than willing, and the other American midwife also had a type that matched. With those two units of blood, her condition stabilized and she slowly began to recover.

Within a few days of Lila's delivery, another patient with profuse bleeding was brought to the hospital. She was in the latter part of her pregnancy and apparently had a condition called placenta previa, where the placenta is implanted at the bottom of the uterus, overlying the cervix, which opens to allow for the birth of the baby. As the cervix starts to open, profound hemorrhaging results and there is no way for the baby to be delivered vaginally. Saving the life of both mother and baby requires an emergency Cesarean section, but this woman refused surgery. She had bled heavily with her previous pregnancy, probably from a low-lying placenta that had not, however, fully covered the cervix, and the baby died. Her only living child had actually been delivered by Cesarean section, and yet she still refused surgery.

I found it impossible to understand. We felt totally helpless, watching her bleed and knowing that if she went home as she wanted, she and her unborn baby would surely die. The hospital director—a dedicated, hardworking, and compassionate man who tended meticulously to the welfare of the patients—made this abundantly clear to the woman's husband. As I stood wondering what could possibly be done, someone inserted an IV into her arm. A sedative in the fluids began to work almost immediately and she was rolled off to surgery. In Afghanistan apparently, only the husband need give consent, and in this case it saved her life. The placenta was found to have grown into the uterine lining and she had to have a hysterectomy. The baby was born severely distressed, but ultimately they both lived. This time, other members of the hospital staff donated blood.

When we were not busy with pregnancy complications or attending births, we saw women in the outpatient clinic. Every morning, the road to the hospital was lined with women in colorful clothing, most in bright blue *burqa*s, walking or being led on donkeys, in search of care for pregnancy or other female-related problems. They often traveled for many hours and then waited in line for several more in order to be seen. What we could offer seemed desperately minimal: if the pregnant women were free of complications, it was usually only advice and a handful of vitamins and iron tablets until the next visit.

Sadly, one of the most common complaints we encountered was the inability to get pregnant. In Afghanistan, much of a woman's value is in her fertility. I was told that a woman who cannot get pregnant is not considered worthy to sit at the table with the family. Even women who had given birth to one or two children told us they grew worried if a few years passed without another pregnancy, fearing punishment or that their husbands would take another wife. Some arrived covered in bruises and, if the wait was too long, some began trembling in fear, because, they said, their husbands—believing they might be seen by a man—had forbidden their visit to the hospital. In a setting where almost all marriages are arranged, the quality of a woman's life is determined by her family's choice of a husband. If the man is kind and the couple cares for each other, her life might be good in spite of harsh living conditions. As in all cultures—for domestic abuse is universal—when the husband is dictatorial or brutal, when he does not allow his wife to leave the house or visit her family, the wife's situation can be deplorable. I can only imagine the added strain on both partners when there are cultural pressures to reproduce and when children are so important in helping to meet demands of daily existence.

We had little to offer women with fertility problems. Drugs commonly used in the West to induce ovulation were not available. An adequate evaluation required a trip to Kabul and expenses far beyond these families' means. Knowing that Western health-care providers were working at the hospital, the women came with high hopes, yet all we could do was look for and treat basic problems such as anemia and infection. Malnourishment was common, but counseling these women about diet and telling them to eat more protein when they might get only one or two meals with meat or poultry a month was an empty gesture.

One day while I was working in the clinic, the hospital director came at a run, urging me to join him in the emergency tent where a pregnant woman was being evaluated for severe trauma from shrapnel. She'd been gathering firewood and inadvertently scooped up some unexploded ordnance, which she tossed into the fire along with the wood. The countryside in Afghanistan is littered with decades of landmines and UXOs—shells, rockets, bombs, and bullets that have been fired but not yet detonated—from the war with the Soviet Union and the factional conflicts that followed. These explosives are located in every conceivable type of terrain. Afghanistan is considered by experts to be one of the three most heavily mined countries in the world. Agricultural land accounts for more than 20 percent of mined areas and grazing land accounts for more than 75 percent.[5] In 2003, sixty people were reported killed or maimed by mines each month, with many more unreported. About 30 percent of the victims were children.

The woman who was admitted that day had wounds to her abdomen, one breast, a shoulder, and her arm, and she had a shattered knee. She was quickly transferred to the operating room, and I was invited to observe and assist. An emergency Cesarean section was required. I was amazed by the speed with which she was thoroughly assessed and prepared for surgery. Unfortunately, trauma of this type is all too common in Afghanistan.

In a very short while, a nearly full-term male baby was delivered with shrapnel wounds covering his back. He was breathless, pale, and floppy, but through the skilled efforts of those in attendance, he was successfully resuscitated. The metal was picked from his back, his wounds were cleaned and dressed, and by the time his mother was treated, stabilized, and dressed back into her blood-soaked clothes, he was ready to be placed into her arms (as with the bedding, there was simply a lack of clean gowns for the many patients the hospital attended). A few weeks later they were discharged—the mother and the baby who had saved her life.

One morning we were interrupted in the clinic by a middle-aged woman with her sister and teenage daughter, who forced their way to the front of the line and insisted on being seen. The staff directed them to the tent where patients were screened and given paperwork and a place in the queue, but the threesome refused to go and managed to work their way through the door and into the examining area where they stubbornly squatted on the floor. Initially, they told the interpreter that the aunt was bleeding, but when we acquiesced to give her our attention, they revealed that the problem was with the girl, who was unmarried and pregnant. This was indeed a dire situation, which the mother dramatized by gestures indicating she and her daughter would both be killed.

Within the confines of the clinic—normally staffed by a rotating handful of midwives from Afghanistan and Tajikistan and their assistants—we required that the women remove their burqas so that we could examine them more thoroughly, but also in order to relate to one another more personally. I was always surprised by how simple it was, when the trappings that so highlight our cultural differences were removed, to feel an easy rapport with these women. Ultimately, issues of health, families, safe child-bearing, and concern for our children are the same among women throughout the world. When these three women disrobed, I was shocked to see how young and stubbornly passive the fifteen-year-old appeared.

Meanwhile, the mother and the aunt were distraught and begged for our help, suspecting that we might have medications or could arrange for a procedure that would terminate the pregnancy. Unfortunately, in Afghanistan, even a vague promise of that possibility could undermine the trust of the community and destroy all of the good that the hospital created.[6] As difficult as it was—knowing that the murder of women by their own family members in circumstances where it is thought necessary to preserve the family honor is still a reality—I nevertheless had to insist that they leave.

The following day, I traveled to Kabul on business and stopped by the hospital in the morning on my way out of town. Suddenly, there was a commotion at the gate, and the three women from the previous day were ushered in. The young girl's clothing was soaked in blood, and we immediately feared the worst: a botched abortion at the hands of someone in the bazaar.

I began attending to her, calling the lab to have her blood typed and trying to assess her bleeding. I sent the interpreter to find out more from her mother. I was busy starting an IV when the interpreter returned and demanded my attention. I was short and impatient, feeling that she didn't understand the severity of the situation, when she managed to convey to me: "That's *not her blood*!" Whatever animal it had come from, the mother had taken an unbelievable risk. The Tajik obstetrician was away, and there was only time to summon the surgeon on call and explain that this girl was pregnant and bleeding before I had to leave. The translator and I had no choice but to decide it was in other hands than ours.

Once in Kabul, I was able to call the hospital and ask after the girl. I was told that she had had an incomplete miscarriage and that they had safely removed "the contents of the uterus." Apparently, the basic ultrasound machine at the hospital was adequate to reveal that she was pregnant but not the status of the fetus. If someone had discovered that the blood was not coming from her vagina and that there was a live fetus in her uterus, I can't imagine what the consequences would have been for the mother. Surely the child's father would have had to have been notified, and perhaps also the police. Not only was the girl pregnant, her mother had faked the bleeding to trick the doctors into terminating the pregnancy. Her gamble had paid off!

Latifa was brought to the hospital, desperately ill, from a very remote village. Her plight touched me deeply. She had given birth to a baby at home, attended by female family members. Sadly, the baby was born dead and the placenta failed to come out following the birth. She'd lain bleeding for twenty days. By the time she reached us, she was severely septic and near death from blood loss. It is remarkable that she survived the journey. Her blood pressure was almost too low to be detected, and her hemoglobin level—a measurement of the blood's ability to carry oxygen—was two, compared with a normal level of twelve to fourteen. This time, the family would not donate blood, and the hospital director went throughout the town and to a local school seeking people willing to help. In this manner, he was able to get four or five pints donated, which raised her hemoglobin to four, but it was not going to be enough.

Latifa had given birth twice before at home. Both times the babies had been stillborn, and the placentas were retained. Her husband had brought her to the hospital following those deliveries, but he had refused to allow her to have her tubes tied to protect her from further obstetric emergencies. This time it looked like she might die. She was given antibiotics and antiseptic solutions were infused into her uterus, in the hope of stabilizing her enough for a needed hysterectomy. During one infusion, worms crawled out of her rectum. She also had a horrible cough, probably tuberculosis. Clearly, she was among the poorest of the poor. Yet, although her condition seemed hopeless, she miraculously rallied and was eventually able to undergo surgery. Our translator and an aid worker from our guesthouse donated more blood, and she gradually began to recover. She was gracious and stoic during her hospitalization, but her situation was all too poignant. She had lost three babies and now her uterus. She would never need to risk another pregnancy, but her value as a wife would probably be diminished.

The fact that these women survived such serious complications is truly incredible. They might well have died from these conditions, even in a modern hospital, and that they did not is a marvelous testament to the skills and determination of the Afghan doctors and nurses (all male) and the Afghan and Tajik midwives (all female), as well as the hospital director and other foreign aid workers. These dedicated people worked hard day and night to meet the full range of health care needs of the surrounding communities while literally building the hospital, both structurally and in terms of its operation: training staff, establishing protocols, and attending to quality assurance and performing in-services, in addition to satisfying all the demands of patient care. I was privileged to work alongside them, however briefly, and honored to have been able to participate in the care of these courageous women.

Before leaving Afghanistan to return to the United States, I traveled to some of the surrounding villages in the province where I was working. The students I had worked with had all committed to return to their villages upon graduation to provide care to child-bearing women out of local clinics. The hospital director invited me to visit some of the clinics in our area. Even with the use of the "ambulance"—a Range Rover outfitted with basic emergency supplies such as blankets, materials to dress wounds, IV fluids, and an oxygen tank—the trip was arduous. The hospital director and a doctor from one of the clinics had to ride in the back and became ill with motion sickness. The roads, at times barely visible, had deep potholes and were often obstructed by large boulders or creeks. Abandoned tanks peppered the landscape, and in some places, painted rocks designated areas now either "mine free" or at risk: white for all clear, red for danger. These were the dangerous routes our patients traveled on foot to get to us, sometimes in labor or bleeding.

We were warmly received in the various clinics we visited. There was always someone in attendance—a doctor, a midwife, or a pharmacist—and that person was delighted and proud to show us around. Some of the clinics were fairly well supplied, with small pharmacies and basic laboratory equipment, whereas others were little more than buildings furnished with chairs and a few exam tables. Presumably the supplies the government can provide, along with donations that the aid workers bring, are doled out to the clinics on the basis of availability and need. Pills were dispensed prudently to hospital outpatients, illustrating the enormous, ongoing need for such basics as prenatal vitamins, iron, antibiotics, birth control pills, and even soap. A commitment by any charitable group merely to provide soap for a year to a particular region in the country would be an incredible gift.

The delivery area, when there was one, typically consisted of a table with a portable sink or basin and buckets to sterilize whatever instruments were available—the first one with soapy water, the second with a disinfectant, and the third with a rinse. Although it might appear primitive, there were often blankets on the table and curtains in the window, and the women who came there (from ever more remote villages) would know they were being attended by someone with training that was as sophisticated as possible and who had the capacity to transport them if necessary.

In one of the villages we took time off to pay a visit to Lila, who had now been home for a few weeks. Her house, like most in the village, was down a narrow dirt lane and behind a door in a high mud wall. The house itself consisted of a sparsely furnished courtyard surrounded by rooms that opened onto it. Outside the main door, we were greeted by a stooped woman who looked like a wizened gnome and stood barely more than three feet tall—Lila's husband's first wife! Just inside the door, a toothless old woman with gray hair proudly held the baby boy out to us. She had attended to Lila and the newborn in the hospital—not Lila's mother, as I had thought, but the second wife.

Lila was busy washing clothes in the courtyard, where several scrawny chickens pecked pointlessly on the barren ground. She quickly assembled chairs for us as the other women doted on the baby. Now fully recovered, I could see how young and vibrant she was. What, I wondered, would her future be as a single parent—an Afghan woman with no education—when her husband and his older wives passed on? Would she be able to return to her family? Would the baby survive? So many do not in Afghanistan, where one out of every five children under the age of five succumb to a disease that would be largely preventable with access to safe water, sanitation, and adequate food.[7]

I still think about Lila and her son. And I think how thankful I am to have had an opportunity to give something to this country and its remarkable people. I feel that I was in the right place at the right time, which is a rare gift indeed.

NOTES

1. I prefer to retain the anonymity of individuals and organizations and their locations because of codes of confidentiality.

2. World Health Organization, *Maternal Mortality in 2005: Estimates Developed by WHO, UNICEF, and UNFPA* (Geneva: WHO Press, 2007). Available at http://www.who.int.offcampus.lib.washington.edu/reproductive-health/publications/maternal-mortality-2005/mme-2005.pdf.

3. P. Leidl, "Dying to Give Life: Maternal Mortality in Afghanistan," *UNDPA*, July7, 2006. Available at http://www.unfpa.org/news/news.cfm?id=822.

4. "Afghanistan," UNICEF, United Nations Population Division and United Nations Statistics Division. Available at http://www.unicef.org/infoby country/afghanistan_statistics.html.

5. Qadeem Khan Tariq,.Mine Clearance Planning Agency Report of the National Survey of the Mine Situation (Journal of Mine Action, 1994). Available at http://maic.jmu.edu/journal/5.3/features/qadeem_tariq/qadeem_tariq .htm and http://www.un.org/cyberschoolbus/banmines/schools/afgbackground .asp.

6. According to a 2009 report by the United Nations Department of Economic and Social Affairs, "The Afghanistan Criminal Code of 7 October 1976 stipulates that the performance of an abortion is a criminal offense except to save the life of the mother." Available at http://www.un.org/esa/population/publications/abortion/doc/afghan1.doc.

7. According to Worldwatch Institute, the leading killers of children under five are diarrheal disease, pneumonia, neonatal disorders, and malnutrition. Afghanistan's child mortality rate for the period of 2002–2005 was 252 per 1,000 live births, three times the rate in Southeast Asia and the third highest in the world (H. Doherty, "Child Mortality," Worldwatch Institute, September 3, 2008, available at http://www.worldwatch.org/node/5875).

CHAPTER 13

Women with Disabilities

Recollections from Across the Decades

MARY MACMAKIN

Nearly every problem Afghan women face in their lives—poverty, widow-hood, lack of livelihood, spousal abuse, lack of education, high mater-nal and infant death rates—has been reported extensively, but, to my knowledge, the challenges faced by Afghan women with physical dis-abilities and the treatment facilities available to them have not been widely reported. A 2004 countrywide National Disability Survey of Afghanistan, conducted by the United Nations to enable intelligent planning for physical rehabilitation programs, found that an average of 2.7 percent of Afghans are disabled, of which fewer than half (1.1 per-cent) are female.[1] The number of these Afghan women and girls whose injuries are caused by buried land mines, bombs, and artillery shelling since the 1979 Soviet invasion is staggering, coupled with increased disease and the challenges of surviving in the economic collapse with the fall of the Taliban in 2001.

The burden on families and the disabled women themselves are of deep concern: How can they afford treatment? Will they get better? Who will cook and keep house? Ingenuity, determination, family devotion, and courage define some of the most basic ways that women and families of the disabled cope, often in unimaginably difficult circumstances.

What follows are anecdotal accounts of my experiences with dis-abled women in Afghanistan as a United States physical therapist work-ing in Afghan clinics and homes from 1961 to 2005.[2] I begin with a brief history.

TRADITIONAL MEDICINE: AN OVERVIEW

Traditional medicine was practiced throughout Afghanistan until around 1900. Common sense and curative wisdom were passed down through generations of healers. Older women, with knowledge of herbs and healing techniques learned from their mothers and grandmothers, were called on in times of sickness. The mullahs had a share in healing practices, using *dahm,* the power of breath and the words of the Qur'an Sharif, folded into a little cloth packet worn around the neck or pinned to the shoulder seam of a child's dress or shirt. For broken bones and joints "out of place," the nearest *shikesteband* (bone setter) was sought for his skills passed down from father to son in setting fractures and reducing joint dislocations. Falling off the roof of a one-story mud brick home is a common risk for children. The shikesteband stabilized a child's wrist fracture with thin wood splints held in place by cloth soaked in egg yolk and secured with string. When dry, this was an effective method of casting.

Larger communities and towns had *hakims,* self-educated men who dosed with powders and potions from their well-guarded boxes and bags. They made the medicines themselves from roots and herbs or purchased them from Indian or Burmese traders. Today, the sources of traditional medicines, other than Afghanistan itself, are generally India and Pakistan. In the *mandayee,* the main bazaar for food staples, Sikhs preside over a colorful array of healing roots, seeds, stones, and powders kept in used kerosene tins. More expensive medicines are stored in smaller tin boxes on shelves behind the shopkeeper, who is knowledgeable about the uses of each one. These various practitioners remain the medical mainstay of rural communities and even continue to practice today in the capital city Kabul.

WESTERN MEDICINE AND THE NEW PRACTICE OF PHYSICAL THERAPY

Western medical techniques may first have been introduced by Amir Abdur Rahman (r. 1890–1900), who imported a Scottish nurse for the women of his harem. The royal family had access to travel in the West and thus experienced the efficacy of Western pills and potions and wanted the same medical care as was available in Europe and the United States. The Amir's grandson, Amanullah (r. 1919–1929) was open to new ideas and had as advisor and father-in-law Mahmud Tarzi, a highly educated and energetic man who started the first newspaper in Afghanistan and motivated Amanullah to introduce the idea of education for girls to a highly resistant population. "What man will want to marry a girl who has been to school?" cried thousands of appalled Afghan mothers.

As an example to his countrymen and particularly the women, Tarzi arranged for girls of the royal family to study nursing in Turkey. These protected young women had an unimaginably hard time under severe Turkish nursing discipline, dealing with men, bedpans, and cleaning up after sick people.

Western medical education soon followed, as young men were sent abroad to study until the 1950s, when Kabul University established its Department of Medicine, staffed and run by the French. The government also began building hospitals, open to all without charge. Women and men were kept in separate wards.

Ibnesina was a teaching hospital for interns and residents from the university medical school and treated a wide range of internal diseases and neurological and orthopedic problems. It was here I first volunteered in early 1963 as a professional physical therapist.[3] Although orthopedics as a branch of medical practice was known to the Kabul community, physical therapy was not, so I had the privilege of demonstrating what PT could—and could not—do.

Among other things, I expected to find the kinds of fragile knees and hips found in American elderly. I looked in vain. Lifestyle appeared to be the answer: in the States, elderly people are pampered and well-cared for. Elderly Afghans benefit from, among others things, walking everywhere and the fact that there are no chairs, so they must use their muscles to get up from the cotton floor mat. This keeps their bones and muscles in good shape with less chance for demineralized femurs and sacrums.

Kabul's Wazir Akbar Khan Hospital was built in the 1960s and was the country's designated orthopedic center. The Japanese government helped develop physical therapy and X-ray departments at WAKH by donating equipment and training technicians. Imamuddin Shams was the first Afghan student sent to Japan to learn physical therapy. He returned to train a core group of nurses. As a result, there was a full range of medical and surgical help, but what about braces for post-polio children,[4] special shoes for foot problems, artificial limbs for amputees, and crutches and wheelchairs?

To fill the crying need for these special appliances, the Ministry of Public Health asked the World Health Organization for help. WHO sent a Swiss orthotics and prosthetics expert from its Regional Training Center in Tehran. With funds raised by the newly established Afghan Society for the Rehabilitation of the Physically Handicapped, young Afghans were sent to Tehran to learn the art of prosthetics and orthopedic shoe-making. This completed the WAKH rehab staff. Having its own trained experts in its own center was a huge leap forward for Afghanistan.[5]

The International Afghan Mission, having built a modern and successful eye hospital called *Noor* (light) and trained men and women to staff it in the early 1970s, saw the need for professional physical therapists of both sexes to be trained according to international standards. They built and furnished a physical therapy school with foreign-trained instructors and graduated several dozen PTs to staff hospitals in Kabul but not yet in the provinces. Work in the provinces has always been shunned by Kabulis as "dangerous," too far from home, and these new PTs felt the same.

In my experience, Afghans are highly persistent and will pursue wellness wherever there is word of someone or someplace with a cure—whether at a hospital in Kabul, at a rural clinic, or from traditional healers. But thousands of people far out in the country—many seeking safety in the mountains from one warlord or another—live at barely subsistence levels with their neighbors, far from even the most basic health clinic. Coping with serious diseases and disabilities requires money and transportation. Families often ask for help from passersby, foreigners in particular. A repeated cry, "*Khoda mehraban ast*" (God is kind), reflects a faith in divine justice that sometimes does not reach far enough but helps people endure until death carries them away.

Years ago, in the northeast corner of Badakshan, a man came to talk to me and my hiking group as we rested by the trail. His daughter was sick. Would I see her? In a dark little room, on dusty old bedding, the twenty-year-old lay emaciated by rheumatoid arthritis, alive despite a damaged heart, unable to eat much of anything. Like so many of the seriously disabled in the remote areas of Afghanistan, she was far from help, sustained by her own weakening life force and the enveloping love of her parents. I felt helpless for there was nothing I could do. I prepared some gruel with flour and water and a little sugar which she gamely tried to eat; I didn't even have the money needed to carry her to a hospital in an urban center. We hiked on, but the picture of that girl in her dusty bed remains with me, thirty years later, and reminds me that the task remains to train male and female students for physical therapy in their home provinces.

THE GREAT DISASTER

In 1973, after forty years of peace and slow but steady progress under King Zahir Shah, the king's cousin Muhammad Daoud Khan staged a bloodless coup and ruled until he and his family were killed in a communist uprising five years later. Afghanistan's accomplishments proved fragile as its leadership fragmented. In 1979, after a year of misrule and further assassinations, Soviet troops and tanks invaded, bearing the slogan, "peace and progress for Afghanistan!"

So began what I label the Great Disaster. Thousands of Afghans became refugees inside and outside the country. Soon after the fighting between the Soviets and Afghan resistance forces commenced, humanitarian non-governmental organizations began setting up hospitals, rehabilitation centers, and clinics in Peshawar, Pakistan, to take care of the war wounded and disabled—the Mujahedin. The hospitals in Kabul continued to operate but under Soviet control. The Mujahedin now were the enemy and could not use these facilities.

The makers of armaments—the United States, the USSR, Sweden, and Israel, among others—apparently entered a sadistic competition to see who could create bullets to maximize flesh shredding and bone splintering. Munitions designed to rip and tear human bodies resulted in lifetime deformities. I first witnessed the results of the arms-makers' "art" in 1988, when I worked in Peshawar in hospitals for the Mujahedin. I am still haunted by those terrible wounds.

Among the NGOs then active in Peshawar, working with rehabilitation for the wounded and disabled were the International Committee of the Red Cross (ICRC), Sandy Gall's Afghanistan Appeal (SGAA),[6] the Swedish Committee for Afghanistan (SCA), Kuwait Red Crescent Society, and the Pakistan Red Crescent Society, which ran a rehabilitation center geared especially for paraplegics. With the withdrawal of Soviet forces from Afghan soil in 1989, most of these agencies shifted their rehab facilities to Kabul.

ICRC provided the most ambitious and complete care, with hostels for men and women with disabilities from distant provinces; a production center for wheelchairs, crutches, artificial legs, and other appliances; and a physical therapy department to ensure the client was able to make use of her appliance.[7] SGAA moved partially to Jalalabad in 1993; the rest of their technicians went to Kabul in 1996, the same year I founded PARSA, Physiotherapy and Rehabilitation Support for Afghanistan, a private, nonprofit NGO working directly with Afghanistan's disadvantaged people, widows, orphans, and the disabled.[8]

Because of the difficulty and expense of transportation from the provinces, ICRC and SGAA also set up orthopedic workshops and rehab centers in Mazar-i-Sharif, Faizabad, and Charikar. In Bamiyan, ICRC instituted a weekly bus service for amputees and other people with disabilities. Nevertheless, there are still villages and communities far from these centers, requiring a long, demanding journey for sick and injured people.

Physical therapy is not the only treatment. In the 1990s, the Swedish Committee introduced a system that had been developed and perfected in Vietnam for training community "rehabilitation workers" to help disabled people in their own communities. The system simplified diagnosis by easily observable signs and encouraged the workers to create crutches, splints, and other devices. Each community had a rehabilitation committee that met regularly, cheered the disabled person to do his or her exercises, and oversaw the work of the rehabilitation workers.

ENCOUNTERS WITH COMMON DISABILITIES

A housewife sent word that she was "sick" to the SCA clinic in Taloqan where I worked and taught from 1992 to 1994. My student PT, Soraya, and I went to her home and found her doing the weekly wash, sitting outside on a tiny stool surrounded by tubs, buckets, a little portable charcoal samovar for boiling water, piles of dirty clothes on one side and the washed ones on the other.

This woman told us her hands were painful. She could not scrub and wring as she wanted. I told her that moving and working the arthritic limbs were among the treatments for arthritis, along with heat and aspirin. Soraya sided with her, however, letting the pain determine how much scrubbing she could do. I found frequently that pain was the guide. Mothers would not insist on treatment for their children if the child cried. "No pain, no gain," the Western therapist's mantra, has no place in traditional mothering, so the pain is allowed to be in charge.

A few girls have been brought to the PARSA clinic with varying degrees of disabling arthritis and some have regained functional use of their hands and arms, depending on how much they trusted the PT and how determined they were. Parents, feeling the pain vicariously in their children, were not much help in the exercises.

The rehab workers who had been trained at the Swedish Committee clinic during my time in Taloqan took me around the countryside to see disabled people they had located and were working with. At one compound we were greeted at the gate by Alida, a girl of about fourteen with rather marked spastic cerebral palsy, who nevertheless had developed a unique way to move around, almost flinging herself forward, swiftly. All the family was away for a few hours and Alida was happy to be the *chowkidar* (doorkeeper). She seemed unconcerned about her unusual gait and condition, showing the natural self-esteem of many Afghans, so I wasn't surprised when she refused treatment at the SCA clinic. The spasticity of cerebral palsy can be reduced and the child's potential for education assessed. But Alida was happy with her family and her life in her own compound and knew she would be teased in another environment.

In Kabul, in 1998, I visited the tiny, neat home of a hairdresser in a suburban hillside community. A very small, bright-eyed, fifteen-year-old girl lay on a cotton mattress in the living room and greeted me with a big smile. Her hair was brushed into two big curls tied with red and blue ribbons. Her mother looked proudly at her daughter, bed-bound with cerebral palsy, and explained that she didn't have the money for a taxi to take her to the physical therapy department of the hospital. The mother was taking excellent care of her daughter, but her daughter would have benefited from speech therapy, as well as a chair and tray table to help her sit up to eat and see people. Unfortunately, Kabul did not have any speech therapists; however, we ordered a PT to come to the house to work with the girl and her mother.

Poverty has forced Afghans to be thrifty. Fuel is costly, therefore in winter the household moves into one room for eating, living, and sleeping. In the countryside, a low, quilt-covered table, a *sandali*, is set up in the middle of the usually small living room, where the whole family sits with the edge of the quilt pulled up to their shoulders and long cushions at everyone's back. A brazier under the table is filled with coals, keeping everyone's lower half warm and cozy. The family gossips, exchanges news, plays word games, eats supper, and drinks tea until it is time to sleep.

My happy memories of these intimate family moments are marred by the children with severe burns on their feet and legs from coming into contact with the burning brazier. During a bomb attack on her village, one terrified mother held her baby under the sandali to escape the bombs, mistaking the baby's screams for fear of the bombs rather than the pain of a burning foot, which was eventually lost.

I once watched a twelve-year-old boy playing soccer on one normal foot and on the other leg he bore his weight on only the bottom point of his tibia. The foot was badly burned under the sandali when he was a baby. He refused to come to the clinic for an artificial foot having earlier experienced painful doctoring, and his father did not insist.

The cruelest aspect of war is the damage done to noncombatants. A neighbor searched the garden where her son had been when a missile struck, but she could not find even a finger of her child to bury. One of my staff lost her two brothers to a random missile as they waited to cross the street. No one in Afghanistan is immune from missiles coming from the air, mines lodged in the ground, or stray bullets from trigger-happy Mujahedin, Taliban, or foreign troops. If not killed outright, the victim might receive a head injury, which means neuromuscular disabilities, similar to a stroke. Or the injury might result in an amputation.

A twenty-one-year-old "daughter of the house," with head injuries from a bomb blast, lives with her parents in a tiny place in one of Kabul's *zurabad* hillside settlements—the crowded mud brick homes of poor folk seeking refuge in the city. Being severely disabled, spastic, and bedridden, this daughter needed total care for bathing, toileting, and dressing by her parents who take care of her as best they can. We suggested she attend literacy classes at a nearby center for people with disabilities and the jobless. We would pay for a taxi. She agreed at first, but then she declined, explaining that carrying her up and down the narrow stairway was too much for her parents to manage. (Unspoken but always present is the unmarried Afghan woman's fear of being seen by unrelated males and the difficulty of toileting.)

The Soviets targeted children with small bombs resembling toys dropped from warplanes. The Ministry of Education and several NGOs had extensive education campaigns to warn children not to touch these tempting objects, but many never heard the warnings. Shepherds, boys and girls, tending their flocks in mountains were most vulnerable. In 1995, at the local hospital in Charikar, a large town north of Kabul, a doctor told me an average of two shepherds a week were brought in with mine injuries, usually in the foot and leg, requiring amputation.

A university graduate was severely injured in a rocket attack, losing her right leg at the hip and her right arm at the shoulder. She was hired by Oxfam International in Kabul, where she could sit in a wheelchair to do her work. I watched her slowly, gamely climb the stairs to her office managing her right leg prosthesis. Normally, disabled women have no chance of marriage and she had no hopes of it, until another Oxfam employee, taken by her beauty and courage, proposed. I saw her a year later at her home, radiant with a baby and a servant girl to help with the chores—one of the fortunate few.

And there is Rahima, a friend from PARSA's early days, who came to the door with her teenage daughters and asked for help. Her flail arm was only one tragedy that happened to her on the day a stray bomb from an abortive coup by an Air Force general destroyed her home and killed her husband and his brother in 1994. (My PT student in Taloqan was widowed during that same brief revolt). The bomb rocked the neighborhood. People ran to help. Rahima called from under the rubble. People rushed to find her. Frantically tossing mud bricks and dirt aside, they saw her left hand and began pulling it. She was dragged from the rubble, thankful for her life, but the nerves in her shoulder and arm were ruptured, leaving the arm flail except for the curling tips of her fingers. A skilled dressmaker, she continued to sew with some help to thread needles, but she and her daughters were homeless nomads.

Eventually, one daughter became my deputy at PARSA and the family could rent an apartment. Rahima became a prolific doll maker and earned a modest income from her Taliban dolls. She is so cheerful, I love to visit her. She is typical of many Afghan women with disabilities I have known: not letting her disability get in the way of her life, her happiness with her family and grandchildren. Whining and victimhood are rarely met with among poorer Afghans—there is no tolerance, no room for them.

COPING AND RESOURCEFULNESS

Habiba, a thirty-five-year-old housewife living in a small farming community near Taloqan, lost her right leg above the knee and was given a prosthesis made by the SCA Orthopedic Workshop. When I visited her, the leg was standing in a corner of her kitchen. She told me that although she appreciated it, the leg was not practical for the frequent sitting and standing transfers she had to make in her daily housework. She was managing well by using a crutch and her one leg.

Afghans live, eat, sleep, wash, and pray at floor level. Homes are not necessarily accessible to disabled women. There is usually no furniture. Mattresses are slept on, then folded in the morning and stored in corners or in the hall, where they will not get dirty until evening and dinner. When a guest comes, a mattress is retrieved and spread.

The floor covering—a well-worn carpet, felt rug, or a tarp in the poorest of homes—is swept every day so it is clean for sitting, but the disabled woman has to stand each time she needs to go to the kitchen or privy. Family members must help with these transfers. Making bread requires strong arms and good balance as the cook slaps the long, flat dough against the inside of the bread oven. This job can be delegated to the eldest daughter, the sister, or an auntie. But the disabled woman may need assistance in bathing, which takes place in a concrete-floored room with a bucket or ewer of warm water, and in toileting outside the mud brick home. Her clothing consists of a long-sleeved dress that hangs below the knees, several layers of underclothing and baggy pants, so dressing and undressing is awkward, especially when using a squat toilet. There is nearly always someone to help. To live alone is practically unheard of, particularly in the country.

Afghan housewives also suffer from a painful elbow apparently caused by forceful scrubbing and wringing of clothing. The musculature is strenuously and continuously overworked and develops symptoms similar to tennis elbow. The elbows can respond well to PT treatment, but many housewives don't consider the pain serious enough to ask someone else to do the washing for the two or three weeks' vacation the elbow requires. Nevertheless, husbands and children often help on laundry day by carrying buckets of water from the well. (Disk protrusions are also common, afflicting women, men, and children, and usually caused by 80- to 120-pound sacks of rice or flour, staples of the Afghan diet, which arrive at the family storeroom on someone's bent back.)

Desperation can be the mother of invention and like many people in impoverished situations, Afghans find ingenious methods to make things work. A friend whose baby was born with spastic CP used her common sense to devise a treatment to overcome the flexion spasticity of the arms and legs by tying them in an extended position with soft flannel strips to the corners of his crib while the baby lay on his back. This gentle, gradual treatment was working and the baby's arms and legs were nearly normal.

The eighteen-year-old sister of a commander, unable to stand due to severe spasticity of both legs, was carried into the SCA clinic in Taloqan. Her X-rays revealed two opposite lateral bends in her spine, forming a perfect "S" deformity from tuberculosis of the spine, with subsequent pressure on peripheral nerves. She needed traction to straighten out her spine, which could be a painful process. She had a strong, devoted mother, who understood the need for treatment, and a brother whose word was law!

A metal cot was found, and a big piece of plywood laid on it to keep the cotton mattress flat. A flannel-covered canvas belt was secured around her upper chest under her arms and attached with a rope to the head of the cot. Traction was then applied by a second flannel-covered canvas belt fitted around her hips from which a rope passed over the end of the cot to a ten-pound rock, producing continuous traction. The only relief she had was when she got up for the toilet. It was a primitive arrangement and painful, but her mother and brother kept her in traction until the leg spasms ceased. I visited a month or so later and was met in the garden by a young woman I didn't recognize at first, now cured by homemade traction.

For the future, disabled Afghan women can expect better care from Afghan PTs, if the recommendations made recently by a British PT and her two colleagues are followed up.[9] The researchers found that, generally, the therapists they studied worked in isolation with little chance to upgrade their skills; more specifically, they recommended the therapists use active rather than passive techniques and use their own reasoning ability to determine better treatment. Techniques for rehabilitation of the disabled will gradually seep into community consciousness as people see them used successfully by the rehab workers and PTs in their communities and as they become part of the traditional knowledge.

Afghan women used to regard disease or a disability as a curse, or Fate, or destiny carved out for her before she was born that she must endure. Most women nowadays, it seems, have transferred their trust to Western medicine's little white, yellow, or mauve pill, or better, an injection. However, I have found this trust is often brief: if the pill doesn't work by the next day, it is rejected and stored away. A friend with frequent aches and pains had a large plastic shopping bag filled with plastic pill bottles and paper squills of the West's best, rejected, and unused but never thrown away.[10]

It is a pleasure to be with Afghan women, with or without disabilities. They are skilled at conversation and at including others in their emotional circles. There is an intimacy that encourages the telling of troubles or gossip or tales from the past. They love visitors; socializing is life and talking a kind of life blood. The visitor brings new stories and never arrives at an inconvenient time. Each guest is received separately and led into a different room, where another family member sits with them, keeps them company, serves them tea. The guest is quickly enclosed in a warm embrace of family, traditional courtesy, lively interest, and undivided attention. Disability disappears and sociability takes over.

I have experienced hard times, pain, hunger, and rejection only vicariously through the stories of Afghan women and their families. I admire their inner resources, their powerful core being, and their spiritual energy, which support and enrich them at all levels of their lives with the certainty of solid traditions and unquestioned and profound belief in Allah and his powers.

NOTES

1. Jean-François Trani, "The National Disability Survey in Afghanistan" (paper presented at United Nations Economic and Social Commission for Asia and the Pacific: Fourth Workshop for Improving Disability Statistics and Management, Bangkok, June 20–22, 2006). Available in its entirety at http://www .unescap.org/stat/meet/widsm4/session4_NDSA_Handicap_Inst.pdf.

2. I changed some of the names to respect the women's anonymity. I apologize for any inaccuracies in time and place.

3. As a volunteer, I joined the CARE-Medico team to do PT follow-up on the patients treated by the orthopedic surgeon. I covered the hospital orthopedic ward and got to know the women patients and staff as my Dari language skills improved.

4. Many Afghan children were visited during the 1950s and 1960s with the scourge of poliomyelitis, as American children had been until the discovery of the Salk vaccine in 1949.

5. WHO later established the prosthetics and orthopedics workshop in a separate building from the hospital, where it was active for about twenty years.

6. Sandy Gall, a British journalist and TV anchor, saw firsthand the need for artificial legs for the hundreds of Mujahedin who had lost one or more limbs in the fighting. He, with his wife Eleanor and daughter Fiona, a physiotherapist, first opened and operated an orthopedic workshop in Peshawar in 1986.

7. The International Committee of the Red Cross Rehab Center was said to be the biggest and most complete in all Asia.

8. In 2005, I turned over my role as executive director of PARSA to Marnie Gustavson. For more about the organization, see http://www.afghanistan-parsa .org/.

9. J. Wickford, J. Hultberg, and S. Rosberg, "Physiotherapy in Afghanistan—Needs and Challenges for Development," *Disability and Rehabilitation* 30, no. 4 (2008): 305–313.

10. One of the unintended functions of the doctors' waiting room is to allow unrelated women to meet. Family histories are exchanged, illnesses reviewed, and opinions on medicines discussed. Since the wars, which made people far less trusting, women aren't so open with their family affairs.

CHAPTER 14

A Question of Access

Women and Food Security

ELIZABETH STITES

This is probably not the first chapter a reader will flip to in her desire to learn more about the experiences of women in Afghanistan. Most people think of food security, when they think of it at all, as either a dry discussion of nutritional measures and market price indices or an apparently obvious cut-and-dried analysis—either you have enough food or you do not. The linkages between women and food security also may at first appear obvious: women are often the primary cooks and main caregivers in a household, and evidence shows that women in many contexts dedicate a higher portion of any earnings to food purchases than do their male counterparts. As mothers, women often decrease their own food intake to ensure that there is enough food for their families in periods of food shortage.

Several key questions are broadly examined here: What did food security look like in Afghanistan in the past, how did this change since the fall of the Taliban, and what is the situation today? If we know what it takes to be food-secure, and we know a fair amount about women in Afghanistan, how do we understand the challenges they face in their efforts to ensure food security for themselves and their families? Finally, how has the role of the international community changed since 9/11 in mitigating food insecurity in times of hardship?

UNDERSTANDING FOOD SECURITY

Exact definitions of food security vary, but the most widely accepted include the notion that all people at all times have access to sufficient nutritious food to maintain active, healthy lives. Food security is built on three main aspects—food availability, food access, and food utilization. Food availability assumes sufficient quantities of food are available on a regular basis. Food access requires enough resources to be able to obtain the quantity of food needed. Food utilization includes having the knowledge, resources (such as fuel and water), and health to make use of the food that is available and accessible. These aspects must exist simultaneously in order for food security to exist. Food insecurity can thus be thought of as a lack of sufficient food, an inability to access sufficient food, or the failure to properly use available food.

We often think of hunger simply as "not enough food," but questions of access and utilization are often just as or more important. For instance, a household may be able to access food (through purchase, production, or assistance) but not have firewood, pots, or water to prepare it. Similarly, a household might not have cash to purchase food or might lack able-bodied labor or rights of access to fields where food is growing. Problems with food access are the most common underlying factors in food insecurity in wealthier nations, as well as in many parts of the developing world.

Afghanistan is an extremely diverse country, and the experiences of Afghan women are equally varied. A chapter of this length cannot offer an adequate discussion of the differences between ethnic groups, religions, wealth groups, and regions, but all these factors influence the relationship between women and food security. This chapter talks primarily about rural women. In painting a broad-brush overview, we miss a great deal of nuance, but factors of variation are noted where possible.

PRE-2001

The rural sector in Afghanistan was largely neglected by the central government throughout the twentieth century, although it was home to the vast majority of the population. Social services and development were focused almost entirely in urban areas. To illustrate, in 1959, the capital Kabul was home to only 1.8 percent of the population but had 74 percent of the country's secondary school students.[1] Prior to the

Soviet era (1978–1989), the central government was highly dependent on external revenues and did not seek to survey, tax, or administer the rural portions of the country. As a result, little statistical information emerged from the countryside.[2] The war between the Soviet-backed government and the United States-supported Mujahedin forces brought massive destruction to the rural sector, with an estimated two-thirds of villages bombed and irrigation and other rural infrastructure and assets destroyed.[3] Up to a third of the rural population was displaced and agricultural production fell to an estimated 45 percent of what it was in the late 1970s.[4] Although conditions in rural areas were harsh in this period, rural communities continued to rely on the local production systems and did not see a catastrophic collapse.

Many Afghans returned to their homes and began to rebuild following the withdrawal of the Soviets in 1989. Agricultural production began to recover after 1992, and by 1997 Afghanistan was meeting an estimated 70 percent of its own food needs.[5] Yields of wheat were higher than in the previous two decades, even against the backdrop of the extensive political upheaval in the 1990s. However, a severe drought that lasted four years began in 1998 and undermined much of the rural recovery.[6] Even so, after two decades of conflict and threats to subsistence survival, the Afghan rural sector and its population had established themselves as highly resilient.

2001–2008

International actors flooded the country after the defeat of the Taliban by coalition forces in the wake of the 9/11 attacks, Most did not recognize— or did not have the time to recognize—the resilience of the rural economy. The standard assumption was that agriculture had either been stagnant or had regressed since the 1970s.[7] This attitude was in line with the "crisis narrative" that emerged in response to the prolonged drought, the Taliban regime (and subsequent collapse), and the lack of data on the actual situation in rural areas.[8]

The situation in rural Afghanistan was not as bad as outside observers working from their own experience and limited assessment data predicted. Afghanistan is highly integrated into a vibrant regional grain market, and the drought was less severe in other parts of Central Asia. Private sector cross-border trade continued into grain-deficit areas. The regional grain markets are now thought to have been the most important source of wheat during the drought years. Furthermore, the decades of war had created of system of human migration well adapted to coping with hardship. Many families remained directly linked to the regional economy through labor migration and the resulting inflow of remittances.[9]

One likely factor in this exaggerated interpretation of the situation was the lack of Central Asian experience of relief workers and organizations. Many of the new arrivals were accustomed to the conditions of the Sahel and sub-Saharan Africa, where markets are less integrated and cross-border social networks less robust. In these locations, the set of conditions in Afghanistan in 2001–2002 would probably have led to much more severe repercussions.

The drought and simultaneous political upheaval did not produce a humanitarian crisis on the order of magnitude that was expected, but the situation in areas of the country was still dire. This is partially due to the fact that the regional grain markets are better linked than internal ones—in other words, grain comes into the country from Iran, Pakistan, and the former Soviet states to the north, but grain does not move as well *within* Afghanistan. Relatively few trade links exist between areas with frequent surplus, such as the north, and areas that commonly experience deficits, such as the central western highlands.[10] This is due to insecurity on the roads, poor winter weather, and a dietary preference for foreign-milled wheat flour.

Data on rural areas from sporadic assessments conducted in the Taliban years did exist when the international aid presence began to ramp up in 2001 and 2002. Communication about these sources of data was lacking, however, and access to these reports was sometimes difficult. The lack of pre-drought baseline data and the political imperative stating that action had to be taken quickly meant that few organizations sought to understand the nature of the rural economy pre-9/11 or the causes and extent of the current food security situation.[11]

Lack of data continued to be a problem once the post-9/11 relief operations were underway. The World Food Programme (WFP), for instance, initially delivered food only in areas where its implementing partners were operational and where assessments were conducted. In the 2001 and 2003 assessment exercises some areas were inaccessible due to insecurity. Some of these locations—such as several districts in Zabul Province in southern Afghanistan—were also particularly hard hit by drought and were thought to be experiencing severe food insecurity.[12] WFP later addressed this problem in Zabul and other areas by using local enumerators and working through local authorities, but this example illustrates the problematic nexus between security, access, and food security for local populations.

The four-year drought ended in 2002, and 2003 saw a record harvest.[13] Reduced rainfall in 2004 and 2006 brought decreased wheat production, but output increased again in 2007. Regardless of these fluctuations, the countrywide average shows little change in own-production (food produced within a household) as a proportion of food access from 2005 to 2008, with the rate remaining at approximately 20–25 percent. Although the overall food output has changed from one year to the next, households still rely on what they can grow for approximately a quarter of their food needs.[14]

TODAY

Based on the picture described above, the rural economy and agrarian sector in Afghanistan are relatively resilient, even in the face of conflict and drought. This does not mean, however, that all people have adequate food or can be classified as food-secure. Differences by region and household can be pronounced, as can rates of change (improvements or declines) in a specific region.

Data compiled by the Afghan Ministry of Rural Rehabilitation and Development (MRRD) and WFP released in May 2008 show that 35 percent of Afghan households were not able to meet their daily kilocalorie requirements. This rate was 5 percent higher than in 2005. In addition, 46 percent of households have both very poor dietary diversity and very poor food consumption. This figure has increased since 2005 except in the southwest, where there was significant improvement, and the east, where there was very slight improvement. The worst-off areas are the west central, south, and north, and each of these areas has seen significant declines since 2005. The report illustrates the broad range of people affected by food insecurity in this period: "[D]ispersed rain and snow during the 2007–08 crop season, high food prices, and very poor cereal supplies have contributed to increased risk of food insecurity and malnutrition, including amongst sedentary farmers, nomads, casual laborers and civil servants, especially teachers, who have little or no direct access to food."[15]

Additional data helps illustrate some reasons behind these high rates of food insecurity. Households dedicate a large portion of their monthly expenditures to food. For instance, in the north of the country, households report that food makes up 85 percent of their expenditures, and the rate hovers around 75–80 percent in the rest of the country. MRRD and WFP have been tracking these figures for several years, and the 2008 numbers were significantly worse than the 2006 numbers.[16] For comparative purposes, the percentage of disposable personal income that American households spend on food (combined measure of money spent on food eaten inside and outside the home) has fallen steadily since the late 1920s, when households were spending an average of 24 percent of income on food. In 2008, average spending on food by American households was just 9.6 percent of total disposable income.[17]

Afghan households are spending high amounts on food for several reasons. For one, food prices have increased dramatically in the past few years, with the price of wheat (the staple crop) up by 160 percent between May 2007 and May 2008. (The price of wheat increased 60 percent just between January and May 2008.) This price increase was due in part to policies in the main wheat exporting countries in the region. Pakistan, Kazakhstan, and Iran all implemented export tariffs and other policies in an attempt to maintain food stocks at home in the face of global price increases. Afghanistan is an overall food-deficit country and imports wheat and wheat flour from these neighboring states. Thus local prices reflect regional food policies.[18]

At the same time that food prices have risen, households have experienced a decline in access to food through their own production in the east, north, and central parts of the country. This means that households are getting less of their food from their fields or gardens. Due to slight increases in other areas, however, the countrywide average shows very little change in own-production as a portion of food access from 2005 to 2008, with a consistent rate of about 20–25 percent.[19]

WFP's 2009 market price index shows a substantial decrease in prices from spring 2008, but prices of wheat were still almost 50 percent higher than in April 2007 and were still very high compared to a normal year. Discrepancies between the Afghan market and the international and regional markets are illustrative of the burden on local consumers: the Afghan wheat price in April 2009 was 65 percent higher than the international prices, 56 percent higher than the price in Delhi, India, and 18 percent higher than the price in Karachi, Pakistan. The positive news for local consumers is that their labor was worth more in terms of wheat in 2009 than in 2008, due to a 5.6 percent average increase in terms of trade between wheat and labor. In other words, the same amount of labor could buy 5.6 percent more food in 2009 than a year earlier.[20]

Although food prices dropped in 2009, allowing Afghan households to have an easier time putting food on their tables, food insecurity still affects many households. Droughts, insecurity (which influences local prices and internal trade), and price hikes are commonly understood as "shocks." In these examples they are external and beyond the control of people seeking to acquire food. Families must therefore find ways to manage and respond to these shocks to guarantee consistent consumption over time.

COPING WITH FOOD INSECURITY

Households engage in a range of strategies to smooth consumption and manage lean periods. Common tactics include reducing food quantity and quality, reducing discretionary spending, and purchasing on credit.[21]

Migration of a family member for better economic opportunity is common, and many rural households have one or more members living in an urban area or in another country and earning wages. In some ways, poorer households are better able to cope with drought-induced hardship and food insecurity than wealthier ones, as poor households have a long history of movement to ensure economic subsistence.[22] There is no guarantee, however, that the family members who remain behind will be better off, and a number of households in a study in 2003 reported that they were worse off following the departure of their (almost always male) relative.[23] The fate of the household depends on the economic situation, local conditions and opportunities in their area, and whether the migrating member is able to send remittances.

Households also cope with food insecurity by diversifying their livelihood strategies. For example, a household that once survived primarily on farming may expand its activities to include work on other farms, weaving, casual labor for wages in towns, trade, and so forth. Multiple studies have shown that many people who live in rural areas are not strictly engaged in agriculture, and many do not work the land at all.[24] Many of these households are landless and already engaged in diversified livelihood activities to get by. Poor households—more apt to be landless—are likely to diversify their livelihoods as a coping strategy to meet basic needs including food, whereas wealthier households are more likely to diversify their livelihood base to take advantage of varied opportunities to increase accumulation.[25]

A study by Klijn and Pain of the Afghanistan Research and Evaluation Unit shows that the use of informal credit is widespread in Afghanistan and is particularly important in enabling households to smooth consumption. People borrow in cash or food and pay their debts through a variety of means, including labor, and often over unspecified and extended time periods. In the three villages sampled, researchers found that households in all wealth groups—ranging from those that experienced occasional shocks to those who could not make ends meet on a regular basis—took on debt for the purpose of consumption smoothing. Potential borrowers often approached relatives and neighbors first and turned to shopkeepers to cover more substantial needs or when their neighbors were unwilling or unable to help. Importantly, even poor households expressed a high level of confidence that they would be able to access credit.[26]

WOMEN AND FOOD SECURITY

Many rural households throughout Afghanistan experience food insecurity to varying degrees. Overall levels would likely be worse in the absence of a resilient rural economy, vibrant private-sector trade with neighboring states, and the widespread use of household-level coping strategies, including economic migration of select individuals, diversification, and accessing informal credit.

Very little of the available data, however, are disaggregated by gender or examine the specific roles and experiences of women, due to a variety of reasons, including the sensitivity of accessing women in rural areas and the prevalence of relatively small or specific studies as a function of the effects of insecurity on the ability to conduct independent research. These small data sets often do not allow for adequate numbers to disaggregate by gender. WFP has the capacity to gather large data sets, but insecurity hampers data collection in many areas and their analysis does not break out the experiences of female-headed households on all indicators.

We can best understand women's experiences of food security by taking what we know about food and analyzing this through a gender lens based on what we know about women. Most women in Afghanistan are in households headed by male relatives—fathers, husbands, brothers, or uncles. Strong cultural and social expectations upon men in Afghanistan mean that most take their roles as the primary providers for their families extremely seriously.[27] The specific experiences of women in these households are interesting, but relatively little data exist on their food security situation, as food security assessments usually take place at the household level. I therefore focus on female-headed households as a specific subset of women.

Female-headed households may be led by widows, divorcees, or women abandoned by their husbands. Many female-headed households are composed of women whose husbands have out-migrated for labor or other economic opportunities. Some may be better off when the husbands are able to send home remittances, but one should not assume this to be the case.

The 2004 National Risk and Vulnerability Assessment conducted by WFP found that female-headed households had poverty rates of more than 70 percent. The poverty rates of male-headed households, in contrast, were much closer to the overall rural poverty rate of 53 percent.[28] Rural Afghan women are involved in production and income-generating activities that contribute to overall household income, but very few have individual ownership of resources such as land and livestock and decision-making control over the finances they bring in.[29] Lack of ownership of and control over resources means that women's income-generating opportunities are fewer than those of men. Grace and Pain explain that these inequities in access to resources "are very real barriers for many rural women, especially those who are financially responsible for their households and who have few income-generating options sufficient to support a family. It is these structural inequities that make some female-headed households particularly vulnerable to poverty."[30]

As shown earlier, own-production accounts for an average of 20–25 percent of food access for Afghan households. Without secure rights to land and livestock, female-headed households have difficulty meeting this portion of their food needs. As discussed elsewhere in this volume, wives and daughters have the right to inherit land based on both Afghan civil law and Shari'a religious law. In reality, however, very few women, especially daughters, inherit as they are meant to, and they often cede their rights in land to their brothers. Widows are more likely to receive land from their deceased husbands, but often they transfer this land to their sons.[31]

Women from female-headed households who do have rights to agricultural land may face obstacles in physically accessing their land due to constraints on female mobility. Restrictions on mobility for women differ greatly based on region, ethnicity, religion, and age. Grace found that settlement size was also a factor—in a small community where people knew and trusted each other, women had greater mobility than they did in more populated areas.[32] Women who cannot access their land must rely on sons or other male relatives or hire casual labor, which is unaffordable for many poor households.

Purchased food makes up the bulk of food needs for most households. To be able to buy food, a household must be able to physically access a food market and must have cash or receive credit. A study conducted by Tufts University in five provinces in 2003 shows that the majority of women reported no access to markets, with a low of 75 percent of women unable to access markets in rural Kabul Province to a high of 99 percent unable to access markets in Badghis Province (regardless of marital or social status). Restrictions were greatest on women in their reproductive years and somewhat more relaxed for older women. Widows of child-producing age faced the greatest difficulties in accessing markets, and female-headed households reported sending a young child to market or paying someone to go to the market on their behalf.[33] Even if they can get to the market, in person or otherwise, female-headed households often face extreme poverty after losing the male breadwinner.[34]

Households use a range of coping strategies to smooth consumption or meet basic needs in times of hardship. Female-headed households face difficulty employing many of these strategies. Out-migration for labor is clearly difficult based on restrictions on female mobility, and a widow with only young children needs her sons to stay at home to serve as her male emissaries and escorts in the outside world. Grace's research in three villages found that some widows and poor women were able to get jobs as casual laborers on other people's land, but constraints on this varied substantially from one area to the next.[35] Diversification into a range of livelihood strategies is a common way to cope with shortages, but female-headed households, especially those with small children, are unlikely to have the skills and demographic composition to make this option viable.[36]

Women are usually unable to access the informal credit that male-headed households use to meet basic needs or cover unexpected costs. Data from the 2003 Tufts study showed that 64–97 percent of rural women in Badghis, Herat, Kabul, Kandahar, and Nangarhar provinces reported being unable to access credit from either traders or relatives.[37] This was due to a variety of factors, including traditional views on providing credit to women, the high risk in lending to people without a stable source of income, and women's general lack of social capital in comparison with men, resulting in a more circumscribed network of contacts that might be in a position to provide a loan. Of interest are the exceptions to the norm. Women who were able to access credit explained that they had first established good relations with the shopkeeper, thereby building up their social capital. Not surprisingly, women who lived farther from the market centers and had little to no interaction with shopkeepers were generally less likely to be able to access credit.[38]

Although women have problems accessing credit to the same extent as men, research by Klijn and Pain shows that the poorest households often receive "assistance"—that is, a gift instead of a loan—instead of credit. Giving to the poor is central to Islam, and widows are often recipients of this practice. Some of these households only take credit when they are not receiving adequate assistance from other community members or relatives. Because widows and female-headed households are seen as more vulnerable, they are more likely to receive charity from others and thus possibly less likely to need credit to meet their food needs.[39]

An aspect of the informal credit system with disproportionate impacts for women is the use of brides and bridewealth to repay debt. For poor families, this debt is incurred most often to cover basic necessities, including food. Families with daughters expect to receive bridewealth when their daughters marry, and the expectation of this eventual windfall acts as a guarantee against lines of credit.[40] In some instances, however, the daughter herself will be promised as repayment on the loan; in other instances, girls will be married at a very young age in order to pay off loans or prevent the need to go into further debt. The practice of marrying off very young girls happens in both female- and male-headed households and is usually a last resort when families are in dire straits.[41]

Some coping strategies are largely female-specific, such as begging. Begging is especially common for widows.[42] Once considered shameful, begging by women increased under the Taliban as women were shut out of economic opportunities. Today begging has become extremely common in Kabul and other Afghan cities, with large numbers of *burqa*-clad women begging outside government offices and international agencies. Child beggars are also common. Men do beg in some areas, but their numbers are significantly lower.

INSECURITY

Revisiting the initial discussion on the underlying aspects of food security, it is apparent that food access in Afghanistan is particularly gendered. Men and women have different constraints that determine how they are able to access food. (Different ethnicities, wealth groups, and generations also experience differences in access, but this is beyond the scope of this chapter.) I have already examined how mobility and access to markets differs for men and women and how this affects food security. But it is important to also consider the links between insecurity and access to food.

Conflict in Afghanistan increased significantly in 2007 and 2008 from already high levels. The United Nations Assistance Mission in Afghanistan classifies the various armed groups into "pro-government forces" (including the Afghan national security forces, the International Security Assistance Force and U.S. forces) and "anti-government elements" (including the Taliban and other armed militia groups). According to the January 2009 report by UNAMA's Human Rights Unit, civilian casualties rose by almost 40 percent from 2007 to 2008. The recent intensification in conflict has brought with it a corresponding rise in civilian casualties and a significant erosion of humanitarian space. In addition to fatalities as a direct result of armed hostilities, civilians have suffered injury, loss of livelihood, displacement, and destruction of property, as well as disruption of access to education, health care, and other essential services.[43]

The expansion of operations by pro-government forces, including air strikes on suspected militant targets, has caused substantial increase in civilian casualties.[44] However, the indiscriminate attacks by the anti-government elements on civilian targets and civilian infrastructure are likely to have had a greater impact upon daily life and the effort to fulfill basic needs. According to UNAMA, attacks by these groups have been part of a widespread campaign of intimidation aimed at instilling fear and terror. Assassinations have been used to terrorize wide portions of the population. Women and children, even when they are not the intended targets, have often been subjected to violence.[45] Middle-class Afghans and their children have been at particular risk of kidnapping for ransom, and many of those who are able to do so have left the country.[46] The nature of this insecurity and the constant threat of violence have profound implications for food access. Traders risk attack on insecure roads and adjust food prices and trade routes accordingly, and civilians fear going to markets in areas prone to violence.

HUMANITARIAN RESPONSE

International donors assisted Afghan refugees living in Pakistan and elsewhere throughout the 1980s, and non-governmental organizations began conducting cross-border activities into Mujahedin-held areas of Afghanistan. The World Food Programme and other UN agencies started work in Afghanistan in the late 1980s, prior to the official end of the Soviet war, and negotiated a formal "humanitarian consensus" with all parties to the conflict.[47] They managed to continue their programs throughout the Taliban period. Antonio Donini, director of the United Nations Office for the Coordination of Humanitarian Affairs in Afghanistan from 1999 to 2002, explains the nature of aid throughout the 1980s and 1990s: "Humanitarian action remained a constant during this period, although its ability to provide assistance and protection to those in need—whose numbers have ranged from 3 million to over 10 million—has ebbed and flowed according to the vagaries of conflict, external intervention, and the international community's fickle attention span."[48]

International agencies gradually built their capacity to provide assistance in the 1980s and 1990s and, in particular, the ability to maintain a neutral and principled stance that allowed access to those in need, regardless of the politics of a given area. This proven neutrality created the humanitarian space required to deliver assistance under the Taliban regime.

The extent of humanitarian space and the associated ability to deliver assistance has changed dramatically in the post-9/11 era.[49] According to Donini's analysis, based on research conducted between 2005 and early 2009, the international community's decision to declare Afghanistan a "post-conflict" situation after the fall of the Taliban has had profound repercussions on the way humanitarian assistance is both perceived and delivered. The separate Office for Coordination of Humanitarian Assistance that had existed since 1988 was disbanded and its functions subsumed into the integrated political UN mission, UNAMA. (There was no humanitarian unit within UNAMA until 2007, and the OCHA office only became a separate entity at the end of that year.) As a political mission, UNAMA has been closely aligned with the U.S.-backed Karzai government, and all actors—from potential beneficiaries to armed groups—see the UN as such. The international humanitarian enterprise has not only taken sides in an ongoing conflict, but the agencies and actors have embedded themselves with one of the belligerents. This makes neutrality impossible and severely compromises the ability of aid agencies to deliver assistance.

Humanitarian capacity has suffered alongside humanitarian neutrality. There has been no common point for information collection and analysis, no adequate logistics capacity, and no coordination of air services, convoys, or customs and tax agreements. Furthermore, because in 2009, Afghanistan was still not classified as a conflict situation, there are few international NGOs in the country with extensive humanitarian experience or a specific humanitarian mandate. NGOs face much pressure from donors to work with the Provincial Reconstruction Teams, civil-military teams under NATO purportedly bringing assistance, including reconstruction and humanitarian relief, to areas alongside political and military agendas. These joint operations themselves have greatly blurred the lines around independent and neutral humanitarian operations, but NGOs are often constrained due to lack of alternatives and a highly insecure operating environment.

The intensification of conflict and the alignment of the UN and NGO community with one of the belligerents to the conflict have greatly increased the risks to agency staff. Aid agency employees are increasingly targeted for attack by anti-government forces, as are civilians who are suspected of any links to an aid agency. UNAMA and the Afghan Independent Human Rights Commission have documented cases in which a victim was threatened or beaten for accepting WFP food aid.[50] Entire portions of the country are essentially off limits to aid agencies and their partners, and it is impossible to have adequate analysis of the situation in much of the south, southeast, and parts of the west. Extrapolating from data from other areas, we can guess that food insecurity in many of these regions will continue and possibly worsen, but it is impossible to assess the situation, let alone deliver food aid.

The collapse of humanitarian space through the politicization of assistance in Afghanistan has had profound implications for addressing food insecurity, either at present or in the event of a return to severe drought or other external shock. As discussed above, female-headed households are often the most food insecure, and we can posit that their access to markets or to credit is even more constrained in Taliban-held areas than in other parts of the country. Ideally, humanitarian assessments would identify these households and relief would follow, but neither of these processes is occurring across much of Afghanistan.

The problem of access is central to understanding women's challenges to being food-secure: due to cultural constraints and practices, women in female-headed households are unable to engage in the coping strategies used widely by other households to manage consumption and mitigate food insecurity. These constraints are recognized by women themselves, and in some cases women have found alternative mechanisms, such as appealing for assistance instead of accessing credit or begging on the streets. There are no official social safety-net mechanisms in Afghanistan, such as welfare or support for widows, and the international safety net of humanitarian relief that assisted many Afghans in the 1980s and 1990s has disappeared in many areas. An issue of great concern at present is the absence of assessment information from many areas of the country—one can assume that food insecurity is particularly severe in certain areas due to poor rainfall, lack of access by traders, and continuing physical insecurity, but there is no way of knowing. The lack of information and inability of the international humanitarian community to respond is directly due to choices made after the fall of the Taliban. These choices, driven by political expediency and the need to be seen as involved in nation building, continue to have profound effects for all civilians.

NOTES

1. Barnett Rubin, *The Fragmentation of Afghanistan: State Formation and Collapse in the International System* (New Haven, Conn.: Yale University Press, 1995).

2. Adam Pain and Jonathon Goodhand, "Afghanistan: Current Employment and Socio-Economic Situation and Prospects," in *Focus Programme on Crisis Response and Reconstruction, Working Paper 8* (Geneva: ILO, 2002).

3. Adam Pain, "Afghanistan: The Context," in *Reconstructing Agriculture in Afghanistan*, ed. Adam Pain and Jackie Sutton (Warwickshire, U.K.: FAO and Practical Action Publishing, 2007), 11–27.

4. Anthony Fitzherbert, "Rural Resilience and Diversity across Afghanistan's Agricultural Landscapes," in *Reconstructing Agriculture in Afghanistan*, ed. Pain and Sutton, 29–48.

5. Pain, "Afghanistan."

6. Fitzherbert, "Rural Resilience and Diversity."

7. Ibid.

8. Andrew Pinney and Scott Ronchini, "Food Security in Afghanistan after 2001: From Assessment to Analysis and Interpretation to Response," in *Reconstructing Agriculture in Afghanistan*, ed. Pain and Sutton, 119–164.

9. Ibid.

10. Ibid.

11. Wendy Johnecheck, "The Evolution of Food Security Information in Afghanistan: A Case of Limited 'Availability,' 'Access' and 'Utilitization', " in *Reconstructing Agriculture in Afghanistan*, ed. Pain and Sutton, 65–91.

12. Pinney and Ronchini, "Food Security in Afghanistan after 2001."

13. Adam Pain, "Rural Livelihoods in Afghanistan," in *Reconstructing Agriculture in Afghanistan*, ed. Pain and Sutton, 49–64.

14. Ministry of Rural Rehabilitation and Development, Central Statistics Office, and World Food Programme, "Afghanistan Food Security Monitoring Bulletin (AFSMB)" (Kabul: MRRD, CSO, WFP/VAM, May 2008).

15. Ibid.

16. Ibid.

17. This and other useful statistics are available from the Economic Research Service of the US Department of Agriculture. See "Briefing Rooms: Food CPI and Expenditures: 2007," USDA Economic Research Service, http://www.ers.usda.gov/Briefing/CPIFoodAndExpenditures/Data/Expenditures_Tables/table7.htm,

18. Ministry of Rural Rehabilitation and Development, Central Statistics Office, and World Food Programme, "Afghanistan Food Security Monitoring Bulletin."

19. Ibid.

20. World Food Programme, Afghanistan Market Price Bulletin (April 2009) (Kabul: World Food Programme/Vulnerabilty Analysis and Mapping, 2009).

21. Ministry of Rural Rehabilitation and Development, Central Statistics Office, and World Food Programme, "Afghanistan Food Security Monitoring Bulletin."

22. Pinney and Ronchini, "Food Security in Afghanistan after 2001."

23. Neamatollah Nojumi, Dyan Mazurana, and Elizabeth Stites, After the Taliban: Life and Security in Rural Afghanistan (Lanham, Md.: Rowman & Littlefield, 2009).

24. Adam Pain and Sue Lautze, Addressing Livelihoods in Afghanistan (Kabul: Afghanistan Research and Evaluation Unit, 2002). Nojumi, Mazurana, and Stites, After the Taliban.

25. Jo Grace and Adam Pain, "Rethinking Rural Livelihoods in Afghanistan," in Synthesis Paper Series (Kabul: Afghanistan Research and Evaluation Unit, 2004).

26. Floortje Klijn and Adam Pain, "Finding the Money: Informal Credit Practices in Rural Afghanistan," in Synthesis Paper Series (Kabul,: Afghanistan Research and Evaluation Unit, 2007).

27. Nancy Hatch Dupree, "The Family During Crisis in Afghanistan," Journal of Comparative Family Studies 35, no. 2 (2004).

28. Cited in Grace and Pain, "Rethinking Rural Livelihoods."

29. Nojumi, Mazurana, and Stites, After the Taliban.

30. Grace and Pain, "Rethinking Rural Livelihoods."

31. Jo Grace, "Who Owns the Farm? Rural Women's Access to Land and Livestock," in Working Paper Series (Kabul: Afghanistan Research and Evaluation Unit, 2005).

32. Ibid.

33. Elizabeth Stites, "Afghan Women, Afghan Livelihoods," in Reconstructing Agriculture in Afghanistan, ed. Pain and Sutton.

34. UNAMA, "Afghanistan: Annual Report on Protection of Civilians in Armed Conflict, 2008," (Kabul: United Nations Assistance Mission to Afghanistan, Human Rights Unit, 2009).

35. Grace, "Who Owns the Farm?"

36. Grace and Pain, "Rethinking Rural Livelihoods."

37. Stites, "Afghan Women, Afghan Livelihoods."

38. Ibid.

39. Klijn and Pain, "Finding the Money."

40. Ibid.

41. Nojumi, Mazurana, and Stites, *After the Taliban.*

42. Grace and Pain, "Rethinking Rural Livelihoods."

43. UNAMA, "Afghanistan: Annual Report on Protection of Civilians in Armed Conflict, 2008."

44. Ibid. In 2008, an estimated 55 percent of the 2,118 reported casualties were attributed to anti-government elements and 39 percent to pro-government forces.

45. Ibid.

46. Antonio Donini, "Afghanistan: Humanitarianism under Threat," in *Humanitarian Agenda 2015: Principles, Power, and Perceptions* (Medford, Mass.: Feinstein International Center, Tufts University, 2009).

47. Antonio Donini, "The Policies of Mercy: UN Coordination in Afghanistan, Mozambique and Rwanda," in *Occasional Paper Series* (Providence, R.I.: Brown University Humanitarianism and War Project, 1996).

48. Antonio Donini, "Humanitarian Agenda 2015: Afghanistan Case Study," in Donini, *Humanitarian Agenda 2015.*

49. This section draws heavily on Donini, "Afghanistan: Humanitarianism under Threat."

50. UNAMA, "Afghanistan: Annual Report on Protection of Civilians in Armed Conflict, 2008."

CHAPTER 15

Psychological Impacts of War

Human Rights and Mental Health

NAHID AZIZ

> Human security comes only with human rights and the rule
> of law. Human rights are the basis for creating strong and
> accountable states without which there can be no political
> stability or social progress.
>
> —Irene Khan, seventh secretary general of Amnesty International

Three decades of war and conflict have left at least two generations of
Afghan women with emotional scars and severe psychological traumas.
This intergenerational trauma is a bitter reality. In addition to negative
consequences of long-lasting war and conflict, severe human rights abuses
have exacerbated Afghan women's psychological and physical well-being.
Eighty percent of Afghan women live in rural areas and have a life expectancy of between forty-two and forty-four years.

Afghan women historically have been strong pillars of society. Yet
Afghanistan has a long history of women's oppression. Cultural and
traditional rules have prevented them from asserting independence or
engaging in self-determination and deprived them of choice. The denial
of their rights reached its peak during the Taliban era (1996–2001)
when they were forsaken, neglected, and ignored.

The United States has been eager to show the world that major changes
have occurred in Afghan society since the invasion in 2001. Special
efforts have been made by the United States to demonstrate many improvements in the lives of Afghan women. Countless non-governmental
organizations provide gender training, promote equal rights, and inform
women of their basic human rights.

Despite the 2001 Bonn Agreement—where Afghanistan pledged its commitment to the establishment of a fully representative government responsive to issues concerning women—the Afghan government has not successfully included them in the political and social sectors. In 2003, the government endorsed the Convention on the Elimination of Discrimination against Women, and in 2004, it signed the Millennium Declaration to support gender equality and to improve maternal and child health. The same year, a new constitution was enacted, guaranteeing the full and equal citizenship of women, including their legal rights and duties. Steps were taken by the Afghan government in 2005 to sign the Protocol for the Elimination of Forced and Child Marriage.[1] In 2006, the Afghanistan National Development Strategy was developed, including among its many goals the eradication of discrimination against women and the encouragement of women leadership.[2] Improvements have been made since the fall of the Taliban, but the majority of Afghan women still suffer from human rights abuses, including discrimination and lack of autonomy, access to health, education, and security.

As human rights abuses continue, Afghan women's mental health has so deteriorated that the Ministry of Public Health labeled it an "epidemic" and made it the number-two priority after maternal and child health.[3] Nevertheless, the process of addressing the mental health of the Afghans, particularly women, has been extremely slow. There is a chronic lack of funding to support mental health activities, including the training of competent mental health professionals. In a country with more than 30 million people, who have suffered three decades of war and displacement, there is an extreme shortage of mental health professionals. According to the World Health Organization *Mental Health Atlas*, in all Afghanistan, there are currently only two psychiatrists, twenty psychologists, and a few untrained psychiatric nurses.[4]

THE IMPACT OF CONFLICT

Afghanistan is well known for foreign invasions and conflicts throughout its history. The country has endured severe, inhumane conditions as a direct consequence of violence caused by political conflicts. During the 1980s and 1990s, thanks to the Soviet invasion in 1979, Afghans composed the largest refugee group in the world. Fully one-third of Afghanistan's population was uprooted and displaced outside the country, deeply affecting the fabric of this traditional, tribal society and contributing to increasing levels of breakdown in social and cultural networks for future generations. This uprooting has manifested in at least three major areas where Afghans, particularly women, experience stress and trauma. The first is related to witnessing human cruelties and horrors perpetrated by the communist regime, including imprisonment and torture of themselves and/or family members. Loss of property, family, culture, and social status as a result of escaping the country were among the worst stressors.

The second and most difficult problem relates to becoming refugees. Acculturation, resettlement, and adjustment in host countries such as Pakistan, Iran, the United States, and others in Europe have caused psychological problems for many Afghans. Most prevalent mental health problems for men and women are pre-migration trauma and loss resulting in depression, anxiety, and physical symptoms, such as back pain and digestive and heart problems. Daily worries created by news and any negative information from Afghanistan were a third major stressor for refugees, leading to psychological uncertainty and loss of hope.

After the Soviet withdrawal in 1989, the country experienced a painful civil war in which, again, the social and psychological consequences were enormous. Violence against women, including rape and intimidation, reached its peak, and a second wave of refugees fled the country. Having lost husbands and close family members during the war and exodus, Afghan widows became the sole caretakers of their families. These were at greatest risk for rape, violence, and torture as they fled to neighboring countries. Because of cultural beliefs that women are the "property" and "honor" of men, rape damages women's purity and goodness, and men's honor is violated and spoiled. During the civil war, Afghan women were targeted as a military strategy by various factions to humiliate and demoralize opponents. Women and girls were raped in front of their family members as a form of psychological torture. Many were kidnapped and forced into marriage by high-ranking officials in the militia, some of whom had as many wives as they wanted, rather than the four allowed by Islam.[5] If they resisted such mistreatment, girls and women could be killed with their families.

It was particularly dangerous for Afghan women and girls crossing the borders between Afghanistan and Pakistan, where many were kidnapped, forced into prostitution, and sold to Pakistani brothels. Often the women believed they were being escorted to refugee camps. The majority of women were widows and young girls who had lost their family members in the war and had no men to accompany and protect them. Many committed suicide to end the shame and guilt associated with rape.

Upon arriving in the host countries, many refugees faced social isolation and loss of social status. These factors made women prone to depression, headaches, heart problems, backaches, digestive problems, and other psychosomatic symptoms, as well as symptoms of post-traumatic stress disorder.

Though the civil war left women with everlasting psychological scars, the situation reached its extreme in 1996, when the fundamentalist Taliban stepped in to fill the power vacuum, ruling with brutal oppression and tyranny. Afghan society as a whole endured enormous challenges, but women's suffering was incomparable. They were completely denied access to basic health care and education. They were not allowed to work outside their homes and punished harshly and indiscriminately. Claiming to protect women's "honor," the Taliban committed inhumane and violent acts against already traumatized Afghan women.[6] This treatment was based on pre-Islamic tribal codes of behavior, which prescribe that women be socially segregated. The Taliban government sponsored a religious police force, called the Department for the Preservation of Virtue and Prevention of Vice, an institution similar to one found in Saudi Arabia. The police publicly beat and flogged women and girls for displaying any part of their faces or bodies, for leaving their homes without a male family member, and for talking to unrelated men. Alleged female adulterers were stoned to death. The Taliban murdered thousands of people and kidnapped and raped countless women. Women lived in abject fear. And such public violence against schoolgirls and women teachers, female professionals, and women in the media, among others, continues today.[7]

HUMAN RIGHTS

The "Universal Declaration of Human Rights" issued in 1948 by the United Nations comprises thirty articles wherein equal rights for all are clearly stated in simple terms: "Everyone is born free and equal in dignity and rights." The UDHR defines human rights as including, among others, access to health, education, and basic needs, such as shelter, food, and human security. [8]

As an Afghan woman, psychologist, academician, and human rights activist, who knows firsthand what it's like to adjust to new cultures and societies, I view the occurrence of mental health problems among

Afghan women as associated with chronic and repeated violations of their human rights. Although there has been some improvement in the lives of Afghan women since the fall of the Taliban in December 2001, particularly in Kabul, the situation remains largely unchanged for the majority. Amnesty International reports that women and girls remain at highest risk for abduction, rape by armed males, sexual violence, forced marriages, domestic violence, and chronic trauma. Underage marriages are routine and young girls are traded for financial settlements and tribal disputes and debts. Women continue to face discrimination in education, health care, and employment, and they are always limited by the threat of violence.[9]

In order to understand the current condition of Afghan women's mental health, one must take into account their long history of oppression, gender inequality, and violence. Patriarchy and fundamentalism prevail in today's government, where many female Afghan parliament representatives—though guaranteed their positions in a reserved-seat system—fear for their lives when they voice their opinions. Afghan women's political participation has increased since 9/11, Amnesty International reports, but conditions still remain constrained by "social prejudice and violence."[10]

Empowerment can never occur until Afghan men accept human equality and admit that Islamic principles are based on honoring women. Afghan women are firm Muslims, whose attitudes and personalities are shaped in accordance with Islam. The Qur'an accords equal status to men and women in economic, social, and political spheres, because both sexes originated from one living being. The dignity of the sexes is accepted in equal measure and women and men must bear equal responsibility, as well as enjoy the same freedoms. There are, however, major contradictions between the words in the Qur'an—revolutionary among Abrahamic religions—and the day-to-day reality of Afghan women's lives. Women suffer from deliberate misinterpretations of the Qur'an. It is not the religion of Islam but patriarchal power that has always contributed to the unfortunate inequalities inside Afghanistan.[11]

Women have no protection from domestic violence. Those who flee abusive marriages are frequently imprisoned, prosecuted for running away or alleged adultery. The violence has many other faces besides inflicting verbal, physical, and psychological harm, including forced, underage marriage and denial of education and economic opportunities. Women lack legal awareness, and there are no functioning fair and just courts to help them.[12]

The connection between human rights violations and mental health problems has long been established. It has been observed among survivors of torture and in countries where political conflict is a bitter reality. Women are at much higher risk for human rights violations in conflict situations and/or traditional societies. In 1998, Physicians for Human Rights found that violations of the human rights and dignity of Afghan women are inextricably linked to detrimental physical and mental health consequences. Most of the women surveyed have had deteriorating mental health since the beginning of the Taliban regime. An alarming 97 percent of Afghan women interviewed met the criteria for a diagnosis of clinical depression, 42 percent met full criteria for a diagnosis of post-traumatic stress disorder. The report concluded that the primary reasons for these diagnoses were the ongoing war and deteriorating human rights conditions.[13]

THE CURRENT CONDITION

The World Health Organization defines mental health as "a state of complete physical, mental, and social well-being, and not merely the absence of disease." It is notable that the WHO's definition of mental health includes "social well-being."[14]

In 2001, the WHO estimated that out of a population of 30 million, 5 million Afghan women and men suffer from mental distresses such as PTSD, depression, anxiety disorders, and substance abuse and dependence.[15] Assessment and discussion of the current condition of women's mental health is extremely challenging and by far one of most demanding aspects of the work facing the majority of health professionals. Nevertheless, there have been a number of limited and preliminary studies that begin to provide an overall picture of the current mental health conditions among Afghan women.[16]

The lack of mental health professionals and culturally sensitive assessment tools and knowledge also creates a barrier to accurate assessment and treatment of mental disorders in the population, especially because Afghan women live under strict gender segregation imposed by cultural norms and therefore cannot be seen under the usual clinical conditions. In 2009, there were two trained psychiatrists (neither practicing their profession due to other governmental obligations) and a smattering of psychologists and psychiatric nurses. Professional capacity in mental health is completely lacking. However, with the help of

European and other international NGOs, mental health structure is slowly taking shape.[17]

The Dutch HealthNet TPO has been providing mental health services and training in Nangarhar Province since 2002, with two major programs. The Basic Psychiatry Program aims to integrate basic mental health care into the primary health-care system, and the European Commission and other organizations have funded the expansion of this program to ten more provinces. The Community Based Psychosocial Program strives to address the psychosocial needs of the primarily rural population.

International Assistance Mission's mental health activities are mostly concentrated in Herat, Ghor, Badghis, and Farah provinces. It first became involved in 1996 when the suicide rate among women rapidly increased during the civil war and the Taliban era. Since 2006, IAM has provided training to physicians, nurses, and other health professionals in basic mental health.

Mental health is explicitly named as a priority by the Afghan government, specifically in the Afghanistan National Development Strategy: "As a direct consequence of the years of conflict, Afghanistan has a large number of disabled and mentally ill people for whom treatment and rehabilitation services need to be developed and for whom assistance will be required in order to re-integrate them in the daily life of the country."[18]

Mental health is also an important element in the Ministry of Public Health's key documents, such as the "Basic Package of Health Services" and the "Essential Package of Hospital Services." The ministry has had a functioning mental health department since 2005, established with financial support from the European Commission, as part of the HealthNet TPO activities, and the U.S. Substance Abuse Mental Health Administration Services.

A main source of women's fears and psychological dysfunction is related not only to ongoing abuses but also to memories of abuses—rape and other sexual violence—committed by war criminals. But reporting and vocalizing sexual violence is challenging, because of women's subordinate status, family concern with "honor," saving face, cultural taboos, and thus women's own reluctance to share details of the traumatic assaults. It has been shown frequently that repeated sexual violence leads to extreme anxiety, depression, irritability, emotional liability, attention problems, personality changes, behavioral disturbances, insomnia, and nightmares, as well as psychosomatic symptoms, such as lack of energy, extreme back pains, muscle weakness, and heart problems.

According to a study headed by Barbara Lopes Cardozo in 2004, Afghan women exhibited significantly lower mental health conditions and poorer social functioning than Afghan men. The study emphasizes the negative consequences of war, restrictions in freedoms, and socio-economic adversity, and it indicates that 62 percent of the respondents reported experiencing four traumatic events in a ten-year period from 1992 to 2002. These included lack of food, water, and shelter, and violent attacks. Data also suggested that in eastern Afghanistan, the rate of exposure to traumatic events was much higher, from eight to ten. These included displacement, deprivation, and exposure to U.S.-led coalition bombardments.[19]

A 2004 in-depth survey by Willem Scholte and colleagues in Nangar-har Province confirmed the high figures of depression and anxiety, in particular among women, with elevated scores on depression questionnaires in 58.4 percent of all women, anxiety symptoms in 78.2 percent, and PTSD symptoms in 31.9 percent of the female respondents.[20] The study found a clear relationship between the number of traumatic events and the likelihood of developing psychopathology. It is also worth mentioning that women who lived in regions under Taliban rule were at higher risk for developing psychological problems.

The pervasiveness of domestic violence in Afghanistan endangers physical and mental health, productivity, and security not only of women but of society as a whole. Many Afghan males returning from long-lasting wars are now at greater risk for developing aggression, hypervigilance, high levels of anxiety, flashbacks of traumatic memories, and other trauma-related symptoms. Left untreated, these have negative impacts not only on the normal functioning of men but also on their families. Depression and substance abuse are the most frequently occurring psychological problems many Afghan males face. In addition, unemployment makes many vulnerable to domestic violence.

Severe traumatization stemming from violence can have effects for generations. The difficult conditions under which women and girls live and their social isolation have additional negative effects. This is compounded by the failure of the state to implement laws to protect the victims of domestic violence and bring the perpetrators to justice.

It must be noted that depressive and trauma symptoms are expressed differently by women living in traditional cultures than by women typically seen in the West. Without a culturally sanctioned vocabulary to express their pain, women tend to express their emotions psycho-somatically. For example, it is not uncommon for Afghan women to complain about physical ailments for which there are no perceptible medical causes. Due to the lack of mental-health training, medical professionals often misdiagnose and prescribe medications that don't address the actual problems. Psychosomatic expressions are in many ways culturally appropriate, because mental illness can easily lead to social stigmatization. According to studies on the occurrences of trauma-related symptoms among Afghan women, PTSD is less prominent than more culturally specific exhibitions of distress. Women avoid talking about their traumatic experiences altogether in the belief that discussing negative experiences makes the situation worse. Afghan women also tend not to speak directly of their pain for the fear of becoming a "burden on others." Psychological symptoms are usually disclosed through the verbal expression *jigar khun*. In Islamic cultures, the liver (*jigar*) is the seat of the emotions. *Khun* means "blood." Combined they describe a deep state of sadness.[21]

Afghan culture promotes female modesty and rewards women for being obedient and not displaying happiness. They are expected to exhibit a certain level of melancholy, to demonstrate humility. Thus, it is not uncommon to observe women asking for forgiveness from God (*toba*) when they find themselves laughing aloud or experiencing joy and pleasure. This is reinforced by fatalistic beliefs that excessive pleasure brings negative consequences. The concepts of *gham* (anguish) and *ghusa* (worry) are common among Afghan women to express their internal pain.[22] These constitute how Afghan women feel about themselves.

Mental health problems are traditionally believed to be caused by evil spirits (*jinn*). Consequently, many Afghans seek solutions to their psychological problems from a religious leader (*mullah*) and cultural healer (*dowa khan*). It is thought that saying prayers and practicing religious rituals ease suffering. Mullahs often advise women to have patience (*saber*), already a well-known virtue among Afghan women. It is believed that through patience one's pain dissipates and God rewards with eternal comfort.

As an Afghan woman and psychologist, I argue that depression becomes a major part of women's identity as it involves culturally ordained sadness and low self-esteem. Extreme levels of gender segregation begin at the birth of a female. Upon delivering a baby girl, rather than being congratulated, the mother is consoled that the next child will be a boy. Some women endure physical violence from husbands who accuse them of not being good enough wives to give birth to sons. Others may be subjected to psychological punishment, such as deprivation of affection, being ignored, and being denied sexually by their husbands. This treatment leads to depression, anxiety, and fear with each pregnancy that the child will be a daughter. Afghan women are thus conditioned to dislike their own gender.

In recent years, there have been increasing numbers of self-immolations, the act of burning oneself as a means of suicide. Self-immolation is defined as the "destruction of the self—specifically by burning, or the deliberate sacrifice of oneself, especially by fire."[23] To understand the underlying reasons, the Afghanistan Independent Human Rights Commission and medica mondiale conducted reviews of individuals who survived self-immolations. In 2006, 106 cases were reported in Herat, Wardak, and Kabul provinces. In addition to standard statistical considerations, and taking into account sociocultural aspects, it can be safely assumed that many more cases go officially unnoticed and unreported. There is simply no institutional body to detect and prevent women at risk, making the situation even more complicated. Researchers and social scientists are struggling to discover the etiology of this trend and different theories have been proposed. Frequent reasons documented are forced and child marriages and violence committed by husbands, in-laws, and husbands' other wives. Thus, self-immolation occurs because of gender-based disempowerment, and it becomes a political tool in order to be heard.

Self-immolation seems to occur more frequently in western Afghanistan, in and around Herat, particularly among women who lived in Iran, where this violent and excruciatingly painful act accounts for a high number of all forms of suicides. Self-immolation can be quickly modeled and is sensationalized and idealized in the media. Although the region is doing relatively better than eastern Afghanistan in terms of security and frequency of insurgency, these suicides seem to be a reaction to the extreme patriarchy and Shi'a Islam, which calls for even greater suppression of women's freedom and mobility.[24]

Medications overdose is a common method of suicide in the West, but it is rarely an option for women in Afghanistan due to limited availability of pharmaceuticals and high levels poverty. Fuel is relatively cheap and more accessible to many women as they use it daily to cook.

Nevertheless, increasing numbers of women are abusing drugs as a form of self-medication to cope with their psychological suffering. In

2008, the AIHRC conducted research to identify the factors that affect women's addiction and the general living conditions of addicted women. Researchers conducted interviews in twenty-one provinces. Not surprisingly, the use of opium occurs more frequently in provinces such as Ghazni, Wardak, and Paktia, where it is cultivated. The researchers found that women abuse substances for pain management, insomnia, fatigue, sexual dysfunctions, hemorrhage, cough, diarrhea, sadness, and grief. Women cited heavy workloads and psychosocial stressors, such as pressure from family members and peers, as well as mistreatment, marital dissatisfaction, family trauma, and loss of family members as reasons for drug use. Although it was difficult to establish a causal relationship between poverty and drug addiction, the commission concluded that without access to health care, low-income women were more likely to abuse drugs.[25]

The Afghanistan Research and Evaluation Unit also conducted research in 2008 to determine the misuse of psychotropic medication in Afghanistan. Painkillers and tranquillizers such as Diazepam (Valium) were found to be most frequently abused. Diazepam is cheap and commonly available from pharmacies and other sources, and many Afghan physicians tend to overprescribe it to address symptoms such as anxiety, depression, and sleep disorders. Patients are rarely informed of side effects and risk of dependency. Self-medication—and the resulting addiction—with opium and psychotropic medications has become a treacherous reality for many Afghan women. Drug abuse and addiction is of special concern, as well, since women's ability—as primary caregivers—to meet their children's needs is greatly diminished. And children often model their mothers' behavior, becoming addicts as well.[26]

RECOMMENDATIONS

Thirty years of war and conflicts have left Afghanistan and its people with devastating psychological consequences. Afghans have been uprooted and demobilized and have suffered socially and economically. Direct, often daily, exposure to violence and fear has adversely affected the mental health condition of all Afghans, particularly women. Social and family structures that for centuries sustained Afghans, especially women, have been destroyed.

There is a great need for epidemiological studies on the occurrences of psychiatric disorders in Afghanistan. With extremely few professionals, the Ministry of Public Health has tried to integrate mental health into primary health care, one of the main objectives of the ministry's "Basic Package of Health Services," but it has been a slow process. Chronic lack of funding is the biggest obstacle in treating psychological problems. Reconstruction of mental health in Afghanistan has been one of the lowest priorities of the donor countries. To date, neither the United States Agency for International Development nor the World Bank has contributed any funding to promote mental health activities in Afghanistan. The majority of the limited funding to promote mental health has come from the European Commission.

Not only do most Afghan women still lack basic health-care services of any sort, but only the barest, minimal mental health services are available from an extremely small number of qualified professionals, mainly in large cities. There is an urgent need for training of mental health professionals, who can provide culturally sensitive services.

Community development, such as the opening of schools, the creation of income-generating activities, and increased security and stability, will help vast numbers of women, as will long-term peace, reconciliation, security, and guaranteeing basic human rights.

Women's mental health must be addressed at local and governmental levels. First and most urgently, the government must implement laws to protect women. This includes protecting victims of domestic and other violence against women and prosecuting the perpetrators. Justice must be served and awareness raised among Afghans of the relationship between post-conflict mental and psychosocial disorders and their direct impact on generations to come.

Reconstruction efforts in mental health must address the following needs:

- Human resource development through the training of health professionals, including medical doctors, nurses, midwives, and community health workers, is essential. This will speed the integration of mental health into primary health care.

- Programs aiming to increase public mental health education and life skills for women and families must be financially supported and extended to rural areas in Afghanistan.

- The provision of culturally relevant mental health services should be encouraged and financially supported. Interventions need to be community based and include the family and community of which the women are an integral part.

- Psychosocial help and approaches have been shown to have a positive impact on the overall mental health of Afghans. Thus, daily stressors must be addressed through the implementation of psychosocial approaches.

- Chronically ill individuals need specialized mental health services provided through inpatient care, by trained psychiatrists, who understand the uses, subtleties, and risks of psychotropic medications and other treatments.

- Continuous research must be supported to determine the prevalence of psychological disorders, the effectiveness of evidence-based treatments, and barriers to seeking help.

It is vital to remember that despite many adversities, Afghan women are still relatively well functioning. They should not be easily pathologized, and their agency and psychological resilience must be acknowledged. But until basic human rights are established in practice as well as on paper, it cannot be claimed that their status has changed since the fall of the Taliban or that the lofty goals described in the 2001 Bonn Agreement have been met. Until then, women's well-being will continue to be compromised and healing cannot begin.

NOTES

1. The *Convention on the Elimination of All Forms of Discrimination against Women* was adopted by the United Nations in 1979 and is an international bill of rights for women, a comprehensive and detailed international agreement seeking the advancement of women. Division for the Advancement of Women, Department of Economic and Social Affairs, United Nations Office of the High Commissioner of Human Rights, http://www.un.org/womenwatch/daw/cedaw/committee.htm

2. Anita Raj, Charlemagne Gomez, and Jay G. Silverman. "Driven to a Fiery Death—The Tragedy of Self-Immolation in Afghanistan," *The New England Journal of Medicine.* 358, no. 21 (2008): 2201–3302.

3. Dr. Amin A. Fatemie, Afghanistan's Minister of Public Health, spoke on May 13, 2009, in Washington, D.C., at the Conference on Health Security in Afghanistan.

4. World Health Organization, *Mental Health Atlas* (Geneva: World Health Organization, 2005).

5. In order to feed the "war machine," the Taliban practiced barbaric customs and sold women and girls to wealthy Saudis. See Sally Armstrong, *Veiled Threat: The Hidden Power of the Women of Afghanistan* (New York: Penguin Books, 2002).

6. Ibid.

7. Sippi Azarbaijani-Moghadam. "The Arrested Development of Afghan Women," as quoted in Alexander Their, ed., *The Future of Afghanistan* (Washington, D.C.: United Institute of Peace, 2009), 63–73.

8. "The Universal Declaration of Human Rights" is a milestone document in the history of human rights. Drafted by representatives with different legal and cultural backgrounds from all regions of the world, the declaration was proclaimed by the United Nations General Assembly in Paris on December 10, 1948. See "The Universal Declaration of Human Rights," United Nations, http://www.un.org/en/documents/udhr/.

9. Amnesty International, *State of the World's Human Rights* (Washington, D.C.: Amnesty International, 2009), http://thereport.amnesty.org/en/regions/asia-pacific/afghanistan.

10. Afghanistan Independent Human Rights Commission, "Evaluation Report on the General Situation of Women in Afghanistan," 2006, http://www .aihrc.org.af/rep_eng_wom_situation_8_march.htm#_ftnref6.

11. Afghanistan is not alone in this misinterpretation of the Qur'an. Most patriarchal societies interpret it to suit male-dominated ideologies, social structures, and beliefs. According to Asghar Ali Engineer—an Indian Muslim and Islamic scholar—interpretation of the Qur'an "is not in keeping with what is intended by it, but is based on our own fixed opinion. Thus to conform to our opinion, we twist the meaning of the Qur'an." Asghar Ali Engineer. *The Rights of Women in Islam* (Elgin, Ill.: New Dawn Press Group, 2004), 4.

12. Human Rights Watch, *World Report* (New York: Human Rights Watch, 2009), 213. Other chapters in this volume address female imprisonment, penal codes, and legal defense.

13. Vincent Iacopino and Zohra Rasekh, "Education, a Human Rights Imperative: The Case of Afghanistan," *Health and Human Rights* 3 (1998): 98–108.

14. "Fact sheet N°220," World Health Organization, September 2007, http://www.who.int/mediacentre/factsheets/fs220/en/index.html.

15. World Health Organization, *The Invisible Wounds: The Mental Health Crisis in Afghanistan* (Geneva: WHO Special Report. Central Asia Crisis Unit, November 6, 2001).

16. Iacopino and Rasekh, "Education, a Human Rights Imperative"; Barbara Lopes Cardozo et al., "Mental Health, Social Functioning, and Disability in Post-War Afghanistan," *JAMA* 292, no. 5(2004): 575–584; and Willem Scholte et al., "Mental Health Symptoms Following War and Repression in Eastern Afghanistan," *JAMA* 292, no. 5 (2004): 585–593.

17. As of 2009, the international NGOs working with mental health issues include Holland's HealthNet TPO, Caritas Germany, International Assistance Mission (an international association of Christian organizations), and medica mondiale Germany.

18. "Pliiar V: Health and Nutrition," *Afghanistan National Development Strategy 1387–1391 (2008–2013),* vol. 2? Islamic Republic of Afghanistan, Ministry of Public Health, Approved February 25, 2008.

19. Lopes Cardozo et al. "Mental Health, Social Functioning, and Disability."

20. Willem F. Scholte et al., "Mental Health Symptoms."

21. Kenneth E. Miller, Patricia Omidian, Abdul Samad Quraishy, Naseema Quraishy, Mohammed Nader Nasiry, Seema Nasiry, Nazar Mohammed Karyar, and Abdul Aziz Yaqubi, "The Afghan Symptom Checklist: A Culturally Grounded Approach to Mental Health Assessment in a Conflict Zone," *American Journal of Orthopsychiatry* 76, no. 4 (2006): 423–433.

22. Ibid.

23. Medica mondiale, "Dying to Be Heard: Self Immolation Research Report," 2007, http://www.medicamondiale.org/fileadmin/content/07_Infothek/Afghanistan/Afghanistan_Dyingtobeheard_self_immolation_medica_mondiale_2007.pdf .

24. The strong conservatism of Shi'a Afghans is illustrated in a controversial 2009 marriage law that condones marital rape, requiring a wife to submit to her husband's advances every four days and stating that she may not leave the house without his permission. As of this writing, the law had been minimally revised thanks to a huge outcry and protests in the streets by women. Among other reports, see Ben Farmer, "Afghanistan Revises Marriage Law but Women Still Required to Submit to Sexual Intercourse," *UK Telegraph*, July 9, 2009, http://www.telegraph.co.uk/news/worldnews/asia/afghanistan/5790702/Afghanistan-revises-marriage-law-but-women-still-required-to-submit-to-sexual-intercourse.html.

25. Afghanistan Independent Human Rights Commission, "Effective Factors Associated with Drug Addiction and the Consequences of Addiction among Afghan Women" (Kabul, 2008).

26. Afghanistan Research and Evaluation Unit, "Afghanistan's Hidden Drug Problem: The Misuse of Psychotropics" (Kabul, 2008). The report states that as of 2005, there were 920,000 drug-addicted persons in Afghanistan. Women accounted for 120,000 of the total number.

PART IV

Making the Rubble Bloom

A widow draws water from a well in her small back yard. She is part of the PARSA (Physiotherapy and Rehabilitation Support for Afghanistan) Widow's Garden Program founded by Mary MacMakin. This women's economic development program—conceived by Zarguna Hashimi, PARSA's former director of Literacy and Early Childhood Development Service, who lost her husband during the Soviet War—serves twenty widows in an area just outside Kabul.
Photo by Sheryl B. Shapiro, 2003.

CHAPTER 16

Mending Afghanistan Stitch by Stitch

How Traditional Crafts and Social Organization Advance Afghan Women

RACHEL LEHR

When Ghulam Sakhi Rustamkhan—Sakhi—contacted me in 2000, he was a refugee in Lahore, Pakistan, desperately seeking a way to improve the lives of his immediate and extended family. Sakhi and I had been students together in Dushanbe, Tajikistan, in the early 1980s but had lost contact in the intervening years. When he approached me all these years later, his family was living in appalling conditions in Lahore's slums, along with other Afghan refugees from their home region.[1]

As a scholar, textile artist, and teacher, I decided to create a sustainable, grassroots enterprise focused on traditional textile techniques, local skills, and literacy. Jennie Wood, a textile industry consultant, joined the initial effort and gave the organization its name, Rubia.[2] Sakhi, educated in economics, kept the community central to all aspects of planning and helped contextualize the Afghan family system as he guided Rubia's programs around existing cultural norms, values, and social structures.

As illegal residents in Pakistan, these Afghan refugees were not in camps, were not registered, and did not have access to refugee "services." They were concerned with avoiding detection and attracting as little official attention as possible, but they urgently needed economic relief. Women's literacy, cultural preservation, health care, and handcrafts were secondary concerns. Taking account of their own skills and experience, the founders examined available resources and abilities within the community and quickly realized there would be no funding for equipment, infrastructure, or large-scale enterprise.

PRODUCTION AND CONTEXT

The Lahore neighborhood of Khanjurwal was a maze of narrow streets. Ditches conveyed sewage, female sanitary products, and rubbish. The stench was palpable, and Afghan women often made a big show of holding their noses with a bit of cloth as they walked in the street.[3] Many newly arrived refugee women found themselves disoriented and saddened by their displacement. Although adaptable, they were out of their element—many had never traveled before. The refugees in Sakhi's community were from the villages of Darrai Nur, a region in Nangarhar Province, eastern Afghanistan, where they cooked over open fires, baked bread in tandoor ovens, relaxed beyond the *qala* (compound) walls in the shade of mulberry trees,[4] and walked through fields to visit relatives; the foreshortened horizon of the neighborhood was oppressive. They were accustomed to the forgiving dusty floors of their mud brick *hawli*s (inner courtyard of the qala), and the cramped brick quarters were hard by comparison.

This is the neighborhood where Rubia was born in 2000.

Women and teenage girls, homebound by the tradition of *purdah* (social segregation)[5] and still practicing the age-old Afghan craft of embroidery, were an available and an invaluable indigenous resource. By harnessing their fine embroidery skills, and targeting a Western audience through well-designed products, we could build an indigenous enterprise to serve the community's needs. Rubia's model of sustainability was founded on competitive market awareness and economic returns. All the work produced in the Lahore slum district, Khanjurwal, was to be sold in the United States and the proceeds returned to pay for more materials and more embroidery.

The women were interested in working but had no "work" experience. Although many had basic embroidery skills, they lacked vocational behavioral skills that prepared them to take instruction, improve their work, accept criticism, work in a timely fashion, and keep all their work clean. It became clear that basic health and literacy classes would also serve to model vocational behavior skills necessary for the success of each woman's embroidery enterprise.

Sakhi invited Hafiza and her husband Zalmay into the early planning of Rubia. Hafiza was the only educated woman in the community. She was also a master embroiderer. In order to work with Hafiza, Rubia had to hire her husband as well. This happened several times with local talented women. Their husbands joined in, assisting their wives in pattern transferring, collecting embroideries, record-keeping, and payments to embroiderers. They were the necessary escorts for the women to be able to go out to work at all. They also became part of the family enterprise.

Hafiza was delighted. Although she had been reluctant to take on this work at first, concerned that it might not be sustainable, she found that the demands of the project lifted her mood and sorrow about the loss of opportunity she had once enjoyed in Afghanistan. Her prominence among the women grew. As she became Rubia's assistant director, her roles encompassed embroidery skills training, literacy training, and overseeing the distribution and production of products. New acquisitions in the household indicated she had more say in how money was spent at home.

In the Pashai community,[6] as in other Afghan tribal groups, family relations are organized along two lineages. A man's lineage determines clan membership (*qaum*), descent, and tribal affiliation. When a woman marries, she gains those affiliations. A women's lineage determines who is considered *khish* (matrilineal relatives) or kin. Even after a woman marries she retains connection to her khish and they become the relatives of her children as well. Even where first-cousin marriage predominates, this widens the circle of a woman's interactions. In the neighborhood of Khanjurwal, many women lead lives interwoven between khish and qaum. Rubia's recruitment of women took advantage of these social networks. Women were invited to participate and they invited other neighborhood women, often along family ties.

There was no need to strategize how to get the men in the community to support Rubia. Men were involved from the inception, because all planning was done within the family context. Long conversations, revisited repeatedly, gradually shifted families toward Rubia's enterprise, resulting in widespread endorsement and investment in the effort.

Some organizations and consultants have objected to the perpetuation of women's traditional handwork—rug weaving, embroidery, tailoring—arguing that it limits women's opportunities, keeping them bound to the domestic sphere.[7] Pay associated with typical women-based projects is poor, and the job places an additional burden on women when working at home. Intermediaries often take most of the profits, leaving women with even less income from their hard work. However, embroiderers, who work through fewer male intermediaries, tend to keep the money they earn. Most homebound women have not had hands-on training to improve their techniques, learn patterns and design innovation, color selection, or quality control. These skills distinguish the poor quality products from the best. Studies have shown that women who are provided the materials and supervision for commission work produce higher quality, more marketable products, which in turn provide better pay.[8]

Rubia, aware of these significant socioeconomic issues, formulated its projects to incorporate the positive aspects of home-based, traditional work into its planning and avoid the pitfalls of other projects. Its design was to not only train but also employ its women and pay a living wage equivalent to what their husbands might earn. It was designed to fit into the lives of rural Afghan women without adding to their burdens. In Rubia's organization, men are not intermediary traders and do not receive their wives or daughters wages. Though long-held normative values will not change quickly with development, the vocational behavioral skills gained by Rubia-trained women are transferable and prepare them for other employment opportunities.

WORK PATTERNS

Rubia never set up an office in Khanjurwal. Organizing work within the space of the domestic sphere matched the resources and needs of the planners and community perfectly.

Women worked at home, between their chores, following the rhythm of life in the neighborhood. Skills training and education took place at home, work was gathered and collected at home, and payment was made through home visits. The conception of the project was connected to the lives of the participants. Because many of these women spent most of their time in household-related chores—preparing dough, cooking, washing laundry, in addition to child care—the handwork had to fit between these activities. Women were offered only enough work to fit into their lifestyle. Earnings from embroidery were supplemental household income. Equipment, mobility, and portability were primary considerations in planning a home-based project. People changed houses frequently and shifted configurations within those homes based on marriages, family feuds, and migrations between Pakistan and Afghanistan. Nothing seemed simpler than a needle, a hoop, some fabric, and thread.

Many planning discussions took place on the floor of Hafiza's house over bottomless cups of astringent green tea and sugar candies, her seven children hopping around, with one still nursing in her lap. Much of her instruction of other women occurred with babies on knees and at breasts. It was individualized, slow paced, and congenial. Women who have little else have this skill—passed from the fingertips of mother to daughter. Like themselves, the embroidery did not have a public audience; this is an exclusively women's craft. Vast networks of embroiderers in Afghanistan have always worked at home, selling their textiles to traders who take it beyond the village. Unbeknownst to the women, their embroidery reaches world markets through multiple traders and buyers. The Darrai Nur women were never before part of that network, but now their embroidery, too, would enter these exchanges. The difference was that they knew where their work was going and who was selling it.

All instruction for women was held in the home—the private, bounded space where women congregate. While any and all women have access to this sphere, only men with the most privileged relationship to the family may mingle. Anyone else invited into this sanctum is accorded a relationship of trust. In a setting where women are not expected to earn income, Rubia's programs use domestic space to protect the privacy of the embroiderers, removing them from the scrutiny of outsiders.

Classes held in Hafiza's second room were scheduled six mornings a week, but women came throughout the day to seek embroidery advice or go over lessons. Often a younger brother or sister was sent to Hafiza with a question. Lifting the textile out of a plastic bag they asked: "Does this color go here?" "Should this area be filled with chain stitch or couching?" Because the embroiderer could not leave home without prior arrangement—permission from her husband or a suitable escort— the young boys and girls played an important role, able to retrieve anything their elders wanted or needed: a pack of cigarettes, a needle and thread, salt for cooking. Along with those errands, children could be seen skipping along with plastic bags of embroidery dangling from their fingers.

All embroidery had to be completed to the specified standard before being accepted and paid for. Pieces were often sent back for another line of stitching to cover the drawn outline or to fill in an area left blank. Children were frequently the messengers conveying these explicit instructions. What may have seemed inefficient, worked quite well to engage entire families in the development of their enterprises. Women embroidered at their convenience. Once at an engagement party, I noticed three women sitting together, embroidering portions of a Rubia shawl they were eager to finish.

Hafiza's husband Zalmay kept records of all the piecework; payments were made on an itinerant basis. Sakhi and Zalmay visited the homes of the embroiderers to pay them, or their proxies, directly. The money earned belonged to the embroiderer and although she usually spent it on household needs—food, medicine, rent, or clothing—she could also spend it on a special piece of fabric for a dress to wear to a wedding or for gold earrings as an investment against harder times to come. I heard many women discuss ways they would spend their income; gold jewelry was often at the top of the list. I witnessed an increase in washing machines, where, despite the squalor, there was running water and electricity in most homes. Women lacked these conveniences in Afghanistan, but in Lahore, an appliance could relieve the burden of housework. (These washing machines returned to Afghanistan and are stored in mud brick homes with the hope that one day electricity and plumbed water might find their way to the village.)

LITERACY AND HEALTH

Barakat, a Massachusetts-based nonprofit, provided Rubia with a small grant to launch the women's embroidery and education project and continues to support Rubia's home-based education program in Afghanistan. Literacy courses are held within the bounded space of women's spheres. In addition to literacy and numeracy, emphasis has always been placed on basic hygiene and vocational behavioral skills. All these courses help the women develop their embroidery into small, family-run businesses. Nazia, Najiba, and Gulbanu, three unmarried sisters, explained that because Nazia was the faster, finer embroiderer she did most of the stitching, whereas Najiba and Gulbanu did most of the cleaning and cooking. That way they pooled their collective energies to meet their family's needs.

About six months into the program the women requested a school for their children, whose education had been neglected through the course of war and displacement. The Afghans did not allow their children to attend local Pakistani schools because as illegal immigrants they were afraid of being noticed, investigated, and deported. In organizing a primary school, Rubia took pains to remain invisible.

Two rooms on a second floor between the houses of two Afghan families were rented, one assigned for girls and one for boys. In order to avoid unwanted attention no signs were posted and there were no school uniforms; everyone who needed to knew just where to go. Fathers in the community who could read and write were hired as teachers. It may have been unseen but it was not unheard. A chorus of children's voices carried out into the alley as they recited their lessons in call and response.

The literacy component in Rubia's original conception was intended to link education with economic opportunity. Embroidery would be the economic incentive, the hook, to bring the women along educationally. Originally we planned that all the embroiderers would attend literacy classes. Sakhi explained that some of the embroiderers' families would not send their girls and women to class. It might happen eventually, he said, but not right away. Rubia was committed to a long-term engagement with the community. We would have to be patient. There has always been an overlap in interest in embroidery and literacy, and many women have taken advantage of both. Across eight years, many embroiderers have come to classes, but so have girls and women beyond the embroidery community thanks to the inherent trust in local leadership, reinforced by an extended presence in the community. The men played a significant role in trusting their wives and daughters to Rubia classes.

The challenge of keeping work clean increased manyfold when embroiderers returned to Afghanistan and traded the brick environment of Pakistan for the dusty, muddy countryside. Thus, Rubia began to incorporate very basic health practices into the embroidery program. In order to assure that they kept their work clean, embroiderers were dispensed "clean embroidery kits," soap for hand washing, and sheets of clean flowered fabric in which to wrap their embroidery and to place on their laps while sewing. We reasoned that as long as free soap were available, it would become more widely used in households. Women who could not keep their work clean would not be given additional work.

RETURNING TO AFGHANISTAN

The small Khanjurwal project was poised to succeed: it had a manage-
able number of women who lived close enough to one another to make
working together easy, with a ready supply of fine materials, convenient
shipping from Pakistan, relative security, electricity, and running water.
Then, on September 11, 2001, the world changed.

Within six months, families were sending emissaries back to Afghanistan to investigate a return. We felt it would be better to establish
Rubia on Afghan soil, where we could grow without being constrained
by fear of detection. Besides, international aid funds were flowing. The
Rubia community in Pakistan was not abandoned, and we maintained
embroidery and education programs in Lahore, even as we established
projects in Afghanistan. By early 2003, enough community members
had returned to Afghanistan for Rubia to become an official non-
governmental organization in Afghanistan.

As villagers from an outlying area, the Darrai Nuris did not have the
strong connections in Kabul necessary to steward proposals. Ministers
and ministries continually shuffled their responsibilities, jurisdictions,
and requirements. New application forms identical to the previous
forms had to be completed again and again.[9] The frustration these Afghans experienced dealing with their own government's capricious policies was mirrored in the attempts to gain access to development funding. Rubia needed funds for "capacity building" but did not have the
capacity to access these funds. The circularity was paralyzing. My role
became intercessor with the international community. I visited one
donor after another, trying to find funding to support Rubia's income-
generating project and marketing component, education, and capacity
building for the core staff. I bounced from the United Nations Development Fund for Women to the United States Agency for International
Development to the International Organization for Migration. When I
was not in Afghanistan, this effort came to a halt because none of the
Darrai Nuris had the language skills to address the donors. Donors did
not speak the Afghanistan national languages, Dari and Pashto. Hafiza,
Zalmay, and Sakhi could run their own office and business and oversee
the embroidery of more than 100 women, but they were locked out of
pursuing funding in their own country. They spoke many languages but
not English. Rubia lacked the funds and connections to hire an Afghan
with these skills.

At first, communication between Darrai Nur and Kabul was arcane. Mobile phones were expensive (now they are not) and satellite phones prohibitive. There were no cell towers in the countryside. We had to travel between farms and villages and send someone ahead to inform them of our arrival and to scout out the way for security. The few hours it took to visit embroiderers and collect materials in Khanjurwal took days of travel in Afghanistan. The lack of water and electricity made it even harder for the women to keep their work clean. Quality embroidery materials were not readily available in Afghanistan. Shipping from Afghanistan to the United States was not yet established.

GENDERED SPACE

Some of the women Rubia trained in Lahore repatriated to Kabul, whereas others went back to Darrai Nur. Life in Kabul was expensive. The deep pockets of the international aid community caused a spike in rentals; many Afghans were squeezed out. Rubia was caught between the need for a presence in Kabul and in Darrai Nur. In Darrai Nur, it made sense to work at home. This was consistent with Rubia's practice in the past. But in order to promote our women's embroidery to the international community in Kabul, we needed an office.

Hafiza and Zalmay soon moved to Kabul and began coming to the office every day for work. Women heard about the project and began seeking embroidery work. The tailor met with staff at the office and foreign visitors came to see what we were doing, to shop in our showroom. The transition was not comfortable and did not fit everyone's needs. They were caught between social space as office and social space as home. Typically in an Afghan office, food is provided by the employer. Many of the tasks that were part of housekeeping before became the responsibility of the office staff, including cooking, cleaning, and guarding. The fluid way that handwork could fit into a home schedule was lost in the office environment. At home, one of Hafiza's daughters would cook, another would clean. Children took care of each other and turned to their mother only when something needing her attention arose.

In Kabul, she had to leave all this behind to go to an office, even taking her youngest child with her. She was not accustomed to this arrangement and found it difficult to meet her commitment to come to work. Sometimes groups of women came to the office to turn in or receive work. Often they came in pairs, or with a *moharram* (escort)—a husband, brother, or even a small son. The office gave them a legitimate destination, both for business and pleasure. They brought picnics or sat down for tea and candy. Though women preferred to embroider at home, those who paid regular social visits to the office were investing in their businesses and securing more responsibilities. Men came to the office seeking work for their wives, delivering goods, or picking up new orders.

With many local businesses and non-governmental organizations in Afghanistan, the office soon became home and hostel. All the Darrai Nuris visiting Kabul now had a place to sleep. What was a workshop by day became a dormitory at night. This increased Rubia's prestige among Darrai Nuris and provided security in the numbers of men who were there at night. It also burdened its resources and made starting work in the morning troublesome. Sometimes overnight "guests" did not clear out early enough in the morning. Gendered use of space became problematic. In the Pashai schema, gendered space at home was clearly established. In Lahore, Sakhi and Zalmay had shared the private sphere with one another's families. Being invited into each other's private family area displayed trust and mutual respect. They knew whose houses they could enter and whose they could not. The Kabul office presented conflicts on many social levels. Soon the mixed-gender gatherings that took place there—including guards, cook, tailor, and male visitors—evoked too much gossip or fear of gossip. Hafiza wanted to be considered a cosmopolitan Kabuli—her husband's family did not. She struggled to hold onto her access to the office despite her sporadic attendance. She began to work more from home. It became impossible for her and the other women to feel comfortable coming to the office, and because it did not fit the Darrai Nuris' familiar framework of gendered space, it could not provide a work environment. Like many other small organizations in Afghanistan, Rubia moved locations, opened and closed and opened offices, and continues to struggle with professionalism and the ideal way to integrate work with office needs.

SCALING UP GRASSROOTS ORGANIZING— WORM'S-EYE VIEW

Our first major grant from USAID was an opportunity to deepen roots in Darrai Nur, employ women trained in Pakistan to teach others, and expand the base of women trained in Rubia's techniques, systems, and standards. This grant offered an opportunity to more women to earn income. Evenings at home were spent sitting on cots in the dark courtyard of the qala, backlit by *arekina*s (kerosene lanterns). Men and women sat together discussing who would fill which positions. They factored, in their casual way, which women had the most mobility due to age, widowhood, sons, and neediness and which women could visit which women's houses. Sakhi did not think there would be much interest in the project and suggested that we work with those who we knew from Pakistan, figuring that when others in the village saw the work was desirable, they'd want to join. Lists of women were written and scrapped repeatedly as we tried to distribute 200 positions fairly.

Sakhi returned from Jalalabad late one evening, delayed by two flat tires. This tardiness prompted his nephew to walk down the Darrai Nur road in the dark to find him, armed with an AK47. Sakhi's household was in uproar because they had received a note from the *uluswali* (district office) requesting Sakhi's presence the next day. Because he had not returned by nightfall, they were sure he was in some kind of trouble. The anxious relatives advised him to "get out of the valley tonight, forget about this funding, it isn't worth it." No one knew what the uluswal wanted, but it couldn't be good. Rural Afghans want as little as possible to do with officials; their *maliks* and *khans* (leaders), and *shura* (leadership) councils intercede for them.

In the morning Sakhi drew his support around him and headed up the valley, counting among them some young soldiers with their weapons. Prestige and power are associated with the size of one's entourage; he wanted to show he could hold his own in front of the uluswal. Waiting at home, his sister-in-law Basri—the rapid-fire rumor mill—assured me he would be arrested for something to do with this accursed fund. But happily, later that morning, he returned triumphant. Now, as word got out that Rubia was going to pay women to stay home and embroider and that this task would not conflict with household chores, we were inundated with requests to participate.

Men from throughout the valley approached Sakhi to insist he include their wives, daughters, and sisters in the program. The most equitable solution Sakhi arrived at was to invite the maliks of each of the ten major clans to choose twenty women each to participate. It was a clever strategy to diffuse and deflect responsibility. This solution not only dissolved the conflict in Zalmay and Sakhi's previous recruitment enrollment, but it also brought more men, and the advice of their womenfolk, into the process. It was truly grassroots and was publicly acknowledged as fair for all.

In order to keep the work at the local level and involve as many people in the planning and implementation as possible, Rubia constructed a scaffold-like network of mentors, dispensers, record keepers, and storage centers that suited the local population. Mentors trained by Hafiza in color and technique were each responsible for a number of women—often older or widowed and more mobile—in their vicinity, whose work they supervised and collected.

The mentors gathered regularly to discuss problems, clarify questions, and inspect and record trainees' work. They sat together at Sakhi's house for a midday meal. It was as if they had formed their own council. These women did not normally meet with one another and never in this type of setting. Sometimes their paths crossed at weddings, but not necessarily—that depended more on khish and qaum. This gathering crossed those boundaries. A great deal of village news and gossip was passed through this informal channel. Sakhi's Darrai Nur house, a mud-brick qala, became the de facto office. Storage units—enormous aluminum trunks—were kept in one of the four rooms. Finished embroideries, pillow blanks, threads, hoops, and needles were protected from the dust of the compound. The finished work remained with each woman until she was paid. Sakhi or Zalmay visited each mentor's home to dispense payments. Payments were made public, so that everyone knew what the others received, a successful procedure designed by the participants themselves to reduce jealousy and exploitation.

PRESERVING CULTURAL HERITAGE

Afghan embroidery ranges in styles and techniques. Some take advantage of the fabric's grid structure to produce complex geometric patterns. The embroiderer counts the spaces in between the warp and weft to design and produce patterns. It is incredibly exacting work; stitch size is determined by the matrix of the fabric. Embroidery requires fine motor coordination, precision, and attention to detail that develops with time and repetition.

Rubia's patterns are inspired by historical Afghan textiles representing a range of tribal designs and subject matter. Some are abstract and graphic, others representational and symbolic. Rubia's commitment to reviving traditional textile techniques extends to using historical dyes. We work with local Afghan dyers to color the embroidery yarns with plant dyes, preserving a natural palette. In Rubia's free-form and curvi-linear style, each embroiderer's stitches are like a thumbprint, unique and recognizable, through stitch size, tension, consistency, angle, and twist of the thread.

All embroideries are signed by the embroiderer, an emblem of her new skills in literacy. But for many women just learning to use the al-phabet, their most authentic signature is in the stitches themselves. Rubia provides the materials, fabric, and color guides; the embroiderer provides her interpretation, taking liberties that add to the delight and surprise in the color combinations and variety of choices for the con-sumer. Knowing that each piece was made by an actual individual, the consumer can begin to take an interest in the broader story of Afghani-stan and a less insular view of the world.

Despite disruptions by decades of war, embroidery as a craft contin-ues to be practiced in rural Afghanistan. Women stitch tablecloths, hand-kerchiefs, bedroom sets, prayer rugs, cosmetic bags, and other textiles to enhance their surroundings and to prepare their wedding trousseaus. The thread of stitchery runs through the fabric of rural Afghan. Now that some traditionally hand-embroidered textiles are being replaced by machine-embroidered ones, there is an even greater urgency to preserv-ing the craft.

Rubia has always sought and supported artistic collaborations. Ru-bia's finest craftswomen have worked for high-end fashion designers who create hand-embroidered garments shown on the runways in Paris and Milan. Rubia's fine embroideries have become components of custom-upholstered furniture in the United States. Rubia embroiderers have in-spired members of the Women's Caucus for Art, a national advocacy or-ganization for U.S. women artists to create a collaborative quilt that is on a national tour. Rubia's aim to promote creative collaborations between artists and artisans also brings women together in healing.

Needlework, like many activities that focus on small achievements and keep hands engaged, is therapeutic. Rubia has reached out with "stitch therapy" to the patients at the Sanga Amaj Women's Drug Treat-ment Center in Kabul. Patients at the center have completed a community-generated tapestry. The colorful tapestry—with themes of poppies, poi-son, and sayings from the Qur'an and the Hadith[10]—embodies Afghan aesthetics and ethics.

Rubia's model is embedded in a threefold commitment: working at the grassroots level, working in the Afghan family context, and preserv-ing cultural heritage. Rubia's retrospective approach of employing traditional methods—in crafts and social organization—is succeeding in advancing Afghan women.

Afghan women, and the country as a whole, benefit primarily from international assistance that focuses on capacity building from the grass roots. Bottom-up, community-run organizations ensure the development of capacity and the longitudinal sustainability of economic security. This requires measuring sustainability from a human perspective rather than quantifying numbers of women served and measuring profits as a primary indicator of success. Afghan women's and men's agency develop through their community involvement and by ownership of and decision-making in the direction and growth of economic projects. Small-scale programs, such as Rubia's, have the opportunity to gain a deep understanding and affiliation with Afghan family life and culture and are subsequently more likely to succeed in the long term. Rubia's motto, "Mending Afghanistan stitch by stitch," highlights our commitment to intentional, deliberate, and traditional steps that help to fortify this community.

NOTES

1. I would like to thank Ruth Mandel, Jennifer Fluri, and Jean Kissell for comments, questions, and generous editorial assistance in the preparation of this chapter.

2. *Rubia* is the Latin genus name for the dye plant *Rubia tinctorum*, better known as madder root, used throughout Central Asia as a natural source of red dye.

3. Bound by tradition and culture, many Afghan women wear the *chadari* or *burqa*. This veil protects a woman's privacy and provides her with the mobility and security to negotiate public spaces.

4. The *qala* is a fortress-like structure and typical architecture in eastern Afghanistan.

5. The word *purdah* means "curtain" or "veil." As a custom it refers to the system of gender segregation typically practiced in Afghan communities. This practice has ancient origins and different cultural manifestations throughout the Middle East and South Asia.

6. Pashai is an ethno-linguistic community in eastern Afghanistan. The language, Pashai, is a minority language in Afghanistan with Indo-Aryan roots. The cultural practices of Darrai Nur are similar to the Pashtun in that region.

7. Antje Bauer, *Afghan Women and the Democratic Reconstruction of Afghanistan: Findings and Interviews from a Journalist's Field Trip* (Berlin: The Berghof Research Center for Constructive Conflict Management, 2002), 43.

8. Zardozi Markets for Afghan Artisans, "Market Survey Report of the Embroidered Garment and Handicraft Subsector in Rural and Urban Afghanistan" (Final Report Submitted to Oxfam Novib, October 15, 2007).

9. After navigating many discouraging bureaucratic hurdles, Rubia finally succeeded in becoming a registered NGO in July 2008 with the assistance of the Welfare Association for the Development of Afghanistan.

10. Hadith, or *al-hadith*, are oral traditions relating to the words and deeds of the Islamic Prophet Muhammad.

CHAPTER 17

Rural Women's Livelihood

Their Position in the Agrarian Economy

JO GRACE AND ADAM PAIN

Much of the writing about Afghan women over the last twenty years has emphasized their condition, portraying it in two ways. First, it has been described in absolute terms making reference to international indices of women's well-being (related to health, education, etc.) on which counts Afghan women undeniably score extremely poorly. Second, attention has been drawn, and again with good reason, to the relative and poor position of women (in relation to men) with respect to their rights, social participation, and exposure to violence. Afghanistan is a patriarchal society and the levels of gender inequality are profound.

But to focus only on the outcomes of structural inequalities does not help us understand how women live within or challenge such structures nor how women act and negotiate to give their lives meaning and satisfaction. There is considerable evidence that women find ways to gain power to act and to achieve outcomes that benefit their lives and the lives of their families. But how can we build understanding of this? There are two potential analytical traps. The first is to assume that we can assess women's lives and what they have by direct comparison with what men possess. There has been a lively debate in the literature, not specific to Afghanistan, about the potential role of land ownership for women's empowerment, with Bina Agarwal arguing the case for it and Cecile Jackson contending that one cannot assume that men and women want the same things.[1] A key part of Jackson's argument hinges on the fact that most women in rural Asia (and elsewhere) live within married relationships and therefore occupy a multitude of positions—as wife, mother, mother-in-law, sister, and daughter—each with its own interests, commitments, and loyalties. The position of women therefore must be seen in relation to men and other women.

The second trap is the danger of prioritizing the capacity of women to act as autonomous economic agents. This reduces an understanding of women's position and activities to simply their ownership of assets and the income that they generate. This denies for women as for men the commitment to the institution of marriage to which most devote their lives and from which they draw material, as well as social and emotional, resources and security. The institution of marriage is of particular significance in Afghanistan. In a context where the state is dysfunctional and fails to provide even the most basic security and where markets are subject to all sorts of informal regulation,[2] these two key institutions (the state and the market) thus fail to provide the benefits and services that might be expected, leading to a context of acute risk and insecurity. This means that investments in and loyalty to both the family and community matter for the security that they can provide. But this has benefits and costs. The focus on marriage, children, and inheritance is significant in this respect as they constrain the pursuit of individual advantage and desires that libertarian capitalism would advocate.

However, the institutions of family and community are far from uniform in Afghanistan. One source of difference is that of economic class, and there are major differences to be found in the opportunities for and constraints on women in landed and landless households. Another source of variability is that of age and the scope for action by women according to whether they are young and unmarried, married with children, daughters or daughters-in-law; whether they are one of several wives within a polygynyous household and their position within it; or whether they are old and/or a widow. Further there are enormous cultural differences. Thus in the southern and most socially conservative areas among Pashtun populations in 2003, only 15 percent of women groups in a national survey reported women in income-generating work.[3] In contrast, in northern Afghanistan, more than 90 percent of women groups reported women working. In a country with a long history of migration, one often finds villages with different ethnicities, languages, and religious beliefs just several kilometers apart. In summary, it is necessary to be extremely cautious when making universal statements about what rural women in Afghanistan do.

One must also take into account the dynamics of change and the consequences for households and their ambitions. Many households have been through seismic events—experiences of conflict or being refugees, drought, the rise and fall of an opium economy—all of which have offered both challenges and opportunities and changed perspectives on life. The work that Afghan women are engaged in is often explained away by the catch-all phrase, "culture." It is "the culture" for women to work less outside the house; it is "the culture" that women do or do not work in agriculture; and it is "the culture" that women are less involved in direct income-generating work. Yet culture is not static and unchanging but is affected by contextual changes—culture adapts. Economically this has meant that many households have become stretched over space, with male migration for urban work both within and outside Afghanistan being an increasing feature; this has consequences for the women left behind and their roles and responsibilities. Therefore, the meaning of rural is far less clear given the significance of remittances from urban economies to many rural households. Equally, increasing access to and demand for education is driving changed expectations within households.

With these considerations in mind, this chapter reviews the evidence on selected aspects of women's role in the rural economy as economic agents (in relation to agriculture, carpets and textiles, and credit systems) and their access and control over land and livestock.

GENDER ROLES IN AGRICULTURE

This section outlines some of the key and differing activities of rural women to show aspects of the contribution they make in agriculture. It is based on the findings of three studies that covered a total of twenty-eight villages in eight provinces of Afghanistan,[4] together with the findings on gender and rural employment from the Nationwide Risk and Vulnerability Assessments conducted in 2003 and 2005, which covered nearly 12,000 households and 23,220 rural households, respectively.[5]

Many women in rural Afghanistan are involved in agriculture, more so than is commonly perceived. However, social norms around what women's roles should be vis à vis men's roles, together with their largely restricted mobility—the degree of which varies between different religious groups—in part determine the extent of women's involvement in agriculture and give rise to regional differences.[6] Tradition is not based solely on religion, which intersects with ethnicity, location, and wealth.

It is also cut across by other factors, such as economic status, age, position in the household, household composition, location of village (close to versus far from a road), village size, and access to knowledge. Thus what women "should" do, as dictated by tradition, is not necessarily the same as what women actually do.[7]

Social norms can be transgressed by various factors, one of which is poverty. Poorer women tend to be more involved in agriculture than wealthier women, working in tasks such as weeding, clearing stones from the land, harvesting, threshing, and cleaning seeds. Markets can also bring about change and opium poppy with its high labor demand has in recent years brought female labor gangs visibly into the village fields to weed where they had not been seen before, and there are reports that women have been able to negotiate comparable wage rates to men.[8]

However, women's roles can change over time. Economic status is not fixed. In some parts of the country, women in richer households were in the past less involved in agriculture when production was good and there was cash to hire agricultural labor. War and drought have impoverished households so that more women have become involved in helping to increase food production.[9] In the northern Faryab Province, people cited the presence of the Taliban as leading to a change in income-generating activities and a declining role for women. Women's ability to work on the land was restricted, so carpet weaving became one of the few income-generating activities possible. In some cases, women's weaving generated most of the household income.

Though not always visible, women from wealthier landowning households are also often involved in agricultural activities inside the house, helping to clean and prepare the seed for storage, separating the wheat from the husk, or taking care of small livestock. But there are exceptions. In Sar-i-Pul Province, in one family with no sons, the wife was involved in many stages of agriculture, from sowing to harvesting to processing. Where a household can afford to hire labor, women's roles are much reduced. In poorer, sharecropping households, women tend to work more on the land alongside the men in their households. However, the kind of work women do varies by age and the demands of domestic work.

Household composition and size, the number of women and the ratio of women to men, affects the activities different women carry out. One study found that women were said to work less in crop agriculture, and in a few cases not at all, if there were "enough" men in the household. Conversely, where there were few men in a household, women transcended the boundaries of the "normal" activities they carried out in agriculture.[10]

The number of females in a household can determine whether certain activities are undertaken. Some cannot keep livestock because there are not enough women in the household to look after them as well as carry out other domestic and agricultural work. Although some women work both on land and with livestock, it is not always the same women carrying out both types of activities. If a household contains more than one family, there will be several females in the house and the tasks may be split, with some women working with livestock and others with crops. This is especially the case in households where women migrate to a pasture area (*ailoq*) for several months at a time. The skills and age of household members can also affect roles. For example, in carpet-weaving households it is usually the younger skilled women who weave as it is physically demanding and requires good eyesight. Carpet weaving is considered to be a very profitable activity and may be prioritized over agriculture for women, although seasonally they may shift between activities.

The marital status of women also affects their activities. Unmarried women, especially if near marriage age, are less likely to be allowed to carry out agricultural tasks outside the house. Yet women in female-headed households are more likely to be engaged with agriculture and livestock. This does not always mean that they carry out the activities on the land themselves, but they may recruit day laborers or give their land to a sharecropper to work. This also depends on whether they have male children. If the sons are old enough, they may work on the land instead of laborers. In most cases widows and the few temporary female-headed households (where husbands had migrated for work) are able to manage the land.

The sale of agricultural (or any other) produce is mostly the domain of men and this may make it more difficult for women to make decisions over how money is spent.

CARPETS AND TEXTILES

Women and carpets are iconic images of Afghanistan to the external world, and historically women have played the major role in carpet and kilim weaving. The production of high-quality carpets, such as those prized in the West, has been associated largely with Turkmen and Uzbek women from the north.

There have been hopes that the development of Afghanistan's traditional carpet markets would offer particular opportunities for women. A degree of caution, however, is required. For a start, carpet production is distinctly gendered with women being the major producers but largely invisible in the actual marketplace, which is controlled by men. However, the terms of trade on the market and how it is structured—controlled by key traders with a majority of producers now working on a wage or profit-share basis—and increasing control of style and design by external markets are more likely to allow producers to survive but not to thrive.[11]

Along with carpets, women have long been engaged in a handicraft industry based around embroidered garments, but again this is most visible and active in the north. A recent survey has revealed the extent and significance of a market that has been largely invisible and in which women dominate the production side.[12] In the city of Sherbegan, in Jawzjan Province—a largely Uzbek area—and in specific locations around Kunduz in larger bazaars and independent of them, women were found to be active in trading the textiles they had produced. In Sherbegan, women, all in burqas, came from nearby villages and occupied an edge of a larger market, where they sold machine-embroidered materials. In a number of small towns around Kunduz, on a twice-weekly basis, there are open markets given over entirely to the sale of embroidery for traditional Baluch garments. These are occupied entirely by women, although they serve as a hub for the exclusively male traders of sales agents to purchase. Again, producers are from both the small towns and surrounding villages. What is significant about this market is that it is entirely geared toward export.

It must be emphasized that the location of women almost exclusively at the production end of the value chain provides pretty minimal returns on their labor—ranging from less than half a dollar per day to two dollars a day, although it was reported that this income largely remained at their disposal inside the family.[13] The trading side of the market is almost exclusively under the control of men. There are examples where the development of these textile markets has allowed room for female sales agents to operate and for independent women to set up small businesses, but these are exceptions rather than the rule.

CREDIT

The use of credit is pervasive in rural Afghanistan. Field evidence clearly points to women being active in the management of both informal and formal credit at household and village levels.[14]

> We get credit from the one who knows us, who has good manners, who does not come every day to our house asking for their money even though we do not have money. We go to those who do not fight with us. We go to cousins, relatives, and friends; not our paternal cousins because they have no money, their life is the same as ours. We go to those with a good life, who have a good economy, and good manners.[15]

In describing how and from whom she accesses credit within her village, Shafiqa, a woman in northeast Kapisa Province, illustrates a number of significant features and widespread characteristics about rural credit in Afghanistan. First and foremost, it is an illustration of the need for credit not as is often assumed for productive investment but simply as a means to buy food when cash is not available and food supplies run out.[16] This need for informal borrowing in cash or kind to meet consumption shortfalls is experienced by many rural households and is indicative of the precariousness of rural livelihood security in Afghanistan.

It also illustrates the widespread availability of informal credit in rural Afghanistan. As many expressed, they know "how to find money" and invest in building social relations to access informal credit both for consumption purposes and for marriage. Significantly, much of this informal credit is on interest-free terms. Although the nature of informal credit defies quantification, its extent and scale in rural household lives has been largely ignored by donors and government.[17] There has been an assumption of an absence of credit in rural areas, which has been used to justify microcredit programs. There has also been a lack of appreciation of the fact that if households constantly have to borrow in order to achieve food security, accessing credit for productive investments, a focus of microcredit, is likely to be secondary in household borrowing requirements. This point is returned to below.

The third feature of Shafiqa's comment illustrates the role women play through their connections in the village in managing access to and obtaining informal credit. A further study on microcredit also illustrates the role of women in informal credit systems:

> Zarifa in Bamyan limits her credit involvement due to concerns about repayment, maintaining ties only with family or friends. She has her own recipro-

cal credit link with a female neighbour to whom she lent 1000 Afs ($20) one month prior to the interview, for which she received bricks in repayment because she was improving her house.[18]

The study on microcredit was also revealing about the use that women made of microcredit facilities.[19] Although microcredit institutions can be unfriendly to women—for example, locating offices distant from villages where it was difficult for women to travel—some microcredit providers have specifically targeted women's groups. The study found cases from these that not only illustrated the interplay between formal and informal credit—the use of formal credit for consumption purposes, for instance—but also the role of women in obtaining group credit and using it for practices that breach lending rules. One woman in Bamiyan used her female relations, friends, and neighbors to obtain a group loan, which she hoarded for herself, so that her husband could buy a car.

WOMEN'S ACCESS TO LAND AND LIVESTOCK

As with gender roles in agriculture and textiles, access and control over assets is determined by a complex interplay of sociocultural factors, to which the gender construct is fundamental. Assets are essential (but not sufficient) for improving and protecting livelihoods, yet in many cases women lack control over them. This section focuses on women's access to two of the most crucial assets for rural livelihoods: land and livestock. Access is not possible for all nor is it necessary, but by focusing on land and livestock, an understanding of the difficulties women face and how they address them can be provided.

Despite women's involvement in agriculture, few women own land and where they do, few exercise control over it.[20] Access to land in Afghanistan is largely obtained through inheritance. According to Shari'a law, women can inherit land as daughters or as wives upon the death of a husband. The Civil Code of 1978 governs inheritance law in Afghanistan and is based on Islamic jurisprudence. Widows are to receive one-eighth of the property or one-fourth if they have no children. Where there is more than one wife, this proportion is shared among them. Provision for widows is priority. Daughters should receive half of their brother's share.

Although the law dictates that women have rights to inherit as daughters and as wives, the reality is different, particularly for daughters.

Inheritance of land is affected by numerous factors that largely stem from the position of most women in the household. Usually when an Afghan woman is born, she is economically dependent on her father and (as with boys) her life is then partly determined by the parental decisions over who she will marry. When she is married she is largely economically dependent on her husband and his natal family, but she often seeks to preserve relations with her brothers, who can be drawn upon in times of need (for example, desertion, divorce, widowhood). Women thus tend to give their land to their brothers, who will marry and be responsible for providing for their own families.

Until the division of land, daughters are often considered to have a share of land. However, to accept ownership over a parcel of the family's land is often seen as a direct affront to male heirs, threatening the need women have to maintain relationships with their brothers for livelihood security. The offering of a share is often merely a ritual, and few women (except perhaps where land is plentiful) accept their portion citing that "we love our brothers." In most cases, the explanation given was that "it is not our culture" as the reason why girls do not inherit, reflecting local social norms. Women who accept are not well thought of in many communities and relations with brothers can be severed if a woman chooses to accept or claim her legal rights.[21] Where women do inherit as daughters, they often lose effective control of their land anyway when they marry.

There are cases of people wanting to give land to their daughters, but the cultural pressure is often too strong to allow it. Two widows interviewed in Badakhshan Province expressed a desire to give land to their daughters, but one said she could not because the rules say that you should give it to your sons; and the other said that when she told her sons she would like to give some land to her daughter, they got angry and argued that "it is not their culture and they will give her a dowry instead." In some cases a woman's husband may encourage her to claim her inheritance from her brothers. In other cases, he will not accept her claim, as "people will say you're dependent on your wife—you can't stand on your own two feet." In one instance, a widow desperately tried to get her daughter to accept all of her land because her sons had not taken care of her when she was ill, but her daughter refused. However the overall land shortage and the decreasing size of holdings as land is continuously subdivided through generations are also cited as reasons for not giving it to female siblings.

Inheriting land as a widow rather than as a daughter is perhaps more common, though this is ultimately constrained by a number of factors. A widow living separately and not with other families appears to have fewer problems inheriting her husband's land, as he will often although not always have received his share of the land when he separated from the joint household. Therefore when the husband dies, it is clear this land belonged to him and will be inherited by his family. Several widows specifically gave this as the reason they faced no problems in receiving their share of the land. In contrast, several cases were found where widows living in joint households in which land had not been divided faced problems and had to claim their rights usually through customary procedures at the village level.[22]

Where women were found to own land, particularly as widows, they were able to use it productively, though their level of control over those assets varied. Unable to work it themselves, many sharecrop it out, largely to male relatives, if they do not have older sons. Young widows will often remarry, particularly if they are too poor to support themselves. The relation of the person they marry varies from place to place. In many Pashtun areas, a woman usually marries a brother of her husband. In contrast in Bamiyan and Badakhshan, for example, a widow normally does not marry a brother of her husband and may have to take the hard decision to leave her children behind with her deceased husband's family. This arises where widows have not inherited land from their parents or are from landless families and find it extremely difficult to generate sufficient income to support a family by themselves. Most of the widows in the study who had not remarried had inherited a share of their husband's land and so were able to keep their children with them, though many still struggle.

Divorced women also face many problems, as few receive any property despite the fact that they are usually pledged an amount of money and sometimes land and livestock when they marry. In theory, this can be claimed at any time upon divorce, but no one interviewed could cite any cases of women receiving this. Without property and few income-generating opportunities, most women have to remarry (if young enough) or be, to some extent, dependent on family members.

Women's access to land is tied to a system that prioritizes land ownership by men as the breadwinners of the family, increases women's economic dependence as wives and later as sisters (in the event of widowhood, divorce, or desertion), and necessitates women's compliance with these rules to assure livelihood security. The nine cases in seven villages in three provinces found in the study of women actually claiming land that was not given were those in which systems of support either from brothers or in-laws had broken down.

The number of women claiming land is not known as it largely is settled by customary law at the village level. Women face difficulties taking their cases to formal law courts in distant district centers, unless they are elderly, because they generally need to be accompanied by a male relative and require money for the fees.

Given the above constraints and the overall land pressure in Afghanistan, other means for generating income at the household level are also necessary. Livestock can be one such asset that women can access and look after, though the extent to which they can generate income is again dependent on several factors. Women appear to have more control over livestock than land, particularly chickens, goats, sheep, and cattle. Often they care for the household livestock, and in mountainous areas, they migrate with men for several months to summer pastures. Livestock raised on a more commercial scale are largely managed by men on account of the need to maintain credit and trade relations with outside buyers, thereby excluding women.[23]

At the time of marriage, women traditionally receive small household items and clothes from their parents. These gifts are seen as a dowry and given as another reason for women not to receive a share of property later in life. Women in some areas also receive livestock through a tradition known as *pie wasi*, the first visit of a new bride to her parental home after marriage, a form of pre-mortem inheritance. The woman takes the animals to her marital home, where in theory, the animals belong to her. But whether this ownership is respected, and whether it translates into control over the animals and their produce, varies from household to household. The husband's parents might take control and even sell the animals without asking the woman's permission. Yet in other households, members may consult her before making decisions over the animal and its produce.

As with land, aside from inheritance, there are few other means of accessing livestock. Not many women have sufficient income to purchase animals. In some areas women access and increase their livestock through a creative system of borrowing animals from wealthier households. For example, a woman from a household with little or no livestock can borrow a female animal from a household that has more and then mate it with a male animal belonging to a neighbor until it produces offspring. During that time, the woman feeds and milks the animal and makes dairy products, a share of which goes to the household that lent it. Once the animal has finished nursing the offspring, the adult is returned to the owner and the woman who looked after it keeps the progeny.

This system can provide a major source of income—extra livestock can be an asset that is sold to make up a shortfall in grain. Some women manage to rear several animals without having to sell them. The livestock provides produce used for household consumption and the *qrut* (dried yoghurt) is sold where possible, if the woman needs goods or money. If the household needs more income to buy food, the animal can then be sold.

Sometimes, as women are fully responsible for arranging this, they are considered to own the animals, though this again appears to depend on the relations inside the household. Several women said they have all authority to sell the animals they brought through this system without anyone's permission, and that if anyone else wants to sell them they have to ask the women. In a few cases, where women had brought several animals through these means, men said the women were allowed to keep one of the animals that they brought and could decide what to do with it. If the women choose to sell it, they could decide how to use the income. Where women cannot control decisions about the sale of an animal, they nonetheless often have some control over the animal produce, which women in all the villages were found to trade inside the village. In some cases, they could also decide how to use the income.

Ownership of land, and to a lesser extent livestock, is crucial for women in enabling them to support their families in times of widowhood or divorce, to act as a bargaining tool to ensure security in old age, and in reducing their dependence and increasing their decision-making power.

The focus of much research and most aid and development programming is still on the "household." This focus often obscures intra-household gender relations and roles—crucial factors in determining access to, and control over, what individuals have and do. It ignores the differences that exist between women, between men, and between men and women. As a result, not enough is known of the extent to which diverse men and women are able to benefit from different activities or how programs and policies impact women and men differently.

Women find a variety of ways to navigate the structural constraints that affect their lives and act for their interests. But they do so within a context where the family and conjugality may provide the only means of achieving a degree of security. As Agarwal puts it, "The appearance of compliance need not mean that women lack a correct perception of their best interests; rather it can be a survival strategy stemming from the constraints on their ability to act overtly in pursuit of those interests."[24]

NOTES

1. Bina Agarwal, "Gender and Command over Property: A Critical Gap in Economic Analysis and Policy in South Asia," *World Development* 22 (1994a): 1455–1458; Cecile Jackson, "Gender Analysis of Land: Beyond Land Rights for Women?" *Journal of Agrarian Change* 3 (2003): 453–480.

2. Sarah Lister and Adam Pain, *Trading in Power: The Politics of "Free" Markets in Afghanistan* (Kabul: Afghanistan Research and Evaluation Unit, 2004).

3. Hector Maletta, "Gender and Employment in Rural Afghanistan, 2003–5," *Journal of Asian and African Studies* 42 (2008): 180.

4. Jo Grace, *Gender Role in Agriculture: Case Studies of Five Village in Northern Afghanistan* (Kabul: Afghanistan Research and Evaluation Unit, 2004); Jo Grace and Adam Pain, *Rethinking Rural Livelihoods* (Kabul: Afghanistan Research and Evaluation Unit, 2003); Jo Grace, *Who Owns the Farm? Rural Women's Access to Land and Livestock* (Kabul: Afghanistan Research and Evaluation Unit, 2004).

5. Maletta, "Gender and Employment."

6. Ibid.

7. Grace, *Who Owns the Farm?*

8. Adam Pain, unpublished field observations, Badakhshan 2004 and Balkh 2007.

9. Grace, *Who Owns the Farm?*

10. Grace, *Gender Role in Agriculture.*

11. Adam Pain and M. Ali, *Understanding Markets in Afghanistan: A Case Study on Carpets and the Andkhoy Carpet Market* (Kabul: Afghanistan Research and Evaluation Unit, 2004).

12. Zardozi. *Market Survey of the Embroidered Garment and Handicraft Subsector in Rural and Urban Afghanistan* (Kabul: Novib, 2007), 76.

13. Ibid.

14. Floortje Klijn and Adam Pain, *Finding the Money: Informal Credit Practices in Afghanistan* (Kabul: Afghanistan Research and Evaluation Unit, 2007); Paula Kantor, *From Access to Impact: Microcredit and Rural Livelihoods in Afghanistan* (Kabul: Afghanistan Research and Evaluation Unit, 2009).

15. Interview with Shafiqa, in a village Kapisa Province, in Klijn and Pain, *Finding the Money,* 1.

16. Klijn and Pain, *Finding the Money.*

17. Ibid.

18. Kantor, *From Access to Impact*, 34.

19. A number of national and international NGOs specifically support microcredit for women; see http://www.unhcr.org/home/SUBSITES/4497b28a2 .pdf. They include the Aga Khan Development Network (AKDN) and Bangladesh Rural Advancement Committee (BRAC). See also www.areu.org.af for various village case studies (Paula Kantor and Erna Andersen, *Microcredit, Informal Credit and Rural Livelihoods: A Village Case Study in Kabul Province* [Kabul: Afghanistan Research and Evaluation Unit, 2007]; Erna Andersen, Paula Kantor, and Amanda Sim, *Microcredit, Informal Credit and Rural Livelihoods: A Village Case Study in Bamyan Province* [Kabul: Afghanistan Research and Evaluation Unit, 2008]) on microcredit provision and its impact.

20. Grace, *Gender Role in Agriculture*; Grace and Pain, *Rethinking Rural Livelihoods*; Grace, *Who Owns the Farm?*; Alan Roe. *Livestock, Water Management and Opium: Natural Resource Management, Farming Systems and Rural Livelihoods* (Kabul: Afghanistan Research and Evaluation Unit, 2008).

21. Grace, *Who Owns the Farm?*

22. Ibid.

23. Roe, *Livestock, Water Management and Opium*.

24. Bina Agarwal, A *Field of One's Own: Gender and Land Rights in South Asia* (Cambridge: Cambridge University Press, 1994), 430.

CHAPTER 18

Chadari Politics

Translating Perceptions into Policy and Practice

LINA ABIRAFEH

Women's rights and roles have been an ongoing part of political processes throughout Afghan history, from fueling conflict to "liberation."
Afghan women recognize their political roles, and yet, from the perspective of those outside, they remain bound by a pervasive symbol that
has also taken on a political role: the *chadari*. Images of women enveloped in blue chadaris played a significant role in instigating calls for
liberation and in providing the moral backbone for the subsequent
"war on terror."

Unfortunately, it is not unusual for any act of veiling to be miscon-
strued as a denial of women's agency. Afghanistan is not unique; many
have documented a history of Western obsession with the veil.[1] Despite
this obsession, Afghan women repeatedly fail to conform to stereotypical images. The most facile of constructs is the use of the chadari as
a barometer to measure social change—or lack thereof. Images surrounding this garment have contributed in no small part to the formulation of policy guiding gender and development interventions in
Afghanistan.

To illuminate this path, this discussion begins with an examination
of popular perceptions of Afghan women. This is followed by a brief
analysis of book covers with chadari images, to better understand how
Afghan women are represented in popular media. Although seemingly
benign, book imagery in fact conveys or reinforces political messages.
These political messages can be linked to gender and development poli-

cies as they are ultimately informed by similar shortcomings: a denial of Afghan women's agency and a belief that liberation will only be possible with outside intervention. These policies, in turn, manifest themselves as interventions that fail to represent Afghan women's realities.

This work is part of a larger study conducted first through an examination of policy texts and media discourses, then through an investigation of program practice, drawing on the perspectives of policy makers and policy implementers. The findings are then weighed against perspectives and experiences of women and men in Afghanistan. It is essential to examine the implementation of policies in light of promised transformation of women's rights and roles. Indeed, Afghanistan is facing a unique set of development challenges: poverty, insecurity, gender inequality. It is in this context that the following discussion takes place.

POPULAR PERCEPTIONS OF AFGHAN WOMEN

The chadari is not a new object of Western obsession. In 1985, well before Afghan women were objects of public interest, Nancy Hatch Dupree wrote that women in Afghanistan "dismiss the stereotyped image depicted by most Western media which insist on picturing Afghan women forever enveloped in billowing veils."[2] Over ten years later, in November 1997, United Nations Special Advisor on Gender Issues and the Advancement of Women Angela King wrote the following in her report after an interagency gender mission to Afghanistan: "External observers and interlocutors often mistake symptoms and causes: the *burqa* . . . is not considered a major problem for most Afghan women with whom the Mission spoke, but is treated as such by many assistance workers in the country, agency personnel at headquarters and sometimes, opinion-makers outside the country."[3]

In March 2005, I tested popular perceptions and media influence to better understand images surrounding Afghan women. I was invited to speak on the issue of Afghan women at the Women as Global Leaders Conference in Dubai, United Arab Emirates. At that point I had already been working in Afghanistan for nearly three years. I used the conference as an opportunity to gauge public opinion on the situation of Afghan women more than three years after their "liberation" and their virtual disappearance from the media. The audience comprised forty female participants, mostly American, including students, academics, and development practitioners. At the beginning of the two-hour session, I circulated a questionnaire to the participants and asked that they complete it immediately. The answers then served as the starting point for the discussion on images of Afghan women.

The discussion started with general descriptions of Afghanistan after the Taliban—not very positive. Images of Afghan women included the chadari and veil, noting that Afghan women are "oppressed but wanting change." Most of the participants mentioned the chadari, but it is significant that all of them used the word "burqa." In fact, none of them were familiar at all with the word "chadari." It was interesting to note the contradiction in each answer as many conveyed the sense that things are bad but hopeful. For instance, one response was, "Hidden but struggling to better the life of their people."

The respondents largely felt that the media contributed to whatever negative images they might have had about "helpless women who don't have rights or privileges," perpetuating "negative images of repressed women, veiled unhappy victims." They felt that there is currently very little focus on Afghan women, particularly since world attention shifted to Iraq and other issues. Another said: "We see images of women under the burqa but we hear George Bush tell us that women's rights have been restored." The media presented a biased and sensationalized view, presenting Afghan women "as either victims, or as victims-turned-success stories."

CAN WE SEE "BENEATH THE BURQA" YET?

Popular literature plays a role in reinforcing the political messages of the day. Imagery used on book covers promotes symbols that carry political messages to entice readers. For books on Afghanistan, images of women in burqas have become the primary means by which audiences identify the women as Afghan. As a result, these books perpetuate images that may have certain effects, reinforcing the victimization of Afghan women. In a brief analysis, using Amazon as the search engine and "Afghanistan" and "women" as the keywords, 715 books emerged in the search results. As I began my review, I noticed a collection of book covers with images of women in chadaris, the covering used for centuries by Afghan women. I thus narrowed my search to books focused exclusively on Afghan women with a chadari on the cover.[4]

Researcher Gillian Whitlock's analysis of books about Afghan women noted that "these texts are carefully positioned to project the gender apartheid imposed by Islamic fundamentalism towards a receptive [read: Western] market."[5] Whitlock states that these life narratives are geared for American women in particular. "To pull Western eyes under the burqa in this way is a powerful rhetorical strategy; it elicits both sympathy and advocacy that can be put to quite different political and strategic uses."[6] The crux of Whitlock's argument is that these auto-ethnographies are employed as propaganda to justify a military intervention with the surface objective of liberating Afghan women from the oppressive clutches of Islamic fundamentalism.[7] Many parallels have been made concerning the cooptation of Afghan women for the war on terror.[8]

Books reviewed frequently refer to Afghan women's "inferior status," their abuse under the Taliban, their shared oppression along with other Muslim women, and United States President George W. Bush's successful "liberation" of the women of Afghanistan. For example, *Off with Their Heads: Traitors, Crooks, and Obstructionists in American Politics, Media, and Business* asks: "Why do so few pay attention to the wonderful work the United States has done in freeing the women of Afghanistan from subjugation?"[9] This is followed by another popular misconception: "In Afghanistan women threw off their burqas when American forces arrived."[10]

Other books reinforce the image of Afghan women as victims. *The Mobilization of Shame: A World View of Human Rights* states that "among all the horror stories about the degradation of women around the world, the abuse of females in Afghanistan has a special place."[11] *Faith in Conflict: Christian Integrity in a Multicultural World* refers to the "savage repression of women in Afghanistan."[12] Similarly, *Humanitarian Challenges and Intervention: World Politics and the Dilemmas of Help* discusses "subordinate women (for instance, in Afghanistan)."[13] In *A Just Response: The Nation on Terrorism, Democracy, and September 11, 2001*, the author asks: "Are there any people on earth more wretched than the women of Afghanistan?"[14]

The covers of *My Forbidden Face: Growing Up Under the Taliban: A Young Woman's Story* and *Three Women of Herat: A Memoir of Life, Love, and Friendship in Afghanistan* present close-ups of women in chadaris, indicating that the books bring the reader as near as possible to Afghan women.[15] Such pictures and provocative titles entice the reader with a verbal "unveiling" and much-desired view of the "forbidden faces" of Afghan women. The cover of *Three Women of Herat* goes one step further: a woman peeks tenuously from beneath her partially removed chadari, covering her mouth with her chadari-enveloped hand, in a seemingly willing effort to reveal herself.[16]

The Story of My Life: An Afghan Girl on the Other Side of the Sky, is about a young woman living in the suburbs of Chicago.[17] Here, the book cover depicts an unveiled Afghan woman, presumably revealing what she looks like on the "other side" (read: the "unveiled" side; further read: the West). Finally, many of the books on Afghan women present a full image of the chadari or several chadaris. *Zoya's Story: An Afghan Woman's Struggle for Freedom* does just that,[18] as does *The Silenced Cry: One Woman's Diary of a Journey to Afghanistan*, with its lone white chadari on the cover.[19]

LIBERATION FROM GENDER APARTHEID

Jan Goodwin's *Price of Honor: Muslim Women Lift the Veil of Silence on the Islamic World*, with three chadaris on the cover, takes the discussion on images and stereotypes further.[20] Goodwin's book, as Uma Narayan writes, "seems to have had a more significant public presence and influence than most 'academic' writing, and not because there are no 'scholarly' examples of these same problems."[21]

Price of Honor opens with a chapter titled "Fundamentally Different?" in which Goodwin recounts the story of Maria, an Afghan refugee she encountered in Pakistan. Maria's life is one of abuse, forced marriage, and a series of tortures and thus inspires Goodwin to embark on her research to "unveil" the mysteries behind the Muslim world. She writes: "It was because of Maria that I began this book. Was what happened to her merely a daily occurrence in underdeveloped nations throughout the world—children born into deprivation, raised in ignorance? . . . Or was her experience intrinsic to her culture?"[22] In addition to myriad uses of the veil, veiling, and its imagery, Goodwin describes the chadari as a "body-bag for the living . . . which would eventually become an international symbol of the Taliban's oppression of women."[23] Said "body bag" would also be the galvanizing point for many American feminist groups.[24]

Academic Deniz Kandiyoti writes of the debates that ensued among transnational feminists on their roles in supporting women in Afghanistan. She explains that "these exchanges followed the familiar tropes of women's rights as universal human rights versus 'feminism-as-imperialism,' reflected in a spate of articles in both the popular press and academic journals."[25] Afghanistan specialist Sippi Azarbaijani-Moghaddam reinforces this point: "Complexity and nuances notwithstanding, unprecedented international interest, misinformation, and hysteria have surrounded the situation of women and girls since the Taliban set foot in Kabul. In recent years Afghan women have been used by countless media, political, and humanitarian entities, as well as publicity hungry women's rights' groups, to pursue their own objectives."[26]

Jan Goodwin's book is an example of literature's transition into policy. Goodwin's writings on Afghan women had a particular influence over perceptions Americans have of Afghan women, leading to her pivotal role in the launching of the so-called Gender Apartheid campaign.[27] Although high-profile campaigning on behalf of Afghan women might serve well in terms of consciousness-raising, it has created difficulties for aid operations on the ground.[28] Such campaigns, philosopher Alison Jaggar has argued, waged by North American feminist activists, limit discursive openness by centering their agendas on certain moral convictions, therefore stifling debate. These agendas then become the foundation for the group's moral perspectives.[29] Many articles by Afghan women activists were released during that time, expressing concern with the campaign and the possibility that it could alienate the very women it was trying to help. These Afghan voices were relatively silent in comparison, however, despite their concern that "the true needs and wants of the Afghan people are largely absent from campaigns waged on their behalf in the United States."[30]

The Gender Apartheid campaign was deemed successful with the 2001 "liberation" of Afghanistan—and therefore of Afghan women— from the Taliban. Many years after the campaign, images of Afghan women as oppressed creatures beneath chadaris still permeated popular perception, although the media's silence led spectators to believe that Afghan women had been liberated and there was no further need to discuss them. One author expressed the views of many: "The veil was probably the clearest example of the perverse nature of media coverage. . . . The fall of the Taliban has led to the virtual disappearance from the media agenda of the issue of the veil, and indeed of Afghan women in general."[31]

Indeed, the cause of Afghan women had been taken up by North American feminists and subsequently forgotten, while Afghan women continued to struggle under external pressure to defend their agency and their cultural integrity. Meanwhile, Afghan women had "good reason to suppose that if their lives were to become the subject of feminist discussion, their own perspectives might be discounted."[32] Jaggar has been a critic of this sudden interest in the perceived victimization of women in non-Western cultures. She argues that this "incomplete understanding distorts Western philosophers' comprehension of our moral relationship to women elsewhere in the world and . . . also impoverishes our assumptions about the intercultural dialogue necessary to promote global justice for women."[33] Indeed, there is arrogance in the notion that the aid apparatus knows better than the women involved about their needs and interests.

These images and perceptions present a good starting point for a discussion of policy formulation from the perspectives of those actively involved. Given the tenacious nature of the perceptions surrounding Afghanistan and Afghan women, one might question the extent to which these images have informed aid interventions.

EXAMINING POLICY TEXTS

It is essential to question how far national and international instruments have been influenced by pervasive images of Afghan women. In this vein, a brief investigation into policy formulation begins here with a textual analysis of aid and gender policy papers of the large aid institutions operating in Afghanistan.[34] These policy papers determine the course of action for gender interventions in Afghanistan.

For this study, five aid institutions were selected based on their roles as core members of a high-level body charged with supporting the Ministry of Women's Affairs and providing strategic direction on all things gender in Afghanistan. I thus examined policy texts with a view to the presence of gender issues—and the quality of that presence. My approach was informed by a number of studies where aid policy documents have been analyzed for their gender content or to discern their approach to women and gender. I was further concerned with the extent to which gender has been "mainstreamed" in the document. Despite rhetoric, very often gender is *not* a cross-cutting issue but has in fact been isolated in the document. It merits questioning when a claim to mainstream gender issues is substantiated by an isolated paragraph on gender.

Viewing gender issues in isolation leaves little room for aid interventions to accurately assess progress made for women. "Progress" is therefore measured in terms of quantity—money spent, women trained, and so on—in lieu of actual improvements made in women's lives.

A further contradiction entails the mention of men in so-called gender documents. In these cases, men are included in the document only as obstacles to women's development or when making negative comparisons with women.[35] This is also reflected in popular perceptions of Afghan women and is problematic as it negates men's roles in women's development—and negates the importance of their own development. As a result, interventions assume that gender relations and power are a zero-sum game, and that interventions for women should offer no alternatives for men.[36] In addition, simplistic formulations and facile analyses label man-as-exploiter and woman-as-exploited. Imagery of chadari-clad women also supports these deductions.

Most texts make lofty claims to instigate social change, yet they provide few practical applications to bring this to fruition. A textual analysis therefore should include an understanding of the presence of terms such as "empowerment" and "gender" in order to illuminate the extent of this intervention priority shift on paper.

One report makes vague references to women, such as "women and men of Afghanistan," and makes negative comparisons of women's suffering as compared to men's. There is little indication of women's agency and in fact emphasis is placed on women's poor condition. No mention is made of solutions to address this condition. The report further refers vaguely and unconstructively to "gender issues" and a "gender-sensitive approach," but fails to define what the terms might mean in Afghanistan. Therefore, although "gender issues" are present, they lack a robust definition. In addition, use of the term is concentrated in the paragraph on "human rights and gender issues" and not throughout the document.

Another report fails to provide definitions or operational guidelines on how to address the various gender issues it raises. References to gender include "gender training modules," "the gender perspective," "gender task force," "gender-sensitive amendments to law," and others. All of these are used in the abstract, without a clear understanding of how they might be put into operation—beyond the technical solution of adding women to existing efforts and isolating women as an "object" of aid interventions. These reports also give little indication of women's agency in Afghanistan, implying that the presence of the aid institution is therefore justified as it is the only way to achieve gains for women.

Yet another report juxtaposes the Taliban ("the problem") with the organization's activities ("the solution"). This plays into popular perceptions of how to "solve" Afghan women's "problems." Each statement regarding Afghan women's poor condition is qualified by Taliban abuses. This constant justification for action, coupled with a moral imperative to act, is simplistic at best. It is also important to note the frequent employment of liberation rhetoric for such purposes. Additional documents from this organization advocate fast responses to what it calls political problems. One might argue that Afghanistan needed precisely the opposite. It also assumes that aid interventions are equipped to provide political solutions. The solutions proposed are hardly political but are in fact technical. Claims of improving women's roles in society are articulated but not substantiated. No mention was made of analyses defining what women might believe to constitute an "improvement"—or whether they sought this improvement in the first place. Further analyses have revealed that such projects are not founded on Afghan community needs and demands. Afghan women have articulated that they were not consulted and felt compelled to accept the projects that were designed to benefit them as a fait accompli.

Such efforts likely would have benefited from a contextualized understanding of Afghanistan's social dynamics—particularly gender issues. This was notably absent from most public discussions on "the situation of Afghan women." Neglect of this understanding demonstrates the propensity to offer technical solutions to political problems and the tendency for elevated claims that could not be met through these technical solutions. Further, moving from program rhetoric to reality was extremely challenging and met with much resistance.

Another organization did not finalize its gender strategies or release them to the public. Such documents frequently employ vague terminology that recognizes Afghanistan's "cultural context"—viewing it as a static element that presents a constraint to the women's liberation agenda. It was implicit that—though neither a workable definition of gender nor a plan to mainstream was provided—aid interventions are best suited to do the "mainstreaming," whatever that entails. This gender policy was not specific to Afghanistan, but was, according to one official, built from gender policies in other countries and "tweaked for the Afghan context."

Other reports reflect similar trends. The uses of the term "gender" do not represent a contextualized understanding and lack any definition of the term. More often than not, the term is used in place of "sex," such as gender-disaggregated data. The reports refer sporadically to women's "vulnerable" status and to their suffering under the Taliban. Beyond language referring to "gender imbalances" and the subsequent need for "special attention" to be paid to women, there is little reference as to how to rectify imbalances. Such documents leave no alternative beyond that of aid intervention to rectify imbalances and bring equality. Through such texts, it is made clear that only the aid apparatus can bring liberation to Afghan women, and that this liberation can only come in the form of technical solutions that constitute the standard package of interventions.

This analysis of texts from reputable institutions in Afghanistan is used to illustrate the similarities in the discourse and the pervasive extent of this particular discourse. This would likely also be the case if popular media and reporting on Afghan women was to be examined through a similar lens.

The texts share a few key commonalities. First, they offer no definitions for terms used or an understanding of the application of these terms in Afghanistan. Practical applications are notably absent, making it challenging for "gender" to translate from paper to practice. Gender issues might be sprinkled strategically throughout the documents, but the value is lost and mention is largely tokenistic.

Next, they offer no recognition of Afghan agency but instead leave room to justify their own existence by problematizing "the women issue" in a way where the only solution is an aid intervention. The rhetoric uses gender terminology but reflects a women-in-development approach. In this case, women's empowerment is a means to achieve economic development.

A parallel can be made between textual references to gender and agency and Sylvia Walby's progression of engagement with gender issues.[37] I extend this approach to address men's issues in gender programming using a five-phased process. The first phase, near neglect, sees men only as perpetrators and therefore women as victims. The second phase exposes the previous neglect, addressing men as obstacles to women's development. The third phase entails engagement with men only to advance women's interests. The fourth phase is that of exceptions: men who are advocates and supporters of women's issues. Finally, full integration of men—the fifth phase—entails working with men in their own right. Most of the texts sit in phase one. None of the texts have moved beyond phase two.

The documents all frame women's issues as social problems, stripping them of any political content. And yet the texts all promise transformation that they cannot deliver on. Proposed transformation is not met by real interventions. Strategic interests are not embedded in the texts and only receive lip service without practical applications. Some prefer to focus on technical solutions with outcomes that are quick and visible (to their constituents and countries). All of the documents treat mainstreaming as a technical project well suited for aid interventions.

CHADARI POLITICS AND PERSPECTIVES

The analysis of policy texts reveals a constructed image of Afghan women, fueled by the media and popular perceptions. In so doing, Afghan women's problems are framed as social, enabling aid institutions to create a situation to fit their standardized solutions.[38] Subsequent calls for liberation were met with technical packages of aid institutions. Academic and contextualized analyses might not have created the space for such packages, revealing instead Afghan women's historic ability to act on their own behalf.

A senior gender advisor with an international institution explained that the discourses and images are typically employed by aid institutions and the media.[39] She elaborated: "This is orientalism and racism. . . . The media has to have shorthand ways because it has a short time to convince anybody of anything. . . . It's also the need to have symbols that are very easily translatable." As a result, images of women in burqas become dominant and the only way to tell that the women are Afghan.

Indeed, "more responsible action in the use of images is needed,"[40] particularly regarding the use of the chadari as a tool to advance Western campaigns for Afghan women. The pervasive image of the chadari was reduced to a symbol of Afghan women's oppression. As a result, many of those interviewed viewed representations of—and focus on—this garment as part of a larger confusion regarding the intersection between Afghan women, culture, and religion. In fact, the obsession with the chadari obscured other gendered consequences of the Taliban's decrees for men. The Western construction of this garment fosters an artificial construct of Afghan men against Afghan women.[41] A gender specialist elaborated:

> Too much focus can push women into a position of defending their culture and it can become a symbol of resistance to "tyrannical Western influences" against "good Afghan women." It also simplifies the complex situation of gendered identities and roles within Afghan culture. By this I don't mean to suggest that women do not have less access to power or control of resources in Afghan cultures but that it's too simplistic to suggest that once women remove their burqas they are free and everything has been made right.

The head of an aid institution working with women expressed it this way:

> The world's image of Afghan women was that they were horribly oppressed and abused—the worst image of women anywhere in the world. This has continually fuelled programs attempting to help Afghan women. That burqa is the ultimate symbol of the backwardness of Afghanistan. Westerners gasp at its sight. There is nothing more reproachable in terms of the absence of women's rights. Even though the quantity of coverage [of Afghan women] has obviously reduced, the quality hasn't. It's still catchy to talk about how oppressed and wretched they are.

This garment can be credited with bringing much (read: largely Western) attention to Afghanistan. It continues to play a prominent role for the aid apparatus, particularly the Western media, producing myriad documentaries, articles, and photographs claiming to offer a glimpse "behind/under/beneath the burqa."[42] This unconstructive image of Afghan women serves only to feed stereotypes and deny Afghan women's agency.

Afghans employ the word "burqa" in discussions with foreigners as this corresponds with foreign images of Afghan women. Afghans also recognized that "burqa" was used more frequently in the aid apparatus and among non-Afghans. However, Afghans continued to use the more common, and in fact more appropriate, term "chadari" in their daily discussions with each other. "Burqa" is an Arabic/Urdu term, whereas Afghans use the Dari/Persian term. This reveals the extent to which the preferred terms of the aid apparatus have become part of Afghan daily discourse.

In the words of another head of an aid institution:

> We live through symbols, through assumptions. Because it is too difficult to understand. The assumption is that a woman who is more Western in terms of dress is empowered. That will take you to a conclusion that all European women are empowered, which is not correct. It will also take you to a conclusion that there is gender equality if there is no burqa.

In my own capacity as the director of a non-governmental organization, I was approached by many journalists about the chadari, to explain why it remains in "post-liberation" Afghanistan. One American journalist told me that, during a five-day visit in early 2002, he estimated that 95 percent of Afghan women were wearing it. He returned for seven days in November 2002 and told me that now perhaps 90 percent of Afghan women still wore the chadari. As a result, he said, he felt that I had failed to do my job in liberating Afghan women. To him, the chadari was *the* tool of oppression. The aid apparatus was the means by which liberation would occur. Therefore, the persistence of the chadari on Afghanistan's streets indicated a failure of the aid apparatus. His words remained with me during my four years in Afghanistan.

This journalist might note with dismay that the chadari persists. And yet, as Afghan men and women clearly articulate, the presence or absence of this garment does little to indicate liberation. It is more important, however, to distinguish between the transformation of customs—such as veiling and the prevalence of Western clothing—and institutional change in the form of laws and women's sense of their rights and roles. In fact, one might assume that men have been "transformed" based on the prevalence of Afghan men in Western dress. The change in men's clothing style does not constitute a Western influence, nor is it an indication of liberation. Indeed, the assumption is that culture is static when it comes to women, and that the sex of the actors is a determining factor in labeling a change "Western" or not.[43]

Both Afghan women and men interviewed for this study noted that the chadari served as the image under which all others were determined. As part of a reflexive journal, the following excerpt was written in my capacity as NGO director in September 2002 to document my first impressions:

> My sense is that Afghan women long for choice. The choice to wear a veil, or a burqa, or nothing at all. The issue extends well beyond the actual fabric of the burqa. It is more important to address the psychological burqa, and its progeny—the fear burqa and the poverty burqa. Social evolution is a slow process, and our task in this is to offer women the tools with which they can achieve self-sufficiency, a choice, and a voice.

And yet, today Afghan women's choices are few—and their voices are notably absent. And the chadari remains the preferred garment. Afghan women repeatedly expressed exasperation with this facile construct, saying that the world thinks "Afghan women are only burqas." As a result of this image, the world felt compelled to "save" them. An Afghan woman explained that the world thinks of them as oppressed and weak. This is not accurate, she said, "but the world wants to see us this way."

The chadari should be viewed in its sociopolitical and historical context. A nuanced understanding reveals that the chadari can also be seen as a symbol of resistance. Its earliest uses by the Pashtun elite provided freedom of mobility and anonymity. During the Taliban era, the chadari was used strategically "as a shroud of anonymity and disguise" to transport messages, weapons, cameras, and banned publications.[44] According to the senior gender officer of a UN agency:

> Empowering women is not a self-evident process. . . . For many, the burqa actually protects them and gives them a freedom they feel they could not have without it. We as Westerners and development agents need to learn to disassociate the burqas from oppression, need to acknowledge emotionally that Afghanistan is not the West, and need to support Afghan women in a manner meaningful to them, whatever that is.

The liberation discourse employed in popular perceptions and popular literature has played no small part in creating a particular image of Afghan women. This image—an oppressed Afghan woman beneath a chadari—in turn contributed to the design of programs and aid interventions. Media-driven images of women-as-victims shift focus from women's agency and facilitate the creation of technical solutions to a political problem, clearly designating space for an aid intervention as the only solution to liberate Afghan women.

NOTES

1. Uma Narayan, *Dislocating Cultures: Identities, Traditions, and Third World Feminism* (New York: Routledge, 1997); Edward W. Said, *Orientalism* (New York: Vintage, 1979).

2. Nancy Hatch Dupree, "Women in Afghanistan: A Brief 1985 Update," *Women in Afghanistan*, ed. F. Rahimi (Kabul: Paul Bucherer-Dietschi, 1985), 14.

3. United Nations Secretary General, "The Situation in Afghanistan and Its Implications for International Peace and Security," General Assembly Security Council (New York: United Nations, 1997).

4. I did not include resulting books on Afghanistan that did not provide a cover image, nor did I include any books on "the situation of Muslim women." Many of these books have provocative titles about Islam, veiling, and so forth. I also omitted published reports as these come without a cover image and are generally produced for the aid apparatus or academia. Although this search yielded 715 books, not all of these are exclusive to Afghan women. They make mention of Afghan women but are not necessarily devoted exclusively to the subject.

5. Gillian Whitlock, "The Skin of the *Burqa*: Recent Life Narratives from Afghanistan," *Biography* 28, no.1 (2005): 64.

6. Ibid., 55.

7. Ibid., 56.

8. See Vron Ware. Info-War and the Politics of Feminist Curiosity: Exploring New Frameworks for Feminist Intercultural Studies, Gender Institute, London School of Economics, 2006.

9. Dick Morris, *Off with Their Heads: Traitors, Crooks, and Obstructionists in American Politics, Media, and Business* (New York: Regan Books, 2004), 147.

10. Mark LeVine, Viggo Mortensen, and Jodie Evans, *Twilight of Empire: Responses to Occupation* (Santa Monica, Calif.: Perceval Press, 2003), 57.

11. Robert F. Drinan, *The Mobilization of Shame: A World View of Human Rights* (New Haven, Conn.: Yale University Press, 2001), 44.

12. Vinoth Ramachandra, *Faith in Conflict: Christian Integrity in a Multicultural World* (Downers Grove, Ill.: InterVarsity Press, 1999), 43.

13. Thomas G. Weiss and Cindy Collins, *Humanitarian Challenges and Intervention: World Politics and the Dilemmas of Help*, (Boulder, Colo.: Westview Press, 2000), 138.

14. Katrina Vander Heuvel, *A Just Response: The Nation on Terrorism, Democracy, and September 11, 2001* (New York: Avalon Publishing Group, 2002), 164.

15. Latifa, *My Forbidden Face: Growing Up Under the Taliban: A Young Woman's Story* (New York: Hyperion, 2001).

16. Veronica Doubleday, *Three Women of Herat: A Memoir of Life, Love and Friendship in Afghanistan* (London: Tauris Parke, 2006).

17. Farah Ahmedi and Tamim Ansary, *The Story of My Life: An Afghan Girl on the Other Side of the Sky* (New York: Simon & Schuster, 2005).

18. John Follain and Rita Cristofari, *Zoya's Story: An Afghan Woman's Struggle for Freedom* (New York: Harper Collins, 2002).

19. Ana Tortajada. *The Silenced Cry: One Woman's Diary of a Journey to Afghanistan* (New York: St. Martin's Press, 2004).

20. Jan Goodwin, *Price of Honor: Muslim Women Lift the Veil of Silence on the Islamic World* (New York: Plume, 2003).

21. Narayan, *Dislocating Cultures*, 106.

22. Goodwin, *Price of Honor*, 6.

23. Ibid., 76.

24. Kay Hymowitz's article reflects many of these issues and also refers to the chadari as "blue alien-creaturely shapes," to add to the imagery. Kay S. Hymowitz, "Why Feminism Is AWOL on Islam," *City Journal*, Winter 2003.

25. Deniz Kandiyoti, "The Politics of Gender and Reconstruction in Afghanistan," *Occasional Paper* (Geneva: United Nations Research Institute for Social Development, 2005), 1.

26. Sippi Azarbaijani-Moghaddam, "Afghan Women on the Margins of the Twenty-first Century," in *Nation-Building Unraveled? Aid, Peace and Justice in Afghanistan*, ed. Antonio Donini, Norah Niland, and Karin Wermester (Bloomfield, Conn.: Kumarian, 2004), 100.

27. For more information on the "Gender Apartheid" campaign, see Feminist Majority at http://www.feministmajority.org. I do not dispute that the situation of Afghan women at that time was dire. Despite criticism, I credit Jan Goodwin and Feminist Majority for bringing to light the situation of Afghan

women and for serving as strong advocates to raise awareness and funding in the United States. Kandiyoti writes that "Feminist Majority's 'Campaign to stop gender apartheid in Afghanistan' scored some U.S. political victories for Afghan women's rights. Through a series of petitions and lobbying activities, they played a significant role in 1998 in persuading the UN and the U.S. to reject formal recognition of the Taliban. They also put pressure on U.S. energy company Unocal to back out of a $3 billion venture to put a pipeline through Afghanistan that would have given the Taliban $100 million royalties." Deniz Kandiyoti, "The Politics of Gender and Reconstruction in Afghanistan," *Occasional Paper* (Geneva: United Nations Research Institute for Social Development, 2005).

28. Judy Benjamin, "Afghanistan: Women Survivors of War under the Taliban," in *War's Offensive on Women: The Humanitarian Challenge in Bosnia, Kosovo, and Afghanistan,* ed. Julie Mertus (West Hartford, Conn.: Kumarian, 2000).

29. Allison M. Jaggar, "Globalizing Feminist Ethics," *Hypatia* 13, no. 2 (1998): 8–9.

30. Sima Wali, "Afghanistan: Truth and Mythology," in *Women for Afghan Women: Shattering Myths and Claiming the Future,* ed. S. Mehta (New York: Palgrave Macmillan, 2002), 1.

31. Gilles Dorronsoro, *Revolution Unending: Afghanistan: 1979 to the Present* (New York: Columbia University Press, 2005), 291–292.

32. Jaggar, "Globalizing Feminist Ethics," 10.

33. Alison Jaggar, "'Saving Amina': Global Justice for Women and Intercultural Dialogue," *Ethics and International Affairs* 19, no. 3 (2005): 55–75.

34. I have elected to retain the anonymity of individuals and organizations because of codes of confidentiality.

35. Francis Cleaver, ed., *Masculinities Matter! Men, Gender and Development* (London: Zed Books, 2002).

36. Ibid., 1.

37. Sylvia Walby, "Gender Politics and Social Theory," *Sociology* 22, no. 2 (1988): 215–232.

38. James Ferguson, *The Anti-Politics Machine: "Development," Depoliticization, and Bureaucratic Power in Lesotho* (Minneapolis: University of Minnesota Press, 1994).

39. As both an academic and a practitioner, in addition to retaining the anonymity of individuals and organizations, I find it is not constructive to personalize issues and obstruct from a more useful discussion on improving delivery of gender-focused aid.

40. Rosemary Skaine, *The Women of Afghanistan Under the Taliban* (Jefferson, N.C.: McFarland, 2002), 29.

41. It should be noted that the Taliban also did their part to pit men against women by requiring that men enforce the edict that "their women" wear the chadari. Failure to do this would result in severe punishment. "In this way, the Taliban accomplish control over both men and women. They not only obliterate women's presence but also by usurping what was the purview of the family, they put to shame the men of the family, thus rendering them disempowered."

Nasrine Gross, "The Messy Side of Globalization: Women in Afghanistan" (speech, Symposium on Globalization and Women in Muslim Societies, Library of Congress, Washington D.C., 2000).

42. Lina Abirafeh, "Burqa Politics: The Plights of Women in Afghanistan," *Chronogram,* October 2004.

43. Narayan, *Dislocating Cultures,* 23.

44. Gillian Whitlock, "The Skin of the *Burqa*: Recent Life Narratives from Afghanistan," *Biography* 28 no.1 (2005): 57.

CHAPTER 19

When the Picture Does Not Fit the Frame

Engaging Afghan Men in Women's Empowerment

ASHRAF ZAHEDI

In no area of international development is the gap between
stated intentions and operational reality as wide as it is in the
promotion of equality between men and women.
—Kirsten Lewis and Nadia Hijab[1]

Throughout Afghanistan's history, reforms aimed at improving the status
of Afghan women have caused political tensions and backlash. In the
1920s, King Amanullah's efforts to advance women's standing in the
family and society sparked opposition by traditional forces and led to
his abdication of the throne. The reforms initiated by the pro-Soviet
regimes of the 1980s ignited violent opposition. As in the past, claims
were made that the reforms were un-Islamic, corrupting Afghan women,
and incongruent with Afghan culture. Undoing these reforms and "au-
thenticizing" Afghan women served as the ideological claims of the
Mujahedin and the Taliban.

In contrast, an ideology of "saving" and liberating Afghan women
provided one justification for the United States-led invasion in 2001.
This ideology effectively characterized Afghan men as oppressors, treating them as a homogeneous group, decontextualizing their resistance to
women's advancement, and ultimately reflecting on the design and implementation of gender policies in Afghanistan.

With the fall of the Taliban, governmental and non-governmental
organizations, along with international donors, once again embarked

upon improving the status of Afghan women. Following the Bonn agreement,[2] the Ministry of Women's Affairs was established in 2002 and charged with advancing Afghan women's causes. The ministry has been made responsible for policy development, but its weak position within President Hamid Karzai's cabinet and the Afghan parliament has undermined its capacity and authority.

Pressured by international donors, the United Nations Development Programme and the United Nations Development Fund for Women, Karazai and MOWA took up "gender mainstreaming" as the main strategy for improving Afghan women's socioeconomic and political status. Yet in adopting the policy, they have not drawn on historical lessons about women and development in Afghanistan.[3] Nor have they, in their decision-making processes, included Afghan women's organizations and other civil societies, whose input could have impacted the choice of policy approach.

Gender mainstreaming has been adopted and implemented throughout the world. I would argue, however, that it is not the best policy approach for Afghanistan.

GENDER MAINSTREAMING

Over the past five decades much has been done to raise awareness about women's unequal status worldwide. Driven by women's advocates and supported by some national governments and international donors, many policy approaches have been developed to improve the lives of women. The "Women in Development" policy approach of the 1970s mainly focused on women's productive role and their integration in economic development. Although this approach to some extent improved the material conditions of women, it did not have much impact on changing their subordinate status. Addressing the shortcomings of WID, in the 1980s, gender analysts presented a new approach, "Gender and Development," which focused on gender relations, examining unequal power between men and women and the ideologies and institutions that sustain women's subordinate position.[4]

Gender refers to both men and women and their "comparative or differentiated roles, responsibilities, and opportunities" in a given society.[5] Gender is socially and culturally constructed and continues to change according to societal changes. Gender, rather than women, has become the core concept in policy approaches.

"Gender mainstreaming," articulated and advanced by gender analysts, academics, and practitioners, evolves out of the previous policy approaches. In recognition of the fact that women and men have been differently affected by public policies and often women have been marginalized, gender mainstreaming advocates that all policies be analyzed for their gender impact. It is an organizational strategy that seeks to ensure that women's and men's "concerns and experiences are integrated to the design, implementation, and evaluation of *all* legislations, policies and programmes so that women and men benefit equally and inequality is not perpetuated."[6]

To reveal the existing gender inequalities, gender mainstreaming draws on sex disaggregated quantitative data on inequalities between men and women in terms of access to education, health care, financial credit, political office, and the like and supports policies and legislations that would address these inequalities. In so doing, gender mainstreaming relies on gender specialists operating in institutions and organizations to evaluate each policy and legislation for its impact on men and women, monitor implementation of gender mainstreaming, and promote gender equality as an achievable goal.

In 1995, at the Fourth UN World Conference on Women in Beijing, women's advocates and representatives of various countries endorsed gender mainstreaming as an internationally agreed-upon strategy to promote gender equality.[7] It has been adopted and implemented in developed and developing countries and has had varying degrees of success based on cultural and structural constraints.[8] Nevertheless, no country has yet fully implemented gender mainstreaming.

Gender mainstreaming is a sophisticated and complicated model. Although praised for its goal of gender equality and transformative change, it has been criticized for its lack of conceptual clarity. To begin with, there is a lack of understanding of the meaning and concept of gender. Olena Hankivsky points out the limitation of gender as the male-female dichotomy, questions prioritization of gender as the "axis of discrimination," and thus regards gender mainstreaming that rests on this concept as "inherently limited."[9] Gender mainstreaming does not address the other forms of discrimination and the interfaces between gender, social class, race, ethnicity, and sexuality that have significant bearings on women's life choices, a serious shortcoming for a development model. Mary Daly considers gender mainstreaming an "underdeveloped" concept that demands rethinking,[10] whereas Suzette Mitchell notes that "mainstreaming" of gender does not have identifiable and measurable criteria for success and is difficult to monitor.[11]

Furthermore, not enough attention is being paid to gendered aspects of the mainstream. While the mainstream refers to the "prevailing thinking of the majority of people, men and women,"[12] due to the historical dominance of men, the existing mainstream reflects only men's interests. Thus implementation of gender mainstreaming requires orchestrated efforts to transform the mainstream and create a favorable environment that would facilitate and support gender equality.

After more than a decade of promoting gender mainstreaming by governments and international agencies, its shortcomings are well documented and its universal application questioned. According to Mitchell, executive director of the International Women's Development Agency: "At the IWDA Gender and Development Dialogue, held in Brisbane, July 2003, stakeholders from academia, development NGOs, United Nations (UN) agencies, women's organizations, consulting firms, bilaterals and gender specialists unanimously agreed that gender mainstreaming—as a term and strategy—is problematic."[13]

Some gender analysts even believe gender mainstreaming as a strategy "has largely failed."[14] A host of reasons have been cited for this failure including conceptual confusion, unreliable sex disaggregated data, limited resources, lack of political will, and problems of monitoring and accountability. These and other reasons pose tremendous challenges to gender mainstreaming in Afghanistan.

GENDER MAINSTREAMING IN AFGHANISTAN

The existing socioeconomic and political realities of Afghanistan indicate that gender mainstreaming faces many obstacles and therefore is unlikely to achieve its objectives in the near future. A number of factors impede its success.

To begin with, "gender" is a foreign word and there is no equivalent term in Dari or Pashto. The closest translation, *jensiyat*, refers to sex and not gender. Some gender specialists have even tried to create a new word, *jensiyat ejtemai*, or "social gender," but this lacks cultural and linguistic connections. Thus many Afghans regard gender as a foreign import and Western imposition.

Research by specialists in Afghanistan indicates that there is confusion about the meaning of gender at every level of its usage.[15] Most use gender to refer to "women"; others use it to refer to "equality." Although Afghans generally do not fully understand the term "gender," some exploit it knowing it pleases international donors, who are more likely to finance or sponsor gender-focused projects.

Gender mainstreaming requires a stable and strong central government. It needs effective state machinery to support women's advancement. This is not the case in Afghanistan. Although Afghanistan's ministries have agreed in theory with gender mainstreaming, in practice few have demonstrated any serious commitment to it. Part of the problem is again limited understanding of the concept of gender, as well as the monitoring and evaluation process, compounded by the lack of budget and expertise. Gender mainstreaming requires significant budget to collect sex disaggregated data and to train gender specialists needed for monitoring and evaluation of policies.

Furthermore, the lack of political will at all levels of the Karzai administration has impacted negatively on the implementation of gender mainstreaming. Most ministers are political appointees, chosen based on nepotism and tribal and political alliances rather than on capability or experience in modern governance. They have competing agendas, pursue different interests, and have limited degrees of commitment to women's issues.

An important component for promoting gender equality and building gender issues into social policies is the active presence of women's groups to exert pressure on the state and sustain the longevity of gender policies. But Afghan women's groups find it difficult to be effective, thanks to the Karzai administration's lack of commitment to women's causes and opposition from Karzai's cabinet members, who have prevented integration of gender issues into social policies and undermined allocation of budget at local and national levels.

The "war on terrorism" has also undermined the prospect of gender mainstreaming. Political alliances made in the name of national security have restored power to warlords and forces opposed to women's rights, eclipsing many gender programs. Political tensions and insecurity have further complicated women's public presence and in turn limited their involvement in women's groups and organizations.

Economic development and political stability also affect the success of gender mainstreaming. Three decades of war, destruction, and internal displacement have destroyed Afghanistan's infrastructure. Its economy is supported by foreign aid and its fragile political system secured by foreign forces. The rate of poverty is high at 36 percent.[16] Any policy that addresses women's equality will have limited impact if it does not also address the dire economic status of Afghan men.

Addressing these constraints to gender mainstreaming, if at all possible, would take much time and significant resources. What's more, whereas gender mainstreaming in theory does not preclude implementation of other policy approaches, in practice its adoption as the "main" strategy effectively diverts resources away from other approaches. Thus, instead of prioritizing gender mainstreaming as the main strategy for gender equality in Afghanistan, it is better to use multiple strategies and policy approaches. Using the empowerment approach and addressing women's needs through grassroots projects can serve them better and provide more immediate results.

WOMEN'S EMPOWERMENT

Women's empowerment as a framework for development projects emerged in the 1980s. Activists and feminists in developing countries were discontent with top-down economic, deterministic development models of the 1970s and thus compelled to advance a grassroots approach that would be more relevant to the realities of women's lives and the complexities of their struggles.

"Empowerment" entails addressing both the personal and social dimensions of power and how they manifest in society. Unfortunately, overuse of the term and its one-dimensional presentation as an individual's "state of mind" or "sense of financial gain" by economic determinists or marketing outlets have stripped it of its original meaning, which relates to the individual in the context of structural inequalities and access to resources. Empowerment involves "awareness raising, building self-confidence, expansion of choice, involvement in decision making and increased access to and control over resources."[17] Women's empowerment does not refer to "power over" men. The negative definition of power, as Jo Rowlands explains, should be "contrasted with an 'energy' definition of power, 'power to' or 'power with.' This model of power is not zero-sum; one person's increase in power does not necessarily diminish that of another."[18] What is more, this individual sense of empowerment needs to be complemented with women's social, political, economic, and legal empowerment to have any significant and lasting impact on their lives.

Awareness, choice, and access to resources are crucial for empowerment. Often women, as in Afghanistan, internalize their low social status and view it as personal deficiency. Awareness-raising efforts direct women's attention toward structural and cultural causes of their disempowerment and restore their confidence in their own abilities. "The very first outcome of awareness generation is likely to be rejection of the legitimacy of subordinated social status for women."[19]

Empowerment relates to agency and one's "ability to define one's goals and act upon them."[20] Women's ability to set goals and achieve them, however, has been undermined by lack of access to and control of resources, limiting their choices. The paths to women's empowerment can be paved by addressing their practical as well as their strategic needs.[21]

"Practical gender needs" refer to women's needs in their socially accepted roles pertaining to child care, living conditions, access to food and water, employment, and the like. Addressing practical gender needs, though highly important, does not challenge the patriarchal power structure directly or in the short term. Yet it contributes to the improved position of women in the long term.

"Strategic gender interest" refers to a transformative change in power relations between men and women that leads to gender equality, the goal of gender mainstreaming. Addressing strategic gender interests is an ideal that needs to be pursued and planned for, but it should be accompanied by measures that address women's immediate and practical needs.

Women's empowerment must be "culturally specific and women must find their own way and their own appropriate means."[22] Efforts should be made to directly engage Afghan women, allowing them to articulate their needs and preferences in terms of access to resources and social services. Likewise, Afghan men need to be part of this engagement, giving them the opportunity to be partners with women and supporting their causes. Drawing on input from Afghan women and men, the Afghan government and the national and international NGOs should provide social services and resources that facilitate and support women's empowerment. These incremental changes, in the long run, will pave the way for achieving gender equality in Afghanistan.

ENGAGING AFGHAN MEN IN WOMEN'S EMPOWERMENT

Afghan men have been projected as oppressors and as unified groups opposed to women's advancement. But the truth is that many Afghan men, from all walks of life, have supported women's causes, including during the Taliban regime.[23] Nevertheless, all Afghan men have been shamed for the misogynist attitudes of some Afghans. The outsiders' ahistorical and slanted views of Afghan men have created an artificial divide between Afghan men and women and effectively narrowed Afghan women's base of support. Indeed, some Afghan men oppose women's advancement, but their opposition, in large part, has been to a particular policy model and context of its implementation and not necessarily to women's improved status.

The pro-Soviet regimes of the 1980s best exemplify how ill-conceived implementation can undermine a policy. For example, though many Afghan men and women were in favor of women's education in principle, they were offended by the regime's parading of dancing female students in the street and televising their dance nationwide,[24] showcasing the women as the embodiment of their policy success. Thus some Afghans turned against the regime and women's education. Rural compulsory education suffered from ill implementation as well. The use of force rather than persuasion and long-term engagement with the opponents derailed a progressive policy that could have positively impacted gender relations. Accordingly, when the government aggressively pushed for rural women's education and "forced men to send their wives and daughters to the literacy centers," it provoked bitter public reaction.[25]

Although patriarchal culture is strong in Afghanistan and has left its imprints on women's private and public lives, not all Afghan men are opposed to all aspects of women's advancement, and these differences need to be recognized. To begin with, men's resistance and opposition to women's access to education, health care, and employment need to be contextualized and addressed by the Afghan government and international donors involved in Afghanistan's reconstruction.

In general—despite sensational accusations to the contrary—Afghan fathers, brothers, husbands, and sons are not against female members of the family seeking medical care. Yet access to medical facilities located far from rural villages, where transportation is scarce and roads unsafe, is a major problem throughout the country. The high costs of visiting doctors and purchasing medicine frequently force families to have to decide between medical care and feeding themselves. The limited number of existing free clinics can hardly meet the demands. Investment in public safety, medical facilities, and availability of low-cost or free medical services staffed by women would improve women's access to health care.

Many men are indeed in favor of education but fear abduction of their children and public violence. Access to school often means long distances to travel on foot on unsafe roads. Considering the risks, some fathers naturally oppose their daughters' education out of affection and for their own good.

Some men are opposed to women's education on the ground that it is un-Islamic. They associate educated women with promiscuity and view urban women as immoral. A national campaign by the government to establish permissibility of women's education in Islam would set the stage for diminishing men's opposition. Some efforts have already been made in this direction but need to be expanded substantially to have any lasting impact.

Men's resistance to women's employment needs to be contextualized within Muslim men's financial responsibility toward female members of their family. According to the Qur'an, men are assigned the task of financially maintaining the family, particularly female members.[26] Providing for family members is an important construct of Afghan masculine identity and concepts of honorable manhood. Even when women have financial resources, they are not expected to support the family (yet it is usually welcomed when the need arises). When men cannot provide for their families, it puts enormous stress on everyone. The sense of shame and inadequacy may turn these men against women's employment. Improving men's employment opportunities would restore men's confidence in their ability as providers and lower their opposition to women's employment and self-employment. It needs to be noted that, until relatively recently, men resisted women's employment, even in the West. Yet across time and with socioeconomic and political developments, men's attitudes toward women's employment have significantly changed. Such change is most likely to occur in Afghanistan as well.

The cited examples illustrate that men's concerns are contextual, and contexts are not static but continue to change. They also show that most men do support women's causes. Even the outlooks of men who do not currently favor women's causes can be turned around. That could only happen through culturally appropriate ways of gender awareness. Awareness-raising can indeed benefit women as well, because many have internalized and accepted their low social status.

Though it would have been ideal to carry on a nationwide gender awareness campaign, it is not practical at this early stage. Considering the existing realities in Afghanistan, too much emphasis on women has been counterproductive. Some Afghan men view publicity surrounding women's status as the imposition of Western concepts of individualism and women's self-centeredness that run counter to Afghan culture and Afghans' familial, communal, and tribal belonging and identities. Responding to a question about what should be done for Afghan women, Rahmat, a 56-year-old chemical engineer stated with frustration, "Let me tell you something. You need to take this question in Afghanistan terms, not American."[27] Najib, a 28-year-old medical student, echoed the sentiment: "Afghanistan is not America or Europe. We believe in women's modesty and do not want our women to imitate Western women and dishonor our family and community."[28]

Raising awareness on the status of Afghan women can take place in decentralized forms through mosques, local councils, and NGOs working at the grassroots levels. The mass media, particularly radio, can play an important role. Content and language must reflect Afghanistan's diverse culture and incorporate culturally relevant concepts such as respect, generosity, pride, and the Islamic notions of equality, rights, and social justice.

Awareness-raising needs to be accompanied by education on women's rights in Islam. Efforts have been made in this direction, and some NGOs have built gender awareness and human rights education into their programs. But more is needed, and with the support of the government and international donors, human rights education through community development for both men and women can be expanded. These men would be more likely to support and participate in women's empowerment. But how to translate men's awareness into their engagement in women's causes is the key.

Experiences of countries such as Yemen show that small-scale and community- based programs work best when they are issue-specific and relevant to men's and women's lives. Yemen is not an ideal model for gender equality, due to its similarity with Afghanistan in terms of gender relations, but it can serve as an example of a beginning. In Yemen, Oxfam along with its partners from civil society organizations started by raising men's awareness through egalitarian Islamic codes, gaining men's and women's trust, securing their commitment, and establishing shared goals.[29] By engaging men in women's empowerment, effectively women's social base of support grows and the possibility for reform in their status naturally increases.

It is imperative to bring Afghan men and women together through shared goals and projects and to draw on their collective energies and resources to advance women's causes, allowing them to chart their own paths to empowerment and work toward gender equality. Policy approaches, including gender mainstreaming, are merely the means to achieve the goal of gender equality. The policy approach advancing this goal must correspond to the context of operation, and the policy frame must fit Afghanistan and its cultural and socioeconomic realities.[30]

NOTES

1. Kristen Lewis and Nadia Hijab, *Transforming the Mainstream: Gender in UNDP* (New York: UNDP and UNIFEM, 2003), 3.

2. The Bonn Agreement was signed on December 5, 2001, under the auspices of the United Nations, outlining the terms of re-creation of the Afghan state after the fall of the Taliban.

3. Shireen Burki's chapter in this volume describes in some detail the various attempts at reform. For more detailed account of the reforms, please refer to Valentine Moghadam, *Modernizing Women: Gender and Social Change in the Middle East* (Boulder, Colo.: Lynne Rienner, 2003).

4. For more information on policy shifts, see Shahrashoub Razavi and Carol Miller, *From WID to GAD: Conceptual Shifts in Women and Development Discourse* (Geneva: United Nations Research Institute for Social Development, United Nations Development Programme, 1995).

5. "GM Glossary," *Gender Mainstreaming Learning Manual and Information Pack,* United Nations Development Programme Learning Resources Centre, http://www.gdrc.org/gender/mainstreaming.

6. Helen Derbyshire, *Gender Manual: A Practical Guide for Development Policy Makers and Practitioners* (London: Department of International Development, 2002).

7. For adaptation of this policy approach, see "Coordination of the Policies and Activities of the Specialized Agencies and Other Bodies of the United Nations System" (New York: United Nations Economic and Social Council, 1997).

8. For more information on gender mainstreaming and its implementation, please refer to Shirin Rai, ed., *Mainstreaming Gender, Democratizing the State? Institutional Mechanisms for the Advancement of Women* (Manchester: Manchester University Press, 2003); Astrida Niemanis, *Gender Mainstreaming in Practice: A Toolkit* (Slovak Republic: United Nations Development Programme, 2007), http://www.undp.org/women/mainstream/docs/Gender_Main streaming_in_Practice__A_Toolkit.pdf; Maitrayee Mukhopadhyay, Gerald Steehouwer, and Franz Wong, *Politics of the Possible: Gender Mainstreaming and Organizational Changes Experience from the Field* (Oxford: Oxfam Publishing, 2006).

9. Olena Hankivsky, "Gender Mainstreaming vs. Diversity Mainstreaming: A Preliminary Examination of the Role and Transformative Potential of Feminist Theory," *Canadian Journal of Political Science* 38, no. 4 (December 2005): 977–1001; quote on page 978.

10. Mary Daly, "Gender Mainstreaming in Theory and Practice," *Social Politics: International Studies in Gender, State & Society* 12, no. 3 (2005): 433.

11. Suzette Mitchell, 'What Lies at the Heart of Gender Mainstreaming: The Strategy or the Implementation?" *Development Bulletin* 64 (2004): 8.

12. Lewis and Hijab, *Transforming the Mainstream*, 5.

13. Mitchell, "What Lies at the Heart of Gender Mainstreaming," 8.

14. Pamela Thomas, "Introduction: Gender and Development: Bridging Policy and Practice," *Development Bulletin* 64 (2004): 4. Despite its shortcomings, gender mainstreaming is still popular with international donors. Meanwhile, the latest policy approach, "Women, Culture and Development," is getting the attention of gender analysts. This approach emphasizes the role of culture and the lived experiences of women. It advocates placing women at the center and culture on par with political economy in development. Yet this approach is still developing and needs to be tested at operational levels. For more information on this policy approach, please refer to Kum-Kum Bhavnani, John Foran, and Priya Kurian, eds., *Feminist Futures: Re-imagining Women, Culture and Development.* (London: Zed Books, 2003).

15. Anna Wordsworth, *Moving to the Mainstream: Integrating Gender in Afghanistan's National Policy* (Kabul: Afghanistan Research and Evaluation Unit, 2008), 26; Lina Abirafeh, *Lessons from Gender-Focused International Aid in Post Conflict Afghanistan. . . . Learned?* (Bonn: Friedrich-Ebert-Stiftung, July 2005), 10.

16. Central Intelligence Agency, The World Fact Book. Washington (online), https://www.cia.gov/library/publications/the-world-factbook/fields/2046 .html?countryName=Afghanistan&countryCode=af&regionCode=sas&#af.

17. Carolyn Hannan, "Transforming Empowerment and Gender Mainstreaming" (speech, International Symposium on A new Vision for Gender Policy: Equality, Development and Peace, Seoul, April 17–18, 2003), 2, http://www.un .org/womenwatch/daw/news/speech2003/CH-Empmainstream-Korea.PDF.

18. Jo Rowlands, "What Is Empowerment?" in *Empowering Women for Development,* ed. Haleh Afshar and Fatima Alikhan (Hydarabad, India: Booklines Corporation, 1997), 47.

19. Sharada Jain, "Awareness Generation, Women's Mobilization & Gender Sensitization: Challenges for 1990," in *Empowering Women for Development,* ed. Afshar and Alikhan, 11.

20. Naila Kabeer, "Discussing Women's Empowerment: Theory and Practice," *SIDA Studies* 3 (2002): 23.

21. The terms "practical gender interests" and "strategic gender interests" were first introduced by Maxine Molyneux in "Mobilization without Emancipation? Women's Interests, the State, and Revolution in Nicaragua," *Feminist Studies* 11, no.2 (1985): 232–233.

22. Afshar Haleh and Fatima Alikhan, "Introduction," in *Empowering Women for Development,* ed. Afshar and Alikhan, 3.

23. Elaheh Rostami-Povey, *Afghan Women: Identity and Invasion* (London: Zed Books, 2007), 36.

24. Senzil Nawid, "Afghan Women under Marxism," in *From Patriarchy to Empowerment*, ed. Valentine Moghadam (New York: Syracuse University Press, 2007), 67.

25. Hafizullah Emadi, *Repression, Resistance and Women in Afghanistan* (London: Praeger, 2000), 102.

26. M. H. Shakir, trans., *The Qur'an* (New York: Tahrike Tarsile Quran Inc, 1987), Surah IV: 34.

27. Interview conducted by Amina Kator, April 2009.

28. Interview conducted by the author, December 2008.

29. Magda El Sanous, *Strategies and Approaches to Enhance the Role of Men and Boys in Gender Equality: Case Study of Yemen* (New York: United Nations Division for the Advancement of Women, 2003).

30. I would like to thank Valentine Moghadam and Wahid Omar for reviewing the first draft of this chapter and providing insightful suggestions. My thanks also to Mojgan Rastegar for her help with literature review and Amina Kator for interviews.

PART V

"Don't Eclipse My Happy New Moon"

Two girls pose in a candy shop in Kabul.
Photo by Sheryl B. Shapiro, 2003.

CHAPTER 20

Empowering Women through Education

Recipe for Success

SAKENA YACOOBI

A few months ago I went to the city to visit a doctor. I asked about the address of the doctor from the people on the street. They all answered me, "The doctors have sign boards. You easily can find the doctor if you carefully read their sign boards." They did not know that I could not read and write. Since that day I decided to go to the AIL center in my village to be able to read and write. Now I am in grade three and I am able to read books, newspapers, and doctors' sign boards. I can write letters. Now I don't need to ask others. I can do things myself.

—A female student at one of AIL's Women's Learning Centers in a village in Afghanistan

Afghan women are among the most oppressed groups of women in the world, but, through education, they are gaining new freedoms in Afghan society. They are learning to read and write and to express themselves. They are learning skills that allow them to support their families and discovering how to maintain a healthy lifestyle. Most important, Afghan women are learning about their rights under Islam and under generally accepted human rights principles. They are finding new respect for themselves and a greater confidence in what they can do. As a result, how they are viewed and how they are treated is also changing for the better.

For thousands of years, Afghan tradition and culture placed women in a position that was less than men, with few rights. It was believed that Afghan women should not be educated. In the middle of the twentieth century, ideas concerning education for women began to change. Some girls in large cities and towns began to go to school, but even then access to education was available to relatively few.

After the invasion of Afghanistan by the Soviet Union in 1979, the few gains that had been made by Afghan women were lost, and if anything, their situation became worse. The core values of the society were destroyed by years of fighting, poverty, and isolation. More than half the Afghan people left Afghanistan and became refugees. Living in foreign lands with strangers, separated from extended family, thousands of women and children were confined to their tents or mud homes in order to ensure their security.

Under these extreme conditions of daily life, traditional Afghan hospitality became impossible, and cultural engagement, marriage, and other celebrations were curtailed. Over time, many customs and values—such as honesty, personal responsibility, mutual respect, basic social manners, and the concept of peaceful resolutions—were lost. Oppression and abuse of women and children escalated, increasing even more with the Taliban's rise to power, and unfortunately, Islam was wrongly used to justify it.

Although efforts have been made to advance the status of women since the fall of the Taliban in recent years, false biases and assumptions about Islam (as well as an unwillingness to look beyond the *burqa* to the real and immediate problems of Afghan women) have often subjected women to even more hardship.

The problems faced by Afghan women are complex and multifaceted. However, when they are offered an education contextualized in Afghan religion and culture (based on a credible assessment of what they perceive to be their actual needs and including topics on ethics, values, health, and family), they are empowered to stand up for their rights and choices. Access to education allows them an equal place as contributing members of society, at home, in the workplace, or in public arenas.

The Afghan Institute of Learning (AIL) is a women's nongovernmental organization (NGO) founded in 1995 in Peshawar, Pakistan. Initially, AIL provided education and health services to Afghan refugee women and children in camps in Pakistan. At the request of the community, we began with training female teachers. Afghans needed to see how we would train women before they would consider additional schools for their girls. When we began our teacher-training program for Afghan women teachers, we supported schools for 3,000 female students. By the end of one year, we had gained the trust of the communities we worked in and our program grew to support schools for 15,000 Afghan girls. This tremendous explosion in enrollment would not have been possible had the principles of community engagement and empowerment not been used.

Working at the grassroots level with proven educational models, AIL has helped to empower Afghan women and reestablish core ethics and values in Afghan society, while working to change the ideas of men about the role of women in the civil society. Originally formulated and used successfully with refugee women in Pakistan, the concepts described below have also been applied successfully in Afghanistan. Since its founding, AIL has provided services to 7,700,000 Afghans and has supported 319 grassroots schools, educational learning centers, and health centers. More than 90 percent of the schools and centers have either achieved their goals or are continuing and self sufficient. AIL presently supports twenty-six centers in Afghanistan and Pakistan.

TEN STEPS TO SUCCESS

1. Begin at the grass roots with locally identified needs.

When beginning new programs, particularly for women, AIL discovered that it is essential to listen to what the women—and men—in the community want rather than design programs to address needs perceived by program officials. The community served must identify the problems and needs and request help in order for the program to achieve optimum success. Input and involvement from all members of the community must be gathered.

Afghan women, like women everywhere, are an integral part of family and community life, working hand in hand with men. To ensure relevancy, therefore, it is crucial not to omit men when working to establish programs for Afghan women. It is necessary to meet with the men in the community, to encourage their input, listen and respond to their concerns, and gather their support. This includes overcoming their suspicions, giving them a chance to express their concerns, and completing social formalities. Agreements about services to be provided and the responsibilities of the service provider and the community are best developed together. Then it is crucial for the provider to follow through on promises.

For example, when AIL began to work with Afghan refugees, only a few girls' schools had been started in refugee camp communities by local people. Although international NGOs had recognized the need for more girls' schools, many people who lived in the camps were suspicious of and resistant to the idea of educating girls. In order to establish a strong foundation for girls' education in the region, the most appropriate starting point for developing such a program had to be identified.

In Pakistan, Afghan school administrators and political party leaders had voiced a need for teacher training and school support. Most important, it had been recognized and articulated by Afghans involved in the existing schools that the female teachers of these girls' schools could benefit from training. This is the starting point we chose for our program to improve education for Afghan girls.

2. Start with the least controversial service in the least conservative area.

When we began training teachers for girls' schools in Afghan refugee camps in Pakistan, we focused on empowering and educating women. Education and teacher training for girls and women has been a historically controversial issue for Afghans. There are traditional concerns about the need and relevance of education for girls, concerns about the religious and cultural appropriateness of the curriculum, and suspicion about education from foreign agencies potentially embedded with foreign values and political agendas. Many Afghans remain staunchly opposed to education for girls and women. However, teacher training had been requested by a few schools. With these issues in mind, AIL chose its first site for teacher training in a less-conservative urban area and employed a teacher-training curriculum that had previously been accepted and used to train Afghan male teachers. This seminar curriculum was acceptable to the community because it was culturally sensitive and based in Islam.

3. A well-conceived program should not impose services on a community.

We found that it is important to make participation in the service offered truly voluntary. It is unwise to relate a person's choice to participate in the training offered with receipt of other services or support for other programs. Incentives should not be offered for participation.

When services are truly voluntary, the amount of participation is a true measure of the quality and appropriateness of the training.

When AIL announced its first teacher training in Peshawar, near the refugee camps in 1995, only a few schools responded. Apparently, the community wanted to evaluate the training before determining whether to participate in greater numbers. Our first teacher-training program was offered in three schools and was well received. Participants endorsed the training and recommended it to the larger community. Soon after, the program had a long waiting list.

4. *Offer high-quality, culturally sensitive programs, incorporating feedback from participants.*

Respecting local customs is imperative for successful Afghan women's programs. A combination of war, culture, politics, and religion has forced a stricter version of *purdah* (social segregation) upon Afghan women in the confined environment of refugee villages and in Afghanistan. Keeping this history and the culture and the religious values of Afghans in mind, appropriate strategies can be developed to provide health and education services to women and girls.

Some examples of culturally appropriate strategies used in our work include establishing facilities only for women, selecting sites for providing programs that are close to where the women live so they can freely attend, and respecting local dress codes. By hiring and working with local Afghan females, we were able to develop trainings that responded to the needs and concerns of the community. We also had staff that understood and respected local customs. Additionally, the teacher trainers who taught the seminar were well trained, credentialed, and highly qualified. They held high expectations for participants, and the participants greatly respected and admired them.

Additionally, trainers solicited periodic feedback from participants during the training by asking what they liked least and best and why, as well as what they best remember about the training or seminar as a whole. Trainers incorporated this feedback into future trainings by self-evaluating each training and writing a report detailing changes that needed to be made. These methods for collecting and utilizing the input of local community members help ensure that the training is of high quality and culturally sensitive.

Initially developed and piloted for Afghan male teachers, the twenty-four-day teacher-training seminar included intensive application-focused learning activities. The quality of the curriculum had been assured through testing and evaluation based on participant and teacher-trainer feedback over the course of three years.

The seminar had demonstrated results. When teachers returned to the classroom and began applying their new skills, student performance improved dramatically. Before participating in the seminar, teachers reported that students learned to read after three years of instruction. Using skills learned through seminar participation, teachers reported that they were able to teach students to read in three months. Both teachers and students were empowered by these successes.

As word spread, interest in further training workshops for broader segments of the community quickly mounted. Our trainings developed a reputation for being secure, safe, relevant, and observant of religious and cultural norms. With our demonstrated commitment to quality programs, respect for local institutions, and protection for our staff, we began to attract more and better staff, which improved the quality of the trainings even more. Soon, we were managing waiting lists for future trainings and receiving requests for new services, including support for schools. Requests for training and support began to come from conservative rural camps, not just the cities.

5. Act at the request of the community when expanding services and go only where invited.

Soon after the success of our first teacher-training seminars, we began to receive requests to support girls' schools in the refugee camps. Trust had been developed. The Afghan communities, having seen that our teacher-training program improved the quality of education for their children and was designed within the context of Afghan and Islamic values, were now willing to let us into their communities to support girls' schools.

6. Require that the community contribute to the development of the new program.

When the community is required to donate security, volunteers, space, and other materials to the establishment of a new program, its members become invested in the outcome of the program and its long-term sustainability. Community donations also raise the self-esteem of the community, as its members realize that they have something to contribute and that their contributions are valuable.

With AIL's agreement to provide school support to communities at their request and invitation, we sign a contract that specifies their and our responsibilities. Generally, communities were responsible for finding teachers (female teachers were preferred), gathering students, beginning a school, and finding a building for the school. Our program paid the teachers, provided materials to the school, trained and supervised the teachers as they implemented newly learned techniques in the classroom. Our programs always began with the assumption that local people were capable of contributing to the program, had something valuable to contribute, and wanted to help educate girls. We did not allow stereotypes, such as "Rural Afghan men do not want women to be educated," to interfere with these basic assumptions.

7. Recognize that in Afghan culture, trust and relationships are personal not organizational.

In using our core principles, we were able to build trust between ourselves and the communities we served with teacher training and support for girls' schools. However, it was important for us to realize that these Afghan communities had built trust and personal relationships with the individual members of our staff, not just our organization. New staff members could not assume that, because they represented a credible organization, they would or should be trusted. Building trust takes time.

Staff members built and maintained trust and personal relationships by modeling the principles discussed here, as well as by behaving in a way that was consistent with the norms and values of the community in both their personal and professional lives. Staff had to be respectable members of the community, wear the *hijab*, model Islamic values, treat people respectfully, value the family, and be knowledgeable about Islam.

8. Set flexible rules in order to respond quickly to emerging needs and issues.

In our program, we never refused to provide educational services to boys or men. However, because our focus was on women and girls, we implemented a policy of serving at least 50 percent females with our programs. This policy allowed us to maintain our focus on women and girls without the risk of alienating the community by excluding some people. Additionally, we enforced a policy of nondiscriminatory hiring practices on the basis of age, region of birth, religious sect, ethnicity, or gender. Policies and practices that facilitate inclusiveness foster broad participation and do not fuel existing divisions.

9. Hold *high standards, have high expectations, and model them.*

By remaining committed to providing only the highest quality of education and by enforcing expectations for staff behavior and community donations, we minimize our security risks and maximize the core mission and values of our programs. Also, when the staff and community find that they are able to meet these high expectations, their dignity and self-esteem increases.

For example, we require that seminar participants arrive on time and not be absent without a compelling reason (death in the family, severe illness, etc.). Although all participants are told of this requirement, there are occasionally those who—based on their experience in other programs—believe this requirement will not be enforced. One participant, who had been warned about being late, was very surprised when she was told the second time that she would not be allowed to attend any more if it happened again. The reasons for this were explained to her. Astonished, she noted that she had never encountered a program that truly wanted participants to learn and was willing to exclude those who were not ready to fully participate. She was not late again, nor did she or others object to the preparatory work they were asked to do outside of class.

It may seem easier to compromise on some issues, but it is worth the time and effort required to build relationships with the community up front and help the staff and the community to meet expectations. Compromising standards and lowering expectations is disempowering, alienates people, and detracts from the long-term sustainability and impact of the program.

10. *Offer more controversial programs in a voluntary, culturally sensitive way after trust has been established.*

In 1998, we decided to expand our program to offer human rights workshops for women. We revisited the principles discussed above, including starting in the least conservative area and making participation truly voluntary.

The human rights workshop was first offered in Peshawar to any interested woman. Women were not given stipends for participating so that it could not be claimed by men or others in the community that they were being paid to attend. Because of our program's reputation for culturally sensitive education and training, the participating women were confident that their participation would not put them in jeopardy.

In human rights workshops, women are told of their rights and how they can be respected within their cultural and religious context. Most women are not aware that they have fundamental rights under Islam to such things as education, good health, safety, and respect. Finding out about their rights helps them to understand how they might be able to change their lives. One of the most important things they learn in the workshops is how to communicate effectively about their rights. Women who have participated in human rights workshops return home to their families and convince their husbands, fathers, sons, uncles, and brothers not only that it is acceptable for women to be educated under Islam but also that it is very beneficial. After the workshop, women are able to use the Qu'ran to point out that Islam freed women from slavery, men and women are equal, and both have the right to education.

As a result of participation in the human rights workshops, women began to flock to literacy, enrichment, and skills training classes and began to send their daughters to school. And, all of this was supported by the men in their households. Indeed, by involving the community at every level, with cultural and religious sensitivity, the demand for human rights workshops increased, even in more conservative areas. Their success reinforced demand for our educational programs for women and girls and resulted in further expansion.

The core concepts outlined above are used with every program that AIL presently runs. As AIL's reputation for offering culturally and religiously sensitive programs for women and children has spread, AIL has been able to offer training to women in areas that would have been unheard of in years past. Because of the trust that people have for AIL and its staff, AIL can work in rural, conservative communities where previously there were no schools for women and girls.

AIL now routinely offers leadership and human rights workshops to rural and urban women. At the request of both women and men, the workshops are also offered to men. Women and girls are studying to be nurses, midwives, and health workers. Women are also learning about reproductive health, HIV/AIDS, and self-immolation. In AIL's centers, women are learning skills and starting home businesses to support their families.

Both women and men are being reintroduced to the basic values and ethics of a civilized society that have been lost through Afghanistan's turbulent history. Through classroom and one-on-one discussions, AIL promotes the values of honesty and integrity; personal responsibility—for one's self, health, and jobs, for family members, and the local village and country—rather than simply accepting handouts or waiting for someone else to do things; mutual respect for elders, children, and others; basic social manners, such as how to greet one another and demonstrate polite behavior; and the concept of peaceful resolutions, such as women and men working together to find nonviolent and nonconfrontational solutions. Our staff models this behavior by always being on time, having lesson plans completed, respecting the students, and, at the same time, expecting the same behavior from the students.

Significantly, because of AIL's belief in involving the community in all of its programs, the women's communities and families are supporting the programs, and Afghans are rediscovering the value of working together to implement the visionary, multifaceted programs supported by AIL.

In early 2003, AIL began supporting the Woman's Learning Center for women and girls outside a major Afghan city. The community donated a house, and AIL provided floor coverings, blackboards, sewing machines, and salaries for three teachers. At the time, there were no girls' schools in the village and almost none of the females were literate. Three women from the village who had no more than an eighth-grade education served as teachers.

About 40 percent of the female villagers came to the classes. All of those women and girls have now completed a tailoring class and are sewing clothes for their families and neighbors, and students in the literacy class are now in the fourth grade. There is such interest in education that a girls' school has opened in the village and one of the WLC students is a teacher there. Recently, AIL began the Community Health Worker (CHW) program out of its nearby clinic. Had it not been for the Women's Learning Center, there would not have been a literate female capable of being trained as the CHW.

> My name is Malika. I am twenty-six years old and a student in the WLC classes. It has been wonderful for me and my family. My family did not think a woman of 25, with two children and the heavy workload every woman in the village has, would be able to learn new things.

My hand was not used to holding pen and chalk. I had never seen anyone in my family write or read. It was hard for me in the literacy classes to write a word or make a sentence, but my teachers encouraged and helped me. They said not to believe that "older people can't learn how to read or write." I wanted to be literate so I could help my children with their lessons. Five years have now passed and I am in the fifth grade. I have not only become a literate person, but know many things, like famous poets, writers, Afghanistan history, geography, religion, and the Pashtu language. I have knowledge about the human body and health and I have learned math and geometry. I not only help my son who is in first grade, but also my daughter in fourth grade. We both try to help each other with our lessons. This year, because so many more girls are coming to our center, I became a teacher of the first grade. I earn good money from my sewing skills and use that money for my children's education. If there is any left over, I help my family. I also completed the Holy Qur'an class and am able to teach it to my children. Since I have had all this success, I am eager to learn more and more. Recently I started training in the CHW program in our village. Now I know about diseases, prevention of disease and first aid. I can do dressings, give injections and can prescribe for common illnesses. I give advice to women on reproductive health.

Neighboring villages have watched the progress of this center and now two others have centers supported by AIL. Malika and the other women are helping them organize their centers.

With the rise of insecurity and terrorism in Afghanistan, recently a group of terrorists told Malika's center to close or all of the women would be killed. For a month the center closed. Then, with the support of the entire community, several women approached the terrorists' leader and asked why the center had been closed.

"It is being run by foreigners," the leader said.

"No," the women responded. "This is our center. We are Afghans. We are being helped by Afghans. We are learning to read and write and about health to help our children and our families. We need this center."

The women used passages from the Qur'an and what they had learned about their rights and responsibilities under Islam in the center. In the end, the leader agreed to let the centers continue in several homes.

None of this would once have been possible. When empowered through education, women are able to overcome their circumstances and their self-doubt and exercise more autonomy over their lives.

Education is important for Afghan women and girls. In a practical sense, women and girls must learn to read and write and learn skills that will help them find work. However, it is far more important for women and girls to receive education that will open their minds to analyze, think critically, and consider people and events in new ways. This type of education allows women to make real choices about their actions and their lives.

In order to be truly empowered, women must also be able to make choices about the type of education they receive. Education that is developed using these core concepts allows women to make that choice. These core concepts are a vital part of education that truly empowers women to make their own decisions. They respond to the women's voiced needs and emphasize what they can do for themselves.

CHAPTER 21

From Both Sides of the Mic

Women and the Media

AUNOHITA MOJUMDAR

In a country emerging from years of political, social, and cultural isolation, where links to the external world were deliberately broken, the media, particularly radio and television, have become essential. They fill a three-decades-old vacuum, spreading information and ideas otherwise inaccessible.

The decades of war destroyed Afghanistan's most precious resource—education—resulting in a generation of youth with inadequate skills. Social and cultural interactions that exchange knowledge and generate fresh concepts through discussions or shared literature also ended during the wars. Traditional storehouses of knowledge passed on within communities were disrupted as families were displaced. Re-creating all these avenues for information, debate, and cultural exchange is a process that will take generations. Media can help fill the vacuum and act as a facilitator to the growth of these avenues. It has the potential to foster national identity, assist the democratization process, challenge information from insurgents, and expose corruption in government, thereby eventually creating more trustworthy and honest leadership.[1]

The role of media is especially significant for Afghan women, who face far greater social and public restrictions than men. Media provide platforms that can give women a voice and allow them to participate in social discourse. Calling into talk shows, participating in roundtable discussions, or being interviewed by journalists provides a forum for articulating their views, when they are too often silenced and customarily denied roles in traditional community councils. Women are also, by and large, excluded from decision-making positions in government and the private sector and therefore have fewer means of influencing and shaping discourse, policy, and social attitudes. Over the long term, it is believed, as Afghan society gets more used to listening to women and hearing their views, the presence of women in the media will influence outlooks, opinions, and behavior.

Yet, in recent years, participation in the very public medium of television proved lethal for Shaima Rezayee, an anchor for Tolo TV, as it did in 2008 for Shokiba Sanga Amaaj, an anchor for Ariana TV. Both were murdered in mysterious circumstances in their homes in the capital Kabul, amid rumors that their "lifestyles," on and off screen, contributed to their killings. Zakia Zaki, who ran a station called Radio Solh (Radio Peace) in Jabbal Sarraj, an hour north of Kabul, was also murdered in 2008.[2] For the many women who continue in the profession, it is an act of bravery.

THE EMERGENCE OF MEDIA

In the aftermath of the Taliban regime, in December 2001, the international community understood media to be vital components of the democracy project and poured funding into the country. By the end of 2002, about 200 magazines, newspapers, and newsletters had emerged, some only to survive one or two editions. Media groups, local and international, such as Aina, the Open Media Fund, United Nations Education Scientific and Cultural Organization, and the Afghan Media Resource Centre, sought to help establish print media, whereas other organizations, notably Media Action International and the Institute for War and Peace Reporting, stepped in to provide professional training to journalists.[3] Donors such as the United States Agency for International Development distributed funds directly to independent private media such as Moby Capital's Arman FM Radio, which was soon followed by the group's Tolo TV.[4]

Young men and women surged forward to take advantage of these opportunities, as did journalists returning from exile, whose careers had been interrupted by the conflicts. Najiba Ayubi attributes her interest in journalism to a lifelong love of literature and writing. In the early 1980s, after completing school in Parwan Province, north of Kabul, she began contributing to the local print media and eventually moved to Kabul in order to work at the national level.

"There were a great number of women in journalism at that time, though most of the media was controlled by the [communist] government. We were greatly respected as journalists," she recalled. The fall of Najibullah, the last president of the Communist Democratic Republic of Afghanistan in 1992, and the beginning of the civil war between Mujahedin factions meant Ayubi and other women "were scattered, moving place to place to avoid the violence. It became difficult even to go to work."

The advent of the Taliban ended all opportunity. "It was as if a vocal person had been struck dumb. We could not say anything." Ayubi smuggled articles out of the country for publication in Pakistan, until finally in 1999, she and her family left for Tehran. Iran, she said, provided no opportunities to practice journalism, but after her return to Kabul in 2002, she picked up the threads and joined the Killid Media Group in 2004, where she became media director.[5]

Radio Free Europe provided Neda Farhat with her first job. In her twenties, Farhat needed work when her family returned to Afghanistan from Pakistan in 2002. She loves being a journalist, and works in hard news for BBC's expanding Persian service. What she likes most about her job is the access to information, which helps her understand the country to which her family thought they would never return. The job, she said, has made her a different person. "I was shy and avoided people. As a journalist, I have to go into crowds with a microphone. I never thought that one day I would be questioning the president of Afghanistan."[6]

Ayubi also says the job has made her stronger: "Besides expressing myself—an Afghan woman—I can express the voices of thousands of other Afghan women. I can express the problems of women better than men can." And Farhat notes that she is able to approach and interview women, unlike her male colleagues, who are not permitted to meet females outside their intimate family circles.

Nilab Habibi became a photojournalist by accident. She is one of two women and two men serving the Pajhwok Photo Service, part of Pajhwok Afghan News, the first multilingual news agency in Afghanistan.[7] She was working as a reporter when a training course conducted by Aina exposed her to photography and she found she liked recording reality through the camera.[8] She prefers to show the unusual face of Afghanistan. "I don't like taking pictures of poor, deprived people always. I would like to take pictures that also show people happy.

"I am going to be a strong woman and a big journalist," she said.[9]

Habibi's colleague, Safya Saify, came to photojournalism through portraiture during her university education in Kabul. She, too, trained at Aina, but fearing opposition, didn't tell her family she was taking the course until she got her certificate of proficiency. Her conservative mother discouraged her but has slowly come to accept her daughter's work. Partly, Saify said, she earned this respect when she was able to pay half the expenses for her brother's marriage through her own earnings.

Saify believes her role as a journalist is in transforming people's lives. "I want to reflect the reality, so people can see it and do something about it." She recalls proudly how a destitute widow she found begging on the streets now has a home, shelter, and food after Saify published her picture.[10]

Saify, Habibi, and Ferhat, whose work involves recording public reactions and images, all face discomfort on the streets. Although the public in Kabul has gotten somewhat accustomed to their presence, the sight of women journalists venturing out still evokes harassment, mockery, and overwhelming curiosity. They are surrounded by crowds, jostling to get closer. Nevertheless, they're determined. It is far worse for female journalists in the provinces, where the concept of unaccompanied women venturing onto the street, into markets, or government offices is generally not acceptable. And whereas a journalist in Kabul may be permitted by her family to travel to work without a *burqa*, a journalist even in the cities of Herat or Mazar-i-Sharif probably would not be. What's more, there are enormous cultural differences at play, so that even within the same city, different tribes have different social codes, one stricter than another depending on the situation.

Working conditions for women journalists vary widely. There are no unions, so conditions depend on management, usually staffed by men— although there are a few women such as Najiba Ayubi who hold senior editorial positions. Conservative male managers who do not allow the women in their own families to step out without a burqa or male escort, let alone work around strange men, often see the women in their offices as having low moral standards. Repercussions can range from harassment and taunts to professional discrimination, especially if the women are seen as competing for contested positions. Media managers make allowances, however, for family pressure—allowing women in newsrooms to leave in the late afternoon, because many families do not permit women to stay out in the evening. But no matter how good they are professionally, women are excluded from the decision-making circles, and there are very few Afghan organizations that promote female journalists as star reporters. Ambition is considered inappropriate for women and is rarely encouraged.[11]

THE ROLE OF MEDIA IN THE CURRENT CONTEXT

In the fragmented polity and society that has emerged from decades of conflict and where the alien has constituted a constant threat, media can be a unifying tool for expanding the limits of participation. A 2004 public opinion survey conducted by the Asia Foundation captured the space for political tolerance. Only 30 percent of those surveyed said they did not mind if political parties they didn't like were allowed to hold meetings in their areas, whereas nearly a quarter said they would end a friendship if the friend supported an opposing party. However, more than 60 percent said they were interested in either attending a meeting where different politicians could be questioned or in hearing the broadcast of such an event on radio.[12]

The media provide nonconfrontational and easily accessible platforms. It is nonintrusive, can be controlled at will, and can be accessed in the privacy of the home. These advantages are especially meaningful for women.

In some parts of Afghanistan women are forbidden to leave their homes for any reason whatsoever unless accompanied by a *moharram,* an escort, usually defined as a close male relative. In large parts of the country, they also need the permission of the male head of the family to leave the house. Only 12.6 percent of Afghan women are literate.[13] Television and radio offer information they cannot access through books, magazines, or newspapers and can disseminate ideas about women's rights and mobilize direct participation in the electoral process. According to Asia Foundation's annual report of 2008, 84 percent of households surveyed said they owned a radio and 44 percent listened to it every day. The access to television was lower, with only 38 percent owning a TV set and 21 percent watching it daily.[14]

In May 2009, Afghanistan's Independent Election Commission announced that not a single woman candidate had registered for provincial council elections in eight provinces.[15] A week from the deadline for registration, several media organizations, including Salaam Watandar, a radio station supported by Internews,[16] took up the challenge and quickly produced a number of stories and interviews to highlight the issue and created an outreach campaign targeting potential female candidates. The message to women was that it was their duty to run for provincial council. Three hundred and thirty-three women registered as candidates—compared with 242 in 2005.[17]

Increasing violence has meant decreasing mobility for parliamentarians, especially women. USAID's Afghanistan Parliamentary Assistance Project, conceptualized and contracted Internews to implement radio roundtables between members of the Afghan parliament, which is located in Kabul, and citizens in provinces too dangerous to reach.[18] The resulting broadcasts on provincial radio stations allowed citizens to call in with their complaints, questions, and requests. Nasima Niazai, an MP from Helmand, used the occasion to ask women to stand for provincial council elections. But again, violence prevented many women from voting in 2009, and numbers were low, particularly in the Taliban-dominated areas in the south.[19]

Internews has also supported a weekly radio program called *Da Pulay Poray* (On the Borderline), which broadcasts on either side of the tense Afghanistan-Pakistan border. The show has tackled sensitive issues such as the psychological and health consequences of girls marrying and conceiving at young ages; the practice of *baad*, exchanging girls to end disputes or repay debts; and the prevention of women getting medical care due to the stigma against women going out in public. The program used women journalists to tell the stories.[20]

BBC World Service Trust's Afghanistan Educational Program receives funding from the UK's Foreign and Commonwealth Office for *Afghan Woman's Hour*, a radio program broadcasting weekly in both Dari and Pashto. The program, which uses women reporters, focuses on women's empowerment and women's participation in political and public life, as well as programming on health, education, and other social issues.[21] BBC audience research has shown that a majority of listeners feel the program has inspired them to change their own situation and solve problems.[22] The program is broadcast on BBC, through the national media organization, Radio Television Afghanistan.[23]

The Killid Group is a not-for-profit public media initiative of Development and Humanitarian Services for Afghanistan.[24] Killid utilizes a variety of platforms: book and magazine publishing; civic radio; training of Killid and other Afghan media journalists about human rights and war crimes investigative reporting techniques; production of original Web content; and cosponsorship of conferences and workshops on media and development. In 2006, it developed a program—in which Najiba Ayubi was involved—about domestic violence, funded for one year by the European Commission. Using fourteen affiliate radio stations, the program called *Why Violence* used a variety of techniques—roundtable discussions, quizzes, dramas, public service announcements, interviews, reports, and special editions of the *Killid Weekly* and of the *Mursal Women's Magazine*—to focus on the issue.[25]

The programs gave lawyers, physicians, academics, and social researchers, as well as government and civil society representatives, including women's organizations, opportunities to explore—with the public—forms of domestic violence and its impact and consequences, legal framework and remedies, Islamic law or Shari'a, and how and where to seek assistance. [26]

In her paper, "Development Communication Strategies and Domestic Violence in Afghanistan," Sarah Kamal, a former consultant for the United Nations Development Fund for Women, discusses how UNIFEM used direct and protracted media interventions combating violence against women in Afghanistan.[27] UNIFEM developed a toolkit for advocacy on gender concerns that could be used by the media, a valuable resource where conflict has destroyed data banks and the tools to access them. The toolkit advocates sensitivity in approaching taboo subjects, for example, turning the issue of forced marriages around to discuss it in terms of men's powerlessness in the face of clan pressure, rather than simply the victimization of women. Kamal writes:

> In some ways, the media has been used to compensate for the central government's limited judicial and enforcement mechanisms. Insecurity and poor infrastructure in rural Afghanistan have discouraged development agencies from having a significant physical presence outside of Kabul or other major urban centers. As a consequence, the radio—a cheap, battery-operated, and accessible medium without literacy requirements—has been a central vehicle for extending development efforts and disseminating messages on voting and the political process across the country. Extension of the central government's judicial framework has followed a similar logic with the texts of legal documents, such as the Afghan Constitution and/or laws regarding, for example, marriage registration or the minimum age of marriage, being broadcast to rural areas. These broadcasts have intended to spread information that would present opportunities for self-regulation or lend weight and authority to negotiations for practices more in line with the central government's legal frameworks in areas otherwise inaccessible to the formal justice system.[28]

Kamal acknowledges the limitations of media campaigns but points out that "the power of the media lies in the intangible rather than the institutional, in re-creating boundaries of what is permissible, and instilling questions about existing norms."[29]

EXTENDING THE BOUNDARIES

Moby Capital's popular Arman FM radio station and Tolo TV have been redrawing the boundaries of what is permissible quite effectively in the social sphere. Its mixture of entertainment and serious programming has proved to be an enormous commercial success, allowing the Afghan group to turn commercial quickly after its inception, using donor money from USAID and others. Based in Kabul, Tolo currently telecasts to fourteen cities through terrestrial broadcasting and satellite. Its popularity has allowed it to continuously expand the content of its programming, including several programs dedicated to female audiences.

Banu is a television call-in show hosted by both male and female anchors, during which women discuss their problems related to domestic issues, which are then addressed by a panel featuring a doctor and a psychologist. In *Beauty and the Beast*—a weekly show directed at both men and women, in roundtable format with parliamentarians, social activists, and others as guests—humor is used to tackle sticky issues, such as women's right to decision making.

Arman FM's *Subah o Arman* (*Good Morning, Arman*) show also uses humor, whereas a more serious youth-oriented weekly program tackles problems related to love and family. The radio station gets calls not only from urban centers but also the remote provinces.

"Radio can reach everywhere," said Masood Sanjar, head of productions for Tolo and Arman.[30] The medium, he noted, allows an intimacy that would not be possible in face-to-face encounters in Afghan society. In talk shows he himself hosts, he has young girls from Kandahar chatting and joking with him on the phone as they could never do in person. The medium also allows families to participate in such talk shows as a group, creating virtual spheres of social interaction not yet possible physically, as social mores do not permit interactions between men and women who are not family. Talk shows worldwide mimic social interaction, but in Afghanistan, they are slowly leading the way to expanding spheres of communication. Since Sanjar began in 2003, he has seen an extraordinary change in the range of subjects discussed and how they are discussed. Equally important, the show allows people, especially youth, to vent their frustrations in the absence of psychological counseling.

Pure entertainment programs also play a role in extending social boundaries. Tolo TV's *Afghan Sitara (Afghan Star)*, a program modeled on *American Idol*, has provided space for female singers to emerge as entertainers on stage. Several of the women who have participated in the show have gone on to record their own songs and become professional musicians.[31] Cooking, health, and even programs about beauty tips are also valuable.[32] Decades of war destroyed much of the traditional repository of knowledge in such ordinary skills.

Media, especially radio, can help overcome physical and geographical barriers to literacy.[33] The function of media, especially radio, in Afghanistan is essential, helping to overcome physical and geographical barriers. And for women, for whom the hurdles to accessing information, participating in social interactions, and engaging in the public sphere are frequently insurmountable, the media begins to provide a forum to fill in the blanks.

NOTES

1. Of interest: Adam Serwer, "The Importance of Media in the Afghan Conflict," *The American Prospect, Tapped: The Group Blog of the American Prospect*, August 12, 2009, http://www.prospect.org/csnc/blogs/tapped_archive ?month=08&year=2009&base_name=the_importance_of_media_in_the; Feroz Mehdi, "Reconstruction, Democratization and the Role of Independent Media in Afghanistan," *Alternatives International*, February 7, 2006, http://www .alternatives.ca/article2498.html. In March 2007, a two-day international seminar titled "Media *Is* Development: Afghanistan Media Civil Society Forum," organized by the Killid Group and IPS-Inter Press Service and held in Kabul, explored "the role played by media and civil society in efforts to support the transformation towards a peaceful democracy." The Killid Media Group is a not-for-profit public media initiative of Development & Humanitarian Services for Afghanistan, http://www.thekillidgroup.com/. IPS-Inter Press Service is a global news agency, http://www.ips.org/institutional/. For further information about the "Media *Is* Development" conference, see Inter Press Service News Agency, http://ipsnews.net/afghanistan/forum.asp.

2. Golnaz Esfandiary, "Afghanistan: Latest Female Journalist's Slaying Highlights Plight." *Radio Free Europe*, June 6, 2007, http://www.rferl.org/content/ article/1076958.html.

3. Edward Giradet and Jonathan Walter, *Crosslines Essential Field Guides to Humanitarian and Conflict Zones: Afghanistan*, 2nd ed. (New York: International Centre for Humanitarian Reporting, 2004), 84–94; interviews with various reporters based in Kabul, 2003–2005.

4. Interviews with journalists, media NGOs, and donors, Kabul, 2003–2005.

5. Interview with Najiba Ayubi, Kabul, June 25, 2009.

6. Interview with Neda Farhat , Kabul, June 26, 2009.

7. Pajhwok Afghan News (http://www.pajhwok.com/) produces news in English as well as in Afghanistan's two major languages, Dari and Pashto.

8. Aina is a French-based NGO founded by photojournalist Reza Deghati and various French entrepreneurs and dedicated to developing civil society, by creating independent Afghan media and training local journalists, men and women, in all media. "AINA (organization)," *Wikipedia*, http://en.wikipedia.org/wiki/AINA_(organization).

9. Interview with Nilab Habibi, Kabul, June 25, 2009.

10. Interview with Safya Saifi, Kabul, June 25, 2009.

11. Interview with woman journalist who requested anonymity, Kabul, 2005.

12. Craig Charney, Radhika Nanda, and Nicole Yakatan, "Voter Education Planning Survey: Afghanistan 2004 National Elections, a Report Based on a Public Opinion Poll," The Asia Foundation, July 2004, http://asiafoundation.org/resources/pdfs/afghanvotered04.pdf.

13. *The National Human Development Report: Afghanistan* (United Nations Development Programme, Kabul, Afghanistan Country Office, 2007), 24.

14. Ruth Rennie, Sudhindra Sharma, and Pawan Sen "Afghanistan in 2008: A Survey of the Afghan People" The Asia Foundation, Annual Survey 2008, http://www.asiafoundation.org/resources/pdfs/Afghanistanin2008.pdf.

15. Independent Election Commission of Afghanistan, press release, May 7, 2009. http://www.iec.org.af/eng/.

16. Internews Network is an international media development organization whose mission is to empower local media worldwide, funded in Afghanistan by USAID, http://afghanistan.usaid.gov/en/Partner.69.aspx.

17. "A Woman's Place Is in the Council Chambers: Radio Programming Inspires Afghan Women to Run for Office," Internews Newsletter, May 13, 2009, http://www.internews.org/prs/2009/20090513_afghan.shtm.

18. Personal communication with Afghan Parliamentary Assistance Project, http://www.sunyaf.org/news.htm.

19. As of this writing, there are no official figures for how many women actually voted in 2009, though it is known that female voter turnout was low especially in violence-prone areas such as Kandahar. However, in Bamiyan Province, which has a woman governor, Habiba Sorabi, the turnout of women voters was strong.

20. BBC World Service Trust, Afghan Education Projects, http://www.bbc.co.uk/worldservice/trust/asiapacific/story/2007/11/071101_afghan_womens_hour_diaries.shtml.

21. Information provided by Andrea Wenzel, Project and Training Manager, BBC World Service Trust Afghanistan, June 28, 2009.

22. " 'Shoulder to Shoulder': Radio for Gender Parity in Afghanistan," BBC World Service Trust, Afghan Education Projects, http://www.bbc.co.uk/worldservice/trust/whatwedo/where/asia/afghanistan/2009/03/090304_shoulder-to-shoulder.shtml and "A Trusted Friend for Afghan Women," BBC World Service Trust, Afghan Education Projects, http://www.bbc.co.uk/worldservice/

trust/whatwedo/where/asia/afghanistan/2008/03/080222_afghanistan_
womans_hour_project_overview.shtml.

23. Radio Television Afghanistan began as Radio Kabul in 1925 during the reign of King Amanullah (r. 1919 to 1929) and is a broadcasting organization of the Afghan government, based in Kabul, with one national television station, one national radio station, and sister channels, such as Herat TV and Balkh TV, in other major cities. "Radio Television Afghanistan," *Wikipedia*, http://en .wikipedia.org/wiki/Radio_Television_Afghanistan.

24. Public media was added to Development and Humanitarian Services for Afghanistan's portfolio in 2002. Its stated mission is to promote civic media, free speech, and open discourse in Afghanistan and to strengthen the press as an independent source of information for the Afghan people. Development and Humanitarian Services for Afghanistan, http://www.dhsa.af/.

25. Killid Media Group, http://www.thekillidgroup.com/c/highlights/high lights_media_capacity.html. Killid also publishes *Mursal*, a woman's weekly magazine, with a print run in 2009 of 15,000 and geared toward semi-literate women: http://www.thekillidgroup.com/c/divisions/mursal.htm.

26. Interview with Najiba Ayubi, Killid Media Group media director, Kabul, June 25, 2009.

27. Sarah Kamal, "Development Communications Strategies and Domestic Violence in Afghanistan," in *Change from Within: Diverse Perspectives on Domestic Violence in Muslim Communities* (Great Falls, Va.: The Peaceful Families Project, 2006), http://www.peacefulfamilies.org/kamal.html.

28. Ibid., 9.

29. Ibid., 10. See also, Sarah Kamal, "Disconnected from Discourse: Women's Radio Listening in Rural Samangan, Afghanistan" (working paper 7, The Inter-University Committee on International Migration, February 15, 2004). Kamal found that 44 percent of households she surveyed in the northern Samangan Province owned working radio sets, though 6 percent of those were out of batteries. She reported that "radio sets were predominantly controlled by the man/men in the households and that in eighty-eight percent of the households with working sets, only men turned the radio on and off" (7).

30. Interview with Masood Sanjar, Kabul, June 27, 2009.

31. A documentary, *Afghan Star*, directed by Havana Marking, was created in 2008 and aired on HBO.

32. Of the women surveyed by Kamal in "Disconnected from Discourse," 12 percent reported listening to the radio, and of those, the most popular programming was the BBC and Radio Afghanistan. "If they were to influence radio programming, women wanted broadcasts of 'good news.' They wanted music, news about a peaceful world, and justice. They cited preferences for educational programming, which could help them out of their *koohi* (uncivilized) state. Iranian radio was seen as a source of good Islamic programming. Women also enjoyed Iranian programs that offered advice on raising children and fostering a harmonious family life. . . . They also wanted the radio to emphasize 'not to marry girls early.' A recurring theme was the need to understand their rights and 'wife and husband roles' as practiced outside of the village" (8, 12).

Across the decades, radio has been profoundly effective in educating populations in Africa, Canada, Latin America, Australia, and Europe. According to
A. W. Bates, "Worldwide experience suggests four basic models of radio ownership and control: commercial, public broadcasting, open access, and radio
schools. The models have profound implications for the way radio is used for
adult literacy." A. W. Bates, "Literacy by Radio: Lesson from Around the
World" (paper presented at the International Symposium of Popular Literacy
by Radio, Santo Domingo, July 1990), Education Resources Information Center, http://www.eric.ed.gov/ERICWebPortal/search/detailmini.jsp?_nfpb=true
&_&ERICExtSearch_SearchValue_o=ED329654&ERICExtSearch_SearchType
_o=no&accno=ED329654.

33. In Kabul, I checked with UNESCO, UNICEF, and various media NGOs,
but could find no information on radio literacy classes in Afghanistan.

CHAPTER 22

Painting Their Way into the Public World

Women and the Visual Arts

LAURYN OATES

The distinction between the social and the political makes no sense in the modern world because the struggle to make something public is a struggle for justice.[1]

In 2008, the first Women's Arts and Modern Painting Exhibition was held in Kabul, organized by the Center for Contemporary Arts Afghanistan. For the first time in Afghan history, the public crowded into a small gallery during the harsh Kabul winter to view the work of Afghan women artists. The artists, aged between sixteen and twenty-five, had created a collection that burst away from any semblance of tradition and that the curator, Rahraw Omarzad—a passionate advocate of contemporary art and veteran of Kabul's turbulent art scene since the 1970s—described to me as "symbolically expressing their experiences from life in the framework of new artistic concepts."

Five hundred years ago, Herat, the Afghan cultural capital of the Timurid period (c. 1370–1507) was Central Asia's spiritual, scientific, and artistic hub. Miniatures, illuminated and illustrated manuscripts, tile work, and distinct new forms of architecture made their way to Persia, the Ottoman Empire, and the Indian kingdoms. The land that is now Afghanistan had its own schools and produced some of the world's great artists, such as the Herati miniature painter Kamaluddin Behzad (c. 1450–1535), who illustrated, among other works, the *Khamsa* (Quintet) of the

Persian poet, Nizami.[2] Although the historical record excludes mention of female artists, women were patrons, commissioning and financing art and architecture. The tomb of Herat's Queen Gowar Shad, who reigned during the fifteenth century, is a place of reverence for modern Heratis. Evidence of her philanthropy still exists everywhere in the city, including a women's garden, which she caused to be built and which was renovated in recent years.

Although the Timurid period is largely considered to be the peak of Afghanistan's artistic glory, the region was also situated along the famed Silk Road and became a crossroads for cultural exchange from North Africa, the Near East, and Europe into Asia. India's Mughal Empire was launched in 1526 from Kabul by the Timurid prince Babur. Its cultural zenith is thought to have taken place from 1556, with the reign of Jalaluddin Mohammad Akbar (Akbar the Great), through the death in 1707 of Emperor Aurangzeb, although the empire continued for another 150 years, bringing the arts of the known world together in a great flourishing.

In 1924, King Amanullah (r. 1919–1929) established the Kabul Museum, which grew to house one of the largest, most valuable collections in Central Asia. Western art styles were beginning to encroach on Afghanistan, and in the 1930s, Ghulam Muhammad Musawwer Maimanagi opened what became the Kabul Fine Arts College in 1955, now the Maimanagi Afghan Traditional Arts Training School, which teaches miniature painting, calligraphy, woodworking, painting, sculpture, embroidery, and jewelry-making to male and female students. Kabul University opened its art department in 1967.

Nancy Hatch Dupree, Afghanistan's best-known resident historian, described the tenuous foundation of visual art in the mid-twentieth century:

> Artists failed to experience the same surge in popularity as the musicians and actors. The work of urban artists was fundamentally eclectic, following various styles from bucolic pastoral scenes to Picasso and Grandma Moses without any assimilation of recognizable Afghan characteristics to satisfy Afghan cultural values. Some leading artists actively sought to revive the traditions of the Timurid School in Herat. Official patronage of talent in the provinces brought to prominence two Khirghis artists from the Wakhan and an elderly gentleman from Aibak whose work celebrated epic heroes. But generally, artists failed to win public support. To collect Afghan art never became fashionable among Afghans or even foreign tourists, so it was a discouraging road for most artists. Efforts to open an art gallery to encourage artists did not materialize at this time.[3]

With the Soviet invasion in 1979, Afghanistan came to be associated more with Kalashnikovs and refugees than with exquisite artwork. The civil war following the Soviet withdrawal in 1989 between Mujahedin factions centered in Kabul, accelerated the erosion of the arts. In 1994, a rocket destroyed much of the Kabul Museum and many of its artifacts. The university art department was destroyed, along with most of the rest of the school. When the Taliban came to power in 1996, they made the obliteration of art, particularly pre-Islamic art, an official policy. Eighty percent of what remained of the museum was looted.[4]

Those who continued to make art clandestinely risked their lives. Most artists fled. Nevertheless, Afghanistan is full of remarkable stories of defiance during the Taliban years. Men and women not only ran underground schools for girls and health clinics for women, they also kept arts and culture alive. Children played in the streets of Herat to guard against Taliban police while mixed-sex literary circles took place inside homes under the guise of sewing circles.[5] Musicians risked death to hear the sounds of their *rabab*s and buried their instruments to safeguard them from destruction, only retrieving them years later.[6]

Little more than a decade later, the arts in Afghanistan are reemerging, and this time, the women are there, not as patrons or the subjects of Timurid miniatures but as artists in their own rights. They are leaving their mark on the country's nascent new wave of contemporary artistic expression, bold, defiant, and full of potential. They are not so much filling a void as diversifying the art scene from women's traditional artistic activities—embroidery, carpet making, silk weaving, pottery.

The Center for Contemporary Art Afghanistan's 2008 exhibition featured painting and sculpture, which often expressed the grim realities many Afghan women face in their daily lives, speaking to experiences of deprivation and oppression but also to hope and imagination. The young artists avoided representation and displayed a wide array of modern and contemporary art forms. Reactions from the media and public came from all directions: some wildly negative criticisms from Afghans unaccustomed to abstract art, as well as heaps of praise from those welcoming a renaissance in the stagnant arts scene. Rahraw Omarzad, who founded the CCAA, was overwhelmed with pride. It was a watershed moment and, he hoped, just the beginning.

Two hundred women showed up to register for classes when the center opened in 2004. Instruction is offered in everything from installation and video art to photography, painting, and drawing. The founding group of Afghan female and male artists, backed by an international advisory board, decided to place a heavy emphasis on supporting women. The Female Artistic Center is the school's hallmark program. In 2009, sixty women were enrolled in painting and drawing classes.

By contrast, only 10 percent of students at Kabul University's rebuilt Fine Arts Faculty are female. In any event, the few Afghans with the means to attend the country's four universities are not turning to art as their first choice in studies. As in many Western countries, art in Afghanistan is often seen as frivolous compared with "serious" professions that will help feed families and contribute to the country's much-needed reconstruction and economic development. As Constance Wyndham, cultural projects officer at Kabul's Turquoise Mountain Foundation wrote, "Art can seem superfluous in a country that doesn't yet have proper roads."[7]

Admittance into engineering, law, and medicine is highly competitive, requiring just the right mix of money and merit. Kabul University's Fine Arts Faculty, however, is a dusty Soviet-era corner on campus with few resources and little prestige. Upon returning to her country of birth for the first time since childhood, Afghan American video artist Lida Abdul recalled, "My going there to do art seemed rather inconsiderate. Did they really need art classes?"[8] Misgivings abound, yet something still draws artists back to their homeland—and it is hardly frivolous.

Basic humanitarian assistance is limited. More is needed, including cultural capital to infuse a scarred population with pride and enthusiasm for a different kind of future. Aid givers are beginning to think of "development" in new ways, seeing art as anything but superfluous. Viable reconstruction in Afghanistan and its peace-building ambitions depend as much on repairing the social and cultural fabric of the country as on building physical infrastructures and institutions. Imagination and invention are required for lasting change. Dupree believes that Afghans' "determination to remain true to the essence of their culture is innate. The nation is traumatized, but the culture still lives."[9]

In a country of wide ethnic, linguistic, and tribal differences, the sparse threads that bind are the profound love of poetry, the persistence of folk songs and tales, a reverence for jokes and proverbs and the skills to tell them, and music, art, and literature that cross all boundaries. These instil pride, national unity, and a deeper sense of heritage among people struggling to make sense of what it means to be Afghan in this little splash of land pulled apart repeatedly by internal and external spoilers.

But for women, art can mean even more. Living in the delicate aftermath of gender apartheid, there are few spaces—conceptual or physical—where women find visibility and voice. Ancient customs of social segregation keep many women relegated to the private sphere. Despite a constitution that guarantees equality and a quota of secure seats in parliament, the chasm is still wide between Afghanistan's daring women parliamentarians and its female masses.[10] For many Afghan women, their most profound political act might be to step outside their home compounds without permission or a male chaperone, or to sign up for a basic literacy class. Families resist sending a daughter to art school and are often uncomfortable when men and women study together, so for now, CCAA offers women-only art classes. Exposure to the public realm can be risky business.[11]

How might this divide be narrowed? The worlds of art and culture could hold a key. Visual art may be a relatively safer mode of self-expression than other forms, which are often poisoned by self- and official censorship. What you cannot say aloud or in print, you can describe in paint, charcoal, or pencil. Perhaps this explains why abstract and other forms of nonrepresentational art are growing roots among young Afghan women such as those at the Center for Contemporary Arts Afghanistan. Art is a means of resistance and healing, as well as an outlet for suppressed talent. It provides a platform for articulating beauty, drawing out caches of memory and happiness in an environment often preoccupied by the consequences of violence. It empowers the artist and the viewer.

As a refugee in Pakistan, Yalda Noori was exposed to painting when she enrolled in a course in Islamabad. After returning to Afghanistan, she picked it up again, but this time, at CCAA, she had fewer limits on her creativity. Her paintings are adorned with lamp shades, "unsustainable," she says in an artist's statement, "just like dreams."[12]

Twenty-four-year-old, Mariam Formuly says her art is rooted in sorrows common to many Afghan women: the deaths of loved ones in war, forced marriage, and suicide—themes that come up repeatedly. Some of her pieces are made of fabric, sharp edges juxtaposed with ragged ones, contrasting the ideal with the disorder of reality.

Ramzia Tajzada depicts injustice against women, but Moqaddesa Yuresh specifically avoids "harsh and frustrating realities," concentrating on expressions of hopefulness.[13] One Yuresh painting is composed of three squares in bright red, blue, and yellow on a white backdrop, two diagonal slices offering a slight opening, disrupting the perfection of the squares.

Omarzad's dream is to open women's art centers across the country. For now, the CCAA, like so many organizations in Afghanistan, is strapped for cash, space, and supplies, restricting its ability to accept new students even in the face of growing demand. The Open Society Institute is one of the center's few funders, along with the Women of the World Foundation.[14] Traditional arts, such as the Khamak embroidery of Kandahar and the famous blue pottery of Istalif (a village north of Kabul), have found support among donors for commercial development and expansion. Yet art for art's sake, as the human right to self-expression or even as a form of therapy, is a tough sell to donors who want to see tangible outcomes for their dollars, easily measured in numbers.

Omarzad is undaunted. He knows, as Dupree also emphasizes, that the right to make and access art is fundamentally linked to cultural renaissance and national identity, unity, and stability. His long to-do list includes establishing a contemporary visual arts high school for girls, opening a women's graphic design center to enable distance-learning opportunities, giving women artists the chance to exhibit their work abroad (shows have already been held in Berlin, Istanbul, New York, Kazakhstan, and Switzerland), and making it possible for women to earn graduate degrees in fine arts. His track record suggests Omarzad will eventually realize these projects. Meanwhile, the center has many new undertakings: a textile design program and classes in multimedia exhibition techniques, among others. To help enlighten Kabul's residents about contemporary art, CCAA is building a mobile cinema unit to travel around the city showing films about art.

Omarzad was born in Kabul in 1964, a time of peace, stability, and promise. He remembers looking at paintings for sale in tourist shop windows in the 1970s, when Afghanistan was an essential stop on the Hippie Trail. He studied fine arts at Kabul University, and then taught there. He also illustrated books for deaf children. He fled the country in 1993, settling in Peshawar, Pakistan, where he continued teaching art. He returned to Kabul in 2002, and he now lectures at the university and has founded the country's only art magazine, *Gahnama-e Hunar* (*Art Periodical*).

The practice of what he calls "copying" leaves Omarzad uninspired. Clichéd representations of landscapes, women in burqas, elderly bearded men, or games of *buzkashi* are stifling,[15] leaving little room for self-expression. And there is no need to be bound to historical legacies. For there to be a new Afghanistan, Omarzad believes, there must be new art by new artists, a fresh start. "We cannot answer the complexity of today's life with the manifestation of yesterday's realities," Omarzad says, quoting Wassily Kandinsky, the artist credited with painting the first modern abstract works. There is nothing more avant garde, Omarzad adds, than to nurture the artwork of women in Afghan society. His vision is of an artistic sector with women inherently linked to the development of an open society. He believes that women's involvement in art promotes well-being in a place where healing is urgently needed.[16]

The Center for Contemporary Art Afghanistan is one key player in a reviving arts sector. Kabul's Foundation for Culture and Civil Society serves as an exhibition and performance space, welcoming men and women. Here, everyone has the opportunity to interact and consider what a resurrected cultural landscape might look like when peace arrives.

Meanwhile, Herat University's Fine Arts Faculty—perhaps in the spirit of Queen Gowhar Shad—has reopened its doors to women, and in Kabul, the Afghan Vocational School of Arts and Music recently came alive after a wartime hiatus with funding from Polska Akcja Humanitarna (Polish Humanitarian Organization), offering calligraphy, painting, ceramics, and sculpture classes to high-school students.

Zolaykha Sherzad runs a design studio in Kabul where she and her team of female and male master tailors produce Afghanistan's haute couture. Her clothing, artful blends of traditional textiles and styles with modern cuts, is worn by President Hamid Karzai, Afghan diplomats, and Kabul's expatriate community. She has displayed her work on runways in Dubai, Paris, London, Delhi, and New York. "I want to show people that Afghanistan is not all about war and orphanages and burqas. It is also about textiles and history and culture. It is about beauty."[17]

This nascent art scene is a critical infusion into a broader civil society and cultural development movement, and its survival is in part due to those artists, musicians, and poets who persevered to keep the country's artistic heritage alive through their underground activities. Whereas the international effort must prioritize support to emergency humanitarian assistance and the establishment of basic services, women's participation in arts and culture can ultimately dismantle some of the structures that facilitated Afghanistan's descent into chaos.

"The advancement of women and their empowerment," Omarzad says, "is an integral part of the process of democratization and civilization."[18]

NOTES

1. Seyla Benhabib, *Situating the Self: Gender, Community and Postmodernism in Contemporary Ethics* (New York: Routledge, 1992), 94.

2. "The Timurids: 1387–1502," Art Arena, http://www.art-arena.com/timurid.htm. Although Herat is today a city in Afghanistan, it has had a turbulent history as part of the Persian Empire. Behzad is considered to be a Persian artist, but those lines were obscure.

3. Nancy Hatch Dupree, "Cultural Heritage and National Identity in Afghanistan," *Third World Quarterly* 23, no. 5 (2005): 977–989.

4. According to Robin Clewley, the staff at the Kabul Museum destroyed the catalog of the museum's collection and buried the most precious objects deep underground so they could not be destroyed. In March 2001, the Taliban blew up Bamiyan's giant, sixth-century Buddha statues, which had been carved directly into a mountain by the pre-Islamic Kushan people. These were the largest Buddhist statues on Earth, a UNESCO world heritage site. Robin Clewley, "Afghan Archivist of Culture," *Wired*, November 6, 2001, http://www.wired.com/culture/lifestyle/news/2001/11/47842.

5. Christina Lamb, *The Sewing Circles of Herat: A Personal Voyage through Afghanistan* (New York: HarperCollins, 2002).

6. Radio Free Europe-Afghanistan, "Afghanistan: Musicians Struggling to Revive Classical Heritage after Taliban," *Human Beams*, November 21, 2005, http://lifeatlarge.humanbeams.com/index.php/lifeatlarge/comments/lf1105rfe_rl_afghanistanmusic. A rebab is a stringed instrument.

7. See Constance Wyndham, "Afghanistan's Artistic Side: The Afghan Contemporary Art Prize," *The Financial Times*, July 2, 2008). In 2008, the Turquoise Mountain Foundation participated in the launch of the Afghan Contemporary Art Prize. Out of the seventy-five male and female entries, ten won the competition. Turquoise Mountain Foundation's mandate is to invest "in the regeneration of the historic commercial centre of Kabul, providing basic services, saving historic buildings and constructing a new bazaar and galleries for traditional craft businesses. It has established Afghanistan's first Higher Education Institute for Afghan Arts and Architecture, training students to produce works in wood, calligraphy, and ceramics. The Institute has been used to develop new Afghan designs, promote Afghan handicrafts through national and international exhibitions and media campaigns, open new markets, restore key parts of the Kabul Museum collection, renovate public spaces, and build capacity in the government and universities." www.turquoisemountain.org.

8. Lida Abdul, "Works in the Exhibition "Nafas,'" *Nafas Art Magazine*, May 2006, http://universes-in-universe.org/eng/nafas/articles/2006/nafas_special/nafas_exhibition/artists/lida_abdul.

9. Dupree, "Cultural Heritage and National Identity in Afghanistan."

10. Women's organizations, post-2001, pushed for women's representation on the Constitutional Drafting Committee, and submitted specific recommendations to ensure that the constitution guaranteed women's rights. See Lauryn Oates and Isabelle Solon Helal, *At the Crossroads of Conflict and Democracy: Women and Afghanistan's Constitution-Making Process* (Montreal: Rights and Democracy, 2004).

11. Numerous women with public presences have been murdered, including women's rights advocate Sitara Achekzai in 2009; Kandahari police officer Malalai Kakar in 2008; Zakia Zaki, a female broadcaster on Peace Radio and Shokiba Sanga Amaaj, of Shamshad in 2007; and Safia Ama Jan, a teacher and women's rights leader in Kandahar in 2006. And in 2004, the Taliban claimed responsibility for bombing a bus carrying female election workers in Jalalabad, killing two women.

12. The artists' statement is on CCAA's website: www.ccaa.org.af.

13. Ibid.

14. The Women of the World Foundation was founded by United States art collector Richard C. Colton and conceptualized by Claudia DeMonte.

15. *Buzkashi* is a popular Afghan horse sport, which developed on the plains of Mongolia and Central Asia.

16. Recent studies have found exponentially high rates of post-traumatic stress disorder among Afghan women, as well as a dangerously high prevalence of anxiety and depression. See Barbara Lopes Cardozo, Oleg O. Bilukha, Carol A. Gotway, Mitchell I. Wolfe, Michael L. Gerber, and Mark Anderson, "Report from the CDC: Mental Health of Women in Postwar Afghanistan," *Journal of Women's Health*, 14 no. 4 (2005): 285–293. One organization, Rubia (described in "Mending Afghanistan Stitch by Stitch," in this volume), has also recognized the power of art to heal psychological wounds, supporting women in a drug clinic to use embroidery for recovery.

17. Quoted in Aryn Baker, "Building a Bridge with Style," *Time Style and Design* (Fall 2008).

18. I am grateful to Afghan-American artist Gazelle Samizay for her review of an early draft of this chapter, to Rahraw Omarzad for putting up with many nagging emails from me and sending photos of art over a slow Internet connection, and to my friend Abdulrahim Ahmadparwani for his passion for Afghan art, literature, and cultural heritage and for helping to instil this passion in others.

CHAPTER 23

A Hidden Discourse

Afghanistan's Women Poets

ZUZANNA OLSZEWSKA

Poetry is a slippery thing. It enables the poet to express her innermost thoughts while hiding behind layers of convention and metaphor. It reveals even as it conceals, and the poet must maintain a delicate tension between these two acts. That tension is all the more delicate in the case of Afghan women, for whom abiding by traditional distinctions between appropriate behavior in public and private carries dramatically higher stakes than it does for men. It can be particularly risky for women to stand somewhat apart from society and speak its unspoken truths— such as the reality of romantic love. Despite these challenges, poetry is an art that women of what is today Afghanistan were already pursuing at the dawn of recorded Persian literature in the tenth century. The love of poetry runs deep in the veins of anyone brought up on the rich literary traditions of the region—whether male or female, literate or non-literate, rich or poor, a speaker of Persian, Pashtu, or any of the dozens of languages of Afghanistan. But women have always had to be particularly judicious in balancing creative expression with safeguarding their honor and upholding public moral codes; for many, this has come at the heavy price of silencing or even death.

History has also not been kind to Afghan women poets. Few female names have come down to us in the classical canon, and only a few more in contemporary times. There is no reason to assume that young Afghan girls across the ages, in the first flush of romantic feeling or creative fervor, have not tried to shape their inner thoughts into polished strings of words to the same extent as boys. But even if they succeeded in reaching audiences beyond a few confidantes or all-female gatherings, there was no guarantee that they would remain for long in the very selective, male-dominated historical records. Today, young Afghans are likely to remember the chilling legend of the first recorded female poet of the Persian language, Rabi'a of Balkh, a noblewoman who was murdered by her own brother for the crime of falling in love with a slave in the tenth century. She is said to have written her last poem with her own blood on the door of the bathhouse in which, her throat cut, she was left to die:

> His love has thrown me in chains again—
> all my struggles have been for nothing!
> I tried to flee like a wild horse, little did I know
> that the harder you pull on the lasso, the tighter the noose.
> Love is a sea whose shores cannot be seen.
> When would you swim across it, poor creature!
> If you wish to carry love with you to the end,
> you must bear every disagreeable thing:
> See evil and suppose it good,
> eat poison and think it sweet.
> Rabi'a Balkhi[1]

It is regrettable—but perhaps no accident—that few remember the remarkable women of the Timurid era in Herat. That dynasty yielded not only the powerful queen Gowhar Shad, one of the instigators of Herat's fifteenth-century cultural renaissance, but also many other aristocratic ladies who were active patrons of architecture, music, painting, and literature—or were themselves notable poets.[2] The literary soirées of Mir Ali Shir Navai (a courtier of the fifteenth-century Sultan Hussein Bayqara) were famous for their refined, witty banter, verbal virtuosity, and extemporaneous poetic composition. Female as well as male poets participated in them. Some of them were married to other poets and composed teasing jibes to their husbands in verse, mocking them, for example, for their old age. Female poets of the Timurid era included Mehri, Mughul Khanum, Nahani, Afaq Jalahir, and Bibi Esmati. They were educated noblewomen, well known for their intellect and wit, and were able to participate in intellectual exchanges with men. One, Nija Munajjima, was also an accomplished astronomer and wealthy enough to endow several mosques. Indeed, she engaged in a rivalry of mosque building and a contest of wits with the great Sufi poet Jami!

It is recounted that Mehri, a companion of Queen Gowhar Shad, was married to an older man by the name of Abdul Aziz Hakim, but she was in love with Gowhar Shad's nephew Masoud Mirza. One night, she sat with Masoud at the top of a tower. On seeing her husband crossing the courtyard below, she extemporaneously composed the following couplet:

> I let my moon appear at the top of a tower
> Beware, O Hakim, don't eclipse my happy new moon!

This revealed her considerable talent, given her ability to spontaneously weave together several layers of meaning: the lover's youthful, beautiful face is often compared to the moon in classical Persian poetry, and the phrase "happy new moon" (tali-i masoud) was in fact a play upon her lover's name, Masoud, which means "the happy one."[3]

These poets' verses circulated throughout Herat, among both the elites and the common people, and remained in people's memories long after their authors' deaths—sadly, Jami is the only one who is commonly remembered today, whether male or female.

In more recent times, three women poets stand out for their talent and prolific poetic output. They are known by their poetic noms de plume: Mastourah of Kabul (1846–1872), Seyyedah Makhfi of Badakhshan (1879–1963), and Mahjoubah of Herat (1906–1966). They were all well-educated daughters or sisters of notable officials and men of culture, encouraged in their work by their families.[4] But they had to take pains to protect their reputations, and in this their choice of noms de plume is telling: Makhfi and Mastourah both mean "the hidden one," whereas Mahjoubah means "the veiled/modest one."[5] This is a tactic they shared with Bibi Esmati ("the chaste"), Nahani, and other women poets from across the Persian-speaking world in previous centuries.[6] Such pseudonyms perhaps functioned like symbolic veils in allowing these women's words to enter the public sphere while keeping their honor and privacy intact. Indeed, Farzaneh Milani, in a book on women's writing in neighboring Iran, says it is no accident that a strong current of women's literature emerged at the same time as efforts to unveil women in the early twentieth century.[7] But perhaps poetry itself could be seen as a shimmering smoke screen: a display of verbal virtuosity that can distract from the fact that it is women who are speaking behind it, smuggling their thoughts out to their readers. Makhfi never married, which undoubtedly gave her more time for literary pursuits, but Mastourah apparently died in her youth due to abuse by her husband, and her collected works have never been published.[8]

Makhfi and Mahjoubah, although they were never able to meet and were twenty-seven years apart in age, struck up a lively literary correspondence. One would write a *ghazal* (five to fifteen couplets with a single rhyme, usually about love) and the other would reply, continuing the theme and following the same rhyme scheme and meter. In one of Makhfi's letter-poems to her friend, she shares with her these words of wisdom, advising a stoic attitude in the face of religious conservatism:

> Those who would dispute over the things of the world
> are like children fighting over a soap bubble.
> Nobody in this world has ever reached fulfillment.
> Why should the wise quarrel over such a mirage?
> O preacher, don't ask the religion of the wine-drinking libertines—
> better you sit in a corner of your madrassa and argue with your books.
> Don't listen to the brainless preacher's advice and keep quiet;
> O Makhfi, who can argue with one who permits no answer?
> Seyyedah Makhfi Badakhshi[9]

In Afghanistan's vibrant oral tradition, women have been composers of folk poetry on a par with men, even if their verbal performances were usually confined to the domestic sphere or to female audiences at celebrations. Even in the twentieth century, among increasingly secular and educated urban dwellers, the tradition continued. Zohra Saed, an Afghan-born poet who lives in the United States and writes poetry in English, describes it beautifully: "While the majority of our grandmothers could not read or write, they learned classical and modern Dari poetry through the rich oral tradition and passed it down to their children. Our kitchen was always buzzing with gossip and poetry, religion and fairytales, philosophy and recipes."[10] Even well-known male poets often speak of the powerful influence their mother's lullabies or stories had on their awareness of the magical music of words.

There are some genres of folk poetry that are strongly associated with women, such as the *makhta* (elegy or lament sung by women in times of mourning) among the Hazaras, and the *landay* (short poem, whose first line is nine syllables and second line thirteen) of the Pashtuns. But women may also compose in other oral genres, such as the ghazal and *charbeiti* or *dobeiti* (folk quatrains), and perform large repertoires of poetry and folktales (*afsanah*). At traditional Hazara weddings, for example, many of the poems composed for the occasion may have been authored by women even if they were sung by men.[11] What is striking in the folk poetry of women are its earthiness and the strong strand of rebellion and provocation in it and its praise of romantic love, as in these *landays* translated from Pashtu:[12]

> *I love! I love! I shall not hide it. I'll not deny it.*
> *Even if that's why you with your knife will cut off all my beauty marks.*
>
> *Last night I was close to my lover, oh evening of love not to return*
> *again!*
> *Like a bell, with all my jewels and deep into the night, I was chiming in*
> *his arms.*[13]

The Hazaras, too, have a similar tradition in their own dialect of pithy short poems with amorous themes:

> *My love, do not make any noise, I am in the middle of cooking*
> *Kiss me discreetly, so that my husband may not see.*[14]

In the first years following the fall of the Taliban in 2001, there was an atmosphere of excitement and optimism in what was seen as a cultural rebirth after the harsh restrictions of the theocratic regime, which had banned poetry and music. Even during those years, however, women had attended underground schools and literary gatherings.[15] Something of women's hunger for literature and knowledge is seen in the voracious reading habits of a budding young poet during Taliban times: "She studied the poetry of Saadi, Hafez of Shiraz, Mowlana of Balkh (Rumi), Bidel of Delhi, Mehdi Soheili, Sohrab Sepehri, Nima Yushij, Fereidoun Moshiri, Forugh Farrokhzad, Parvin Etesami, Qahar Asi, and the novels of Jalal Al-e Ahmad, Sadeq Hedayat, Fahimeh Rahimi and Nasrin Samani," all famous classical and contemporary writers from across the Persian-speaking world. At the same time, "editing the literary works of other young writers for the Herat Literary Association and household chores were all part of her daily routine."[16]

This precocious young woman was Nadia Anjoman, one of the rising stars of poetry in Herat. She was able to study Dari Literature officially at Herat University after 2001 and published her first book, *Gol-e Dudi* (Smokey Flower) to great acclaim in 2005. She was hailed for introducing a fresh language and youthful point of view into Dari poetry, particularly in her ghazals.

She once described her poetic work: "For as long as I can remember, I have loved poetry, and the chains with which six years of captivity under Taliban rule bound my feet led me to haltingly enter the arena of poetry with the foot of my pen. The encouragement of like-minded friends gave me the confidence to pursue this path, but even now when

I take the first step, the tip of my pen trembles, as do I, because I do not feel safe from stumbling on this path, when the way ahead is difficult, and my steps unsteady."

VOICELESS CRIES

The sound of green footsteps is the rain.
They're coming in from the road, now,
thirsty souls and dusty skirts brought from the desert,
their breath burning, mirage-mingled,
mouths dry and caked with dust.
They're coming in from the road, now,
tormented, girls brought up on pain,
joy departed from their faces,
hearts old and lined with cracks.
No smile appears on the bleak oceans of their lips;
not a tear springs from the dry rivers of their eyes.
O God!
Might I not know if their voiceless cries reach the clouds,
the vaulted heavens?
The sound of green footsteps is the rain.

Nadia Anjoman
July/August 2002[17]

Indeed, poets in Herat acknowledge that in the past few years, there has been a blossoming of women's poetry, with a large number of young women taking up the pen. One (male) young poet said: "In the past, if there were female poets in Herat, unfortunately they were followers of great poets who were men, but gradually we are witnessing the emergence of a number of women who are just themselves. They don't try to imitate any other poet, at least not an Afghan man. The prominence of Forugh is one of the factors that has led them to turn to themselves and try to create specifically women's poetry from now on."[18] He was referring to Forugh Farrokhzad, the celebrated Iranian modernist poet whose work in the mid-twentieth century represented a milestone for female expression of intimate emotions—including sexuality—in free verse, and continues to be well-loved today.

Twenty-two-year-old poet Somaiyah Ramesh is outgoing and optimistic about the level of literary activity around her in Herat, "the cradle of civilization and culture," and sees poetry as a form of rebellion and social protest. But she complains of certain hindrances. One is the gap between generations and styles: "There is nobody to encourage young people. The great poets prefer classical styles [with their conventionalized form and imagery], but not the younger ones. They prefer new poetry and blank verse. That's why there have been some conflicts." There are also difficulties specific to women, in the form of the traditional values that they must confront: "There have always been barriers for Afghan women, in any area. In writing, too. Women cannot speak their minds. That fear still exists. For example, they still cannot write erotic poetry, nobody would accept that here. Perhaps some do write it, but nobody has found the courage to read it out."[19]

Khaledah Forugh, one of Afghanistan's leading female poets and a professor of literature at Kabul University, agrees: "A literary woman finds herself confronting the morality, religion, and traditions of Afghanistan's society, and thus it is much rarer for her to achieve full maturity as a writer. In most cases these difficulties result in self-censorship. That is to say, a woman poet cannot express her feelings with the same directness as a man, even when he is writing about taboo subjects. This has happened to me time and again. When I have wanted to express myself in this way, I have either been unable to, or have had to change the subject according to what was morally and socially expedient."[20]

ALWAYS FIVE IN THE AFTERNOON

The purple lines carve into my gaze
                              uselessly.
With a pen that is a cloud,
they take my words
and break them
syllable by syllable
so that I may not read a single verse of love.
They have cut off my voice.
Though bloody,
though wounded,
I will be recorded on love's cardiogram!
But hopelessness is stronger yet.
My steps are not familiar with moving forward,
and movement is the unforgivable sin of the age.
They have always counseled my mirror
        to sit and break and be silent.

The clock of our time
always shows five in the afternoon.
It has never been five at dawn,
and memory's cradle can never forget
that movement is the unforgivable sin of the age.
The smell of sunset always brings sorrow to my senses.
The form of a mountain is sculpted inside me,

but every night after long weeping,
I fall apart.
The city of screams has rusted shut,
                    spent.
The window of our house is a wrinkled word.
It shares with the wall
an awareness of things it hadn't yet known.
This time, the rain –
        all around the wind blows
and throws the hands of the trees thoughtlessly
to the ground.
Flute.
One must play the reed flute of aloneness.
Khaledah Forugh[21]

Khaledah Forugh, at least, has married into a family of poets who understand her endeavors. Many female poets are not so lucky, she says, giving the example of her contemporary Maryam Mahmoud, who published one volume of poetry and never wrote again. The generation of girls who bravely defied Taliban orders to attend clandestine writing workshops (the famous "sewing circles") in Herat have since gotten married and one by one have fallen silent. Poets in Herat talk about three young women whose writing careers have been threatened or cut short by marriage. The husband of the first, although he does not care much for literature, accompanies her to every literary gathering, presumably to keep an eye on her. The second, a law student and exceptionally talented writer of ghazals is not allowed to print her name under her poems when they are published. And the third was Nadia Anjoman. She faced severe restrictions from her in-laws and died in unexplained circumstances after a dispute with her husband in 2005. Aged only twenty-five, she left behind her first book of poetry and a baby boy. Thousands of fans and sympathizers attended her funeral in Herat, and her work continues to be popular in Persian-speaking countries among young people of both sexes.

LIGHT BLUE MEMORIES

O exiles of the mountain of oblivion!
O the jewels of your names, slumbering in the mire of silence.
O your obliterated memories, your light blue memories
in the silty mind of a wave in the sea of forgetting:
Where is the clear stream of your thoughts?
Which thieving hand stole the pure golden statue of your dreams?
In this storm which gives birth to oppression,

where has your ship, your serene silver mooncraft gone?
After this bitter cold which gives birth to death—
if the sea should fall calm,
if the cloud should release the heart's knotted sorrows,
if the moonlight maiden should bring love, offer a smile,
if the mountain should soften its heart, adorn itself with green,
become fruitful—
will one of your names, above the peaks,
burn bright as the sun?
Will the rise of your memories,
your light blue memories,
in the eyes of fishes weary of floodwaters and
fearful of oppressive rain,
become a reflection of hope?
O, exiles of the mountain of oblivion!

Nadia Anjoman
November/December 2001[22]

Afghan women in exile have fared somewhat better. Some, who were already established writers before the war began, fled to Europe and continued their work there, although sundered from a literary milieu in their mother tongue and left adrift on the sea of their own nostalgia. Some of them nonetheless achieved acclaim for their work, such as the short-story writer Spojmai Zariab, who has lived in France since 1991.[23] In contrast, those Persian-speakers who grew up in Iran found themselves in a dynamic literary scene in their own language. That language was living and changing, as were its poetic forms. In addition, the benefit of Iran was that its public sphere had been turned into an *Islamic* space and was therefore considered more wholesome by families. Large numbers of Afghan refugee girls were educated in Iran, and many became involved in literature.[24]

Mahboubah Ebrahimi is a native of Kandahar who grew up in Iran, has a degree in public health, and is an award-winning poet who recently published her first book. She grew up listening to her grandmother's stories and reading the poetry of Hafez and Parvin Etesami (an early twentieth-century Iranian female poet), trying her hand at writing her own poems from a young age. Living in Tehran, she and her husband were literary activists who published a cultural magazine and organized poetry gatherings and a highly popular festival of Afghan youth literature, called *Qand-e Parsi* (The Sweetness of Persian), held annually in Tehran from 2002 to 2007. Young women always had a strong presence at this festival, confidently presenting their poems on a diverse array of topics and in some years sweeping up many of the prizes—a major encouragement in their poetic careers. A festival on such a scale and with such broad female participation remains a dream in Afghanistan at present, but women—and men—writing in the diaspora are perhaps Afghanistan's greatest literary hope.

MORNING, NEWS OF WAR

Today the television sets showed you once again
and shook the morning of contented people once again.
You, the blackest hole of man's existence on this earth,
were shown to all the carefree people of the world again.
It didn't matter how the morning started out for you
or why your birds were dying by the score, by the score.
The angels standing guard upon the shoulders of the earth
taught the children how to fly to heaven once again.
Once again a world of hearts briefly bled for you—
today the television sets showed you once again.

Mahboubah Ebrahimi
Written shortly after September 11, 2001[25]

Interviewed in a Tehran park in 2005, Ebrahimi spoke with calm confidence of the growth of women's literature: "I'm certain that in twenty or twenty-five years we will have a generation of female writers and poets in Afghanistan. And this, alongside all the difficulties of exile, is a blessing that has been given to us, that women have had space to breathe in a cultural environment like that of Iran, but based on our own cultural foundations. . . . We hope to introduce ourselves to the world—to countries which only see the face of poverty of Afghanistan . . . however, from the cultural perspective, we are a rich people. We want to promote the face that is not seen in the world, to translate our work!"[26] Two years later, in 2007, her first volume of poetry, *The Winds Are My Sisters*, was published in Iran.

In the same year, she and her family returned to Afghanistan for good, making their home in Kabul, where I spoke to her again. She seemed tired and dispirited; she and her infant daughter had just recovered from an illness, and she was disillusioned by her fruitless search for a job and persistent security threats. Her previous ambition and enthusiasm seemed to have dimmed. This was not the homeland that she had dreamed of returning to but a country in which several women had recently been killed for their work in television or journalism; a country in which the optimism of several years before was increasingly being eroded by fear. More and more educated women were once again staying at home—this time by choice. Although her husband, also a poet, was in the same difficult situation as she was, it seemed easier for him to think in the abstract. He was already sketching out his next work, a surreal dialogue between a poet and a jinn, a commentary on the state of Afghan society. As we sat in the gathering darkness just before *iftar* and before the night's few hours of electricity lit up the bulbs, Mahboubah confessed her own plans in a sad voice. "I've decided never to write poetry again. All it's left me with is a world of sorrow." Hers is a sorrow, perhaps, of expectations raised and then shattered.

PEACE

A rifle on your shoulder
you come out to greet me,
disheveled, dressed in rags.
This
is not you.
You were supposed to be
a rider on a red horse . . .
Upon my hair you place
a crown of opium blossoms—
Roses?
You smile
and half-dead butterflies
fall to the dust.
Release me!
I'm afraid of you.
You've hidden minefields in your pockets.
They've killed people
and thrown them into the wells of your heart.

Your kisses say—
But your voice,
tired and hoarse, reaches me:
Come, let's go home.
If you kiss me,
the mines will be disarmed,
the guns,
the poppies.
Your kiss
is a white dove
with a delicate flower in its beak.
Mahboubah Ebrahimi[27]

NOTES

I would like to express my deep gratitude to Sayed Asef Hossaini for his contributions to this article—including suggesting the title, interviewing Khaledah Forugh, helping with translations, and locating sources—and for his ongoing encouragement and friendship, which have been invaluable to me throughout my research.

All poetry translations are by Zuzanna Olszewska unless otherwise specified.

1. Persian original in Masoud Mirshahi, ed., *Sher-e zanan-e Afghanistan* [Afghan Women's Poetry] (Tehran: Nashr-e Shahab, 2004), 53.

2. The colorful lives and works of these women are described in a unique sixteenth-century biographical work on female poets by Fakhri Heravi, a Herati who migrated to India, called *Javahir al-Ajayib* (Jewels of Wonder). See Nushin Arbabzadah, "Women and Cultural Patronage in the Timurid World" (master's thesis, Cambridge University, 2002).

3. Arbabzadah, "Women and Cultural Patronage," 41, translated by Arbabzadah.

4. This was typical of female poets across the Persian-speaking world whose names have survived in historical accounts: almost all were members of the royal courts or the aristocracy. See Farzaneh Milani, *Veils and Words: The Emerging Voices of Iranian Women Writers* (Syracuse, N.Y.: Syracuse University Press, 1992), 55.

5. Interview with Khaledah Forugh, March 2008.

6. For example, the seventeenth-century Mughal princess Zeib un-Nisa in India (whose nom de plume was also Makhfi) and another Nahani of Shiraz, also described in *Jewels of Wonder*: *Nahani* is yet another word for "the hidden one."

7. She writes: "Iranian women, for centuries, were suppressed physically and verbally by the conventions of the veil and public silence. The norms and values that regulated women's physical concealment applied equally to their literary expression. Theirs was a private world, where self-expression, either bodily or verbally, was confined within the accepted family circle" (Milani, *Veils and Words*, 46). And: "Significantly, the movement to unveil in Iran is associated with women's attempt to break into print as writers" (ibid., 7).

8. Described in entries in the *Daneshnamah-ye adab-e farsi* [Encyclopaedia of Persian Literature], vol. 3, *Afghanistan* (Tehran: Moassesah-ye Farhangi va Entesharati-ye Daneshnamah, Vezarat-e Farhang va Ershad-e Eslami, 1996), 882, 934.

9. Persian original in Amir Fuladi, *Makhfi Badakhshi va Mahjoubah Heravi*, Jadid Online, October 3, 2007, http://www.jadidonline.com/story/03102007/makhfi_mahjoubeh.

10. Zohra Saed, Introduction to "Special Feature: Afghan Women's Writing," *How2* 1 no. 7, (Spring 2002), http://www.asu.edu/pipercwcenter/how 2journal/archive/onlinearchive/v1_7_200/current/afghan/ index.htm.

11. See, for example, Sayd Bahodine Majrouh, *Songs of Love and War: Afghan Women's Poetry* (New York: Other Press, 2003); Sayed Askar Mousavi, *The Hazaras of Afghanistan: An Historical, Cultural, Economic and Political*

Study (Richmond, Va.: Curzon Press, 1998), 82–88; Inger W. Boesen, "Conflicts of Solidarity in Pakhtun Women's Lives," in *Women and Islamic Societies: Social Attitudes and Historical Perspectives*, ed. Bo Utas (London: Curzon Press, 1983); Margaret A. Mills, "Gender and Verbal Performance Style in Afghanistan," in *Gender, Genre and Power in South Asian Expressive Traditions*, ed. Arjun Appadurai, Frank Korom, and Margaret Mills (Philadelphia: University of Pennsylvania Press, 1991), 56–77.

12. Benedicte Grima offers a dissenting view, arguing that Pashtun women do not compose love poems, which simply "represent women in men's folklore and fantasy." Instead, they are more likely to recount narratives of the sorrows they have experienced in their lives. Grima, *The Performance of Emotion among Paxtun Women: "The Misfortunes Which Have Befallen Me"* (Austin: University of Texas Press, 1992), 154.

13. Majrouh, *Songs of Love and War*, 5, translated by Majrouh and Marjolijn de Jager.

14. Mousavi, *The Hazaras of Afghanistan*, 84–85, translated by Mousavi.

15. As described by Christina Lamb in *The Sewing Circles of Herat: A Personal Voyage through Afghanistan* (New York: HarperCollins, 2002), 141–180.

16. M. Shafie Noorzaei, "Nadia Anjoman Biography" (quote translated from the Dari version), Exil-Archiv, Else-Lasker-Schüler-Stiftung, undated, http://exil-archiv.de/html/biografien/anjoman.html.

17. Persian original in Nadia Anjoman, *Gol-e Dudi* [*Smokey Flower*] (Kabul: PEN Association of Afghanistan, 2006), 49–50.

18. Interview with Masoud Hasanzadah, September 10, 2007.

19. Interview with Somaiyah Ramesh, September 10, 2007.

20. Interview with Khaledah Forugh, March 2008.

21. Persian original reprinted by Khaledah Forugh in her blog, *Dar khiabanha-ye khab o khaterah: Sherha-ye Khaledah Forugh* [In the Streets of Dreams and Memories: The Poems of Khaledah Forugh], http://www.neervana .blogfa.com, Azar 9, 1386/December 20, 2007.

22. Persian original in Anjoman, *Smokey Flower*, 42–43.

23. For an interview with Zariab, see Jasmina Sopova, "Spôjmaï Zariâb: A Pen Against a Nightmare," *UNESCO Courier*, March 2001, http://www .unesco.org/courier/2001_03/uk/dires.htm.

24. See Homa Hoodfar, "Families on the Move: The Changing Role of Afghan Refugee Women in Iran," *Hawwa* 2 no. 2, (2004); Zuzanna Olszewska, "Stealing the Show: Women Writers at an Afghan Literary Festival in Tehran," *Bad Jens: Iranian Feminist Newsletter*, 2005, http://www.badjens.com/afghan .lit.html.

25. Persian original in Mahboubah Ebrahimi, *Badha khaharan-i man and* [*The Winds Are My Sisters*] (Tehran: Sura-ye Mehr, 2007), 14. English translation first published in Zuzanna Olszewska, "Four Afghan Poems," *Modern Poetry in Translation* 3 no. 13 (March 2010), 157.

26. Interview with Mahboubah Ebrahimi, September 27, 2005.

27. Persian original in Ebrahimi, *The Winds Are My Sisters*, 42–43. An earlier version of the English translation was published in Olszewska, "Four Afghan Poems," 157–158.

Great Expectations

Mursal listens to her teacher in an Afghans4Tomorrow Vocational and Training Center in Kabul. She wrote the following on a postcard for her English teacher, Marsha MacColl, during a writing assignment: "Hello Hi! My name is Mursal I have two sister and I haven't brother and I have a sweet mother and sweet father I am 12 years old and I am in A4T school in fourth class I love my teachers ok good bye Mursal I am from Afghanistan." Photo by Susan Hall, 2007.

CHAPTER 24

Hopes and Dreams

Interviews with Young Afghans

AMINA KATOR

EDITORS' NOTE: It is appropriate that young people should be given the last word. We conclude with excerpts from interviews conducted by Amina Kator in the summer of 2009. The interviews took place in the Chilsitoon, Mekroyan, Salang, and Shari-Naw areas of Kabul, and the interviewees come from various backgrounds.

Some of the women gathered at the home of a friend, Kator wrote, and "we drank tea and had light-hearted conversations initially and after several hours of talking, we bonded. We talked about the latest movies and the good Bollywood actors. The next day, the women felt comfortable talking to me and I conducted each interview separately and privately."

Kator also interviewed men. One old friend of Kator's father, from before the family fled the country, "was ecstatic to see me, because I am my father's daughter. His reaction and hospitality made the other men much more comfortable with me."

But, she added, "in Afghanistan it is not difficult to get people to open up about their hardships and dreams, once they know they can trust you and that their voices might actually be heard." Kator began with a set of questions, but abandoned them in favor of a conversational mode, which she said is more in keeping with "the Afghan way."

The interviews, which Kator translated, include young men and women and are arranged by age from thirteen to twenty-five. They have been edited for length, not content, and the names have been changed.

These young people—experienced and wise beyond their years— address concerns about their personal lives and their country, including their unease about government corruption and lack of security. They overwhelmingly assert that education is the real key to lasting peace and successful reconstruction. We must listen to them. The future of Afghanistan rests in their hands.

NARGES MANSURY

I am thirteen years old. I am from Kandahar and speak Pashto. I live in Kabul and have ten family members. I am the middle child. Our financial situation is not good, because my parents do not work. My father has lung cancer and my mother has severe asthma. My three older brothers and sisters work and I am the only one going to school right now. My younger siblings are too young. We have relatives in the United States who help us, but not everyone is that lucky.

According to Islam, "Heaven lies under the feet of the mother," and it is very important to grasp the importance of this saying in the Qur'an. God has given the task of the mother to raise His creatures and that is why He has dictated that women be "treated like pearls." One day the Afghan people will embrace the rights of women. If the government encourages it, then it might happen. If not, then Afghanistan will not progress.

Not enough is being done to help Afghan people, especially women. With all the construction taking place, every project is half completed. You will not see one street that has been completely built. You will not see one school that has all the proper equipment and materials. If the basic necessities are tended to, then Afghans can focus on social issues such as human and women's rights. But it will take a long time to address these issues when people are worried about where to live and how to find food.

I want to become a doctor and help those who are crippled and sick. I don't let problems cause me grief. I focus solely on my studies. I study every night and sometimes when the electricity goes out, I light candles so I can continue reading. I love to read, especially mystery books. I feel like life is a mystery and I pray to God to solve it. So far, it seems like education is the only answer.

BICHI OMIDI

I am fifteen years old. I have two older sisters and one younger brother. I speak Dari and am pure Afghan. I don't like to claim an ethnicity, because I feel it has divided us. I hope to become a business woman and make a lot of money so I can help my people.

Men in Afghanistan dominate women, but that is not supposed to be. Women in Islam have more rights, because we populate humankind. Women are mentally stronger and capable than men. We can bear children and go through menstruation. Men have little patience and are hostile to women. They beat them and are verbally abusive. Afghan women tolerate this and it makes them strong. Look at the mullahs here. Yes, they can read the Qur'an beautifully, but do they know what they are reading? No. They are very conservative and want to maintain a dichotomy between men and women, so that women should be in the private sphere and men in the public.

What can we do to bring progress and development to Afghanistan? One possible way is to offer programs to men and women about their rights under Islam and how it benefits men to allow women to work and go to school.

But the government [of President Hamid Karzai] has not done a good job in helping Afghans. All the foreign money is divided between corrupt politicians. There is no accountability. The majority of Afghans live in tents or rent homes at high prices. They are barely making enough to survive. If there's no home, there's no peace of mind.

I hope to earn money after my education so I can help other students receive their educations. Many are not given the opportunity. We youth are the future of Afghanistan. Money really does make the world go around. Without it, no one takes you seriously. I hope to make so much money that it will never concern me again.

RAZIA AZIZI

I am fifteen years old and a student at Zargona School, studying physics and chemistry. I hope to become an optometrist one day and serve my people. My family's financial condition is not good and is getting worse. My father is crippled and my mother is very sick.

I am engaged to a man fifteen years my senior, who lives in Jalalabad, because the dowry was very good. He is my cousin and I will be married as soon as I turn sixteen. I hope he will allow me to continue my education. My parents say I have to do whatever my husband wants. It bothers me that I have not been able to talk in private with my fiancé, because it is not considered appropriate, but I have time, I hope. My mother begged my father to let me wait until I was sixteen to marry, and my mother-in-law is very strict and wants me to have children when I turn seventeen. I want children, but I am young. My sisters-in-law are not friendly. They call me a little girl.

I am taking care of my three younger siblings and helping my mother with cooking, cleaning, and laundry, in addition to going to school. [A non-governmental organization] gives us about three hundred Afghanis [six dollars] a month, and that covers food and other bills. It takes me an hour to walk to school.

At school, I am alive. I want to become as educated as possible. I want to become a candidate in the Afghan elections and support my family as a doctor. I want my children to be proud of me and I want to keep my husband happy, too. He wants eight children and I hope that doesn't get in the way of my education. But if I move to Jalalabad, I don't know how I will pay for my education. In Kabul, the organization is helping me. My fiancé is a taxi driver. I am still trying to figure it out.

GULHAM ASADA

I am eighteen years old, I finished grade twelve and am teaching an English course for third graders. I plan to go to university when I can afford it. I am Hazara and originally from Bamiyan. My family is a little better than poor. I am the oldest son out of five children and my father was a *shaheed* [martyr]. I have to support my family. I want to become an engineer and serve my country. I want to build dams, so sanitation problems can be lessened. There is so much I want to do, but I have to look after my family first. They have to eat.

Afghanistan will progress. We are Muslim and God will protect and help us rebuild Afghanistan. Things have gotten better since the Taliban, but I am worried about security.

Every child needs to be educated. Right now there are so many uneducated Afghans. The government needs to provide more educational opportunities for young and old, scholarships and financial assistance.

Americans think Afghans are backward, but that is not the case. We are one of the world's most hospitable and strong-minded people. There has been so much warfare and it has divided us, Hazara, Pashtun, Tajiks, Panjshiris. Every group has its own allegiance and this disunity is keeping us back, but all of us are Afghan and we need to eradicate all ethnic allegiances and hold hands in unity.

BASHIR SAID

I am eighteen years old. I am Pashtun from Bamiyan Province. I teach English and calligraphy at Payman Muqadas School. I want to become a translator with the coalition forces. I have two older brothers. One lives in England and the other is a shopkeeper here in Mekroyan. We are able to maintain a decent standard of living.

In other provinces, like Kandahar and Helmand, the biggest problem is security. We are not in favor of the American forces being here permanently, but for right now, we need them. Lack of security is why Afghan men don't want their wives or daughters to go to school. What if they are killed or raped or abducted?

There is a great disparity between the rich and the poor. In order for any country to be developed, there needs to be a strong middle class. My family is among the few middle class here, and that's because my brother sends money from overseas. More jobs are needed, but there are none out there. Even teachers or assistant teachers like me make barely enough to survive. I make sixty dollars a month.

Afghans have endured tremendous grief and now just want to rebuild their lives. They are returning to find there is nothing left of the land they fled, so they are starting from scratch and that's why there's so much theft and kidnapping. People are desperate.

I am a young Afghan male. Do I want to grow a beard? No. Do I want women confined? No. Do I want my children to have freedom in all aspects? Yes. So, this I want to make clear: young Afghans of today are extremely open-minded individuals who have a passion and desire to restore Afghanistan and bring it back to the times of King Zahir Shah and President Daoud Khan, before the Soviet invasion. I want women to walk freely in the streets and learn whatever they wish. We need doctors, engineers, and lawyers, but we also need journalists, comedians, actors, investors, directors, singers. We need both men and women to contribute. We as Afghan youth must help Afghanistan flourish in all regards. There is so much to look forward to in life.

LAMBA OTMANI

I am twenty-two years old, from Kabul, and am working right now at the Ministry of Women's Affairs. I attended Preston University [in Islamabad, Pakistan] for two years, but I stopped because my family was sponsored to go to Canada. There is tension for me, because I want to leave Afghanistan knowing there is a better life in Canada, but there is a person I am deeply in love with and we want to get married. He has a great job and is highly educated. He is faithful and comes from a good family. He has been asking for my hand for a year, but my mother always refuses saying I can find someone better in Canada.

I cannot leave the house unless I take one of my brothers with me. Going to a theater or even a park is impossible because there have been so many cases of rape and kidnappings and this is in Kabul. The government is so focused on creating roads and buildings that they have completely abandoned everything else and have done nothing for safety, especially for women. Even these projects are ineffective. [The government] are all corrupt, disgusting men who reap all the money.

The issue is lack of accountability. No one monitors how money is being spent. There need to be programs of self-defense classes for women and programs for these men who roam the streets and are doing nothing with their lives. They need to be taught to respect women and not see them as low as street dogs. The war has shattered so many lives and created these sexually deprived boys.

If such programs could be created in addition to there being accountability, I honestly think that life in Afghanistan would drastically improve. I hope to see an Afghanistan where a woman can go to the market without being harassed, where the government actually cares for its people and creates vocational opportunities for the unemployed and ethics classes about how to treat one another. I hope to see an Afghanistan where I can have the option of wearing a scarf and it is not forced on me, where I can choose the person I want to spend the rest of my life with, where women are treated as equals to men and not as inferiors.

I try not to become discouraged and empower myself by taking English classes and learning as much as I can. As long as I can become as educated as possible, there will be a chance that things might get better. If not, what is the use of living this life?

NAHID SULTAN

I am twenty-four years old. I am Tajik and currently live in Sash Darak, one of the nicest areas in Kabul. I have three brothers and one sister and our financial situation is relatively good because all of us are working. Both my parents are educated, so they have always supported education. My parents never put pressure on me to marry or be a servant in the home. I am fortunate to have such a progressive family.

I am an employee at the Ministry of Foreign Affairs and studying International Development. I will be going to Egypt for two weeks to learn about the policies of different countries.

Many people complain about government corruption, but this really angers me. I ask these people if they were here during the time of the Taliban. It was a very dark chapter in our lives, but it has, thank God, closed and a new one is just beginning. This new chapter, however, has a long way to go before any concrete progress can occur.

I have personally felt the impact of the government policies. I was awarded a scholarship by the government to go to a university in Maryland, because my grades were really high and my exam scores were among the best. Unfortunately, my father would not let met go, because I would have been completely alone and it would have been very difficult for him to be separated from me. But now my older brother is in America, so if I receive another scholarship, my father will let me go.

My hope is that Afghanistan will become a progressive country. The security situation is not good, even in my area. Because our area is considered wealthy, thieves and suicide bombers target us. People are desperate nowadays. [*Note*: The day after this interview, a bomb exploded close to Nahid's home, blowing out all the windows. Her brother, the only family member who was at home, sustained minor cuts and bruises.]

At school, girls are jealous and talk behind my back because I refuse to think about children or marriage for the time being. They still believe that women's role is to raise kids, cook and clean. We as Afghan women cannot afford not to take advantage of the opportunities that are now available to us. We should be supporting women candidates and encourage more political activity. We have a voice, so why should we remain silent? Why should we choke our own throats when we can sing in harmony? I wish that Afghan women would see this and take an active role. They are rarely seen, much less heard. I'm not saying they should completely rebel. They might jeopardize their own lives. But if slowly, slowly they raise their voices and stand up for themselves, men will begin to take notice. It is only with education that women can begin to realize their own self-worth. There need to be day care centers so mothers can go to school. There need to be incentives.

But nothing in Afghanistan is black and white. There is no magic bullet. Everything takes time and we Afghans need to have *sabr* [patience]. Nothing happens instantly, but gradually and by the grace of God, there will be subtle progress and it will be the youth who are leading the way.

HASAN OTMANI

I am twenty-four years old. I completed my bachelor's in Business Finance with a minor in Business Management. I am currently looking for someone to marry. I had thought I found the girl, but it didn't work out.

Things are better for Afghans in areas such as Kabul and Herat, but if you go to Jalalabad or Kandahar, the situation has only gotten worse. It is still very dangerous for women to go outside or for any sort of business to be conducted. The people living there are very backward-minded, extremely traditional, and they want to preserve the lifestyle they have been following for centuries.

The government cares only about seeing how many roads can be paved or how many new hotels they can create. These generate personal income. But what about building homes? Afghans have received no compensation for land forcibly taken from those who lived on it for generations. They are now living in tents. There are so many children roaming the streets and not going to school. They dig through trash piles for scraps of food or walk around the streets begging for money. Why is the government not opening schools for these kids? Why is the government not encouraging parents to send their kids to school or providing incentives or raising their salaries so parents can afford it? Why isn't there a program where parents can receive subsidies from the government to send their kids to school or anything? Sure, new schools have been built, but who makes sure there is transportation available for the students to get to the nearest school? Some would have to walk ten miles. These kids are Afghanistan's future. Considering how much foreign aid Afghanistan is getting, the Afghan government should be doing this. But they are not. They are pocketing the money.

My hope is to open any sort of business so that when I make enough money, I can help these children by opening schools and providing them with food as well as learning materials.

Empowerment for a male is not an issue in Afghanistan. Empowerment for women is the tricky part. There is absolutely no freedom for women here. I personally am a very open-minded guy. I don't care if my sister wears a scarf or wants to go to the movies. The problem is that the safety situation is so horrendous that I don't want to jeopardize her life by allowing her to go outside alone or not wear her scarf. It is out of fear that Afghan women rarely go outside alone. The men are like dogs here. My hope is that one day my sister can walk out of the house and I won't fear that something will happen to her. I am already empowered, but I want her to be empowered as well. I want her to live like a human being and not a caged bird. Unfortunately, it is going to take a long time.

HALIMA ASMATI

I am twenty-five years old and a Tajik. I finished grade twelve and right now am taking courses in English and computer programs such as Excel and Word. I am also teaching eighth graders chemistry at Setara School. I wanted to go to a university for higher education, but it was cut short when I got married at seventeen. He was my cousin, much older than me, and my family forced me into it. I have been divorced for about two years and it was devastating, but my husband was a drug addict and I became one, too, for awhile. My relatives are bitter that I divorced, but after what happened to me, my father no longer listens to them but allows me to do what I want.

The government is doing nothing for women like me. I am not asking for money but rather for programs that will empower women and allow them to stand on their own two feet. My hope is that women in Afghanistan will never need to rely on these chauvinist men for any financial support. Even with the Taliban gone, women are still considered inferior. They must bear one child after another. The concept of birth control is either unknown or looked down upon. The only way to change it is to encourage women to stop having so many kids. There should be posters and hospitals should provide free condoms or birth control pills and explain how to use them. Nowadays you see posters promoting education, but they should be promoting contraception.

I don't have kids and probably never will. I have decided never to marry again and focus on returning to school and becoming a professor in the sciences.

There has to be a way to get the Afghan government to realize that it is a good thing for women to go to school. There is a saying in Afghanistan that you can't make a donkey move unless it wants to. So we have to wait for those who are donkeys to make the decision to change.

Selected Bibliography

Abirafeh, Lina. *Gender and International Aid in Afghanistan: The Politics and Effects of Intervention.* Jefferson, N.C.: McFarland, 2009.

Agarwal, Bina. *Cold Hearths and Barren Slopes: The Woodfuel Crisis in the Third World.* London: Zed Books, 1986.

———. *A Field of One's Own: Gender and Land Rights in South Asia.* Cambridge: Cambridge University Press, 1994.

Ahmad, Eqbal, and David Barsamian. *Terrorism: Theirs and Ours.* Boston: Open Media, 2001.

Ali, Tariq. *The Duel: Pakistan on the Flight Path of American Power.* New York: Scribner, 2008.

Benhabib, Seyla. *Situating the Self: Gender, Community and Postmodernism in Contemporary Ethics.* New York: Routledge, 1992.

Bennett Jones, Owen. *Pakistan: Eye of the Storm.* New Haven, Conn.: Yale University Press, 2002.

Brodsky, Anne E. *With All Our Strength: The Revolutionary Association of the Women of Afghanistan.* New York: Routledge, 2003.

Coll, Steve. *Ghost Wars: The Secret History of the CIA, Afghanistan and Bin Laden, From the Soviet Invasion to September 10, 2001.* New York: Penguin, 2004.

Constable, Pamela. *Fragments of Grace: My Search for Meaning in the Strife of South Asia.* Washington, D.C.: Potomac Books, 2005.

Denker, Debra. *Sisters on the Bridge of Fire: One Woman's Journey in Afghanistan, India, and Pakistan.* Tucson, Ariz.: Schaffner Press, 2001.

Donini, Antonio, Norah Niland, and Karin Wermester, eds. *Nation-Building Unraveled? Aid, Peace and Justice in Afghanistan.* West Hartford, Conn.: Kumarian Press, 2004.

Dupree, Louis. *Afghanistan.* Oxford: Oxford University Press, 1997.

Dupree, Nancy Hatch. *The Road to Balkh*. Kabul: The Afghan Tourist Organization, 1967.

———. *The Women of Afghanistan*. Stockholm: Swedish Committee for Afghanistan, 1996.

Ellis, Deborah. *Women of the Afghan War*. Westport, Conn.: Praeger, 2000.

Emadi, Hafizullah. *Culture and Customs of Afghanistan*. Santa Barbara, Calif.: Greenwood Press, 2005.

———. *Repression, Resistance, and Women in Afghanistan*. Westport, Conn.: Praeger, 2002.

Fitzgerald, Paul, and Elizabeth Gould, with Sima Wali. *Invisible History: Afghanistan's Untold Story*. San Francisco: City Lights, 2009.

Ghaus, Abdul Samad. *The Fall of Afghanistan: An Insider's Account*. Washington, D.C.: Pergamon-Brassey's International Defense Publishers, 1988.

Grace, Jo. *Gender Role in Agriculture: Case Studies of Five Villages in Northern Afghanistan*. Kabul: Afghanistan Research and Evaluation Unit, 2003.

Grace, Jo, and Adam Pain. *Rethinking Rural Livelihoods*. Kabul: Afghanistan Research and Evaluation Unit, 2003.

Gregorian, Vartan. *The Emergence of Modern Afghanistan: Politics of Reform and Modernization, 1880–1946*. Stanford, Calif.: Stanford University Press, 1969.

Grima, Benedicte. *The Performance of Emotion among Paxtun Women: "The Misfortunes Which Have Befallen Me."* Austin: University of Texas Press, 1992.

Hawken, Paul, Amory Lovins, and L. Hunter Lovins. *Natural Capitalism: Creating the Next Industrial Revolution*. New York: Back Bay Books, 2008.

Heath, Jennifer. *A House White with Sorrow: A Ballad for Afghanistan*. Boulder, Colo.: Roden Press, 1996.

Holmgren, David. *Permaculture: Principles and Pathways beyond Sustainability*. Victoria, Australia: Holmgren Design Services, 2002.

Ingalls, James, and Sonali Kolthakar. *Bleeding Afghanistan: Washington, Warlords and the Propaganda of Silence*. New York: Seven Stories Press, 2006.

Jones, Ann. *Kabul in Winter: Life without Peace in Afghanistan*. New York: Metropolitan Books, 2006.

Joya, Malalai. *A Woman among Warlords: The Extraordinary Story of an Afghan Who Dared to Raise Her Voice*. New York: Scribner, 2009.

Kakar, M. Hassan. *Afghanistan: The Soviet Invasion and the Afghan Response, 1979–1982*. Berkeley: University of California Press, 1995.

Kandiyoti, Deniz. "The Politics of Gender and Reconstruction in Afghanistan," Occasional paper, United Nations Research Institute for Social Development, Geneva, 2005.

Kantor, Paula. *From Access to Impact: Microcredit and Rural Livelihoods in Afghanistan*. Kabul: Afghanistan Research and Evaluation Unit, 2009.

Kayeum, Joan. *The Afghan: Hard as a Rock, Tender as a Flower—A Character Sketch Based on Afghan Proverbs*. Privately published, Derwood, Md., March 2007.

Klijn, Floortje, and Adam Pain. *Finding the Money: Informal Credit Practices in Afghanistan*. Kabul: Afghanistan Research and Evaluation Unit, 2007.

Lamb, Christina. *The Sewing Circles of Herat: A Personal Voyage through Afghanistan*. New York: HarperCollins, 2002.

Larson, Anna. *Afghanistan's New Democratic Parties: A Means to Organize Democratization?* Kabul: Afghanistan Research and Evaluation Unit, 2009.

Lister, Sarah, and Adam Pain. *Trading in Power: The Politics of "Free" Markets in Afghanistan*. Kabul: Afghanistan Research and Evaluation Unit, 2004.

Majrouh, Sayd Bahodine. *Songs of Love and War: Afghan Women's Poetry*. New York: Other Press, 2003.

Marsden, Peter. *The Taliban, War, Religion and the New Order in Afghanistan*. Oxford: Oxford University Press, 1998.

Mehta, Sunita, ed. *Women for Afghan Women: Shattering Myths and Claiming the Future*. New York: Palgrave MacMillan, 2002.

Mills, Margaret. "The Gender of the Trick: Female Tricksters and Male Narrators." *Asian Folklore Studies* 9, no. 2 (2001): 237–258.

———. *Rhetorics and Politics in Afghan Traditional Storytelling*, Philadelphia: University of Pennsylvania Press, 1991.

Moghadam, Valentine, ed. *From Patriarchy to Empowerment*. New York: Syracuse University Press, 2007.

Morris, Dick. *Off with Their Heads: Traitors, Crooks, and Obstructionists in American Politics, Media, and Business*. New York: Regan, 2004.

Mousavi, Sayed Askar. *The Hazaras of Afghanistan: An Historical, Cultural, Economic and Political Study*. Richmond, Va.: Curzon Press, 1998.

Mukhopadhyay, Maitrayee, Gerald Steehouwer, and Franz Wong. *Politics of the Possible: Gender Mainstreaming and Organizational Changes Experience from the Field*. Oxford: Oxfam Publishing, 2006.

Narayan, Uma. *Dislocating Cultures: Identities, Traditions, and Third World Feminism*. New York: Routledge, 1997.

Newell, Nancy Peabody, and Richard S. *The Struggle for Afghanistan*. London: Cornell University Press, 1981.

Nojumi, Neamatollah, Dyan Mazurana, and Elizabeth Stites. *After the Taliban: Life and Security in Rural Afghanistan*. Lanham, Md.: Rowman & Littlefield, 2009.

Olesen, Asta. *Afghan Craftsmen: The Cultures of Three Itinerant Communities*. London: Thames and Hudson, 1994.

Ong, Walter J. *Orality and Literacy*. New York: Routledge, 1982

Phillips, Anne. *The Politics of Presence: The Political Representation of Gender, Ethnicity and Race*. Oxford: Clarendon, 1995.

Rahimi, Fahima. *Women in Afghanistan*. Liestal: Stiftung Foundation, Stiftung Bibliotheca Afghanica, 1986.

Rai, Shirin. ed. *Mainstreaming Gender, Democratizing the State? Institutional Mechanisms for the Advancement of Women*. Manchester: Manchester University Press, 2003.

Rashid, Ahmed. *Descent into Chaos: The United States and the Failure of Nation Building in Pakistan, Afghanistan, and Central Asia*. New York: Viking, 2008.

———. *Taliban: Militant Islam, Oil & Fundamentalism in Central Asia*. New Haven, Conn.: Yale University Press, 2001.

Rostami-Povey, Elaheh. *Afghan Women: Identity and Invasion*. London: Zed Books, 2007.

Rubin, Barnett R. *The Fragmentation of Afghanistan: State Formation and Collapse in the International System*. New Haven, Conn.: Yale University Press, 1995.

Said, Edward. *Orientalism*. New York: Vintage, 1979.

Shiva, Vandana. *Earth Democracy: Justice, Sustainability, and Peace*. Boston: South End Press, 2005.

Stewart, Rory. *The Places In Between*. New York: Harvest/Harcourt, 2006.

Skaine, Rosemary. *The Women of Afghanistan Under the Taliban*. Jefferson, N.C.: McFarland, 2001.

Smith D. J. *Challenging Myths and Finding Spaces for Change: Family Dynamics and Family Violence in Afghanistan*. Kabul: Afghanistan Research and Evaluation Unit, 2009.

———. *Decisions, Desires and Diversity: Marriage Practices in Afghanistan*. Kabul: Afghanistan Research and Evaluation Unit, 2009.

———. *Love, Fear and Discipline: Everyday Violence toward Children in Afghan Families*. Kabul: Afghanistan Research and Evaluation Unit, 2008.

Solinger, Rickie, Madeleine Fox, and Kayhan Irani, eds. *Telling Stories to Change the World: Global Voices on the Power of Narrative to Build Community and Make Social Justice Claims*. New York: Routledge, 2008.

Szabo, Albert, and Thomas J. Barfield. *Afghanistan: An Atlas of Indigenous Domestic Architecture*. Austin: University of Texas Press, 1991.

Weber, Olivier, ed. *Afghanistan: La Mémoire Assassinée* [Afghanistan: The Assassinated Memory]. Paris: Editions Mille et Une Nuits, 2001.

Wildman, David, and Phyllis Bennis. *Ending the U.S. War in Afghanistan: A Primer*. New York: Olive Branch Press, 2010.

About the Contributors

LINA ABIRAFEH is a gender and development practitioner and researcher with thirteen years of experience in countries such as Afghanistan, Sierra Leone, Morocco, Bangladesh, Papua New Guinea, and Haiti. In Haiti, she served as the Gender-Based Violence (GBV) Coordinator for the UN Humanitarian Response. Abirafeh set up and directed the Afghanistan office of Women for Women International, an international NGO providing basic services, rights training, and skills training. She completed her Ph.D. in 2008 from the London School of Economics Institute of Development Studies, researching the effects of gender-focused international aid in conflict and postconflict contexts, with a specific focus on GBV. She has published in various books and development journals. Her book *Gender and International Aid in Afghanistan: The Politics and Effects of Intervention* was published in 2009.

NAHID AZIZ is a clinical psychologist and associate professor of clinical psychology programs at Argosy University. She was born in Afghanistan and fled at seventeen after the Soviet invasion, taking political asylum in Germany, where she finished high school and her undergraduate studies in psychology. In the United States, she earned her doctorate in clinical psychology. She specializes in immigrant and refugee mental health; is co-chair of Afghanistan Mental Health Workgroup, providing technical assistance to the Afghan Ministry of Public Health and is the vice president of Afghan Education for A Better Tomorrow.

ANNE E. BRODSKY received her Ph.D. in community/clinical psychology from University of Maryland, College Park, and postdoctoral training at The Johns Hopkins School of Public Health. She is currently associate professor of psychology at UMBC. Her teaching, research, and applied work focus on the resilience of women and the role of women's communities in resisting societal risks and oppressions. She has worked in numerous urban U.S. communities and since summer 2001 has made regular research trips to Pakistan and Afghanistan, interviewing more than 200 Afghan women, children, and men about Afghan women's risk and resilience. She is the author of *With All Our Strength* and more than fifteen academic articles and chapters on risk, resilience, and community.

SHIREEN KHAN BURKI was born in New York City in 1964 to a Pashtun father and an Irish mother. She spent her childhood in Islamabad and the North West Frontier Province. She lived in Peshawar, Pakistan, from May 1987 until April 1989, where she worked as a contractor for the United States Agency for International Development on its Tribal Areas Development Project. Her work involved travel to all seven tribal agencies that abut Afghanistan. She received her Ph.D. from the University of Utah's Political Science Department in 2007 and is currently working on her first book on gender policies of Pakistan and Afghanistan since independence.

PAMELA CHANDLER, RN, MS, is a certified nurse-midwife and a family nurse practitioner, with more than thirty years of experience providing care to women and their families. She has a broad background in both alternative and traditional roles, ranging from a home-birth practice in rural Northern New Mexico to joint faculty appointments in the School of Nursing and the School of Medicine at the University of Colorado Health Sciences Center. She currently has private practices providing integrative care to women and home-based postpartum and newborn care to new families. She has worked as a consultant in Liberia, Haiti, and Afghanistan, among other countries, providing support for midwifery training programs and teaching home-based lifesaving skills.

JO GRACE is the Director of Programs for an international NGO in Mozambique. Having conducted research related to female development and women's land access in India, and with a master's degree in gender analysis in development, she worked in Afghanistan from 2002 to 2007. From 2002 to 2004 she worked for the Afghanistan Research and Evaluation Unit conducting research on livelihood change, gender roles in agriculture, and women's access to land and livestock.

NILAB HABIBI is a photojournalist with Pajhwok Photo Service, a division of the Pajhwok Afghan News Agency in Kabul, Afghanistan. For more, visit http://www.pajhwok.com.

JENNIFER HEATH is an independent scholar, award-winning activist, cultural journalist, curator, and the author and/or editor of nine books of fiction and nonfiction, including *A House White with Sorrow: A Ballad for Afghanistan*, *The Scimitar and the Veil: Extraordinary Women of Islam* and *The Veil: Women Writers on Its History, Lore, and Politics*. Her touring art exhibitions include *The Veil: Visible & Invisible Spaces*. She came of age in Afghanistan and is the founder of Seeds for Afghanistan and co-founder with Judy Hussie-Taylor of the Afghanistan Relief Organization Midwife Training and Infant Care Program, now International Midwife Assistance.

SUSAN HALL traveled with the Global Exchange delegation "Women Making Change" to Afghanistan in March 2005 for an Independent Study Project in photography. She returned to Afghanistan in March 2007, as a volunteer for the

NGO Afghans4Tomorrow, teaching English and photographing in the A4T girl's schools. Her goal as a documentary photographer is: to educate and agitate; to initiate dialogue; to visually document the costs of war; to reject the supposition that we as individuals are powerless to effect change; to inspire the viewer to engage in quantifiable action to advance peace in the U.S. and the world; and to submit that human life is sacred and that killing in any form is uncivilized. For more, visit http://www.susanmhall.com.

MASSOUDA JALAL was born in Gul Bahar in Kapisa Province. She was on the faculty of Kabul University until 1996, when the Taliban government removed her. She is a psychiatrist and pediatrician and has worked at several Kabul hospitals, as well as for the United Nations and the World Food Programme. After the fall of the Taliban, she emerged as a leading voice for the role of women in Afghanistan and campaigned for the presidency. As an outsider in Afghanistan's power structure, she stressed her independence from the warlords and past oppressive regimes. An exit poll taken during the October 2004 election showed Jalal with about 7 percent of the vote among Afghan women. She received 1.1 percent of the vote in the 2004 election, placing sixth among seventeen male candidates. Her candidacy had a positive impact both at the national and international levels. In May 2010, she won the United Nations Global Award on Human Rights in recognition of her continuing fight for the elimination of violence and discrimination against women in Afghanistan and the promotion of women's status in Afghanistan with a national action plan guaranteeing at least 30 percent of women's participation at all levels of public and private sectors and in all layers of power in Afghanistan.

MALALAI JOYA was born in Afghanistan to a former medical student who was wounded while fighting against the Soviet Union. Malalai was four years old when her family fled Afghanistan in 1982 to the refugee camps of Iran and then Pakistan. She finished her education in Pakistan and began teaching literacy courses to other women at age nineteen. In 1998, during the Taliban reign, she returned to Afghanistan to teach girls in secret home-based classes. After the fall of the Taliban, she was elected to parliament from Farah Province. In May 2007, Joya was suspended from parliament on the grounds that she had insulted fellow representatives in a television interview. Her suspension generated protest internationally. *Time* magazine named Joya one of the "Top 100 Most Influential People of 2010," and *The New Statesman* listed her among the "50 People That Matter in 2010."

AMINA KATOR was born of Afghan parents in Peshawar, Pakistan, and is fluent in Dari and conversational Urdu. She received her bachelor's degree in political science with a minor in global poverty and practice from the University of California-Berkeley and plans to attend graduate school for a master's degree in International Policy and Conflict Resolution. In Afghanistan she worked with a nonprofit organization called The Children of War, working with Afghan girls, aged fourteen to seventeen, studying domestic violence and deterrence and assisting students to learn Microsoft programs.

FAWZIA KOOFI is a member of the Afghan parliament, representing the province of Badakshan, and the first woman in Afghanistan to be elected deputy speaker of parliament. Since 1998, she has worked with UNICEF Afghanistan as a project officer for child protection and was an English-language lecturer at Faizabad Medical University. Since 2001, she has been involved in planning various national programs, such as the demobilization, disarmament, and reintegration of child soldiers. She is one of the youngest members of parliament, where her interests are security, anti-corruption, and human and women's rights. She is a widowed mother of two daughters, earned a master's degree in business management from Preston University in Pakistan and is currently enrolled in the Law Faculty at Kabul University.

ANNA LARSON is a researcher in governance for the Afghanistan Research and Evaluation Unit. She has been working in Afghanistan since 2004 on governance and gender issues. She has an MSc in political economy of violence, conflict and development from the School of Oriental and African Studies, London University. Her publications include studies of women's presence and gender interests in the Afghan parliament, gender mainstreaming in Afghanistan, and the role of Afghan political parties in democratization and state building. She is currently working on an ongoing study of parties and democratization for AREU.

RACHEL LEHR, an award-winning artist and scholar, is a founder of Rubia, Inc., and now serves as Rubia's executive director in the United States. Rachel's artistic work and research focuses on the domestic spheres occupied by rural Afghan women, capturing the rhythm and vitality of life in women's private spaces. Her scholarship has focused on dialects of Persian spoken in Iran, Tajikistan, and Afghanistan. She is currently completing her doctorate in linguistics at University of Chicago; her dissertation focuses on Pashai, an endangered language spoken in Darrai Nur, a rural mountain community in eastern Afghanistan.

MARY MACMAKIN worked as a physical therapist in the hospitals of Kabul throughout the 1960s and 1970s until 1980, when she left Afghanistan for a decade. In the early 1990s she was employed by the Swedish Committee of Afghanistan to teach physical therapists in Taloqan, a city in northern Afghanistan. She founded PARSA in 1996 to provide comprehensive services to disabled Afghans and Afghanistan's widows and orphans. She is proud of PARSA's service to Afghan girls with the forty-five home schools it supported during the Taliban regime, ensuring regular education to nearly 1,500 girls. She was imprisoned by the Taliban and exiled to Pakistan, but nevertheless the Afghan female staff continued to run PARSA's projects with clandestine bus trips to and from Kabul while concealed from the Taliban under their *chadaris* (*burqas*).

MARGARET A. MILLS has taught at Ohio State University since 1998. Previously, she was chair of the Department of Folklore and Folklife at the University of Pennsylvania. She is widely regarded as a leading specialist in the popular culture of the Persian and Farsi-speaking world. Her book *Rhetorics and Politics in Afghan Traditional Storytelling* won the 1993 Chicago Folklore Prize for best academic work in folklore. She is the author or co-editor of four additional books, with two others in preparation, as well as numerous other publications.

AUNOHITA MOJUMDAR is an Indian journalist who has reported on South Asia for twenty years and lived in Afghanistan for the past six. Initially working with the media NGO, Internews, and Pajhwok Afghan News, she is now a full-time freelance correspondent contributing to *Himal Southasia*, Al Jazeera, Eurasianet, *Christian Science Monitor*, and the *Financial Times*, among others.

LAURYN OATES is a Canadian human rights activist concentrating on women's rights and education in conflict zones. She has worked throughout the Muslim world, particularly in Afghanistan, where she works in close partnership with a variety of Afghan women's organizations and international charities such as Canadian Women for Women in Afghanistan, Global Rights, Womankind Worldwide, the Afghan Research and Evaluation Unit, the Funders' Network for Afghan Women, and others. She frequently speaks and writes about human rights. Her work has appeared in publications ranging from the *Calgary Herald* to *The Propagandist* magazine. She has called Vancouver, Montreal, and New York home, but she currently lives on Bowen Island in British Columbia.

ZUZANNA OLSZEWSKA is a junior research fellow in Oriental Studies at St. John's College, the University of Oxford. She has a doctorate in social anthropology from the University of Oxford, having completed a dissertation on poetry and its social contexts among Afghan refugees in Iran. Her translations of Afghan Persian poetry have appeared in various collections and in the journal *Modern Poetry in Translation*. She plans to publish her translations in a single volume.

WAHID OMAR was born in Kabul and left Afghanistan shortly before the Soviet invasion in 1979. He lived in France as a political refugee until 1987, received his bachelor's degree in 1991 at the University of Colorado (with a major in international affairs) and his master's degree in French literature at Colorado State University in 1994 and his Ph.D. from the University of Colorado in 2010. He has worked in Afghanistan since 2001 in project development, implementation, and feasibility studies, and as an educational advisor for the United Nations Development Program, training university professors and building capacity at the University of Kabul. Under his leadership forty-five projects have been implemented, ranging from school and community centers, teacher training, water improvement projects, and micro lending, to humanitarian aid and relief efforts. He has won many awards for his teaching and writing, and his work in collecting and preserving Afghan folklore has garnered the attention of the Smithsonian Institution. He is the author of *Afghanistan: A Nation in Performance—A Comparative Study between Medieval France and Contemporary Afghanistan*.

ADAM PAIN is a visiting professor (Rural Development South) in the Department of Urban and Rural Development, Swedish Life Sciences University, Uppsala, and a senior research fellow at the School of Development Studies, University of East Anglia, UK, where he was a faculty member between 1976 and 1987. He was the team leader, from 1987 to 1991, on a regional research program based in Botswana. From 1992 to 2000, he worked in Bhutan as an advisor to the Ministry of Agriculture. He has been working in Afghanistan since February 2001 with the Afghanistan Research and Evaluation Unit on livelihood change and natural resource management issues. He is currently a co-principle investigator on a joint East Anglia–AREU ESRC research grant on poverty changes in Afghanistan.

LIZETTE POTGIETER is a resident multimedia freelance journalist in Kabul, Afghanistan. A native of South Africa, her work has been published by Reuters, medica mondiale Afghanistan, AFP/Getty Images, *Die Burger* (national South African daily), *The Star* (national South African daily), *South African Journal of Philosophy, Seoul Lifestyle & Culture, Korea Times, Morning Calm* (Korean Air in-flight magazine), the *Weekly Chosun Ilbo Magazine* and the *Chosun Ilbo Daily* in Seoul, South Korea, *Korea Focus, South China Morning Post, Afghanistan Alive,* Russia Today TV, YTN TV Korea, and USAID publications.

AZITA RAFAT was a member of the Afghan parliament, representing the province of Badghis. She is deputy chair of the International Relations Committee and chair of the Law Committee for parliament's female and youth caucus. From 1997 to 2000, during the Taliban regime, she was the first female health volunteer with the Red Cross in Afghanistan. She has worked as a teacher trainer and in various sectors of civil society to improve the lives of women in her home province. In 2006, she graduated from the Mathematics Department of the Badghis Teacher Training Institute and she established the first computer and English courses for women in Badghis.

SAFYA SAIFY is a photojournalist with Pajhwok Photo Service of the Pajhwok Afghan News Agency in Kabul, Afghanistan. For more, visit http://www.pajhwok.com.

SIMA SAMAR was born in Jaghori, Ghazni, Afghanistan, and obtained her medical degree in 1982 from Kabul University. She practiced medicine at a government hospital in Kabul but was forced to flee to her native Jaghori, where she provided medical treatment to patients throughout the remote areas of Central Afghanistan. In 1984, she again fled for safety to Pakistan, where she worked as a doctor at the refugee branch of the Mission Hospital. In 1989, she founded the Shuhada Organization and Shuhada Clinic in Quetta, Pakistan, dedicated to providing health care to refugee Afghan women and girls, training of medical staff, and education. Shuhada now runs four hospitals, twelve clinics, and sixty schools in Afghanistan. Samar is chairperson of the Afghanistan Independent Human rights Commission and has been the UN Special Rapportuer on the human rights situation in Sudan since 2005.

SHERYL B. SHAPIRO is a freelance photographer based in Boulder, Colorado. Her passion is photographing indigenous people living traditional lifestyles. She has traveled extensively in the developing world, including Afghanistan, Iran, Iraq, Yemen, North Korea, and Tibet. Her images and stories reflect the humanity and dignity of her subjects, as well as the kindness and hospitality of the people she encounters. Her work has been published in *Practical Horseman,* the *Melbourne Herald Sun,* the *Brisbane Sunday Mail,* and *The Veil: Women Writers on Its History, Lore, and Politics,* to name a few. She teaches courses on independent third-world travel and presents educational slide shows of her journeys for public and private audiences. For more, visit http://www.sherylshapiro.com.

DEBORAH J. SMITH is the senior research manager for gender and health at the Afghanistan Research and Evaluation Unit, where she has managed a research portfolio including customary law and community-based dispute resolution; the representation of women's interests in the *Wolesi Jirga*; gender mainstreaming in government ministries; the problem use of psychotropic drugs; and family dynamics and family violence. Before moving to Afghanistan, Smith worked at the London School of Hygiene and Tropical Medicine, where she conducted health policy research in Malawi and Zambia. She has a Ph.D. from the London School of Economics and Political Science, for which she conducted field work on gender issues in Rajasthan, India.

ELIZABETH STITES is a senior researcher in conflict and livelihoods at the Feinstein International Center at Tufts University. She conducted research in Afghanistan in 2002 and 2003, and is co-author of the book *After the Taliban: Life and Security in Rural Afghanistan*, published in 2009. Her current research projects are in Uganda and Nepal.

ALISA TANG is a native of Red Bud, Illinois, and worked for The Associated Press in Afghanistan from November 2006 to June 2008, focusing on social issues, women, and children. She has reported on an array of stories, including the assassination of a woman journalist for taking on corruption. She is now based in Bangkok.

SAKENA YACOOBI is executive director of the Afghan Institute of Learning (AIL), an Afghan women-led NGO she founded in 1995. Created to provide teacher training, education, and health services to women and children, AIL now provides services to 350,000 women and children annually and has established itself as a groundbreaking, visionary organization that works at the grass roots, empowering women and communities to find ways to help themselves. Dr. Yacoobi has received many recognition-of-service awards in Afghanistan. Internationally her awards include the 2003 Peacemakers in Action Award of the Tanenbaum Center for Inter-religious Understanding, the 2004 Peter Gruber Foundation's Women's Rights Prize, the 2005 National Endowment for Democracy Award, the 2006 Skoll Award for Social Entrepreneurship, the Citizen Leader Award from the University of Pacific, and the 2007 Gleitsman International Activist Award. The first Ashoka Fellow from Afghanistan, Dr. Yacoobi is also on the boards of Global Fund for Women and Creating Hope International.

ASHRAF ZAHEDI, PH.D., is a sociologist and scholar in residence at the Beatrice Bain Research Group at the University of California, Berkeley. She has taught at Boston University, Suffolk University, and Santa Clara University and conducted research at many universities, including Stanford's Institute for Research on Women and Gender. Her research interests include political ideology, social policy, socioeconomic disparities, human rights, social movements, gender and developments, and transnational feminism.

DINAH ZEIGER has written widely on women, war, and nationalism. Her current research focuses on the performance of the First Amendment. She received her Ph.D. from the University of Colorado and presently teaches media law at the University of Idaho.

Index

DATE DUE

TEXT
10/13 Sabon

DISPLAY
Sabon

COMPOSITOR
Westchester Book Group

INDEXER
IndexingPros

CARTOGRAPHER
Bill Nelson

PRINTER
Sheridan Books